£6—00

MICROMETEOROLOGY

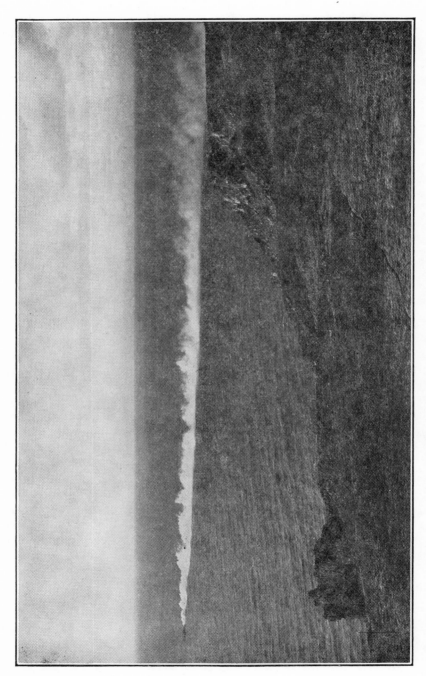

Point-source Smoke Cloud (Crown copyright reserved)

Micrometeorology

A STUDY OF PHYSICAL

PROCESSES IN THE LOWEST

LAYERS OF THE EARTH'S ATMOSPHERE

O. G. Sutton C.B.E., F.R.S., D.Sc.

DIRECTOR OF THE METEOROLOGICAL OFFICE; LATELY DEAN OF THE
ROYAL MILITARY COLLEGE OF SCIENCE, ENGLAND

NEW YORK · TORONTO · LONDON

McGRAW-HILL BOOK COMPANY

1953

MICROMETEOROLOGY

PREFACE

In this book I have attempted to meet the needs of meteorologists, and of workers in other fields, who require detailed information about physical processes in the regions of the atmosphere where life is most abundant. It is my hope that such an account will help to increase the number of micrometeorologists, and to this end the book has been planned, not as an encyclopedic work of reference, but as an integrated course of reading, bringing together the main results of research in certain branches of applied meteorology which are important in the life of a civilized community.

The deeper and more fundamental problems of meteorology have shown themselves to be as stubborn as any in present-day physics. The atmosphere does not yield its secrets willingly, and long experience seems to be an essential prerequisite for success in the more familiar branches of meteorology. The restricted field of micrometeorology, however, presents a less forbidding aspect to the newcomer, and many of the problems of the lower atmosphere are familiar in other branches of applied science, although the approach is often quite different. One of the purposes of this book is to facilitate, as far as possible, the change of outlook which must accompany the transition from the carefully planned experiment of the laboratory to the systematic observation and interpretation of uncontrolled natural processes which are the foundation of meteorology.

Although the subject matter and treatment are mainly of postgraduate level, the techniques required to follow the discussions in these pages should be well within the grasp of a student who has attained the standard of an initial degree in mathematics and physics. As far as possible I have avoided elaborate proofs or any treatment of a problem which seemed to me to display mathematical virtuosity rather than physical insight. Throughout the book I have stressed the continuity of atmospheric physics with more familiar studies, as well as the interrelations of the topics themselves, since I believe that it is hardly possible to over-estimate the value of the all-round view in meteorology. In addition I have followed, wherever appropriate, a method of presentation which my experience as a teacher has shown to be advantageous. Each main topic is introduced by a brief review, in simple language, of the chief problems in the particular field of investigation and their significance in micrometeorology. The precise and logical exposition is given at a later stage, when the necessity for a more sophisticated approach is apparent. This means that there is a certain amount of repetition in each chapter, as in any properly planned series of lectures. I believe that most readers, especially those coming to the subject for the first time, will find this helpful.

The book covers what I conceive to be the most important topics in the physics of the surface air layers and is self-contained in the sense that the detailed discussions of the later chapters are supported by the basic physics and mathematics of the earlier pages. The selection of material is always a difficult matter in a book of this type, and it may be argued that micrometeorology is not necessarily confined to the atmosphere near the ground and that some attention should have been paid to the fine structure of upper air phenomena, especially the microphysics of clouds. There is much to be said for this view, but I feel that to have included these matters in the present work would have made the book unwieldy and would have affected adversely the continuity and internal harmony of the text. It is impossible to separate the detailed study of clouds and rain formation from the larger scale processes of synoptic meteorology, and such a complicated subject deserves a treatise of its own. For somewhat similar reasons I have refrained from discussing the effects of the atmosphere on radio propagation, but here I am fortified in my judgment by the fact that there are now available to the specialist reader several comprehensive accounts of these matters.

In the preparation of this book I have frequently consulted Dr. Geiger's "Das Klima in der bodennahen Luftschicht," which in its latest form contains a vast amount of information about the lower atmosphere. Sir David Brunt's "Physical and Dynamical Meteorology," Professor Haurwitz's "Dynamic Meteorology" and Dr. Goldstein's "Modern Developments in Fluid Dynamics" have always been at my elbow and have proved invaluable. I am greatly indebted to my friend and former fellow worker, Dr. F. Pasquill, who kindly took on the task of reading the whole book in draft form, for many apposite and illuminating suggestions. My thanks also go to my colleagues, Prof. G. D. West and Prof. C. J. Tranter, and to my brother W. G. L. Sutton, for their helpful criticism of the earlier chapters. For permission to reproduce certain figures I am indebted to the Controller of Her Britannic Majesty's Stationery Office, The University Press, Cambridge, The Royal Society, The American Meteorological Society, and The Royal Meteorological Society. Lastly I owe much to my wife for her assistance and advice in revising the manuscript and other tedious but necessary tasks and also to my secretary, Miss E. J. Smith, for her patience in preparing the typescript.

O. G. Sutton

Shrivenham, England
November, 1952

CONTENTS

INTRODUCTION

In the historical development of meteorology, interest has centered chiefly on the broader aspects of climate and weather, processes which involve large regions of the earth's surface and great depths of the atmosphere. In recent years, however, more and more attention has been paid to the systematic study of the fine structure of atmospheric processes and especially to the detailed study of phenomena which occur in the layers of the air nearest the ground.

The term micrometeorology, as used in this book, is intended to denote the intimate study of physical phenomena taking place over limited regions of the surface of the earth, and usually within the lowest layers of the atmosphere. The climate of a region and the weather which it experiences from day to day derive directly from the movements of great air masses over continents and seas, and on such a scale the exact conditions which determine, say, the dispersion of pollution from a factory chimney or the draining of cold air into a valley are insignificant. Although such features are of minor importance when viewed on the climatological atlas or the forecaster's synoptic chart, they may profoundly affect human welfare and economy and for this reason, if for no other, are worthy of serious study.

The physics of the lower strata of the atmosphere is both interesting and important, chiefly because of the large variations in conditions which are found in the layers of air nearest the ground. Such variations are significant, not only for meteorology, but for other sciences. The climate into which a plant first emerges is quite unlike that experienced by man and the larger animals a few feet higher up, for the layers of air within a fraction of an inch of the ground may experience both tropical heat and icy cold in the course of a single day. A detailed study of the effect of climate on vegetation can hardly be based satisfactorily on what the climatologist records in his screen some 4 ft or so above the ground.

The development of micrometeorology as an exact science demands not only the examination and interpretation of highly accurate observations made in the layers of air adjacent to the surface but also a study of the physical processes which give rise to microclimates. This implies a detailed knowledge of the motion of air near a solid or liquid boundary of variable shape and changing temperature. The outstanding feature of such motion is that the flow is normally turbulent, so that considerable mixing takes place. It is to this fact that the lower atmosphere owes many of its characteristic properties on which much of life depends, for it is the turbulence of the wind which is chiefly responsible for the spread of heat from the ground to the air, the exchange of carbon dioxide between plant and animal life, the scattering of pollen and the lighter seeds, and the cycle of water from the earth, seas, and rivers to the air and back again.

In this book, the earlier chapters treat of the basic physics and mathematics required for the study of processes taking place near a boundary, such as the surface of the earth. The later chapters show how the fundamental concepts are applied to yield solutions which, although necessarily approximate, have important consequences in practical problems of hydrology, atmospheric pollution, and agricultural meteorology.

CHAPTER 1

THE ATMOSPHERE AT REST

1.1. Constitution and Physical Properties

The Atmosphere. From the aspect of meteorology, the atmosphere consists of a hypothetical gas called *clean dry air* and the gas *water vapor*. With these are usually found various impurities, such as industrial gases, and a certain amount of matter in suspension, such as water (in the form of ice, snow, or rain), smoke, dust, pollen, etc.

Dry Air. Clean dry air, or more briefly, dry air, is a mixture of gases whose relative proportions remain unchanged up to great heights. Paneth[1] gives the constitution shown in Table 1.

TABLE 1. CONSTITUTION OF CLEAN DRY AIR

Constituent	Volume, per cent
Nitrogen	78.08
Oxygen	20.95
Argon	0.93
Carbon dioxide	0.03
Neon	1.8×10^{-3}
Helium	5×10^{-4}
Krypton	1×10^{-4}
Xenon	1×10^{-5}
Ozone	Variable; about 10^{-6}
Radon	6×10^{-18}
Hydrogen	Doubtful; $< 1 \times 10^{-3}$

Thus 99.99 per cent by volume of dry air is made up of the four gases nitrogen, oxygen, argon, and carbon dioxide.

The chief physical properties of dry air are shown in Table 2.

TABLE 2. PHYSICAL PROPERTIES OF DRY AIR

Density ρ at 0°C and 1000 mb pressure	1.276×10^{-3} g cm^{-3}
Specific heat at constant pressure c_p	0.24
Specific heat at constant volume c_v	0.17
Ratio of specific heats γ	1.405
(Mean) molecular weight M	28.9

Since the constituents of dry air are gases which, at terrestrial temperatures, are far above their critical temperatures, the perfect-gas law applies,

$$p = \frac{R_1}{M} \rho T \qquad (1.1)$$

1

where p is the pressure in dynes per square centimeter and T is absolute temperature. R_1, the universal gas constant, has the value 8.31×10^7 ergs deg^{-1}. In view of the unchanging constitution of dry air it is convenient to write $R_1/M = R$, the gas constant for dry air, whose value is 2.876×10^6 cm^2 sec^{-2} deg^{-1}.

Water Vapor. To the meteorologist, water vapor is the most important single constituent of the atmosphere. This is chiefly because, at terrestrial temperatures, water passes very easily from the vapor to the liquid and solid phases, and vice versa, with a large release or absorption of heat, and thus provides an agency whereby great quantities of heat are transferred from the surface to the atmosphere, and vice versa. The significance of water, whether in the vapor or in the liquid phase, in the maintenance of life needs no emphasis.

Because of its importance in many different processes, the amount of water vapor present in the air is measured in a variety of ways.

The pressure and density of water vapor. According to Dalton's law of partial pressures, the pressure exerted by water vapor in the atmosphere is independent of pressures of other gases. If no condensation or evaporation is taking place, water vapor may be treated as an ideal gas, whose pressure e is given by

$$e = \frac{R_1}{M_w} \rho_w T \tag{1.2}$$

where $M_w(= 18)$ is the molecular weight of the gas and ρ_w its density. The temperature of the vapor, T, may be assumed to be that of the dry air with which the vapor is mixed, since any difference in temperature between the vapor and the air would be quickly smoothed out by the vigorous diffusion which normally accompanies all atmospheric motion. Since $R_1 = RM$, where R and M refer to dry air, the above equation may be written as

$$e = \left(\frac{M}{M_w}\right) R\rho_w T \simeq 1.61 R\rho_w T \simeq \frac{8}{5} R\rho_w T \tag{1.3}$$

or

$$\rho_w = \left(\frac{M_w}{M}\right) \frac{e}{RT} \simeq 0.622 \frac{e}{RT} \simeq \frac{5e}{8RT} \tag{1.4}$$

There are thus two direct ways of specifying the amount of water vapor in any sample of the atmosphere: (1) by the amount of the total pressure which is due to water vapor alone, e; (2) by the density ρ_w of the vapor. The density of water vapor is usually called the *absolute humidity* of the atmosphere.

At the surface, the total pressure of the atmosphere is normally about 1015 mb. Of this, water vapor accounts for a very small amount, of the order of 1 to 2 per cent. The density of dry air at 1000 mb and 0°C is 1.276×10^{-3} g cm^{-3}, and that of water vapor is less than 5×10^{-6} g cm^{-3} at the same temperature. Thus, despite its great importance in atmospheric processes, water vapor forms but a small part of the atmosphere near the ground.

If p is the total pressure of a mixture of dry air and water vapor, $p - e$ is the partial pressure of the air alone, so that the density ρ_m of the mixture is approximately

$$\rho_m = \frac{p - e}{RT} + \frac{5}{8}\frac{e}{RT} = \frac{p}{RT}\left(1 - \frac{3e}{8p}\right) \tag{1.5}$$

We may write this in the form

$$\rho_m = \frac{p}{RT'} \tag{1.6}$$

by defining a *virtual temperature* $T' = T\left/\left(1 - \frac{3e}{8p}\right)\right.$, the temperature at which a sample of dry air would have the same density as the mixture, at the same pressure.

Provided that there is no condensation, a mixture of dry air and water vapor behaves like a perfect gas, obeying the law

$$p = R'\rho T$$

where

$$R' = \frac{R}{\left(1 - \frac{3e}{8p}\right)} \simeq R\left(1 + \frac{3e}{8p}\right)$$

This approximation is often very useful in dealing with air containing only a small amount of water vapor.

Saturation and relative humidity. According to the kinetic theory of gases, evaporation occurs when some of the molecules in a liquid succeed in overcoming the mutual attractive forces and escape from a free surface into the space above, forming a vapor. Some of the molecules in the vapor strike the surface and are recaptured by the liquid, and this process may go on until, ultimately, a state of dynamic equilibrium is attained in which the number of molecules lost by the liquid exactly equals the number gained from the vapor in any given interval of time. When this occurs, the vapor is said to be *saturated*, and for a given temperature there is a definite saturation vapor pressure or saturation vapor density. (It is also possible, in certain circumstances, to obtain supersaturated vapors, but in general such conditions do not concern the micrometeorologist.)

Saturation vapor pressure and saturation density increase rapidly with temperature, and various formulas, theoretical and empirical, have been proposed for this relation. Kaye and Laby[2] state that the Kirchhoff-Rankine-Dupré formula

$$\log e = A + \frac{B}{T} + C \log T$$

is accurate and convenient, and they further recommend for interpolation treating log e as a linear function of temperature. In most meteorological work sufficient accuracy is obtained by the use of tables of saturation vapor pressure, over ice or over water, at 1°C intervals. A few typical values are given below.

SATURATION VAPOR PRESSURES OF WATER IN MILLIMETERS OF MERCURY

Temperature, °C	0	5	10	15	20	25	30
Vapor pressure, mm Hg	4.58	6.54	9.21	12.78	17.51	23.69	31.71

The physical fact of saturation does not depend in any way on the presence or absence of the other gases of the atmosphere. In meteorology there has grown up a loose but convenient way of referring to the atmosphere as "saturated" or "unsaturated"; this means simply that the water vapor which forms part of the air is or is not in equilibrium with a plane surface of water (or ice) at a certain temperature, equal to that of the atmosphere. There is a natural temptation to think of dry air as a kind of sponge which can become saturated with water, but this is entirely wrong. Nevertheless the term "saturated air" has become so familiar in meteorology that it would be pedantic to avoid it entirely, and no harm is done provided that the reader is aware of the exact meaning.

We define *saturated air* as a mixture of clean dry air and water vapor in which the latter constituent is saturated, and *moist,* or *humid, air* as a mixture of clean dry air and water vapor in which the pressure (or density) of the vapor is below the saturation pressure (or density). From these definitions there has emerged the most familiar way of measuring water vapor in the atmosphere, *viz.,* by the *relative humidity f,* defined as the ratio of the actual vapor pressure to the saturation vapor pressure at the same temperature, and invariably expressed as a percentage. Thus,

$$f = \frac{100e}{e_s} \qquad \text{per cent} \qquad (1.7)$$

where e_s is the saturation vapor pressure.

Related measures of water vapor. In problems of diffusion and evaporation, the mathematical treatment is usually in terms of the absolute humidity, or density of water vapor. Observations are usually recorded in terms of vapor pressure, or relative humidity, and the change of units can be quickly effected by means of tables. In air-mass analysis and many other problems of large-scale meteorology another measure, the

humidity mixing ratio x, is very useful.   This is defined as the ratio of
the mass of water vapor to that of dry air in a given volume of moist air.
This is very nearly the same numerically as the *specific humidity q*, defined
as the mass of water per unit mass of moist air.   The algebraic relations
between the various measures are as follows:

$$x = 0.622 \frac{e}{p - e} \simeq 0.622 \frac{e}{p} \qquad \text{since } e \ll p \qquad (1.8)$$

$$f = \frac{100(p - e)}{0.622e_s} x \qquad\qquad (1.9)$$

$$\rho_w = \frac{(p - e)}{RT} x \qquad\qquad (1.10)$$

$$q = \frac{0.622e}{p - 0.378e} \simeq x \qquad\qquad (1.11)$$

The amount of water vapor in the air may also be expressed by the *dew
point*, defined as the lowest temperature to which a sample of moist air
can be cooled, at constant pressure, without causing condensation.
Finally, the *saturation deficit*, defined as the difference between the saturation vapor pressure and the existing vapor pressure, at the same temperature, is also used, especially by biologists.   The alternative name for
this quantity, the "drying power of the air," should be avoided because
the saturation deficit expresses only a partial aspect of the problem of
evaporation.
    A particularly useful property of the humidity mixing ratio of a
volume of air is that it is independent of temperature changes and is
therefore invariable for the volume in question, provided that there is
no evaporation or condensation or mixing with air of different humidity.
In meteorological language, humidity mixing ratio is a *conservative function* of an air mass, but this property is perhaps less useful to the micrometeorologist than it is to those concerned with synoptic meteorology.

1.2. The Hydrostatic Equation and the Variation of Pressure with Height

    The pressure of the atmosphere, as measured by a barometer, is the
weight of a vertical column of air of unit cross section, centered at a given
point and extending upward to infinity.   If z be height above the datum
point, the density, pressure, and absolute temperature of the air will be
$\rho(z)$, $p(z)$, and $T(z)$, respectively.   Considering a slice of thickness δz,
its weight is $g\rho\ \delta z$, and by definition this is equal to the difference of
pressure between heights of z and $z + \delta z$, that is, $-\delta p$.   Hence

$$\delta p = -g\rho\ \delta z$$

or, in the limit as $\delta z \to 0$,

$$\frac{dp}{dz} = -g\rho \qquad\qquad (1.12)$$

This is the fundamental statical equation of the atmosphere, and the relation is strictly true only for an atmosphere free from acceleration in the vertical.

Since, for a dry atmosphere

$$\rho = \frac{p}{RT} \tag{1.13}$$

it follows that

$$\frac{dp}{p} = -\frac{g}{RT}\,dz$$

or

$$p = p_0 \exp\left(-\frac{g}{R}\int_0^z \frac{dz}{T}\right) \tag{1.14}$$

where p_0 is the pressure at the surface $(z = 0)$. If T is known as an explicit function of height, this equation can be used to give a numerical relation between pressure and height. This is the basis of barometric altimetry, in which T is usually supposed to vary linearly with height, a rough but convenient approximation to the actual state of affairs.

In investigations dealing with shallow layers near the surface the change of temperature with height is, in general, so complex that any simple numerical solution of the hydrostatic equation, such as that discussed above, is inapplicable.

The Variation of Density with Height. From Eqs. (1.12) and (1.13) it follows at once that

$$\frac{1}{\rho}\frac{d\rho}{dz} = -\frac{1}{T}\left(\frac{dT}{dz} + \frac{g}{R}\right) \tag{1.15}$$

If the variable temperature $T(z)$ is replaced by a mean value T_m, constant throughout the layer concerned, Eq. (1.15) reduces to

$$\frac{1}{\rho}\frac{d\rho}{dz} = -\frac{g}{RT_m}$$

and so

$$\rho = \rho_0 \exp\left(-\frac{gz}{RT_m}\right) \tag{1.16}$$

where ρ_0 is the density at the surface $z = 0$. If z is measured in centimeters and T_m in degrees centigrade, this becomes

$$\rho = \rho_0 \exp\left(\frac{-3.4 \times 10^{-4}z}{T_m}\right)$$

Thus in an atmosphere of constant temperature the density decreases exponentially with height. Relations of this type (but usually with different numerical constants) have been fitted to observed values of density up to considerable heights and are used to specify hypothetical standard atmospheres, for example, in ballistics. The exponential law of decrease of density with height must be regarded as an expression of average conditions in the atmosphere, and such formulas are of little use in problems of micrometeorology, since near the surface of the earth the temperature gradient dT/dz often attains values which are far too large to be neglected.

From Eq. (1.15) it follows that $d\rho/dz = 0$ if

$$\frac{dT}{dz} = -\frac{g}{R} \simeq -3.4 \times 10^{-4} \,°\text{C cm}^{-1}$$

This particular value of the temperature gradient is frequently called the *autoconvection gradient*, but the term has no particular significance at this stage.

1.3. The Variation of Temperature with Height

The expression for temperature as a function of height above the surface is called the *temperature profile*. Change of temperature with height is one of the most important factors in micrometeorology, for reasons which will become increasingly evident throughout this book. It is a well-known fact that, in general, temperature decreases with height, but this simple statement must be modified for conditions near the ground. On a warm clear day, temperature falls very rapidly with height in the surface layers, but after sunset, especially with clear skies, the temperature of the air in these layers usually increases from the ground upward, a state of affairs called by meteorologists an *inversion*. The theoretical determination of the temperature profile in the atmosphere cannot be achieved directly in general terms, and the problem must be approached by considering certain relatively simple limiting cases, the most important being that which introduces a particular value of the temperature gradient known as the *dry adiabatic lapse rate*.

The problem to be considered is the following: A volume of dry air which is compelled to move, by some means or other, from one level in the atmosphere to another will necessarily change its pressure. We suppose that this change of pressure is according to the hydrostatic equation (1.12) although, strictly, this equation applies only if there are no vertical accelerations and it is further assumed that the atmosphere is uniform in all directions except the vertical. Since the three variables pressure, temperature, and density are connected by the equation of state (1.13), it follows that the change of pressure must bring about changes in the density or in the temperature, or in both, of the volume, such changes depending upon the circumstances of the motion of the volume and on the state of the surrounding atmosphere. The temperature may fall or rise because of lowered or raised pressure but may also vary because of conduction of heat to and from the surrounding air, or by entrainment of external air by the volume during its motion, or by radiation. We consider here only the special case when there is no flow of heat across the boundary of the volume, so that the entire change of temperature is caused by changes in pressure. This means that the density of the air in the volume at any level is completely determined by its absolute temperature. We seek, in particular, the conditions in which the density of the volume is always the same as that of its surroundings, so that finally the problem may be expressed thus: *If a volume of air is displaced from one level to another in an otherwise quiescent dry atmosphere, what must be the temperature profile in the atmosphere as a whole to ensure that the volume always has the same density as its environment, changes of temperature in the volume being supposed to take place without any exchange of heat with the surrounding atmosphere?*

We require certain thermodynamical preliminaries:

Adiabatic changes. A change of state (*i.e.*, of the temperature, pressure, and density) of a gas is said to be *adiabatic* if it takes place without heat being supplied or withdrawn. This condition implies a certain functional relation between the temperature, pressure, and the specific heats of a gas.

It is proved in textbooks of thermodynamics† that the principle of the conservation of energy in the form known as the *first law of thermodynamics* implies that if an infinitesimal amount of heat dQ is communicated to a gas, part serves to increase the internal energy of the molecules $c_v T$ and part does work against the external pressure. In symbols,

$$dQ = c_v \, dT + A p d \left(\frac{1}{\rho}\right)$$

where A is the reciprocal of the mechanical equivalent of heat. Since

$$\frac{p}{\rho} = RT$$

it follows that

$$p d \left(\frac{1}{\rho}\right) = R \, dT - \frac{dp}{\rho}$$

and so

$$dQ = (c_v + AR) dT - A \frac{dp}{\rho}$$

$$= (c_v + AR) dT - \frac{ART}{p} dp$$

$$= c_p \, dT - (c_p - c_v) T \frac{dp}{p}$$

† See, *e.g.*, Zemansky, "Heat and Thermodynamics," 2d ed., p. 101 (McGraw-Hill, 1943).

since

$$AR = c_p - c_v$$

For an adiabatic change, $dQ = 0$. Hence, for such a change, writing $\gamma = c_p/c_v$ ($\simeq 1.41$ for dry air)

$$\gamma \frac{dT}{T} - (\gamma - 1) \frac{dp}{p} = 0$$

or

$$T = \text{constant } p^{(\gamma-1)/\gamma} \simeq \text{constant } p^{0.288} \qquad (1.17)$$

Thus if the pressure of a volume of air is changed and no heat is allowed to enter or leave the volume, the temperature must increase or decrease according to Eq. (1.17).

The dry adiabatic lapse rate. Consider an atmosphere at rest, in which ρ, p, and T are functions of height z. A volume of air in this atmosphere is subjected to a virtual vertical displacement, and we proceed to investigate the changes which take place in the state of the volume if, in the process of adjusting its pressure to that of the surrounding air, it changes its temperature adiabatically. This means eliminating pressure and density from the hydrostatic equation (1.12) by means of the functional relation (1.17) between pressure and temperature for an adiabatic process. Thus, if T' refers to the volume, as distinct from the rest of the atmosphere,

$$\frac{dT'}{dz} = \frac{\gamma - 1}{\gamma} \frac{T'}{p} \frac{dp}{dz} = -\frac{\gamma - 1}{\gamma} g\rho \frac{T'}{R\rho T}$$

$$= -\frac{g}{R}\left(\frac{\gamma - 1}{\gamma}\right)\frac{T'}{T} \qquad (1.18)$$

The most important case is that in which the temperature T' of the volume differs infinitesimally from that of the surrounding air, when

$$\frac{dT}{dz} = -\frac{g}{R}\left(\frac{\gamma - 1}{\gamma}\right) = -\frac{gA}{c_p} \qquad (1.19)$$
$$\simeq -9.86 \times 10^{-5} \,°\text{C cm}^{-1}$$
$$\simeq -1°\text{C per 100 m}$$

This particular rate of decrease of temperature with height, known as the *dry adiabatic lapse rate* and denoted by the symbol Γ (gamma), is one of the fundamental constants of meteorology.

The required temperature profile is thus

$$T(z) = T(0) - \frac{gA}{c_p} z \qquad (1.20)$$

since in an atmosphere possessing such a temperature distribution, a mass of air displaced from one level to another and undergoing only adiabatic changes will always be at the same temperature as the environment and will therefore have the same density as the surrounding air.

Static stability of the atmosphere. This result supplies a criterion of static stability for an atmosphere. If the gradient of temperature in the atmosphere exceeds the adiabatic lapse rate, it is obvious that a volume of air, displaced upward by an infinitesimal amount from a level at which it had the same temperature and pressure as the surrounding atmosphere, will be at a higher temperature than the environment at the new level and will therefore be of lower density than the surrounding air. The force of buoyancy which must result from this condition means that the volume is likely to continue ascending, so that such an atmosphere must be classed as *statically unstable.* Similarly, in an atmosphere whose gradient of temperature falls below the adiabatic lapse rate a mass of air forced upward will be denser than its environment and will tend to sink back to its old level, a necessary condition for *static stability.* The same result holds if the displacements are downward, and therefore generally, provided that the changes are always adiabatic. Hence we may say that a dry atmosphere is in neutral, stable, or unstable static equilibrium according as the rate of change of temperature in the vertical is equal to, is less than, or exceeds the adiabatic lapse rate. The limitations of this analysis are considered below.

Potential temperature. Since vertical motions are of the greatest importance in any meteorological problem, it is convenient to define a temperature which is unaffected by variations in pressure, provided that all changes are adiabatic. The *potential temperature* θ of dry air is defined as the temperature which a volume of air assumes when brought adiabatically from its existing pressure to a standard pressure, generally that at the surface. If p_0 is the surface pressure, from Eq. (1.17)

$$\theta = T \left(\frac{p_0}{p}\right)^{(\gamma-1)/\gamma} \simeq T \left(\frac{p_0}{p}\right)^{0.288} \tag{1.21}$$

where T is the actual (absolute) temperature of the volume.

The gradient of potential temperature may be expressed in terms of the gradient of (absolute) temperature and the adiabatic lapse rate. Differentiating Eq. (1.21) in its logarithmic form,

$$\frac{1}{\theta}\frac{d\theta}{dz} = \frac{1}{T}\frac{dT}{dz} - \left(\frac{\gamma-1}{\gamma}\right)\frac{1}{p}\frac{dp}{dz}$$

$$= \frac{1}{T}\frac{dT}{dz} + \left(\frac{\gamma-1}{\gamma}\right)\frac{g}{RT}$$

and so

$$\frac{1}{\theta}\frac{d\theta}{dz} = \frac{1}{T}\left(\frac{dT}{dz} + \Gamma\right) \tag{1.22}$$

The term

$$\frac{dT}{dz} + \Gamma$$

is the difference between the existing gradient of temperature and the adiabatic lapse rate. At the surface the potential temperature and the absolute temperature are, by definition, equal, and the approximation

$$\theta = T + \Gamma z \tag{1.23}$$

is adequate for moderate values of z and certainly for the surface layers, whose depth rarely exceeds 100 m, which enter into micrometeorology.

Conditions in moist air. The above analysis refers to dry air; the argument becomes more complicated when water vapor is present, especially if motion in the vertical is likely to cause condensation. Provided that the water vapor in the atmosphere is below saturation, the equations for adiabatic processes in moist air differ little from those for dry air. Equation (1.17) is replaced by

$$T = \text{constant} \cdot p^{AR/c_p'} \tag{1.24}$$

where c_p' is the specific heat at constant pressure of unsaturated moist air. Numerically, this differs only slightly from c_p so that, for most practical purposes, Eqs. (1.17) and (1.24) are identical.

For micrometeorology, the extension of the preceding work to a saturated atmosphere is not of first importance and will not be considered here. The reader is referred to any of the standard texts on dynamic meteorology for further information.†

The Significance of the Adiabatic Lapse Rate. The derivation of the criterion of stability given above must be considered carefully before the results are applied to the real atmosphere. There are several points of uncertainty, the most important of which refer to the assumption that the processes involved are adiabatic. If the hydrostatic equation is to be applied, it is clear that the air mass which is in motion should be small, and its movements should be slow, if the conclusions drawn from purely statical arguments are to remain valid. On the other hand, the condition of adiabatic changes generally demands that the motion shall be rapid and the air mass large, in order that any heat exchange with the surrounding air shall be negligible. It follows that the atmosphere near the ground can be expected to attain the adiabatic gradient only in certain special circumstances.

The conditions postulated in the analysis are approached when the sky is thickly covered with cloud and there is a moderate or high wind.

---

† For example, Haurwitz, "Dynamic Meteorology," Chap. III (McGraw-Hill, 1941).

In these circumstances the temperature of the ground does not differ greatly from that of the air immediately above, for radiation is prevented from reaching or leaving the surface in large amounts by the cloud cover. The strong wind means that the air in the lower layers is thoroughly mixed, so that there are no large temperature differences between adjacent patches of air.   (This is borne out by observations of temperature differences between various heights in the lower regions of the atmosphere, which are invariably remarkably free from fluctuations in windy, overcast weather.)   The vertical movements of the air which take place in these conditions are caused not by buoyancy but by dynamic instability, and are rapid and have relatively short paths.   It follows that in these circumstances the gradient of temperature in the vertical should approach fairly closely to the adiabatic lapse rate, since nearly all the conditions of the analysis are fulfilled.

This result is of fundamental importance, but its implications and limitations require careful consideration.   It implies that if a region of the atmosphere, having temperature uniform over any horizontal plane, is subject to mechanical mixing, the result is to reduce all internal vertical gradients of temperature to the adiabatic lapse rate.   On this theory, no amount of stirring can succeed in establishing permanently a smaller temperature gradient, and an isothermal atmosphere cannot be realized by mixing.   The most that such churning can do is to produce an atmosphere of equal potential temperature, and in this sense a condition of uniform potential temperature is to be regarded as a basic equilibrium state, the ultimate effect of turbulent mixing being to reduce any departures from this state to a minimum.   These arguments, however, presuppose that it is legitimate to apply the essentially statical reasoning of the preceding paragraphs to an atmosphere in a state of disorderly motion, and this is by no means obvious a priori.   It cannot be asserted, at this stage, that in the lower layers of the atmosphere, on an overcast windy night, the mean potential temperature is invariable with height.

These arguments have profound consequences in the theoretical treatment of heat-transfer problems in the atmosphere.   In a solid or in an incompressible fluid (*i.e.*, one in which an element of the fluid does not change its density as it moves), the flow of heat across any plane surface is proportional to the gradient of temperature at the level considered, and the laws of thermodynamics ensure that the tendency is for gradients of temperature to be smoothed out.   In the atmosphere, compressibility cannot be ignored except in very shallow layers, and in such a fluid the transport of heat must involve the gradient of potential temperature, the tendency being for the atmosphere to assume a state of uniform potential temperature.

The above discussion takes no account of the influences of water vapor and of radiation.   In parts of the atmosphere remote from the surface layers such additional effects cannot be ignored.   In the upper region of the atmosphere, called the stratosphere, temperature tends to be invariable, or even to increase slightly, with height, a state of affairs usually ascribed to a balance between radiation and absorption.   Below this, and in regions well above the surface layers, the mean gradient of temperature is approximately constant at about two-thirds of the dry adiabatic lapse rate.   A complete explanation of this fact is lacking.   The true surface layers, those below about 100 m, are characterized by a wide range of values of temperature gradient.   The largest gradients, found in the immedite vicinity of the ground, are of magnitudes quite different from those found in the free atmosphere.   In clear weather, gradients of temperature equal to hundreds and even thousands of times the adiabatic lapse rate are a persistent feature of the air within the first meter or so of a closely cropped grass surface.   This property is responsible for many of the characteristic features of the lower atmosphere.

It is important to realize that the analysis, so far, has not dealt with the problem of natural convection, *i.e.*, the motion of air in the vertical because of buoyancy.   There is no justification for asserting, at this stage, that vertical motions arise spontaneously once the temperature gradient exceeds the adiabatic lapse rate.   What has been done is to consider a system in static equilibrium and, by assuming a virtual displacement, to find the forces which act on a volume in the disturbed state, and hence the condition for the *static* stability of the system.   It is shown later (Chap. 4) that it is possible for a thin layer of air to sustain a high temperature gradient without convective motion because of the influence of viscosity and conduction.   The problem then becomes one of *dynamic* stability.

BIBLIOGRAPHY

1. F. A. PANETH, Sci. J. Roy. Coll. Sci., 6, 120 (1933).
2. G. W. C. KAYE and T. H. LABY, "Tables of Physical and Chemical Constants" (London, 1948).

CHAPTER 2

THE ATMOSPHERE IN MOTION. (I) LAMINAR FLOW

2.1. General Aspects of Motion near the Surface of the Earth

The atmosphere over any large area of the globe, and especially in the middle latitudes, is characterized by well-defined dynamic systems, in which the motion of the air is largely determined by horizontal gradients of pressure and temperature. For many purposes in meteorology it is sufficient to regard the atmosphere as incompressible and free from friction; the routine estimation of wind force from the synoptic chart of the pressure field, for example, is based on the assumption that the air adjusts its speed to maintain a balance involving only the pressure gradient and the forces arising from the rotation of the earth. The velocity calculated in this way, known as the *geostrophic wind*, is a useful approximation to the actual wind speed at heights between 500 and 1000 m above the surface.

In micrometeorology, in contrast to synoptic meteorology, the emphasis is not so much upon changes of pressure distribution as upon the effects, direct and indirect, of air movements, and in problems involving wind very near the ground it is usually possible to treat the pressure gradient as a constant driving force and to ignore entirely the effects of the rotation of the earth. In such circumstances the most important factors are friction and the influence of density gradients, the situation being like that met in wind-tunnel investigations, in which the mean air speed is maintained at a constant level by the airscrew and motor, allowing attention to be concentrated upon the changes which take place in the velocity field near a surface or solid body.

In discussing the details of air flow, it is convenient to consider the atmosphere to be divided into a number of horizontal layers (Fig. 1). In the *surface boundary layer*, extending to not more than 100 m above the surface, the effects of the earth's rotation (Coriolis force) may be disregarded in comparison with effects which arise from the surface itself. The wind in this region usually derives directly from the large-scale pressure gradient shown on the forecaster's synoptic chart, but, in certain circumstances, motion in the surface layer is primarily determined by local density effects unrelated to the main pressure field, such as those which give rise to the gravitational (katabatic) winds of hilly country (see Chap. 7). Enveloping the lower stratum, and extending to about a

14

kilometer above the surface is the deeper *friction layer*, or *planetary boundary layer*, a zone of transition from the disturbed flow near the surface to the smooth frictionless flow of the free atmosphere. The problem of wind structure in this layer involves not only the pressure gradient and the Coriolis force but also the residual frictional effects of the earth's surface. The theoretical geostrophic wind is attained between 500 and 1000 m, and above this, in the *free atmosphere*, friction may be ignored except for very exact and detailed investigations.

The most difficult dynamic problems are those encountered in the surface layer, and this is for a variety of reasons. In the first place, the proximity of the boundary means that the surface wind is normally turbulent, and this at once involves the most intractable aspects of fluid

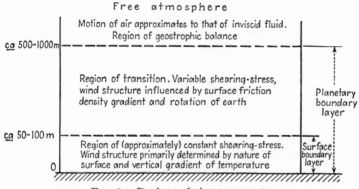

Free atmosphere

ca 500-1000m

Motion of air approximates to that of inviscid fluid.
Region of geostrophic balance

Region of transition. Variable shearing-stress, wind structure influenced by surface friction density gradient and rotation of earth

Planetary boundary layer

ca 50-100 m

Region of (approximately) constant shearing-stress. Wind structure primarily determined by nature of surface and vertical gradient of temperature

Surface boundary layer

0

Fig. 1.   Regions of air movements.

dynamics. Second, the extremely variable nature of the surface makes impossible any strict mathematical specification of the lower boundary, but the characteristic features of the meteorological problem, and the main source of difficulty, arise from the fact that the air layers in contact with the ground often exhibit large diurnal changes in density gradient which affect, in a complicated fashion, the entire character of the flow.

The Mathematical Treatment of Fluid Motion. Although all fluids, whether liquids or gases, exhibit some degree of internal friction or viscosity, it is convenient to consider first the limiting case of a hypothetical inviscid fluid and, for the atmosphere, to make the additional assumption that the fluid is incompressible. The so-called classical hydrodynamics founded by Euler and Bernoulli consists in the application of certain fundamental mechanical laws to such a fluid. The essential principles involved are two: (1) the principle of the conservation of mass; (2) Newton's second law of motion, that the rate of change of momentum of a body is equal, in magnitude and direction, to the impressed force.

The first of these principles leads to the *equation of continuity*, which, for an incompressible fluid, expresses a linear relation between the gradients of the velocity components along their various axes, or, in vectorial language, that the divergence of the velocity is zero. The second principle yields *Euler's equations of motion*. In calculating the acceleration of an element of the fluid it is necessary to take into account the fact that not only does the velocity change during a short interval of time but also that the element has moved a short distance. Thus the terms in the Eulerian equations which express the change of momentum of the element are of the form

$$\rho\left(\frac{\partial u}{\partial t} + u\frac{\partial u}{\partial x} + v\frac{\partial u}{\partial y} + w\frac{\partial u}{\partial z}\right), \text{ etc.}$$

where u, v, w are the component velocities along axes of x, y, and z, respectively, and ρ is the density, assumed constant. These terms have to be equated to the forces which arise from internal pressure gradients ($\partial p/\partial x$, etc.) or from external causes, such as gravity. The solution of a typical problem in classical hydrodynamics thus involves the determination of the velocities and pressure which satisfy the three equations of Euler, the equation of continuity, and the special (initial and boundary) conditions of the particular type of motion being investigated. Such solutions are usually in fairly close agreement with observation in regions of the atmosphere remote from the surface, as in the example of the geostrophic wind.

The inclusion of viscosity results in the addition, to each component equation, of three terms of the type $\mu\,\partial^2 u/\partial x^2$, where μ is the dynamic viscosity. The equations of motion of an incompressible viscous fluid are therefore of the form:

$$\underbrace{\rho\left(\frac{\partial u}{\partial t} + u\frac{\partial u}{\partial x} + v\frac{\partial u}{\partial y} + w\frac{\partial u}{\partial z}\right)}_{inertia\ terms} = \underbrace{\mu\left(\frac{\partial^2 u}{\partial x^2} + \frac{\partial^2 u}{\partial y^2} + \frac{\partial^2 u}{\partial z^2}\right)}_{viscous\ terms} \underbrace{- \frac{\partial p}{\partial x} + \rho X}_{forces\ terms}, \text{ etc.}$$

where X is the x component of the external forces, per unit mass. The three equations of this form are the *Navier-Stokes equations of motion*.

An examination of the various groups of terms throws light on the complexities of fluid dynamics. The terms on the left-hand side, expressing the rate of change of momentum of a fluid element, arise solely because a fluid has mass or density and are therefore appropriately called the *inertia terms*. They involve squares or products of the unknown velocities. The groups of second-order derivatives on the right-hand side (*viscous terms*) express the fact that the fluid possesses internal friction; they are, however, linear. The complete equations, together with the equation of continuity, thus form a set of simultaneous nonlinear partial differential equations of the second order which have to be solved for the three unknown velocity components and the pressure.

The nonlinearity of the complete set of equations is responsible for most of the difficulties encountered in the development of the theory of fluid motion. As yet, no mathematical technique has been found which can deal adequately with nonlinear second-order partial differential equations, and in this sense the Navier-Stokes equations are intractable. The only exact solutions which have been discovered relate to certain limiting cases of very low speeds. However, the nonlinearity of the inertia terms has not prevented the successful development of the inviscid fluid theory in one special case. If the motion is of the type known as irrotational, there always exists a velocity potential (ϕ) which is found not from the equations of motion but from the linear second-order partial differential equation known as Laplace's equation, together with the condition that $\partial\phi/\partial n$ (n = normal) vanishes at the boundary. The introduction of the velocity potential (or, alternatively, of the stream function ψ) effectively reduces a problem in fluid motion to one of kinematics. The equations of motion enter only when, having found ϕ (or ψ) from Laplace's equation, it is required to determine the pressure, and this is possible because the equations have a first integral. Examples of this method are given later in this chapter, in the discussion of air flow over undulating country. With viscosity, irrotational motion is not possible (see page 43), and it is necessary to work with the actual velocities and pressure, and hence with the equations of motion, throughout the entire problem.

It is natural to suppose that, for motion in air, a reasonable approximation could be obtained by omitting the frictional terms because of the low viscosity of gases. Unfortunately, this is true only in regions of the atmosphere remote from the surface. When resistance is involved, as in motion near the ground, the complete omission of viscosity is fatal. Theoretically, a body completely immersed in a uniform steady stream of an inviscid fluid would offer no resistance whatever, since any forces arising from pressure differences over the surface of the body would cancel—a result manifestly far removed from the truth.† Although viscosity, of itself, cannot explain, for example, the destructive effects of a gale, it is nevertheless indirectly responsible for fluid resistance by modifying the velocity field in the proximity of a solid body.

The inertia terms, on the other hand, can be omitted only when the velocities involved are very small. This is so, for example, in the motion under gravity of a very small particle, such as a speck of dust, or a minute drop of water in a fog. The resulting linear second-order equations were

† This is D'Alembert's paradox, summed up neatly by Rayleigh in the sentence "On this theory, the screw of a submerged boat would be useless, but on the other hand, its services would not be needed."

solved for the translational motion of a sphere by Stokes in 1851, giving rise to the so-called Stokes' law, which shows that the ultimate velocity reached by a freely falling small sphere is extremely small, so that such particles can remain in suspension for indefinite periods, even in air. Stokes' law holds with fair accuracy for motion in air provided that the diameter of the sphere does not exceed about $\frac{1}{10}$ mm but fails completely for larger bodies, such as raindrops.

Most practical problems of fluid dynamics are concerned with motion near a solid body and with speeds whose magnitude makes it necessary to retain the inertia terms. The omission of viscosity necessarily leads to the unreal result that resistance is zero, and thus a condition of stalemate is reached, for the equations cannot be solved when both the inertia and the viscous terms are retained.

The difficulty thus created has been largely removed by the development, from 1906 onward, of the *boundary-layer theory* of Prandtl. If a uniform stream of air is allowed to flow over a fixed solid boundary, it is observed that the velocity, which is necessarily zero at the surface itself, attains the free-stream value at a very short distance normal to the boundary. In other words, the entire change of velocity takes place in a very thin layer adjacent to the surface, so that the whole effect of viscosity is confined to this stratum, the so-called *boundary layer*. Inside this layer the velocity gradient is very high, and since the frictional resistance, or drag, of the surface is proportional to the product of the viscosity and the velocity gradient, it is clear that even a fluid of low viscosity, such as air, can produce significant frictional effects when flowing over a smooth plane surface. Using these facts, Prandtl showed how the Navier-Stokes equations can be modified to permit of solution by laborious but not intrinsically difficult methods, and thus to allow the calculation of the skin friction of the surface, as well as many properties of the air flow.

The above is a very much simplified sketch of the development of the boundary-layer concept; in practice, turbulence in the boundary layer and the effects of the irregularity, or "roughness," of a surface often make semiempirical methods unavoidable. Nevertheless, considerable progress has been made on these lines, with profound implications for meteorology.

In the free atmosphere, the motion of the air not only is virtually independent of viscosity but, to a high degree of approximation, may be considered to be irrotational, or free from vorticity. Vorticity cannot arise spontaneously in continuous inviscid fluid but is generated by the action of viscosity and thus is normally found only in the immediate proximity of a solid body, in the boundary layer, and in the remains of the layer in the wake of a body. The general picture of flow near the surface of the earth is one in which a frictionless irrotational flow in the free atmosphere becomes a viscous rotational flow near the ground, and one which normally is highly turbulent. The details of this picture, together with the relevant mathematical theory, will now be considered.

2.2. Kinematics of Inviscid Fluids

The accelerations. Consider a rectangular coordinate system Ox, Oy, Oz, fixed in the field of flow (generally, such a system will be fixed in the earth). Let u, v, and w be the components of the velocity of a particle, or small element of the fluid, at time t, so that $u = \partial x/\partial t$, $v = \partial y/\partial t$, $w = \partial z/\partial t$.

Since $u = u(x,y,z,t)$,

$$\frac{du}{dt} = \frac{\partial u}{\partial t} + \frac{\partial x}{\partial t}\frac{\partial u}{\partial x} + \frac{\partial y}{\partial t}\frac{\partial u}{\partial y} + \frac{\partial z}{\partial t}\frac{\partial u}{\partial z}$$

$$= \frac{\partial u}{\partial t} + u\frac{\partial u}{\partial x} + v\frac{\partial u}{\partial y} + w\frac{\partial u}{\partial z} \tag{2.1}$$

and this is the x component of the acceleration of the particle at (x,y,z,t). Similarly, the y and z components are

$$\frac{dv}{dt} = \frac{\partial v}{\partial t} + u\frac{\partial v}{\partial x} + v\frac{\partial v}{\partial y} + w\frac{\partial v}{\partial z} \tag{2.2}$$

$$\frac{dw}{dt} = \frac{\partial w}{\partial t} + u\frac{\partial w}{\partial x} + v\frac{\partial w}{\partial y} + w\frac{\partial w}{\partial z} \tag{2.3}$$

The physical interpretation of these expressions is as follows: If P is the point (x,y,z), the particle which was at P at time t is at Q $(x + \delta x,$ $y + \delta y,$ $z + \delta z)$ at time $t + \delta t$, that is, we take a step forward in time and another in space. The first terms on the right in Eqs. (2.1) to (2.3) express the former, while the spatial advance gives rise to the remaining terms.

The relations derived above refer to the Eulerian system of hydrodynamics, in which attention is directed to the whole field of flow at any particular instant. The alternative approach, which investigates the life history of a typical particle, is usually attributed to Lagrange although, according to Lamb, this method also was initiated by Euler.

The forces. Consider (Fig. 2) a small element of volume $\delta x\ \delta y\ \delta z$. If p is the pressure at the center of the left-hand face $\delta y\ \delta z$, the total pressure force on this face will be $p\ \delta y\ \delta z$, neglecting terms of higher order. The pressure force on the right-hand face $\delta y\ \delta z$ is

$$\left(p + \frac{\partial p}{\partial x}\,\delta x\right)\delta y\ \delta z$$

Hence the net pressure force acting in the direction Ox is

$$- \frac{\partial p}{\partial x} \, \delta x \, \delta y \, \delta z$$

If X be the x component of any external force, per unit mass, the total force in the direction Ox is thus

$$\left(X\rho - \frac{\partial p}{\partial x} \right) \cdot \delta x \, \delta y \, \delta z$$

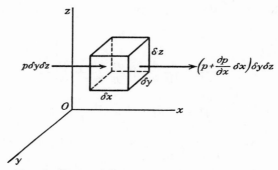

FIG. 2.   Pressure forces on an elemental volume.

The equations.   Since the mass of the element is $\rho \, \delta x \, \delta y \, \delta z$, from Newton's second law of motion,

$$\left(X\rho - \frac{\partial p}{\partial x} \right) (\delta x \, \delta y \, \delta z) = \rho \, \delta x \, \delta y \, \delta z \, \frac{du}{dt}, \text{ etc.}$$

or, for all three components,

$$\left.\begin{array}{l}
\dfrac{\partial u}{\partial t} + u \dfrac{\partial u}{\partial x} + v \dfrac{\partial u}{\partial y} + w \dfrac{\partial u}{\partial z} = X - \dfrac{1}{\rho} \dfrac{\partial p}{\partial x} \\[2mm]
\dfrac{\partial v}{\partial t} + u \dfrac{\partial v}{\partial x} + v \dfrac{\partial v}{\partial y} + w \dfrac{\partial v}{\partial z} = Y - \dfrac{1}{\rho} \dfrac{\partial p}{\partial y} \\[2mm]
\dfrac{\partial w}{\partial t} + u \dfrac{\partial w}{\partial x} + v \dfrac{\partial w}{\partial y} + w \dfrac{\partial w}{\partial z} = Z - \dfrac{1}{\rho} \dfrac{\partial p}{\partial z}
\end{array}\right\} \qquad (2.4)$$

where Y and Z are the components of external force, per unit mass, in the y and z directions, respectively.   These are *Euler's equations of motion of an inviscid fluid.*

The equation of continuity.   Euler's equations are derived from Newton's second law of motion, that the force required to produce an acceleration of any element of the fluid is equal to the product of the acceleration and the mass of the element.   A second physical principle must be invoked, that of the conservation of mass, in dealing not with rigid bodies but with elemental volumes of a fluid of variable density.

Returning to Fig. 2, the quantity of fluid flowing in time δt through the left-hand face is $\rho u \, \delta y \, \delta z \, \delta t$ (neglecting higher order small quantities) and through the right-hand face

$$\left[\rho u + \frac{\partial}{\partial x} (\rho u) \delta x \right] \delta y \, \delta z \, \delta t$$

Hence the net mass outflow in time δt is

$$- \frac{\partial}{\partial x} (\rho u) \delta x \, \delta y \, \delta z \, \delta t$$

with similar contributions from the other faces. Thus the increase in mass due to the net flux throughout the whole volume in time δt is

$$- \left[\frac{\partial}{\partial x} (\rho u) + \frac{\partial}{\partial y} (\rho v) + \frac{\partial}{\partial z} (\rho w) \right] \delta x \, \delta y \, \delta z \, \delta t$$

The mass originally in the volume is $\rho \, \delta x \, \delta y \, \delta z$, and the increase in time δt is $(\partial \rho / \partial t) \delta x \, \delta y \, \delta z \, \delta t$. Hence

$$\frac{\partial \rho}{\partial t} + \frac{\partial}{\partial x} (\rho u) + \frac{\partial}{\partial y} (\rho v) + \frac{\partial}{\partial z} (\rho w) = 0 \tag{2.5}$$

which may be written

$$\frac{1}{\rho} \frac{d\rho}{dt} + \frac{\partial u}{\partial x} + \frac{\partial v}{\partial y} + \frac{\partial w}{\partial z} = 0 \tag{2.6}$$

where d/dt denotes the operator

$$\frac{\partial}{\partial t} + u \frac{\partial}{\partial x} + v \frac{\partial}{\partial y} + w \frac{\partial}{\partial z} \tag{2.7}$$

Equation (2.5) or (2.6) is called the *equation of continuity*.

In a *homogeneous incompressible fluid* the density is the same everywhere, and Eq. (2.6) becomes

$$\frac{\partial u}{\partial x} + \frac{\partial v}{\partial y} + \frac{\partial w}{\partial z} = 0 \tag{2.8}$$

i.e., the divergence of the velocity vector vanishes.

A fluid is said to be *incompressible but heterogeneous* if the density of an element does not alter as it moves, although the density of the fluid as a whole may change from one point to another. In this case $d\rho/dt = 0$, so that Eq. (2.8) is obtained in this case also. The operation (2.7) is called "differentiation following the fluid."

The three equations of motion and the equation of continuity are the basis of the *classical hydrodynamics*. In mathematical physics, a problem is constituted by one or more differential equations, together with a number of special relations, called *initial and boundary conditions*, which particularize the problem. It is important to understand that usually a general solution of the equation or equations is not sought and, more often than not, would be of little practical interest even if it could be found. The equations of mathematical physics are few in number but of great generality; the second-order linear partial differential equation known as Laplace's equation enters into the theories of gravitation, electrostatics, thermal equilibrium, and the motion of fluids, and the respective problems differ chiefly in the boundary conditions, which are thus as much a part of the problem as the equations themselves.

In the dynamics of an inviscid fluid, an essential boundary condition is that the velocity of the fluid *normal* to a fixed solid surface must vanish. This is simply an expression of the fact that the surface is impervious to the fluid. There is no similar restriction on the *tangential* component of the velocity at the surface, and thus an inviscid fluid may be supposed to slip without restraint over a surface. Experimental evidence shows that a real (*i.e.*, viscous) fluid always adheres to a surface, so that the tangential velocity must necessarily be zero at the junction of a fixed boundary and a real fluid. This is perhaps the most important distinction between the dynamics of inviscid and viscous fluids.

Streamlines; Velocity Potential. In problems of hydrodynamics it is frequently convenient to plot the velocity field so that both the direction and magnitude of the speed of flow can be easily envisaged. This is done by constructing a *streamline map*. A streamline, or line of flow, is defined as a curve which at any instant of time is tangential to the motion of the fluid at all points. Thus fluid cannot cross a streamline. A *stream tube* is defined as a region of space bounded by streamlines.

From this definition it is evident that the streamlines must satisfy the differential equations

$$\frac{dx}{u} = \frac{dy}{v} = \frac{dz}{w} \qquad (2.9)$$

When the streamlines retain the same shape at all times, the motion is said to be *steady*. In this case, but not otherwise, the streamlines coincide with the actual paths of the particles of the fluid.

It follows from Eqs. (2.9) that the streamlines are cut orthogonally by the surfaces which satisfy the equation

$$u\,dx + v\,dy + w\,dz = 0 \qquad (2.10)$$

The analytical condition that such surfaces should exist is that

$$u\left(\frac{\partial w}{\partial y} - \frac{\partial v}{\partial z}\right) + v\left(\frac{\partial u}{\partial z} - \frac{\partial w}{\partial x}\right) + w\left(\frac{\partial v}{\partial x} - \frac{\partial u}{\partial y}\right) = 0 \qquad (2.11)$$

If the expression

$$u\,dx + v\,dy + w\,dz$$

is a perfect differential $d\phi$, so that

$$u = \frac{\partial \phi}{\partial x}, \qquad v = \frac{\partial \phi}{\partial y}, \qquad w = \frac{\partial \phi}{\partial z} \qquad (2.12)$$

it follows that each of the expressions

$$2\xi = \frac{\partial w}{\partial y} - \frac{\partial v}{\partial z}, \qquad 2\eta = \frac{\partial u}{\partial z} - \frac{\partial w}{\partial x}, \qquad 2\zeta = \frac{\partial v}{\partial x} - \frac{\partial u}{\partial y} \qquad (2.13)$$

vanishes identically, and (2.11) is satisfied.

The function ϕ is called the *velocity potential* and the quantities ξ, η, ζ defined in (2.13) are the *components of vorticity*, or *spin*. When

$$\xi = \eta = \zeta = 0$$

the motion is said to be *irrotational*, and from the definition of ϕ it follows that if a velocity potential exists, the motion must be irrotational.

For incompressible motion in two dimensions, when $w = 0$,

$$u = \frac{\partial \phi}{\partial x}, \qquad v = \frac{\partial \phi}{\partial y} \qquad (2.14)$$

Hence the equation of continuity (2.8) becomes

$$\frac{\partial^2 \phi}{\partial x^2} + \frac{\partial^2 \phi}{\partial y^2} = 0 \qquad (2.15)$$

This is *Laplace's equation* in two dimensions. This equation, together with the condition that the gradient of ϕ along a normal vanishes at a rigid surface, determines ϕ and hence the velocity field.

Stream Function. Equations (2.9) for the streamlines become, in two-dimensional motion,

$$v\,dx - u\,dy = 0 \qquad (2.16)$$

Since the equation of continuity (2.8) for two-dimensional flow is

$$\frac{\partial u}{\partial x} = \frac{\partial(-v)}{\partial y}$$

it follows that the left-hand side of Eq. (2.16) must be a perfect differential, say $-d\psi$, so that

$$v\,dx - u\,dy = -\frac{\partial\psi}{\partial x}\,dx - \frac{\partial\psi}{\partial y}\,dy$$

or

$$u = \frac{\partial\psi}{\partial y}, \qquad v = -\frac{\partial\psi}{\partial x}$$

The function ψ is called the *stream function*. The streamlines of any motion can be plotted by giving the constant C in the equation

$$\psi(x,y) = C$$

different values.

It is easily verified that ψ also satisfies Laplace's equation (2.15), and since

$$\frac{\partial\phi}{\partial x}\frac{\partial\psi}{\partial x} + \frac{\partial\phi}{\partial y}\frac{\partial\psi}{\partial y} = 0$$

it follows that the equipotential curves $\phi = $ constant and the streamlines $\psi = $ constant cut orthogonally. The stream function may be regarded as an alternative to the velocity potential in the solution of a problem in irrotational flow.

The difference of the values of the stream function at two points represents the flux across any line joining the points. This follows immediately from the definition of ψ; if ds be an element of the curve and θ the angle made by the tangent with Ox, the flux is

$$\int(u\sin\theta - v\cos\theta)ds = \int(u\,dy - v\,dx) = \int d\psi = \psi_2 - \psi_1$$

This property might also be used to define the stream function, whose value at any point P is taken to be the amount of flow across a curve AP, where A is some fixed point in the plane. The name *flow function* is sometimes used for ψ, because of this property.

Circulation and Vorticity. It is shown in kinematics that the motion of a rigid body may be resolved into two components, *translation* and *rotation*. In translational motion, the angular relation of the body with respect to the axes of reference is invariable; the body does not turn about its own center but, apart from this, may describe any path in space, whether curved or not. In pure rotational motion the body varies its angular relation to the reference axes without change of location as a whole.

In a fluid, an elemental volume is free to move about independently of the main motion. In defining irrotational motion for a fluid, attention must be confined to a small element. If the elements of the fluid have no angular velocity about their centers, the motion as a whole is irrotational. Thus we may speak of the irrotational flow of a fluid around a cylinder, or any other body with curved surfaces, without a logical contradiction.

The *circulation* around any closed curve in a fluid is defined as the line integral of the tangential component of the velocity on the curve. In symbols,

$$\Gamma = \int_C q \cos \alpha \, ds$$

where Γ is the circulation, C the closed curve, q the resultant velocity at any point, and α the angle between the direction of q and the element ds of the curve at the point.

If the curve C is chosen to be a small rectangle with sides parallel to the coordinate axes, for two-dimensional flow

$$d\Gamma = \left(\frac{\partial v}{\partial x} - \frac{\partial u}{\partial y}\right) dx \, dy$$
$$= 2\zeta \, dS$$

where ζ is the vorticity defined on page 23, Eq. (2.13), and dS is an element of area. Hence the vorticity may be defined as half the limiting value of the ratio of the circulation to the area of a small element and is thus of the nature of an angular velocity.

It was proved by Stokes that a small element of the fluid, having three equal principal moments about the center of gravity, if suddenly frozen and detached from the main body of the fluid will begin to move with a pure translational motion, if, and only if, $u \, dx + v \, dy + w \, dz$ is an exact differential. This is the reason why motion satisfying this condition is called irrotational. If vorticity is present, the solid will spin like a top and its motion will be rotational as well as translational. The components of vorticity measure the angular velocity of the element about its center.

The mathematical theory of vortex motion in an inviscid fluid has been greatly developed by Helmholtz, Kelvin, Kirchhoff, and others. These studies consider *vortex lines*, defined as lines drawn in the fluid to coincide with the instantaneous axis of rotation of the corresponding fluid element, *vortex filaments* (portions of the fluid bounded by vortex lines through an infinitesimal closed curve), *vortex tubes* and *sheets*. The nomenclature and definitions suggest that the rotational motion is frequently confined to relatively small regions of the space occupied by the fluid, and this is the outstanding feature of the classical theory.

The vortices of the mathematician are idealizations of those found in nature. In the atmosphere there are plenty of examples of well-defined vortices. The most common are perhaps the familiar smoke ring, and the small "whirlwind" which forms at street corners on a windy day. On a larger scale are the "dust devils" of sandy areas and the "tropical revolving storms" of the lower latitudes.

The mathematical vortex of the inviscid fluid has one outstanding property. It is unchangeable, *i.e.*, it cannot be created or destroyed by inertia and pressure forces. This is often expressed as the *principle of the permanence of irrotational motion;* any motion started from rest in an inviscid fluid without surfaces of discontinuity must be forever irrotational. When surfaces of separation of definite masses of fluid are present, vorticity can occur, but only in sheets. A surface of discontinuity, over which the normal component of velocity is continuous, but with the tangential component different on both sides, may be regarded as a sheet made up of an infinity of vortex filaments, which in turn give rise to the discontinuity in the tangential component.† In a real fluid, vorticity arises principally because of internal friction in the fluid, and since the influence of viscosity is most strongly felt in the close proximity of a solid body, it follows that, in the atmosphere, vorticity is most likely to be found in the layers of air adjacent to the surface of the earth. The progressive slowing down of an air stream to zero velocity at a boundary means that an element of air caught in these layers is forced to turn about its own center. At great heights, where the influence of the earth's surface is negligible, the motion of the air approximates to irrotational flow. It is shown later in this chapter that viscosity not only gives rise to vorticity but is also responsible for its spread and ultimate decay in the main body of the fluid.

2.3. Air Flow over Undulating Country

The application of the theory of inviscid flow to the meteorologically important problem of the motion of air over undulating country was initiated by Pockels,[1] whose solution is given below.

The general method upon which the theoretical work is based is as follows: If a pattern of streamlines can be found from the hydrodynamical equation, any one of these streamlines may be supposed to represent the surface of a solid body. This is because an inviscid fluid can move freely over such a surface, and thus a streamline may be interpreted as a solid boundary without modifying the flow in any way.

To obtain the pattern of streamlines over a surface with an undulating profile, consider a two-dimensional irrotational air stream which at great heights is of constant speed V and entirely horizontal. At ground level the flow must conform to a surface consisting of a succession of parallel ridges and valleys, extending infinitely across wind.

† See A. S. Ramsey, "A Treatise on Hydromechanics," Part II, Hydrodynamics, pp. 239–241 (G. Bell, 1947).

Let the axis of x be horizontal and that of z vertical. If ϕ be the velocity potential, the component velocities are

$$u = \frac{\partial \phi}{\partial x}, \qquad w = \frac{\partial \phi}{\partial z} \tag{2.17}$$

For steady conditions the equation of continuity (2.5) is

$$\frac{\partial}{\partial x} (\rho u) + \frac{\partial}{\partial z} (\rho w) = 0 \tag{2.18}$$

The density ρ is assumed to vary in the vertical only. Hence, from (2.17) and (2.18)

$$\frac{\partial^2 \phi}{\partial x^2} + \frac{\partial^2 \phi}{\partial z^2} = -\frac{1}{\rho} \frac{d\rho}{dz} \frac{\partial \phi}{\partial z} \tag{2.19}$$

As a further simplification it is assumed that the temperature of the air is constant at all points, so that density decreases with height according to the law

$$\rho = \rho_0 \exp(-qz)$$

where q is a constant (see page 6). Equation (2.19) now becomes

$$\frac{\partial^2 \phi}{\partial x^2} + \frac{\partial^2 \phi}{\partial z^2} = q \frac{\partial \phi}{\partial z}$$

A solution of this equation which gives $u = V$, $w = 0$ as $z \to \infty$ is

$$\phi = V[x - b \cos mx \exp(-nz)]$$

whence

$$u = \frac{\partial \phi}{\partial x} = V[1 + bm \sin mx \exp(-nz)]$$

$$w = \frac{\partial \phi}{\partial z} = Vbn \cos mx \exp(-nz)$$

provided that

$$m^2 - n^2 = qn$$
$$n = r - \tfrac{1}{2}q$$
$$r^2 = m^2 + \tfrac{1}{4}q^2$$

So far the ground contour has not been specified except in general terms. The surface is supposed to coincide with one of the streamlines, the differential equation of which is

$$\frac{dz}{dx} = \frac{w}{u} = \frac{bn \cos mx \exp(-nz)}{1 + bn \sin mx \exp(-nz)}$$

Integrating,

$$\exp(-nz) \sin mx = -\frac{m}{bqn} + B \exp(qz)$$

where B is the parameter of the streamlines. A particular streamline is chosen as the ground contour by taking $x = z = 0$ to be a point on the profile curve; for these values $B = m/bqn$, so that

$$\frac{bn}{m} \sin mx \exp(-rz) = \frac{1}{q}\left[\exp\left(\frac{1}{2}qz\right) - \exp\left(-\frac{1}{2}qz\right) \right] \quad (2.20)$$

Now q is of the order of $10^{-4}\ m^{-1}$ if z is in meters, and if the maximum height of the undulations is such that

$$\left(\frac{1}{2}qz\right)^2 \ll 1 \quad \text{or} \quad z \ll \frac{2}{q} = 2 \times 10^4\ m$$

(which is certainly satisfied for undulations such as sand dunes or the gentle slopes common to cultivated land), terms in $(qz/2)^2$ and higher powers may be neglected in the expansion of the exponentials on the right-hand side of (2.20). Hence the profile equation is, approximately,

$$z = \frac{bn}{m} \sin mx \exp(-rz)$$

This curve may now be fitted to any given succession of ridges; if λ denotes the "wavelength," or distance between the summits,

$$m = \frac{2\pi}{\lambda}$$

W. R. Morgans[2] has used these results to construct theoretical curves of equal vertical velocity for a succession of mountain ridges of height 2300 m, distance between peaks = 24 km, for which $b = 1270$, $n = 2.066 \times 10^{-4}$, $m = 2.618 \times 10^{-4}$, $q = 1.25 \times 10^{-5}\ m^{-1}$.

From the theoretical solution the following deductions may be made:

1. The maximum velocity of the wind is found at the summit and the minimum velocity at the bottom of the valley, where, in both cases, the wind is entirely horizontal.

2. Along the vertical passing through the middle of the slope, the horizontal velocity is constant and equal to V, the velocity at great height.

3. Along the vertical through the summit, the speed of the wind, which is a maximum at the summit, decreases steadily toward its value at infinity, V. At the bottom of the valley, the wind increases steadily with height to its final value V.

4. The vertical velocity, which decreases with height everywhere, attains its maximum value at the middle of the slope where

$$w = V \tan \alpha$$

α being the angle of slope at this point. Thus the greater the slope, the greater the vertical velocity.

5. Curves of ascending and descending velocities are symmetrical with respect to the vertical through the summit.

Pockel's analysis thus leads to the expected result, that the highest horizontal velocity is attained on the summit, but in addition brings out the nonintuitive feature that the maximum vertical velocity is found at the middle of the windward side of the undulation.

In general, the inviscid-fluid theory of the flow around a solid body is in fair agreement with observation for points on the windward side but usually fails completely on the lee, since it takes no account of the formation of the wake. Agreement with observation must therefore be expected only on the windward slopes of hills.

Idrac[3] used kites to measure vertical velocities above gentle slopes (maximum slope 25°) descending from a ridge about 100 m high to a level plain, and later above undulations about 10 m high. In both cases there is much similarity between the theoretical and observed distributions of vertical velocity on the windward side. The vertical velocity tends to zero, as predicted, at the summit and on the plain and reaches a maximum at the steepest part of the slope. There is also a fair measure of numerical agreement for the maximum vertical velocity; Pockel's formula, for $V = 10$ m sec^{-1} and $\alpha = 25°$ gives $w_{max} = 4.7$ m sec^{-1}, and Idrac's contours show that vertical velocities up to and possibly exceeding 4 m sec^{-1} were measured at the point of greatest slope for a free-stream wind of 10 m sec^{-1}. However, the vertical-velocity field is not symmetrical about the vertical through the summit, as it is in the theoretical solution, and on the lee side a state of disorder prevails.

Koschmeider[4] estimated vertical velocities from observations made with gliders above the Rossitten dunes and found a marked difference from Pockel's theory in that, over the summit, the vertical velocities at first increase with height, and then decrease. Koch,[5] by photographing small puffs of smoke, found that a region of maximum vertical velocity occurs above the middle of the slope, but in general the observations show a much more complicated field of flow than is indicated by the simple irrotational-flow theory. For further details of the experimental work the original papers, or the summary given by W. R. Morgans,[2] should be consulted.

It will be seen from the above that despite the omission of viscosity and the drastic assumption of irrotational flow, the inviscid-fluid theory succeeds in giving a plausible picture of the pattern of flow near a low hill, at least on the windward side. The picture is, however, essentially qualitative and cannot be relied upon for accurate quantitative analysis. The failure is most pronounced on the lee of the hill; it is here that the omission of viscosity (and hence of vorticity) is most felt, since motion behind a bluff body is anything but irrotational.

Sources and Sinks. Flow over a Cliff. The above example indicates how the velocity potential can be employed to obtain the details of inviscid flow near a solid body, relying on the fact that any streamline may be chosen as the surface. The stream function may be used in a similar fashion, by employing the concept of sources and sinks.

A *source* is a point at which fluid is supposed to be appearing at a uniform rate, and a *sink* is a point at which fluid disappears. The fluid is supposed to pass outward from a source equally in all directions along radial lines. Let Q be the *strength* of the source, *i.e.*, the rate at which fluid is being produced. For a source of constant strength,

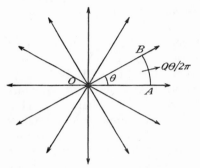

$$Q = 2\pi r u_r$$

where $r = \sqrt{(x^2 + z^2)}$ is distance from the source and u_r is the radial velocity.

The streamlines are straight lines radiating from the source, and, by definition, the stream function ψ is constant along these lines. Any radial line OA may be taken as $\psi = 0$ (Fig. 3).

FIG 3.   Flow near a source.

If B is any point on the streamline making an angle θ with OA, the flux across the arc AB is $(r\theta)u_r = (Q/2\pi)\theta$. Hence

$$\psi = \frac{Q}{2\pi}\,\theta$$

is the stream function for OB.

It should be noted that the source represents a singularity in the field, *i.e.*, the equations of motion are not satisfied at this point. If the source is contained within the streamline which is chosen to represent the surface, the pattern exterior to the chosen streamline will satisfy the hydrodynamic equations at all points and the source becomes simply a mathematical device for representing the effect of the body on the flow.

This method has been used by Glauert[†] to examine the flow of air, supposed inviscid, over a level plain and thence over a cliff. Suppose that a source of strength Q is placed in a uniform stream of velocity $-U$ parallel to the axis of x. By inspection, it is obvious that the stream function for the flow is

$$\psi = -Uz + \frac{Q}{2\pi}\,\theta$$

[†] H. Glauert, "The Elements of Aerofoil and Airscrew Theory," 2d ed., p. 22 (Cambridge, 1948).

being the sum of the stream functions for the two separate flows. Writing $Q = 2Uh$, the expression for ψ becomes

$$\psi = U \left(\frac{h\theta}{\pi} - z \right)$$

The pattern of flow is obtained by taking $\psi = $ constant, where the constant is given a series of values (say 0, 1, 2, 3, . . .), U and h having

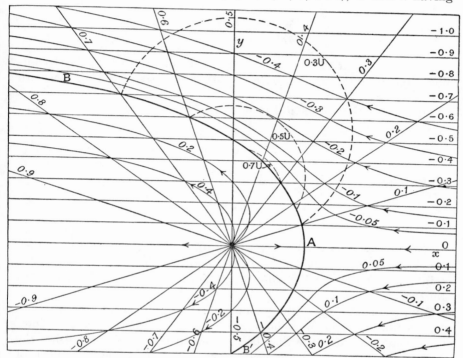

Fig. 4. Flow over a cliff ("The Elements of Aerofoil and Airscrew Theory" by H. Glauert).

been given suitable numerical values. The result is shown in Fig. 4. The streamline $\psi = 0$ consists of the positive part of Ox plus a curve of a parabolic shape, and the pattern is symmetrical about $\psi = 0$. This is supposed to represent a part of the surface of the earth, consisting of a level plain rising to a cliff. The source is entirely within the "cliff" curve and henceforth may be ignored, since the problem is concerned only with the flow exterior to $\psi = 0$.

For the cliff

$$r \sin \theta = z = \frac{h\theta}{\pi} \qquad (0 \le \theta \le \pi)$$

Hence

$$h = \pi r \frac{\sin \theta}{\theta}$$

Thus h measures the maximum height of the cliff as r increases and $\theta \to \pi$. The velocity components are given by

$$u = \frac{\partial \psi}{\partial z} = -U \left[1 - \frac{hx}{\pi(x^2 + y^2)} \right]$$

$$w = -\frac{\partial \psi}{\partial x} = \frac{Uhz}{\pi(x^2 + z^2)} = \frac{Uh}{\pi} \frac{\sin \theta}{r}$$

At the foot of the cliff, $u = w = 0$ (this is the point at which the stream-lines divide symmetrically). Hence the coordinates of the cliff base are $x = h/\pi$, $z = 0$.

The distribution of vertical velocity is given by

$$w = \frac{Uh}{\pi} \frac{\sin \theta}{r}$$

On the cliff, $h = \pi r \sin \theta / \theta$, and so

$$w = U \frac{\sin^2 \theta}{\theta}$$

which attains a maximum value $w = 0.725U$ at the point $\theta = 66.8°$, $z = 0.37h$. This result indicates that soaring flight is possible near this point on the face of such a cliff. Such flight is frequently observed with gulls on a rocky coast.

Solutions of this type, although dealing with problems rendered somewhat artificial by the omission of viscosity, have important applications. In recent years attention has been given to the problem of using the natural wind to supplement coal or water power in the generation of electrical current. The method usually consists in erecting a wind turbine near the summit of a ridge, in order to take advantage of the higher horizontal velocity caused by the crowding together of the stream-lines over the crest. The inviscid-fluid theory gives a first approximation to the solution of the problem of finding the increase in horizontal velocity caused by the ridge.

Waves in the Lee of Hills. Glider pilots have frequently reported what appear to be systems of standing waves in the lee of hills, and it is therefore a matter of some importance for aeronautics to examine the conditions in which such waves may be set up. The corresponding problem for rivers was investigated by Kelvin in 1886, who gave an expression for the deformation of the free surface resulting from small sinusoidal undulations in the bed. An account of this work, and of subsequent extensions, has been given by Lamb.†

In the atmospheric problem there is no free surface, and the interest lies mainly in considerations of waves which have large amplitudes in the lower layers. Lyra[6] and Queney[7] have shown that a wave motion exists in the lee of an obstacle in a wind uniform with height, but on the micrometeorological scale such waves are negligible. Scorer[8] has considered the extended problem of an obstacle in a wind variable with height, together with a stable (positive) gradient of potential temperature. His result is that if the scale is such that the effects of the earth rotation can be ignored, waves of large amplitude can exist near the ground, in the lee of an obstruction. Such surface waves owe their existence, in the main, to the variation of wind with height.

Scorer's analysis is restricted to nonturbulent inviscid flow and his main conclusion is that waves of large amplitude near the ground, and not elsewhere, can be formed over level ground in the lee of hills if the quantity

$$\sqrt{\left(\frac{g\beta}{V^2} - \frac{1}{V}\frac{d^2v}{dz^2}\right)}$$

decreases upward, where $\beta = d(\ln \theta)/dz$, θ being potential temperature and V the undisturbed wind. Such waves decrease upward exponentially and are essentially stable. They occur only if an obstruction is present and would persist indefinitely downstream over level country in the lee of the hill, were it not for friction. The reader is referred to the original paper for diagrams illustrating the flow of air (1) over an isolated ridge in a level plain and (2) down a slope leading to a level plain, in conditions favorable for the formation of lee waves. In these examples the wavelength is a few kilometers, and the diagrams exhibit, in a qualitative fashion, the theoretical counterpart of a real phenomenon in undulating country.

2.4. Winds on a Rotating Earth

Except in very shallow layers near the surface, any discussion of the motion of the air must take into account the influence of the rotation of the earth. This gives rise to the so-called Coriolis, or deviating force, whose magnitude is easily determined. The derivation of the expressions will not be given here, and the reader will find the full analysis in any textbook of dynamic meteorology.‡

---

† "Hydrodynamics," 6th ed., Arts. 242–246 (Cambridge, 1916).

‡ See, *e.g.*, Brunt," Physical and Dynamical Meteorology," 2d ed, Chap. VIII (Cambridge, 1939); or Haurwitz, "Dynamic Meteorology," Chap. VI (McGraw-Hill, 1941).

Consider a system of axes fixed in the earth, with Ox horizontal and drawn to the east, Oy horizontal and drawn to the north, and Oz vertical. If ω be the angular velocity of rotation of the earth and ϕ the latitude, a particle in the atmosphere experiences a force whose magnitude per unit mass has components

$$\left.\begin{array}{r} -2\omega(w \cos \phi - v \sin \phi) \text{ parallel to } Ox \\ -2\omega u \sin \phi \text{ parallel to } Oy \\ 2\omega u \cos \phi \text{ parallel to } Oz \end{array}\right\} \qquad (2.21)$$

where u, v, and w are the component velocities along axes of x, y, and z, respectively. It follows that the direction of the total deviating force is parallel to the plane of the equator and perpendicular to the direction of motion of the particle.

The equations of motion are therefore

$$\left.\begin{array}{r} \dfrac{du}{dt} + 2\omega(w \cos \phi - v \sin \phi) = -\dfrac{1}{\rho}\dfrac{\partial p}{\partial x} + X \\[2mm] \dfrac{dv}{dt} + 2\omega u \sin \phi = -\dfrac{1}{\rho}\dfrac{\partial p}{\partial y} + Y \\[2mm] \dfrac{dw}{dt} - 2\omega u \cos \phi = -\dfrac{1}{\rho}\dfrac{\partial p}{\partial z} - g + Z \end{array}\right\} \qquad (2.22)$$

where X, Y, and Z are component accelerations representative of forces not due to pressure and gravity.

The Geostrophic Wind. In the free atmosphere, the vertical component of the motion of the air, w, is usually very much less than the horizontal components, and it is possible to obtain a useful approximation to the motion of the air, at sufficiently great heights, by assuming that the wind at these levels is horizontal and free from friction. Thus

$$\left.\begin{array}{r} \dfrac{du}{dt} - 2\omega v \sin \phi = -\dfrac{1}{\rho}\dfrac{\partial p}{\partial x} + X \\[2mm] \dfrac{dv}{dt} + 2\omega u \sin \phi = -\dfrac{1}{\rho}\dfrac{\partial p}{\partial y} + Y \end{array}\right\} \qquad (2.23)$$

These equations state that the air is accelerated so as to achieve a balance between the gradient of pressure, the deviating force, and the external forces. For a stationary or very slowly moving pressure system the motion may be considered steady ($\partial u/\partial t = \partial v/\partial t = 0$), and if, in addition, all forces except those due to the rotation of the earth and the pressure field are disregarded, the simple system which results allows a rapid estimate to be made of the wind force once the gradient of pressure has been evaluated from the synoptic chart.

If the acceleration be resolved along the tangent and normal to the path, it is found that usually the tangential acceleration, or change in velocity down wind, is small compared with the centripetal, or normal, acceleration. The force arising from this latter acceleration is directed toward the center of curvature and, on the above assumption, must be balanced by the Coriolis force and the pressure gradient. The Coriolis force is at right angles to the path and hence in the same direction as the acceleration. For a balance to be achieved, the pressure gradient must also be along the same line, which means that the motion must be along the isobars.

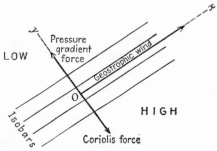

Fig. 5. The geostrophic wind (Northern Hemisphere).

The wind which satisfies this balance is the *gradient wind*. When the isobars are straight or so slightly curved that the centripetal acceleration may be ignored, the resulting motion is the *geostrophic wind*. The geostrophic wind, denoted by the symbol G, is the "free-stream velocity," or "velocity at infinity," for problems involving the surface layers. Writing, for convenience, $2\omega \sin \phi = \lambda$, by definition,

$$G = \text{pressure gradient} \div \lambda\rho \qquad (2.24)$$

and the direction of G is along the isobars, *i.e.*, normal to the pressure gradient. If the isobars are strongly curved, so that the centripetal acceleration cannot be neglected, Eq. (2.24) must be replaced by

$$\lambda(V - G) = \pm \frac{V^2}{r}$$

where V is the gradient wind and r is the radius of curvature of the path.

These considerations suggest that the most natural form of the two-dimensional equations of motion is one in which the components are combined to form the vector $u + iv$, where $i = \sqrt{-1}$. Equations (2.23) then combine to form the single equation

$$\frac{d}{dt}(u + iv) + i\lambda(u + iv) = -\frac{1}{\rho}\left(\frac{\partial p}{\partial x} + i\frac{\partial p}{\partial y}\right)$$

For the geostrophic balance

$$\mathbf{G} = u + iv = \frac{i}{\lambda\rho}\left(\frac{\partial p}{\partial x} + i\frac{\partial p}{\partial y}\right)$$

showing that the velocity vector is normal to the pressure-gradient vector.

Since the direction of the x axis can be chosen at will, Ox is placed along the isobars, so that $\partial p/\partial x = 0$ and $\partial p/\partial y$ is the total pressure gradient. Thus

$$\mathbf{G} = u = -\frac{1}{\lambda\rho}\frac{\partial p}{\partial y}$$

The vector equation of motion is

$$i\lambda(\mathbf{V} - \mathbf{G}) = \mathbf{F} \tag{2.25}$$

where $\mathbf{V}$ is the actual wind at any height and $\mathbf{F}$ represents additional forces, such as those due to motion along a curved path or to internal friction.

2.5. Viscosity and Its Effects

Because of their molecular structure all fluids, whether liquids or gases, exhibit, in greater or less degree, a resistance to deformation, or *viscosity*. This property is most easily recognized in slow motion near a solid boundary, where the fluid ceases to flow uniformly but is *sheared*, *i.e.*, the particles glide over each other in layers parallel to the surface. The inviscid fluid of the classical hydrodynamics is an ideal substance incapable of supporting any shearing stress, however small. In such a fluid there cannot be any dissipation of energy by internal friction. Moreover, as already explained, the boundary of a solid body can exert no tangential force on an inviscid fluid, which is therefore free to move over the surface without dissipation of energy. A real fluid, on the other hand, is compelled by molecular attraction to adhere to a solid boundary, and some of the kinetic energy of its bulk motion is irreversibly changed into heat and thus enhances the energy of the molecular motion.

Viscosity in a Gas. The analysis of viscosity in a gas may be undertaken in two ways:

1. The Newtonian method. The fluid is considered as a continuum, and viscosity is introduced by postulating a system of forces to account for typical effects.

2. The method of the kinetic theory of gases. The fluid is considered as an aggregate of molecules, whose mutual interactions give rise to the effect of internal friction.

Newton's analysis of viscosity. Suppose that a volume of gas is contained between two large parallel plane surfaces, one of which is in steady motion relative to the other (Fig. 6). For reasons which will become apparent later, it is necessary to assume that the speed of the moving plane is very low or that the distance between the planes, Z, is small. In these circumstances observation shows that the relative motion of the solid surfaces ultimately causes the whole body of gas to move parallel to the boundaries. At the boundaries the gas adheres to the surfaces, so that if $u = u(z)$ is the velocity of the gas relative to the fixed plane at distance z from it,

$$u = U \text{ on the plane } z = Z$$
$$u = 0 \text{ on the plane } z = 0$$

where U is the speed of the moving plane relative to the fixed plane. Observation also shows that with this special arrangement, the velocity of the gas changes linearly between the planes, *i.e.*,

$$u = U \frac{z}{Z} \qquad (2.26)$$

$$\frac{du}{dz} = \frac{U}{Z} \qquad (2.27)$$

We call (2.26) the *velocity profile* and (2.27) the *velocity gradient*.

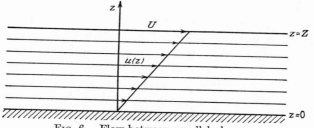

FIG. 6.   Flow between parallel planes.

To maintain the boundary in motion thus calls for a force proportional to U/Z per unit area of the surface, acting parallel to the plane, *i.e.*, tangential to the flow. This force is clearly a *shearing stress*, and so

Shearing stress per unit area $\propto$ velocity gradient

This relation is made precise by the introduction of a coefficient of proportionality, characteristic of the gas, called the *dynamic viscosity*. Generally,

$$\tau = \mu \frac{du}{dz} \qquad (2.28)$$

where τ is the shearing stress per unit area and μ is independent of u and z.

In problems of fluid motion it is often more convenient to use, not μ, but the *kinematic viscosity* ν defined by

$$\nu = \frac{\mu}{\rho}$$

where ρ is the density of the fluid. The dimensions of μ are $ML^{-1}T^{-1}$, while those of ν are L^2T^{-1}.

At ordinary pressures, the dynamic viscosity depends only on the nature and temperature of the gas. Table 3 shows a few typical values

TABLE 3. VISCOSITY OF DRY AIR AT VARIOUS TEMPERATURES

Temperature, °C	0	20	40
μ, g cm^{-1} sec^{-1}	1.71×10^{-4}	1.81×10^{-4}	1.90×10^{-4}
ν,† cm^2 sec^{-1}	0.132	0.150	0.169

† Values of ν appropriate to surface atmospheric pressure.

of μ and ν. In many problems, especially those arising in turbulent flow, the kinematic viscosity enters only as a fractional power, for example, $\nu^{\frac{1}{4}}$. In these cases the relatively small change with temperature may be disregarded without serious error, and ν may be looked upon as an absolute constant. It may be remarked, in passing, that the kinematic viscosity of air is much greater than that of water. In general terms, as will be seen later, this means that certain special features of a motion, such as vorticity, are *diffused*, by the action of viscosity, much more rapidly through air than through water. This property of viscosity is more easily seen from the kinetic-theory approach described in the next section.

Viscosity as a property of an aggregate of molecules. It is now recognized that a gas is not a continuous medium but an assembly of *molecules*, which in many problems may be regarded as discrete bodies, having definite mass and size. As a further simplification the molecules in a gas may be treated as elastic spheres, moving (at normal temperatures) at very high speeds and continually colliding with each other. This is the genesis of the *kinetic theory of gases*, which has been remarkably successful in explaining bulk properties, such as viscosity, by setting up simple mechanical models of a gas on the lines described above.

The molecules of nitrogen, oxygen, and argon, the three principal constituents of air, have diameters about 10^{-8} cm. At normal temperatures and pressures the average speed of these molecules is (about) 4×10^4 cm sec^{-1}, and they travel a distance of (about) 10^{-5} cm (the *mean free path*) between collisions. Something like 10^9 collisions are experienced by each molecule per second, and the property of viscosity arises as a direct consequence of this incessant agitation.

The simplest analysis of this field follows lines originally laid down by Clerk Maxwell in 1860. It is supposed that the molecules of gas are moving, for the most part, in a completely random fashion, with average velocity components equal in all directions. This may be called the "heat motion", normally expressed as temperature, which measures the energy of the motion. Suppose that the gas is moving slowly, as before, between parallel planes (Fig. 6), the additional motion, or drift of the molecular field in a given direction, being too small to affect the distribution of the heat motion along the component axes. A molecule will thus have, at any instant, not only the momentum appropriate to its own random motion, independent of its position in the field, but also a small amount of ordered momentum, in the direction of the general drift and dependent upon the position of the molecule with respect to the boundaries.

Suppose that a steady state has been established for the bulk motion and that a velocity profile $u = u(z)$ exists between the boundaries. A molecule on the plane $z = z$ is supposed to possess an ordered momentum $mu(z)$ appropriate to that level. As a result of its heat motion it will move over the mean free path (l), conserving this momentum, before a collision takes place. A molecule which leaves the plane $z = z$ perpendicularly will thus arrive at the plane $z = z + l$ without loss of momentum, the result being the transport of an amount of ordered momentum equal to

$$mu(z + l) - mu(z) \simeq ml \frac{du}{dz}$$

across a layer of gas of thickness l. The number of molecules crossing the plane at right angles is, on the average, one-third of the total number crossing, since all directions of motion are equally possible. If N is the number of molecules per unit volume and c is the average molecular velocity, the rate at which momentum is carried across unit area of the layer by this process is

$$\frac{1}{3} Nmcl \frac{du}{dz}$$

Since the bulk motion is steady, momentum is passed from one layer to the next as rapidly as it is received, so that a force $-\tau$ is exerted per unit area of the moving plane and a corresponding force $+\tau$ on the stationary plane. Thus

$$\tau = \frac{1}{3} Nmcl \frac{du}{dz}$$

But $Nm = \rho$, the density of the gas. Hence

$$\tau = \frac{1}{3} \rho cl \frac{du}{dz} \tag{2.29}$$

Comparing this with Eq. (2.28),

$$\mu = \tfrac{1}{3}\rho cl \tag{2.30}$$

or

$$\nu = \tfrac{1}{3}cl \tag{2.31}$$

The viscosity is thus expressed in terms of the mean molecular velocity and the mean free path, a fundamental result. The analysis given above is extremely crude, but more refined arguments lead to virtually the same result, and if, for example, the assumption of conservation of momentum over the free path is replaced by more precise considerations (the so-called "persistence" of the molecular velocities), the result is merely to change slightly the numerical factor $\frac{1}{3}$.†

The implications of this analysis should be carefully noted. The effect of the unceasing agitation of the molecules is that there is a continuous transfer of momentum from regions of high bulk velocity to regions of low bulk velocity, and the rate of transfer of momentum across unit area of a plane surface in the fluid is expressed by the product of the viscosity and the velocity gradient. In this sense viscosity causes a *diffusion of momentum* throughout the gas. Second, it should be observed that although there is no net transference of the molecules across a plane parallel to the direction of flow (otherwise the gas would not remain of uniform density), the existence of a gradient of bulk velocity ensures that the random motion brings about a continuous cross-stream transfer of momentum. Finally, the reader should note the important part played by the mean free path in Maxwell's analysis. The free path may be regarded either as the distance over which the molecule conserves its store of momentum or as a rough measure of the depth of the layer of gas in which viscous action takes place. It will be seen in Chap. 3 that these concepts have become of importance in the wider class of problems relating to turbulent motion.

2.6. The Equations of Motion of a Viscous Fluid

The previous section deals with the relatively simple example of flow in one direction between parallel planes, the effect of viscosity being represented by a single tangential stress. In general, there will be nine such stress components on the surfaces of a fluid element (Fig. 7). The three component stresses on any face, resolved parallel to the axes, are denoted by a simple notation. Thus on the face $x = $ const., parallel to the (y,z) plane, the stresses are

$$\tau_{xx} \text{ normal to the plane}$$
$$\tau_{xy} \text{ and } \tau_{xz} \text{ tangential to the plane}$$

The first subscript indicates the face on which the stress acts, and the second subscript denotes the direction in which the stress is acting, a tension being regarded as positive and a pressure as negative. In an inviscid fluid

$$\tau_{xx} = \tau_{yy} = \tau_{zz} = -p$$

while all the tangential stresses vanish, by definition.

† For further details, the reader is referred to the standard works of Jeans or Loeb on the kinetic theory of gases.

Relations between the Components. Suppose that the element of fluid is centered at (x,y,z), with edges of length δx, δy, δz parallel to the axes. Considering a surface normal to the axis of x, the stresses per unit area at (x,y,z) are τ_{xx}, τ_{xy}, τ_{xz}. On the two corresponding faces of the element the stresses are

$$\tau_{xx} - \frac{1}{2} \frac{\partial}{\partial x} (\tau_{xx}) \delta x, \qquad \tau_{xy} - \frac{1}{2} \frac{\partial}{\partial x} (\tau_{xy}) \delta x, \qquad \tau_{xz} - \frac{1}{2} \frac{\partial}{\partial x} (\tau_{xz}) \delta x$$

at the center of the face near the origin, and the same expressions, but with the minus sign replaced by a plus, express the stresses at the center

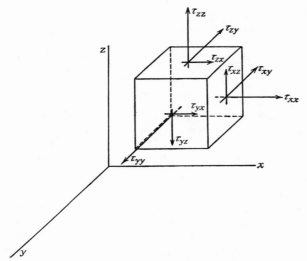

Fig. 7.   Viscous stresses on a fluid element.

of the face remote from the origin. The resultants of these stresses are forces

$$\frac{\partial}{\partial x} (\tau_{xx}) \delta x \, \delta y \, \delta z, \qquad \frac{\partial}{\partial x} (\tau_{xy}) \delta x \, \delta y \, \delta z, \qquad \frac{\partial}{\partial x} (\tau_{xz}) \delta x \, \delta y \, \delta z$$

parallel to the axes Ox, Oy, Oz, respectively, and couples

$$-\tau_{xz} \, \delta x \, \delta y \, \delta z, \qquad \tau_{xy} \, \delta x \, \delta y \, \delta z$$

about Oy, Oz, respectively.

The other two faces may be treated similarly, giving similar forces parallel to the axes and couples

$$-\tau_{yx} \, \delta x \, \delta y \, \delta z, \qquad \tau_{yz} \, \delta x \, \delta y \, \delta z$$
$$-\tau_{zy} \, \delta x \, \delta y \, \delta z, \qquad \tau_{zx} \, \delta x \, \delta y \, \delta z$$

Resolution parallel to the axes yields three equations of motion

$$\left.\begin{aligned}
\rho \frac{du}{dt} &= \rho X + \frac{\partial}{\partial x}(\tau_{xx}) + \frac{\partial}{\partial y}(\tau_{yx}) + \frac{\partial}{\partial z}(\tau_{zx}) \\[4pt]
\rho \frac{dv}{dt} &= \rho Y + \frac{\partial}{\partial x}(\tau_{xy}) + \frac{\partial}{\partial y}(\tau_{yy}) + \frac{\partial}{\partial z}(\tau_{zy}) \\[4pt]
\rho \frac{dw}{dt} &= \rho Z + \frac{\partial}{\partial x}(\tau_{xz}) + \frac{\partial}{\partial y}(\tau_{yz}) + \frac{\partial}{\partial z}(\tau_{zz})
\end{aligned}\right\} \qquad (2.32)$$

where, as before, X, Y, and Z are the components of external force per unit mass.

By taking moments about lines through (x,y,z) parallel to the axes it follows that

$$(\tau_{yz} - \tau_{zy})\delta x \, \delta y \, \delta z + (\text{terms of higher degree in } \delta x \, \delta y \, \delta z) = 0$$

Hence, as $\delta x \, \delta y \, \delta z \to 0$,

$$\tau_{yz} = \tau_{zy}$$
$$\tau_{zx} = \tau_{xz}$$
$$\tau_{xy} = \tau_{yx}$$

so that the nine original components of stress reduce to six. Equations (2.32) express completely the motion of a viscous fluid.

The Equations. As they stand, Eqs. (2.32) cannot be put to practical use, because they contain six unknown stresses as well as the three unknown velocities. The stresses in an element of fluid are obviously independent of any translation or rotation of the element as a whole but are affected by any distortion, *i.e.*, by relative motion of the parts of the element. The most general displacement of a fluid element is made up of a pure strain, *i.e.*, a motion such that lines drawn parallel to a certain set of axes undergo elongation at a uniform rate, a translation and a rotation. The state of stress depends only upon the state of strain.

The detailed analysis, which is long and complicated, shows that the six stresses can be expressed linearly in terms of the so-called principal stresses. These stresses are assumed to differ from their mean value $-p$ by linear functions of the rates of distortion of the fluid element.† The final result is that the viscous stresses can be expressed in terms of the pressure, the viscosity, and the velocity gradients, thus:

Normal stresses:

$$\tau_{xx} = -p - \frac{2}{3}\mu\left(\frac{\partial u}{\partial x} + \frac{\partial v}{\partial y} + \frac{\partial w}{\partial z}\right) + 2\mu\frac{\partial u}{\partial x}$$

$$\tau_{yy} = -p - \frac{2}{3}\mu\left(\frac{\partial u}{\partial x} + \frac{\partial v}{\partial y} + \frac{\partial w}{\partial z}\right) + 2\mu\frac{\partial v}{\partial y} \qquad (2.33)$$

$$\tau_{zz} = -p - \frac{2}{3}\mu\left(\frac{\partial u}{\partial x} + \frac{\partial v}{\partial y} + \frac{\partial w}{\partial z}\right) + 2\mu\frac{\partial w}{\partial z}$$

† For the details of the analysis, the reader is referred to Lamb, *op. cit.*, Chap. XI.

Tangential stresses:

$$\tau_{yz} = \mu \left(\frac{\partial w}{\partial y} + \frac{\partial v}{\partial z} \right)$$

$$\tau_{zx} = \mu \left(\frac{\partial u}{\partial z} + \frac{\partial w}{\partial x} \right) \qquad (2.33)$$

$$\tau_{xy} = \mu \left(\frac{\partial v}{\partial x} + \frac{\partial u}{\partial y} \right)$$

If the fluid is incompressible, the term $-\dfrac{2}{3} \mu \left(\dfrac{\partial u}{\partial x} + \dfrac{\partial v}{\partial y} + \dfrac{\partial w}{\partial z} \right)$ vanishes.

Substitution in Eqs. (2.32) gives the *Navier-Stokes equations of an incompressible viscous fluid:*

$$\left.\begin{aligned}
\frac{du}{dt} &= X - \frac{1}{\rho}\frac{\partial p}{\partial x} + \nu \left(\frac{\partial^2 u}{\partial x^2} + \frac{\partial^2 u}{\partial y^2} + \frac{\partial^2 u}{\partial z^2} \right) \\
\frac{dv}{dt} &= Y - \frac{1}{\rho}\frac{\partial p}{\partial y} + \nu \left(\frac{\partial^2 v}{\partial x^2} + \frac{\partial^2 v}{\partial y^2} + \frac{\partial^2 v}{\partial z^2} \right) \\
\frac{dw}{dt} &= Z - \frac{1}{\rho}\frac{\partial p}{\partial z} + \nu \left(\frac{\partial^2 w}{\partial x^2} + \frac{\partial^2 w}{\partial y^2} + \frac{\partial^2 w}{\partial z^2} \right)
\end{aligned}\right\} \qquad (2.34)$$

If $\nu = 0$, these equations reduce to those of Euler (2.4).

2.7. Flow near a Plane Surface

The nonlinearity of the Navier-Stokes equations and the consequences thereof have already been noticed. If the velocity vector can be derived from a potential, so that the flow is irrotational, it can be shown very simply that this also implies that all terms which are multiplied by μ in the Navier-Stokes equations must vanish identically.† (This may be interpreted as a statement that the frictional forces are in equilibrium, as in a solid body.) Thus solutions obtained for irrotational motion also satisfy the Navier-Stokes equations, but for such motions the vanishing of the second-order terms means that the equations are thereby reduced in order, and this introduces difficulties when it comes to satisfying conditions at a solid boundary. In irrotational flow, the motion is completely determined by the condition that the normal component of velocity vanishes at the boundary, but without the second-order frictional terms there is no way of making the tangential component vanish, except in the trivial case in which the whole mass of fluid is at rest relative to the surface. Hence, unless the frictional terms vanish identically,

---

† Thus, if ϕ be the velocity potential, $\nabla^2 \phi = 0$, where ∇^2 is the Laplace operator, $\partial^2/\partial x^2 + \partial^2/\partial y^2 + \partial^2/\partial z^2$. Hence $\nabla^2 \, \mathrm{grad} \, \phi = \mathrm{grad} \, \nabla^2 \phi = 0$, and so

$$\nabla^2 u = \nabla^2 v = \nabla^2 w = 0.$$

the Navier-Stokes equations must represent motions in which the fluid elements can rotate, *i.e.*, the motion possesses vorticity.

In the following simple but important examples of viscous flow near a plane surface, exact solutions of the Navier-Stokes equations can be found because, in the circumstances of the problems, the nonlinear inertia terms vanish identically.

Couette Flow. Suppose the space between two parallel plane boundaries $z = 0$, $z = Z > 0$ is filled with fluid of uniform density. Let the upper boundary have a steady velocity in the x direction, and let the lower boundary be stationary. It is further assumed that the air moves steadily in planes parallel to the boundaries, so that $v = w = 0$. From the equation of continuity, $\partial u/\partial x = 0$, so that $u = u(z)$. The Navier-Stokes equations become

$$\mu \frac{\partial^2 u}{\partial z^2} - \frac{\partial p}{\partial x} = 0$$
$$\frac{\partial p}{\partial y} = \frac{\partial p}{\partial z} = 0 \tag{2.35}$$

Since all the inertia terms are zero and since u is independent of x, the pressure gradient $\partial p/\partial x$ must be a constant. Hence, from Eqs. (2.35)

$$u = \frac{1}{2\mu} z^2 \left(\frac{\partial p}{\partial x} \right) + Az + B$$

where A and B are constants to be determined by the boundary conditions

$$u = 0 \text{ on } z = 0$$
$$u = U \text{ on } z = Z$$

The required solution is

$$u = U \left(\frac{z}{Z} \right) + \frac{1}{2\mu} \left(\frac{\partial p}{\partial x} \right) z(z - Z) \tag{2.36}$$

The shearing stress at any point is

$$\tau_{zx} = \mu \frac{du}{dz} = \frac{\mu U}{Z} + \frac{1}{2} \left(\frac{\partial p}{\partial x} \right) (2z - Z) \tag{2.37}$$

and the frictional drag per unit area of the lower boundary is

$$\left(\mu \frac{du}{dz} \right)_{z=0} = \frac{\mu U}{Z} - \frac{1}{2} Z \left(\frac{\partial p}{\partial x} \right) \tag{2.38}$$

For Couette motion, $\partial p/\partial x = 0$, and the shearing stress is invariable with distance from the boundary. This stress may be written as

$$\tau_{zx} = \mu \frac{du}{dz} = \rho U^2 \left(\frac{\nu}{UZ} \right) \tag{2.39}$$

The quantity UZ/ν, which is nondimensional, is called the *Reynolds number* of the motion and is denoted by the symbol Re. Thus

$$\tau_{zz} = \text{Re}^{-1}\, \rho U^2 \tag{2.40}$$

The significance of this form will become apparent later.

Diffusion of Vorticity. In the previous example, the motion of the air was assumed to be steady and uniform over any plane parallel to the boundaries.

Suppose now that the restriction of steady motion is removed. Equations (2.35) are then replaced by

$$\rho\,\frac{\partial u}{\partial t} = \mu\,\frac{\partial^2 u}{\partial z^2} - \frac{\partial p}{\partial x}$$
$$\frac{\partial p}{\partial y} = \frac{\partial p}{\partial z} = 0 \tag{2.41}$$

These equations are satisfied by taking $p = \text{constant}$ and

$$\frac{\partial u}{\partial t} = \nu\,\frac{\partial^2 u}{\partial z^2} \tag{2.42}$$

since $\nu = \mu/\rho$. Equation (2.42) will be recognized as that of the linear flow of heat in a solid or of diffusion in a gas (Fick's equation).

Suppose we seek a solution of Eq. (2.42) for the conditions

$$u = U \text{ for all } z \quad \text{when } t = 0$$
$$u = 0 \text{ on } z = 0 \quad \text{for } t > 0 \tag{2.43}$$

This is the problem of a fluid which up to a certain instant ($t = 0$) is moving steadily and uniformly with the velocity U, but which subsequently ($t > 0$) is subjected to the braking action of an infinite stationary plane. The problem is to ascertain how the effect of the stationary plane spreads throughout the fluid.

Mathematically, this problem is identical with that familiar in the theory of conduction of heat, in which one face of a semiinfinite solid, initially at uniform temperature throughout, is thereafter kept at zero temperature (Chap. 4). The solution of the problem is

$$\frac{u}{U} = \text{erf}\,\frac{z}{2\,\sqrt{(\nu t)}} \tag{2.44}$$

where

$$\text{erf } x = \frac{2}{\sqrt{\pi}}\int_0^x \exp\,(-\theta^2)d\theta$$

is the error function.

This solution satisfies the initial and boundary conditions; for $t = 0$, $u/U = 1$, and for $z = 0$, $t > 0$, $u = \text{erf}(0) = 0$. It may also be shown that the solution is unique, *i.e.*, no other function satisfies the equation and the initial and boundary conditions. It follows from (2.44) that as t increases without limit, $u \to 0$ for any finite value of z, so that ultimately the frictional drag of the boundary brings the whole mass of fluid to rest.

The vorticity of the motion is, by definition,

$$\eta = \frac{1}{2}\frac{\partial u}{\partial z} = \frac{U}{2\sqrt{(\pi \nu t)}}\exp\left(-\frac{z^2}{4\nu t}\right) \tag{2.45}$$

The expression on the right-hand side is another familiar solution, representing the spread of heat, initially concentrated on the plane $z = 0$, throughout the infinite solid. Considering the plane $z = 0$ as a vortex sheet, Eq. (2.45) shows that vorticity is diffused by viscosity throughout the entire fluid, exactly as heat is diffused. Thus the fluid, which initially was free from rotation, gains vorticity because of the resistance of the plane $z = 0$. This resistance is due entirely to viscosity. On the other hand, as $t \to \infty$, the vorticity decays everywhere, again because of the action of viscosity. Thus viscosity gives birth to vorticity and ultimately destroys it.

At any finite time t the vorticity, theoretically, is found throughout the whole fluid, but if a convention is adopted, that the upper limit Z of the layer which contains rotation is determined by the height at which η has fallen to some small fraction, say $1/f$, of its maximum value (which is found on $z = 0$) at that time, it follows that

$$Z = 2\sqrt{(\nu t \cdot \ln f)}$$

Hence the thickness of the layer which possesses vorticity is of the order of $\sqrt{(\nu t)}$, a result which might also be deduced from purely "dimensional" arguments.

In considering these results one important limitation should be noted. It has been assumed throughout that the flow is in parallel planes, so that $v = w = 0$, and there is no intermingling of the parallel streams except by the motion of the molecules. Motion of this type, called *laminar*, can be maintained only in certain special circumstances, and one condition is that the velocity is small everywhere. If these conditions are not fulfilled, the motion becomes much more complicated and the inertia terms cannot be assumed to vanish. True laminar motion is comparatively rare in the atmosphere, but the state is approached in flow near the surface of the earth in special circumstances which are by no means infrequent. These will be described later.

2.8. The Theory of the Laminar Boundary Layer

It will be apparent that the analogy between the spread of vorticity in a fluid and the conduction of heat in a body is by no means superficial, and the physical conditions which arise in motion near a solid boundary are more easily grasped by considering the rise of temperature in a fluid near a hot surface. This has been made clear by Prandtl,[11] to whom science owes the conception and early development of the theory of the *boundary layer*. Consider a heated body immersed in a stream of cold fluid. If the velocity of the stream is low, heat spreads in all directions and affects a large volume of the fluid, but if the flow is swift, only a relatively thin layer of the fluid will be warmed as it passes the body. In the hydrodynamic problem, if the velocity of the originally irrotational stream is small, rotation generated by viscosity will be found at great distances from the body, but for swifter streams vorticity will be concentrated in a thin layer of fluid immediately adjacent to the surface, and the flow remote from the body will remain irrotational. These deductions, amply confirmed by numerous experiments in wind tunnels, indicate how the hitherto intractable Navier-Stokes equations may be made to yield results of fundamental importance concerning flow near a solid surface, provided that the viscosity is very small or, to be more exact, that the Reynolds number is very large.

Dynamic Similitude and the Reynolds Number. Because it is impossible to control natural winds, much experimental work in fluid mechanics is done with models, and an obvious first requirement is that the pattern of flow at full scale shall be a magnified but otherwise unchanged version of that found with the model. *Geometric similitude* between two systems means that one may be made to coincide with the other by a suitable change in the unit of length; *dynamic similitude* means that, by suitable changes in the fundamental units (those of mass, length, and time), the equations of motion and the boundary conditions of one system can be transformed into those of the other. There is a simple analytical condition for this.

Consider a fluid of uniform density in which external forces such as gravity produce a certain hydrostatic pressure, which provides a datum above which the actual pressure p is reckoned. In the motion of such a fluid there are three types of forces, expressed by:

1. Inertia terms, such as $\rho \, \partial u/\partial t$, $\rho u \, \partial u/\partial x = \frac{1}{2} \rho \, \partial(u^2)/\partial x$, etc.
2. Friction terms, such as $\mu \, \partial^2 u/\partial x^2$, etc.
3. Pressure-gradient terms, such as $\partial p/\partial x$, etc.

For two motions to be dynamically similar, the ratios of the forces represented by these terms must be identical in both motions, but since in the equations these forces balance, it is necessary to consider only the ratio of two of the above types. These are chosen to be the inertia and frictional forces.

Let U be any convenient reference velocity and l any characteristic length. The inertia terms involve $\rho U^2/l$ and the friction terms $\mu U/l^2$. The ratio of these is $\rho U l/\mu = Ul/\nu$, which will be recognized as an example of the nondimensional quantity called the Reynolds number. Thus a necessary condition for the dynamic similitude of two motions in which the systems are geometrically similar is that they must have the same Reynolds number and be subject to the same boundary conditions. This is the fundamental principle governing all work with models in wind tunnels.

There is, however, another aspect of the above relations. In any given motion, the Reynolds number indicates whether inertia or viscous effects predominate; if the Reynolds number is small (*e.g.*, less than unity), the pattern of flow will be shaped chiefly by viscosity, and very large Reynolds numbers (*e.g.*, tens or hundreds of thousands) mean that inertia effects are far more important than viscous effects. To fix ideas, consider air flowing past a body at moderate speed,† and take l to be any convenient length in the body, such as its diameter. If the reference velocity be the speed of the air at a great distance from the body, the Reynolds number will be high, but if the speed of the air stream be measured very close to the surface of the body, the Reynolds number will be small. In a general fashion, this says that the influence of viscosity will be felt chiefly in the layers of air very near the body, and hardly at all in the free stream.

The importance of the Reynolds number in problems of aerodynamics may be seen from a very general result derived by Rayleigh. The force exerted by a stream on a body completely immersed in it depends upon (1) the density and viscosity of the fluid, (2) the speed of flow, and (3) the size, shape, and attitude of the body. For bodies of similar shape and attitude whose size is specified by a linear dimension l, dimensional analysis then yields *Rayleigh's formula for aerodynamic force*

$$\text{Force} \propto \rho\, U^2 l^2\, \text{Re}^n \qquad (2.46)$$

where U is the velocity of the undisturbed stream relative to the body and n is a pure number which can be found only by exact analysis or by experiment. The component of aerodynamic force parallel to the direction of the undisturbed stream is called *resistance* or *drag*, and for this force Rayleigh's relation is usually written as

$$\text{Resistance} = \tfrac{1}{2}\rho U^2 l^2 C_D$$

where C_D ($=$ const. Re^n) is a factor of proportionality called the *drag coefficient*. An exact solution which illustrates Rayleigh's theorem is that

† The restriction to moderate speed, *i.e.*, a speed well below that of sound waves in air, is necessary in order to exclude the possibility of compressibility effects.

for the shearing stress per unit area in Couette motion [Eq. (2.40)]

$$\tau_{zx} = \frac{1}{2} \rho U^2 \left(\frac{2}{\text{Re}} \right)$$

In this example

$$C_D = \frac{2}{\text{Re}}; \qquad n = -1 \qquad (2.47)$$

Rayleigh's theorem shows that, in incompressible motion, the pattern of flow around a submerged body is completely determined by the Reynolds number, which thus emerges as a basic parameter of fluid motion.

The Equations of Motion in the Boundary Layer. Prandtl's analysis of motion in the proximity of a rigid boundary is based on the physical observation that in a fluid of small viscosity, such as air, frictional effects are significant only in a very thin layer adjacent to the boundary. In this layer the velocity gradient is necessarily large, because the transition from zero relative velocity at the boundary to that of the free stream takes place in a minute depth of the fluid, and, despite the smallness of the viscosity, the viscous and inertia terms in the Navier-Stokes equations may be of the same order of magnitude within the thin layer of strongly sheared motion. Outside the boundary layer the fluid may be regarded as inviscid, with a uniform velocity and a known pressure field.

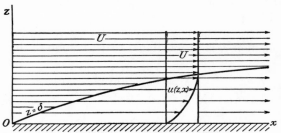

FIG. 8. The laminar boundary layer at a plane surface.

The method consists essentially in an examination of the orders of magnitude of the various terms in the equations of motion and of continuity inside a layer of depth δ, supposed small. For two-dimensional motion the surface is taken to be the plane $z = 0$, the flow proceeding in the x direction. It is convenient to use throughout nondimensional variables ξ, ζ, τ, so that if U be a reference velocity (usually the velocity in the free stream) and l a characteristic length in the x direction (such as the length of the surface down wind), the new variables are defined by

$$\xi = \frac{x}{l}, \qquad \zeta = \frac{z}{\delta}, \qquad \tau = \frac{U}{l} t$$

The boundary layer $0 \leq z \leq \delta$ is now defined by $0 \leq \zeta \leq 1$.

The equations of motion and the equation of continuity become

$$\frac{1}{l}\left(U\frac{\partial u}{\partial \tau} + u\frac{\partial u}{\partial \xi} + \frac{l}{\delta}w\frac{\partial u}{\partial \zeta}\right) = -\frac{1}{\rho l}\frac{\partial p}{\partial \xi} + \frac{\nu}{l^2}\frac{\partial^2 u}{\partial \xi^2} + \frac{\nu}{\delta^2}\frac{\partial^2 u}{\partial \zeta^2} \qquad (2.48)$$

$$\frac{1}{l}\left(U\frac{\partial w}{\partial \tau} + u\frac{\partial w}{\partial \xi} + \frac{l}{\delta}w\frac{\partial w}{\partial \zeta}\right) = -\frac{1}{\rho \delta}\frac{\partial p}{\partial \zeta} + \frac{\nu}{l^2}\frac{\partial^2 w}{\partial \xi^2} + \frac{\nu}{\delta^2}\frac{\partial^2 w}{\partial \zeta^2} \qquad (2.49)$$

$$\frac{1}{l}\frac{\partial u}{\partial \xi} + \frac{1}{\delta}\frac{\partial w}{\partial \zeta} = 0 \qquad (2.50)$$

and $u = w = 0$ on $\zeta = 0$; $u = U$, $w = 0$ for $\zeta \geq 1$.

It is supposed that u, $\partial u/\partial \xi$, and $\partial^2 u/\partial \xi^2$ are $O(1)$ and that large accelerations are excluded, so that $\partial u/\partial t = (U/l)\partial u/\partial \tau$ is also $O(1)$.

From Eq. (2.50) it follows that

$$\frac{\partial w}{\partial \zeta} = O\left(\frac{\delta}{l}\right)$$

Since u changes from zero to U in the interval $0 \leq \zeta \leq 1$, it follows that $\partial u/\partial \zeta$ and $\partial^2 u/\partial \zeta^2$ must be $\bar{O}(1)$. Hence, in Eq. (2.48), all the inertia terms are of the same order of magnitude.

Turning now to the viscous terms in Eq. (2.48), if both ν and δ are small but such that ν/δ^2 is $O(1)$ and ν/l^2 is small, the term $(\nu/l^2)\partial^2 u/\partial \xi^2$ is negligible and henceforth may be omitted. The term $(\nu/\delta^2)\partial^2 u/\partial \zeta^2$ is $O(1)$ like the inertia terms and must be retained. The typical inertia term $(1/l)u\,\partial u/\partial \xi$ and the viscous term $(\nu/\delta^2)\partial^2 u/\partial \zeta^2$ are thus of equal magnitude, and since u is proportional to U, it follows that

$$\delta^2 = \text{constant}\,\frac{\nu l}{U}$$

or

$$\frac{\delta}{l} = \text{constant}\,\sqrt{\frac{\nu}{Ul}} = \text{constant}\,\sqrt{\frac{1}{\text{Re}}} \qquad (2.51)$$

where Re is the Reynolds number of the motion, the constant being of order unity. This result is of considerable importance in the subsequent development of the theory.

Equation (2.49) now reduces to

$$\frac{1}{\rho}\frac{\partial p}{\partial \zeta} = O\left(\frac{U^2\delta^2}{l^2}\right)$$

or

$$\frac{1}{\rho}\frac{\partial p}{\partial z} = O(\delta)$$

so that the rate of change of pressure perpendicular to the wall is negligible. Thus the pressure is constant along any normal to the surface and is therefore determined by the equation of inviscid flow

$$\frac{\partial U}{\partial t} + U \frac{\partial U}{\partial x} = -\frac{1}{\rho}\frac{\partial p}{\partial x} \qquad (z \geq \delta) \qquad (2.52)$$

The equations of motion and of continuity in the boundary layer are thus, in terms of the original variables,

$$\left.\begin{array}{c} \dfrac{\partial u}{\partial t} + u \dfrac{\partial u}{\partial x} + w \dfrac{\partial u}{\partial z} = -\dfrac{1}{\rho}\dfrac{\partial p}{\partial x} + \nu \dfrac{\partial^2 u}{\partial z^2} \\[2ex] \dfrac{\partial p}{\partial z} = 0 \\[2ex] \dfrac{\partial u}{\partial x} + \dfrac{\partial w}{\partial z} = 0 \end{array}\right\} \quad z < \delta \ (2.53)$$

where, in both sets of equations, $\delta = O(\sqrt{(\nu/lU)})$. These are Prandtl's equations.

2.9. Application of the Boundary-layer Theory to Flow over a Plane Surface

A fundamental problem in micrometeorology is that of friction in the air in the immediate proximity of the surface of the earth, supposed plane. This problem will now be solved for laminar motion by a method which, although approximate, succeeds in giving a realistic approximation to the exact solution of the Prandtl equations and avoids the tiresome numerical methods inherent in the full treatment.

In dealing with boundary-layer problems, a difficulty immediately arises concerning the exact definition of δ, the boundary-layer "thickness." At the surface itself, $u = w = 0$, but at the upper edge of the layer, u must pass continuously to U, and $\partial u/\partial z$ must become zero. In the mathematical treatment such conditions usually cannot be satisfied for any finite z. This difficulty is overcome, and δ given a finite value, by the requirement that, on $z = \delta$, u is equal to U to some prescribed degree of accuracy (say, within 10, 1, or 0.1 per cent). For precise analytical work, various definitions are employed, e.g., the so-called "displacement thickness" δ_1, defined by

$$\delta_1 = \frac{1}{U}\int_0^\infty (U - u)dz$$

where the integral is evaluated along a normal across the boundary layer.

This definition gives the amount by which the streamlines of the undisturbed flow are displaced outward near the surface.

Consider a plane AA perpendicular to the surface $z = 0$. The amount of fluid crossing an element of unit width and height dz in unit time is $\rho u\, dz$ (Fig. 9). Before entering the boundary layer this mass was moving

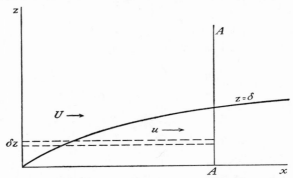

Fɪɢ. 9. Application of the momentum theorem to a boundary layer.

with the undisturbed velocity U, and the loss of momentum is therefore $\rho u(U - u)dz$. The total loss of momentum is, per unit time,

$$\rho \int_0^\infty u(U - u)dz \simeq \rho \int_0^\delta u(U - u)dz$$

This rate of loss of momentum must be equal to the sum of the frictional resistance of the surface up to the point A. Hence

$$\int_0^x \tau_0\, dx = \rho \int_0^\delta u(U - u)dz$$

or

$$\tau_0 = \rho \frac{d}{dx} \int_0^\delta u(U - u)dz$$

where τ_0 is the frictional drag of the surface, per unit area. It is now supposed that the velocity profile is known in the boundary layer, so that

$$u = Uf\left(\frac{z}{\delta}\right) = Uf(\zeta)$$

Hence

$$\rho \int_0^\delta u(U - u)dz = \rho U^2 \delta \int_0^1 (f - f^2)d\zeta$$

A crude assumption concerning the velocity profile, *viz.*, that it is linear in the boundary layer, or

$$f(\zeta) = \zeta \qquad \text{if } 0 \leq \zeta \leq 1$$
$$f(\zeta) = 1 \qquad \text{if } \zeta > 1$$

gives

$$\int_0^1 (f - f^2)d\zeta = \int_0^1 (\zeta - \zeta^2)d\zeta = \tfrac{1}{6}$$

and the momentum loss is

$$\rho \frac{U^2 \delta}{6}$$

The friction at the surface is, by definition,

$$\tau_0 = \mu \left(\frac{du}{dz}\right)_{z=0} = \frac{\mu U}{\delta} f'(0) = \frac{\mu U}{\delta}$$

and so

$$\frac{\nu U}{\delta} = \frac{U^2}{6} \frac{d\delta}{dx}$$

whence

$$\delta = (2\sqrt{3})\sqrt{\frac{\nu x}{U}} \simeq 3.464 \sqrt{\frac{\nu x}{U}}$$

From this the displacement thickness δ_1 can be found,

$$\delta_1 = \frac{1}{U}\int_0^\infty (U - u)dz = \delta \int_0^1 (1 - f)d\zeta = \frac{1}{2}\delta$$

Hence

$$\delta_1 \simeq 1.732 \sqrt{\left(\frac{\nu x}{U}\right)} = \frac{1.732x}{\sqrt{\mathrm{Re}}} \tag{2.54}$$

The friction at the surface is

$$\tau_0 = \frac{\mu U}{\delta} = \frac{0.289\rho U^2}{\sqrt{(Ux/\nu)}} = \frac{0.289\rho U^2}{\sqrt{\mathrm{Re}}} \tag{2.55}$$

and the total resistance from $x = 0$ to $x = l$ is

$$\int_0^l \tau_0\, dx = 0.577 U^2 l \sqrt{\frac{\nu}{Ul}}$$

The above approximate solutions may be compared with the exact solution obtained by Blasius,[9] who considered the equations

$$u \frac{\partial u}{\partial x} + w \frac{\partial u}{\partial z} = \nu \frac{\partial^2 u}{\partial z^2}$$

$$\frac{\partial u}{\partial x} + \frac{\partial w}{\partial z} = 0$$

with the boundary conditions

$$u = w = 0 \text{ on } z = 0$$
$$u = U \text{ along } x = 0 \text{ and as } z \to \infty$$

i.e., steady flow over a plane surface in the absence of a pressure gradient. The solutions obtained are

$$\delta_1 = 1.72 \sqrt{\left(\frac{\nu x}{U}\right)}$$

$$\tau_0 = \frac{0.332\rho U^2}{\sqrt{\mathrm{Re}}}$$

which may be compared with (2.54) and (2.55). It will be seen that despite the crude assumption of a linear profile, the numerical agreement is good. Other approximations have been proposed; Lamb used a profile in the form of a sine function and polynomials of degree three and four have also been employed, with satisfactory results. An account of these is given in Goldstein's treatise.[†]

The main interest in the above solution, however, is not the closeness of agreement in the numerical factors (which in the case of the linear profile is, to a certain extent, accidental) but the implications of the method itself. It has been shown that in this case a knowledge of the velocity profile is all that is required to ascertain the rate of transfer of momentum across the lines of flow, and this has important repercussions for micrometeorology. Direct measurement of the friction of the ground is not easy, and it is often necessary to use indirect methods, such as those given above, to ascertain the magnitude of this quantity.

Kármán's Integral Condition. The above method was used by v. Kármán[10] to obtain a general relation for boundary-layer flow. The Kármán relation can be obtained from the boundary-layer equations as follows: If $u = f(z)$, with $u = 0$ on $z = 0$, $u = U$ on $z = \delta$, integrating the first equation of (2.53) and substituting from the equation of continuity gives

$$\int_0^\delta \rho \frac{\partial u}{\partial t}\, dz + \int_0^\delta \rho u \frac{\partial u}{\partial x}\, dz + [\rho w u]_0^\delta + \int_0^\delta \rho u \frac{\partial u}{\partial x}\, dz = -\delta \frac{\partial p}{\partial x} + \left[\mu \frac{\partial u}{\partial z} \right]_0^\delta$$

Then

$$\int_0^\delta \rho \frac{\partial u^2}{\partial x}\, dz = \frac{\partial}{\partial x} \int_0^\delta \rho u^2\, dz - \frac{\partial \delta}{\partial x}[\rho u^2]_0^\delta = \frac{\partial}{\partial x} \int_0^\delta \rho u^2\, dz - \rho U^2 \frac{\partial \delta}{\partial x}$$

The term $[\rho u w]_0^\delta$ vanishes for $z = 0$, and so

$$U[\rho w]_0^\delta = U \int_0^\delta \rho \frac{\partial w}{\partial z}\, dz = -U \int_0^\delta \rho \frac{\partial u}{\partial x}\, dz$$

$$= -U \frac{\partial}{\partial x} \int_0^\delta \rho u\, dz + U \frac{\partial \delta}{\partial x}[\rho u]_0^\delta = -U \frac{\partial}{\partial x} \int_0^\delta \rho u\, dz + \rho U^2 \frac{\partial \delta}{\partial x}$$

[†] "Modern Developments in Fluid Dynamics," S. Goldstein (ed.), Vol. 1, p. 157 (Oxford, 1938).

The shearing stress $\mu \, \partial u / \partial z$ is equal to τ_0 on $z = 0$ and vanishes for $z = \delta$. Hence finally

$$\frac{\partial}{\partial t} \int_0^\delta \rho u \, dz + \frac{\partial}{\partial x} \int_0^\delta \rho u(u - U) dz = -\delta \frac{\partial p}{\partial x} - \tau_0 \qquad (2.56)$$

This is v. Kármán's general integral relation. It will be observed that for steady motion in the absence of a pressure gradient,

$$\frac{\partial}{\partial x} \int_0^\delta \rho u(U - u) dz = \tau_0$$

as before. In the more general case Eq. (2.56) should be regarded as a relation for δ, which for steady motion is determined as a function of x if the velocity profile and the pressure gradient are known.

BIBLIOGRAPHY

1. F. C. Pockels, Ann. Physik (4), IV, 459 (1901).
2. W. R. Morgans, Aeronaut. Research Committee, R. and M. No. 1456, London (1931).
3. P. Idrac, Etude sur les conditions d'ascendance du vent favorable au vol à voile, Mém. office natl. météorol. France (1923).
4. H. Koschmeider, Z.F.M., 235 (1925).
5. H. Koch, Veröffentl. Forschungs.-Inst. R.R.G. (1928).
6. G. Lyra, Z. angew. Math. u. Mech., 23, No. 1 (1943).
7. P. Queney, Univ. Chicago, Dept. Meteorol. Misc. Rept., No. 23 (1947); Am. Meteorol. Soc. Bull., 29, 16 (1948).
8. R. S. Scorer, Quart. J. Roy. Meteorol. Soc., 75, 41 (1949).
9. H. Blasius, Z. Math. u. Physik, 56, 4 (1908).
10. Theodore v. Kármán, Z. angew. Math. u. Mech., 1, 233 (1921).
11. L. Prandtl, "The Mechanics of Viscous Fluids," Aerodynamic Theory, Durand (ed.), Vol. III, G. (Berlin, 1934).

CHAPTER 3

THE ATMOSPHERE IN MOTION. (II) TURBULENT FLOW

The motion of the air near the surface of the earth is rarely as simple as that described in the examples of the previous chapter. In general, a fluid of low viscosity moving in the vicinity of a solid body will not follow a steady or even a recognizable pattern of streamlines, except in very special circumstances. True laminar flow, in which a particle of fluid always follows exactly the same path as its predecessors, is a mathematical idealization, which must be regarded as a useful but limited approximation to the truth on certain occasions. The *natural* state of fluid motion (using the word in its colloquial sense) is one in which the motion of individual particles is extremely complicated, although among the confusion it is usually possible to recognize a fairly simple mean pattern.

If a body with sensible lateral extension (technically, a *bluff body*), such as a sphere, is suspended in a wind tunnel or other device designed to produce a "smooth" flow, it is possible to distinguish two modes of motion in the vicinity of the body, provided that the velocity of the stream is not too low. Upstream of the object, and often for a certain distance over its surface, the flow remains smooth and conforms to the shape of the body, but toward the rear, and for a considerable distance behind the body, the smooth flow disintegrates into one in which it is impossible to distinguish any steady or regular pattern of streamlines. This type of motion is called *turbulent*. Except in very special circumstances, the wind near the ground is highly turbulent, especially in the neighborhood of obstacles such as trees, houses, and hills. As yet, the mathematical theory of this type of motion is only partially established, and most of the difficulties experienced in the study of micrometeorology are to be traced, ultimately, to the great complexity of the motion of the air in the lower layers of the atmosphere.

3.1. General Aspects of Turbulence

The study of turbulent motion is best approached by considering certain simple experiments on the flow of water in long, straight pipes, first described by Osborne Reynolds in 1883, and now a familiar classroom demonstration. In this arrangement, water from a large reservoir is allowed to flow through a long, straight glass tube, carefully insulated

56

from external vibrations, the nature of the flow being made visible by the introduction of a thin stream of dye from a subsidiary tube near the inlet. If the motion of the water in the tube is sufficiently slow, the filament of dye maintains its integrity from inlet to outlet, and shows little broadening with distance downstream, but if the speed of flow is increased beyond a certain limit, the character of the motion changes. In the new type of flow the filament of dye is quickly broken up and diffused over the whole stream by crosscurrents, so that the tube remote from the inlet becomes filled with dilute color in which it is no longer possible to distinguish the original filament of dye.

The first type of flow is clearly laminar, the motion being permanently along lines parallel to the wall of the tube with no sensible intermingling of adjacent layers of fluid. The second, or turbulent, type of flow is characterized by the existence of large secondary motions transverse to the main flow, causing rapid and incessant mixing of the fluid throughout the pipe. The turbulent motion is obviously strongly rotational, but the vortices do not form any recognizable pattern, and the path of a typical particle is extremely tortuous, although the fluid as a whole moves steadily toward the outlet. Following Reynolds, the flow may be supposed to consist of a relatively simple *mean motion*, on which is superimposed an extremely complicated secondary, or *eddy, motion*, of an oscillatory but not obviously periodic character.

A closer examination of the two types of motion shows the difficulty (or perhaps, at this stage, the impossibility) of framing a satisfactory mathematical definition of turbulent motion. Even in so-called laminar flow, the path of a particle is not completely specified by the solution of the hydrodynamic equations, for the agitation of the molecules of the fluid means that a particle is incessantly bombarded from all sides, so that its path always contains random irregularities. This is the phenomenon known as Brownian motion, but it should be noted that fluctuations of this type are unrelated to the bulk flow and occur even when the fluid, as a whole, is at rest. Turbulence, on the other hand, implies not only that random irregularities are observed in the path of the particle but that such irregularities are on a much larger scale and are related, in some way not yet completely understood, to the bulk motion. These considerations suggest that nonturbulent flow may be defined as one in which any random irregularities in the motion of a fluid element are infinitesimal, *i.e.*, of the molecular scale of magnitude. Turbulent flow is motion containing random oscillations of finite size, leading to irregularities in the path of a particle of scale comparable with lengths which determine the kinematics of the mean motion, such as the shape of the boundary. Such oscillations cause mixing and are therefore quite different in character from, say, regular wave motions, which in general do not bring about intermingling of adjacent layers of fluid.   The main theoretical problem of turbulence, as yet only partly solved, is to investigate the origin of such oscillations and their effects on the mean motion, but this is hardly possible until a satisfactory definition of turbulence has been found.†

From the physical aspect there is often no difficulty in recognizing a turbulent motion because of the pronounced irregularities in the motion and the characteristic appearance of the flow.   Nearly all natural motion, whether of air or water, is turbulent.   A sensitive anemometer erected near the ground reveals that the motion of the air is made up of a rapid succession of gusts and lulls accompanied by simultaneous changes in direction, but the amplitude of the oscillations varies with locality, weather, height above ground, and time of day, and this great variability in the turbulence of the wind is responsible for most of the difficulties of the meteorological problem.   It is sometimes impossible to say with confidence whether a natural wind is turbulent or not.   A pressure-tube anemometer may give, on occasion, a very smooth velocity record, but this particular instrument has a large inertia, and if the same flow were examined by a hot-wire anemometer and a cathode-ray tube, it is possible that significant oscillations, which had been damped out by the pressure-tube instrument, would be revealed.   This illustrates one of the ever-present difficulties of micrometeorology, that of deciding how far the conclusions reached are affected by the characteristics of the instruments used.

3.2. The Origin of Turbulence

In his experiments on flow in long, straight pipes, Reynolds was able to show that the motion became turbulent when the Reynolds number ud/ν (d = pipe diameter) exceeded a certain critical value, of the order of 2000.   The problem of the origin of turbulence has been pursued ever since, both experimentally and theoretically.   It is assumed that turbulence arises as the result of instability of laminar flow, and there have been numerous attempts to determine a general criterion for the transition.   The problem, which has attracted many eminent mathematicians, including Rayleigh, Orr, Heisenberg, Tollmien, and Schlichting, has proved very stubborn.   On the experimental side, it was soon estab-

---

† The above definition is incomplete in that the adjective "random" is not defined mathematically.   It has been suggested that "random" here is equivalent to "not specifically related to the boundary conditions."   This implies that the fluctuating-velocity fields characteristic of turbulence have a kind of universal character, irrespective of the configuration of the boundary over which the fluid is moving.   There is much evidence to support this view, but the statement may not be true for oscillations of the largest length scales.   For further discussion of the definition of turbulence see the record of the Symposium on Atmospheric Turbulence in the Boundary Layer, held at Massachusetts Institute of Technology, June 4–8, 1951.

lished that no matter how great the initial unsteadiness, a flow ultimately settles down to the laminar state if the Reynolds number is below a certain limit, but later investigations revealed that motion can remain laminar at much higher Reynolds numbers if elaborate precautions are taken to eliminate any extraneous disturbances. This suggested that laminar flow is stable for infinitesimal disturbances and that some finite external disturbance must be present to cause the transition.

Micrometeorology deals primarily with motion near a surface, so that investigations into the initiation of turbulence in a boundary layer are of particular interest. The problem of the stability of the laminar boundary layer without a pressure gradient (Chap. 2) was attacked by the mathematicians of the Göttingen school from 1924 to 1935. Tollmien[1] found that the laminar flow, if subjected to a small periodic disturbance, would give rise to unstable waves if $Re = u\delta_1/\nu$ (where u = free-stream velocity, δ_1 = displacement thickness of the boundary layer) exceeded 420. Schlichting[2] gave the critical value as 575. Early tests of this theory (1938) failed to show any such unstable waves in the boundary layer near a plate at these low Reynolds numbers. On the other hand, there was evidence to support a theory, advanced by Sir Geoffrey Taylor, that the generation of turbulence in the laminar boundary layer is related to turbulence in the free stream.

These conflicting theoretical and experimental results have now been reconciled by the work of Schubauer and Skramstad at the National Bureau of Standards.† In brief, the Tollmien-Schlichting unstable waves occur when the turbulence of the free stream is very small, and thus can be observed only in special low-turbulence types of wind tunnel. In an ordinary wind tunnel the free-stream turbulence is the controlling factor, and transition follows lines suggested by Taylor's theory. By themselves, the Tollmien-Schlichting waves do not constitute turbulent flow but give rise to conditions in which unstable vortex sheets are formed, which ultimately roll up into small eddies. Dryden[18] concludes that if the free-stream turbulence is very small, the spectrum of the disturbances originally present is of major importance, whereas for higher free-stream turbulence the intensity and scale of the turbulence matter most. These considerations are particularly important in aerodynamics, and it has been suggested that in the higher atmosphere, where the wind is normally very free from turbulence, the noise created by the machine may well be the factor which decides whether flow over the surface of the wings will be turbulent or not.

Atmospheric Turbulence. The above considerations apply to motion in which density changes are negligible, so that gravitational effects do not arise. In the atmosphere near the ground this condition obtains

† A summary of this work, with illustrations, is to be found in an article by H. L. Dryden.[18]

only when the sky is heavily overcast. At other times large diurnal changes of surface temperature, mainly caused by the opposing effects of incoming short-wave radiation from the sun and outgoing long-wave radiation from the earth, radically affect the air flow. To fix ideas, consider conditions near level ground, either bare or covered with short grass, in the afternoon and evening of a clear day in early summer or in the fall, in circumstances in which the synoptic chart shows only small horizontal gradients of pressure. When the sun is high in the heavens, the temperature of the surface rises considerably above that of the air immediately adjacent to it and the wind is highly turbulent. As the sun sets, the temperature of the ground falls rapidly below that of the air, with the result that the layers of the atmosphere immediately in contact with the ground are chilled and become denser than those above. The maintenance of the turbulent state implies that masses of air are being moved continually in the vertical, so that if the fall of density with height is very pronounced, considerable work has to be done in lifting the denser masses against the gravitational field, at the expense of energy of the mean motion. The inevitable result is that, in such circumstances, the turbulent motion becomes less pronounced and may even die away completely. This, in turn, means that the supply of momentum from the free stream to replace that absorbed by the friction of the ground is reduced because of the loss of mixing, and the flow, as a whole, tends to settle down to slow motion in parallel layers. Provided that the sky remains clear and that there are no large horizontal pressure gradients, this state of affairs will generally continue until dawn, when the incoming radiation raises the temperature of the ground, and ultimately that of the lowest air layers. The position is now reversed, for the less dense air is below, and any tendency to vertical motion is enhanced by the prevailing density distribution. Soon after dawn the near-laminar flow gives place to turbulent motion, which continues throughout the day.

The turbulence of the atmosphere near the ground thus exhibits a pronounced diurnal variation, being high in large lapse rates and small in large inversions. When the sky is completely covered with thick cloud and there is a moderate or high wind, the gradient of temperature remains small and steady and in these conditions the degree of turbulence shows little variation by day and night. The hours during which temperature falls rapidly with height and turbulence is most pronounced will be referred to as the *lapse period*, and the time when the reverse condition obtains (*e.g.*, during a clear night), as the *inversion period*.†

----

† The diurnal change of turbulence in clear weather is easily observed by dwellers in the country, for the smoke from a fire of weeds, which is vigorously scattered by the wind during the mid-hours of daylight, can be seen to drift in thin, dense sheets or plumes for considerable distances, without much mixing, in twilight.

The great difficulties of the meteorological problem arise because, in general, it is impossible to ignore the effects of thermal stratification in the lower atmosphere. Progress in such investigations is bound to be slow for two reasons. In the first place, the introduction of a variable density gradient means that the mathematical theory is considerably more complicated than that for a homogeneous fluid, and at the present time hardly exists. Second, it is a matter of great difficulty to produce in wind tunnels fully developed profiles in substantial layers of fluid having density gradients comparable with those observed in the lower atmosphere, so that there is little in the way of evidence from controlled experiments to guide the worker in this field. The micrometeorologist must rely for his data almost entirely on observations made in the open, where control is impossible and conditions are rarely, if ever, exactly the same on different occasions. It will be shown later that in such investigations the basic parameter is not the Reynolds number but the Richardson number Ri defined by

$$\mathrm{Ri} = \frac{\dfrac{g}{T}\left(\dfrac{\partial T}{\partial z} + \Gamma\right)}{\left(\dfrac{\partial \bar{u}}{\partial z}\right)^2}$$

where $\bar{u}$ is the mean velocity and the other symbols have their usual meaning. An examination of the effects of turbulence in a fluid of variable density gradient thus demands very accurate measurements of the gradients of temperature and velocity.

3.3. The Basic Mathematical Theory of Turbulent Motion

Mean Values and Fluctuations. Let u, v, w be the components of velocity measured at a point (x,y,z). In turbulent flow all three components are functions of time as well as of position. The *mean velocity*, with components $\bar{u}$, $\bar{v}$, $\bar{w}$, is defined at a fixed point and at a time t_0 by the relations

$$\bar{u} = \frac{1}{T}\int_{t_0-\frac{1}{2}T}^{t_0+\frac{1}{2}T} u\, dt; \qquad \bar{v} = \frac{1}{T}\int_{t_0-\frac{1}{2}T}^{t_0+\frac{1}{2}T} v\, dt; \qquad \bar{w} = \frac{1}{T}\int_{t_0-\frac{1}{2}T}^{t_0+\frac{1}{2}T} w\, dt \quad (3.1)$$

where T is an arbitrary interval called the *period of sampling*. In general,

$$\bar{u},\ \bar{v},\ \bar{w} = f(x,y,z,t_0,T)$$

Geometrically, this means that, having obtained a record of u, v, w at a point over an interval of time, the areas between the time axis and the curves $u = u(t)$, $v = v(t)$, $w = w(t)$ are measured over a subinterval of duration T, centered at $t = t_0$, and used to construct average velocities $\bar{u}$, $\bar{v}$, $\bar{w}$, such that the parts of the areas which lie above $u = \bar{u}$, $v = \bar{v}$, $w = \bar{w}$ are equal to the parts which lie below the same lines (Fig. 10). Clearly, if the velocity so constructed is to be characteristic of the motion as a whole, the interval T must be sufficiently long to ensure that an adequate number of fluctuations is included. On the other hand, the universal adoption of a very long period of sampling might mask important changes which are taking place in the flow, *e.g.*, the general level of velocity might be steadily rising or falling during the period chosen, so that the motion could not be properly represented by a single constant mean velocity.

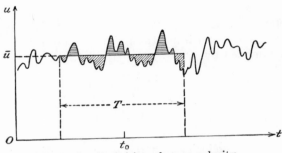

FIG. 10.   Definition of mean velocity.

If circumstances are such that the mean velocity may be regarded as steady, the analysis is greatly simplified. In all cases, a *fluctuation*, or *eddy velocity*, u', v', w' is defined as the difference between the total velocity at any instant and the mean velocity, so that

$$u' = u - \bar{u}; \qquad v' = v - \bar{v}; \qquad w' = w - \bar{w} \tag{3.2}$$

In steady mean flow

$$\bar{\bar{u}} = \bar{u}, \text{ etc.}$$

and

$$\bar{u}' = \frac{1}{T} \int_{t_0 - \frac{1}{2}T}^{t_0 + \frac{1}{2}T} (u - \bar{u})dt = \bar{u} - \bar{\bar{u}} = 0$$

Thus

$$\bar{u}' = \bar{v}' = \bar{w}' = 0 \tag{3.3}$$

but it cannot be asserted a priori that mean values of the squares and products of the eddy velocities (for example, $\overline{u'^2}$, $\overline{u'v'}$, etc.) are necessarily zero.

If the mean flow cannot be regarded as steady, some other restrictive condition must be imposed, usually that changes in u, v, w are sufficiently rapid to allow an interval T to be defined in which $\bar{u}$, $\bar{v}$, $\bar{w}$ vary only slowly. In all cases, Eq. (3.3) must be satisfied, either exactly or to a high degree of approximation, before progress can be made, and this is equivalent to assuming that some measure of regularity exists even in turbulent motion.

The process described above presumes that the velocity at any point can be decomposed uniquely into a steady or slowly varying mean velocity and an irregularly fluctuating eddy velocity. In aerodynamic problems it is usually possible to assume that conditions are such that the mean velocity is insensitive to the period of sampling, so that a single representative mean velocity can be constructed from observations taken over arbitrary intervals of time. This is not always so in the atmosphere, and the influence of the period of sampling is often pronounced in micrometeorological problems. This aspect arises later in dealing with diffusion in detail; for the present it suffices to say that because the fluctuations in the natural wind have periods varying from a fraction of a second to many minutes, the choice of a period for the construction of a representative mean value is usually a matter of importance.

The procedure given above may be used to construct mean values of any other entity which fluctuates because of turbulence. The most important examples are temperature and concentration of suspended matter. Most standard meteorological instruments are designed to give good approximations to the mean value over intervals of the order of a minute or so; others, such as certain types of recording cup anemometers, employ longer periods of sampling. Micrometeorology demands that special attention be given to the accurate recording of the fluctuations themselves and in this respect, if no other, differs considerably in its instrumentation from normal meteorology or climatology.

The Reynolds Stresses. It is readily seen that the Navier-Stokes equations of incompressible motion, in virtue of the definition of the viscous stresses (Chap. 2), may be written in the form

$$\rho \frac{\partial u}{\partial t} = \frac{\partial}{\partial x}\left(\tau_{xx} - \rho u^2\right) + \frac{\partial}{\partial y}\left(\tau_{xy} - \rho uv\right) + \frac{\partial}{\partial z}\left(\tau_{xz} - \rho uw\right) \quad (3.4)$$

and two similar equations for v, w. It is assumed that these equations are equally valid if u, v, w represent the total velocities in turbulent flow, and the problem is to ascertain the equations satisfied by the mean velocities.

In the above equations put $u = \bar{u} + u'$, etc., and take mean values according to the rules established above. The resulting equations are

$$\rho \frac{\partial \bar{u}}{\partial t} = \frac{\partial}{\partial x} \left(\bar{\tau}_{xx} - \rho \bar{u}^2 - \rho \overline{u'^2} \right) + \frac{\partial}{\partial y} \left(\bar{\tau}_{xy} - \rho \bar{u}\bar{v} - \rho \overline{u'v'} \right)$$
$$+ \frac{\partial}{\partial z} \left(\bar{\tau}_{xz} - \rho \bar{u}\bar{w} - \rho \overline{u'w'} \right)$$

$$\rho \frac{\partial \bar{v}}{\partial t} = \frac{\partial}{\partial x} \left(\bar{\tau}_{xy} - \rho \bar{u}\bar{v} - \rho \overline{u'v'} \right) + \frac{\partial}{\partial y} \left(\bar{\tau}_{yy} - \rho \bar{v}^2 - \rho \overline{v'^2} \right)$$
$$+ \frac{\partial}{\partial z} \left(\bar{\tau}_{yz} - \rho \bar{v}\bar{w} - \rho \overline{v'w'} \right)$$

$$\rho \frac{\partial \bar{w}}{\partial t} = \frac{\partial}{\partial x} \left(\bar{\tau}_{xz} - \rho \bar{u}\bar{w} - \rho \overline{u'w'} \right) + \frac{\partial}{\partial y} \left(\bar{\tau}_{yz} - \rho \bar{v}\bar{w} - \rho \overline{v'w'} \right)$$
$$+ \frac{\partial}{\partial z} \left(\bar{\tau}_{zz} - \rho \bar{w}^2 - \rho \overline{w'^2} \right)$$

$$(3.5)$$

Each of these equations has the same form as (3.4) if $\bar{u}$ replaces u, etc., and

The viscous stress τ_{xx} is replaced by $\bar{\tau}_{xx} - \rho \overline{u'^2}$
The viscous stress τ_{xy} is replaced by $\bar{\tau}_{xy} - \rho \overline{u'v'}$
The viscous stress τ_{xz} is replaced by $\bar{\tau}_{xz} - \rho \overline{u'w'}$
etc

$$(3.6)$$

This means that the equations satisfied by the mean values are not simply the Navier-Stokes equations, with mean values of the velocities and viscous stresses replacing instantaneous values, but that certain additional terms, independent of viscosity and depending on the fluctuations, *viz.*,

$$-\rho \overline{u'^2}, -\rho \overline{v'^2}, -\rho \overline{w'^2}, -\rho \overline{u'v'}, -\rho \overline{u'w'}, -\rho \overline{v'w'} \qquad (3.7)$$

have been added to the viscous stresses. These terms, called the *Reynolds stresses*, indicate that the velocity fluctuations, like the molecular agitation, cause transport of momentum across a surface in the fluid. In general, the Reynolds stresses outweigh in importance the purely viscous stresses, which often may be neglected in problems of turbulent motion.

The physical significance of the Reynolds stresses may be seen without difficulty. The normal stresses $-\rho \overline{u'^2}$, etc., clearly represent the additional dynamic pressure caused by the fluctuating velocity; it is for this reason that a pitot tube in a turbulent stream reads slightly higher than the true mean velocity. The tangential stresses $-\rho \overline{u'w'}$, etc., which involve two component velocities, are of fundamental importance in problems of air flow near the surface of the earth and are best explained by an appeal to statistical theory. The correlation coefficient r between two fluctuating velocities u', w', at a point is, by definition,

$$r = \frac{\overline{u'w'}}{\sqrt{(\overline{u'^2})} \sqrt{(\overline{w'^2})}} \qquad (3.8)$$

The magnitude and sign of r thus depend mainly on the mean value of $u'w'$, and the virtual stresses $-\rho\overline{u'w'}$, etc., will differ from zero if, and only if, a correlation exists between the corresponding pairs of eddy velocities at a point. How such a correlation may arise is seen by considering the example of a steady horizontal mean wind near the ground. Let the x axis be in the direction of the mean wind, the y axis horizontal and across the mean wind, and the z axis vertical, so that $\bar{u} = \bar{u}(z)$; $\bar{v} = \bar{w} = 0$. In this system, gusts or sudden increases in the mean wind are denoted by positive values of u' and lulls by negative u', left-hand and right-hand swings of the wind from its mean direction are denoted by, say, positive and negative v', respectively, and upward and downward instantaneous currents by positive and negative w'. If the mean value of a product such as $u'v'$ is not to vanish, there must be a preponderance of terms of the same sign, either negative or positive, which implies that, say, positive values of u' are more likely to be found with positive values of v' than with negative values. There is no reason to associate either gusts or lulls with a tendency of the wind to swing in any particular direction, and the most likely result is that $\overline{u'v'} = 0$. On the other hand, since the steady state is maintained against the effect of surface friction by fast-moving air from above being brought nearer the surface, together with a simultaneous transfer of retarded air masses from below to above, there is every reason to expect that gusts (positive u') will be more frequently found with descending currents (negative w') than with upward currents (positive w'). Hence, $\overline{u'w'}$ will not vanish, and the Reynolds stress $-\rho\overline{u'w'}$ will be significantly different from zero. This quantity, called the *eddy shearing stress*, is the mathematical expression of the transport of momentum, by the velocity fluctuations, across any plane parallel to $z = 0$. Möller,[3] using Scrase's[4] results for winds in the lowest layers of the atmosphere over downland, found a well-marked correlation ($r = 0.8$) between u' and w', with the fast-moving air descending and the retarded air rising. This illustrates the essential reality of the Reynolds stresses in flow near the ground.

3.4. The Analogy with Molecular Processes

Although the introduction of the Reynolds stresses throws considerable light on the general mechanism of turbulence, the mathematical difficulties are not immediately relieved. In general, no analytical method is known whereby these stresses can be expressed in terms of the mean velocities and their derivatives, so that for the most part the equations still remain intractable. Most of the progress which has been made so far in relating theory and observation has followed the introduction, at this stage, of certain plausible but empirical relations between the turbulent stresses and the mean flow. A rational theory of turbulence, comparable with, say, that developed for the irrotational motion of an inviscid fluid, does not exist at present.

Much of the description of turbulent flow which has occupied the preceding pages is reminiscent of the theory of viscosity developed in the kinetic theory of gases (Chap. 2). A fluid in turbulent motion may be supposed to have a kind of granular structure, in which "lumps" of fluid break away from the mean motion and lead (for a short time at least) an independent life, before being absorbed again into the main flow at some different level. This gives a picture of the transfer of momentum and other entities by turbulence which corresponds almost exactly to that envisaged in the simpler molecular models of a gas. The plausibility of this analogy is reinforced by the fact that undoubtedly such motion of small individual masses of fluid can take place, a well-known example being the Kármán "vortex street," the flow observed in the wake of a bluff body at low Reynolds numbers, when vortices are shed alternately from either edge, to float downstream in a well-defined pattern which is dissipated by viscosity only after a considerable time. True turbulent flow might be regarded, very rationally, as a motion in which the vortices are much more numerous and their distribution not as well ordered. It is therefore not surprising that much of the earlier work, and especially that on atmospheric turbulence, was based on a "kinetic-theory" model, in which wandering masses of fluid, called *eddies*, were supposed to behave like molecules, carrying momentum, heat, and suspended matter from one layer to another by a kind of collision dynamics, the final transference of properties being supposed to involve a process somewhat vaguely defined as "mixing with the main body of the fluid."

Before entering into the details of the mathematical development of this analogy, it is as well to be assured that the broad consequences of such a structure agree with the known facts. One of the most striking effects of turbulence is shown by comparing the velocity profiles for laminar and turbulent flow in a long pipe of circular cross section. If the Reynolds number is well below the critical value, the details of the motion in a circular pipe are known from Poiseuille's exact solution of the equations of viscous motion. If z is the radial distance from the center of the pipe and a is the radius, the Poiseuille profile is given by

$$u(z) = \frac{p_1 - p_2}{4\mu l} (a^2 - z^2) \tag{3.9}$$

where $p_1 - p_2$ is the pressure drop over the length l. The velocity distribution is thus parabolic, and the velocity gradient

$$\frac{du}{dz} = -\frac{p_1 - p_2}{2\mu l} z$$

decreases linearly from a finite value $-(p_1 - p_2)a/2\mu l$ at the wall $(z = a)$ to zero at the center of the pipe $(z = 0)$.

When the flow is turbulent, the distribution of mean velocity far from the inlet is very different. The general character of the motion is seen in Fig. 11. The profile is nearly uniform over a central core, with a large velocity gradient at the wall. No exact expression for the profile has been deduced, but it is known that the empirical relation

$$\bar{u} = \bar{u}_{\max} \left(\frac{a - z}{a} \right)^{\frac{1}{7}}$$

represents the measurements with tolerable accuracy, from the wall almost to the center of the tube, for moderate values of the Reynolds number ($< 200{,}000$). For higher Reynolds numbers, smaller values of the index are indicated ($\frac{1}{8}$ to $\frac{1}{10}$), and a more exact expression still,

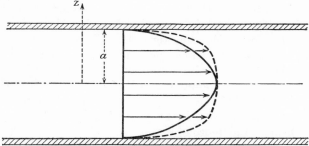

FIG. 11. Laminar (full line) and turbulent (dotted line) velocity profiles in a pipe.

evolved by Kármán, shows that the mean velocity varies as the logarithm of the distance from the wall. Whatever expression is used, it is clear that the variation of velocity with distance from the wall is extremely slow except in the immediate vicinity of the boundary. This is a characteristic feature of turbulent flow, and a similar state of affairs holds in the atmosphere. The wind velocity over a bare or short-cropped grass surface shows only a very slow change with height (except very near the ground) in the lapse period, when turbulence is high, but has a much steeper gradient in the inversion period, when the flow is laminar, or nearly so. This is one of the most important facts in micrometeorology, to be considered in greater detail in Chap. 7.

Such properties are entirely consistent with the kinetic-theory picture of a turbulent fluid. Like the molecules, the eddies transfer momentum from one layer to another, for it is possible to imagine an eddy, originally a part of the main stream in a region of relatively high velocity, breaking away and conserving some or all of its momentum until it mixes again with the mean motion in a region of lower velocity. Such mixing would be revealed as a momentary gust, or increase of velocity, at the new level, and the net effect of incessant secondary motions of this type would be to eliminate large velocity differences, except in the immediate neighborhood of the boundary, where the solid surface severely restricts the cross-current motion. The main effect of turbulence is to cause *large-scale mixing*, a statement which is valid irrespective of the truth or not of the kinetic-theory analogy. The great importance of turbulence in the study of conditions near the ground resides almost entirely in this aspect, for without the continuous mixing caused by the eddy motion the atmosphere would have properties utterly different from those which it now possesses.

3.5. Exchange Coefficients

A natural first step toward a theory of turbulence is to adopt the fundamental ideas of the kinetic theory of gases by expressing the transfer of momentum, or any other suitable entity, by means of virtual coefficients of viscosity, conductivity, and diffusivity, defined in much the same way as their molecular counterparts. Such quantities were called *Austauschkoeffizienten* ("exchange coefficients") by Wilhelm Schmidt, a pioneer worker in this field, who developed the corresponding theory very thoroughly in his classical monograph "Die Massenaustausch in freier Luft," published in 1925. A similar concept had been proposed much earlier by Boussinesq, while, in England, Taylor and Richardson also applied the theory to meteorology.

A fundamental expression for the turbulent flux, independent of any theory of the structure of eddy motion, may be obtained at once. Let E be the amount per unit mass of fluid of any transferable conservative entity such as momentum, heat, or matter in suspension. It is assumed that $\bar{E}$, the mean value of E, is constant over any x,y plane and that the motion is such that $\bar{v} = \bar{w} = 0$. The amount of E transported in unit time through unit cross section of a plane parallel to $z = 0$ is $-\rho E w'$ (the negative sign indicates that the flux is in the direction of increasing z when E decreases with z), plus the small contribution arising from the molecular agitation $k \, dE/dz$, where k is the appropriate molecular coefficient (viscosity, conductivity, diffusivity). Hence, per unit area,

Instantaneous flux $= k \dfrac{dE}{dz} - \rho E w'$

$$= k \frac{d}{dz} (\bar{E} + E') - (\bar{\rho} + \rho')(\bar{E} + E')w'$$

Taking the mean value,

$$\text{Mean flux} = k \frac{d\bar{E}}{dz} - \bar{\rho}\overline{E'w'} - \bar{E}\overline{\rho'w'} - \overline{E'\rho'w'} \qquad (3.10)$$

If fluctuations in density are omitted and $\bar{\rho} = \rho$,

$$\text{Mean flux} = k \frac{d\bar{E}}{dz} - \rho\overline{E'w'} \tag{3.11}$$

Thus the mean flux across a plane perpendicular to the z direction depends chiefly upon the existence of a correlation between the fluctuations in velocity and in the entity being transferred. If momentum is being transferred, $E = u$, $k = \mu$, and thus

$$\text{Mean flux} = \mu \frac{d\bar{u}}{dz} - \rho\overline{u'w'} \tag{3.12}$$

in which the second term will be recognized as the appropriate Reynolds stress, the mean flux of momentum being the frictional force per unit area, or shearing stress. Matter in suspension, such as water vapor, smoke, or dust, implies that E be expressed as grams of matter per gram of air—thus for the diffusion of water vapor E must be the specific humidity, or the ratio of the absolute humidity to the density of the (moist) air, so that ρE is the absolute humidity, or concentration of water vapor (mass per unit volume). The case of heat requires special consideration and is dealt with later (Chap. 4). It is, of course, essential that the entity E be conservative, *i.e.*, unchanged during the transfer process; for example, if the diffusion of water vapor is being considered, condensation must be excluded.

The fundamental problem in the analysis of turbulent mixing is to express (3.11) in terms of the mean entity $\bar{E}$ and its derivatives. The *exchange-coefficient hypothesis* is that the term $-\rho\overline{E'w'}$ can be expressed as the product of a virtual coefficient of mixing and the gradient of the mean entity $d\bar{E}/dz$. If A is this coefficient, on this hypothesis

$$\text{Mean flux} = (k + A) \frac{d\bar{E}}{dz} \tag{3.13}$$

Thus for momentum,

$$\text{Mean flux per unit area} = \tau = (\mu + A) \frac{d\bar{u}}{dz} \tag{3.14}$$

or, writing $K_M = A/\rho$ and $\nu = \mu/\rho$

$$\frac{\tau}{\rho} = (\nu + K_M) \frac{d\bar{u}}{dz} \simeq K_M \frac{d\bar{u}}{dz} \qquad \text{if } \nu \ll K_M \tag{3.15}$$

K_M is called the *eddy viscosity*.

The analysis up to this point has been purely formal, the quantity K_M being defined by the relation

$$K_M = - \frac{\overline{u'w'}}{d\bar{u}/dz} \tag{3.16}$$

which yields no information regarding the behavior of K_M, for example, whether it is a function of $\bar{u}$, u', w', and z, or a constant. An obvious first step is to find the order of magnitude of K_M for atmospheric processes, and to ascertain this, it is assumed, as a first approximation, that K_M is an absolute constant (*i.e.*, independent of position in the field) like its molecular counterpart ν.

3.6. The Approach to the Geostrophic Wind

The wind near the surface of the earth is usually related to the prevailing large-scale pressure distribution and may therefore be regarded as the geostrophic wind modified by friction. If the frictional forces, whatever their origin, are expressed by virtual stresses τ_{zx}, τ_{zy}, the equations of motion of two-dimensional steady mean flow, referred to axes fixed in the earth, are

$$-\lambda \bar{v} = -\frac{1}{\rho}\frac{\partial \bar{p}}{\partial x} + \frac{1}{\rho}\frac{\partial}{\partial z}\tau_{zx}$$

$$\lambda \bar{u} = -\frac{1}{\rho}\frac{\partial \bar{p}}{\partial y} + \frac{1}{\rho}\frac{\partial}{\partial z}\tau_{zy}$$

(3.17)

These are Eqs. (2.23) of Chap. 2 with friction included. The problem to be solved is that of finding how the geostrophic wind, which is the free-stream velocity, is modified in magnitude and direction near the surface of the earth ($z = 0$) by the virtual stresses arising from the turbulence.

If molecular friction is disregarded (a step justified later), the stresses are given by

$$\tau_{zx} = A_x \frac{\partial \bar{u}}{\partial z}; \qquad \tau_{zy} = A_y \frac{\partial \bar{v}}{\partial z}$$

(3.18)

in accordance with the exchange-coefficient hypothesis. As a first approximation it is assumed that $A_x = A_y = A = $ constant, and the frictional terms in Eqs. (3.17) are replaced by $K_M\, \partial^2\bar{u}/\partial z^2$ and $K_M\, \partial^2\bar{v}/\partial z^2$, respectively, where $K_M = A/\rho$ is the eddy viscosity.

The main effects of eddy friction are seen from a study of the simplified problem in which the pressure gradients and the density are the same at all heights and the isobars are straight and parallel. If the x axis is placed along the isobars, as in Chap. 2, it is easily seen that Eqs. (3.17) reduce to the single equation.

$$i\lambda(\mathbf{V} - \mathbf{G}) = K_M \frac{\partial^2 \mathbf{V}}{\partial z^2}$$

(3.19)

where $\mathbf{V} = \bar{u} + i\bar{v}$ and $\mathbf{G}$ is the geostrophic wind. The problem is completed by the inclusion of the boundary conditions

$$\mathbf{V} = 0 \text{ on } z = 0$$
$$\lim_{z \to \infty} \mathbf{V} = \mathbf{G}$$

Hence $\bar{v}$, the velocity component perpendicular to the isobars, vanishes at great heights, since the geostrophic wind blows along the isobars.

The appropriate solution is easily found by a trial substitution of an exponential function. Resolved into real and imaginary parts, the

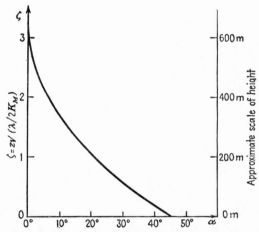

FIG. 12.   Angle between wind and geostrophic direction.

expression for the ratio of the variable wind to the constant geostrophic wind is

$$\frac{\mathbf{V}}{\mathbf{G}} = 1 - \left(\cos z \sqrt{\frac{\lambda}{2K_M}} - i \sin z \sqrt{\frac{\lambda}{2K_M}} \right) \exp \left(-z \sqrt{\frac{\lambda}{2K_M}} \right) \quad (3.20)$$

Writing $z\sqrt{(\lambda/2K_M)} = \zeta$, the component velocities are

$$\bar{u} = \mathbf{G}(1 - e^{-\zeta} \cos \zeta)$$
$$\bar{v} = \mathbf{G}e^{-\zeta} \sin \zeta$$

The graph of $\bar{u}$ against $\bar{v}$, for positive ζ, is an equiangular spiral with $\bar{u} = \mathbf{G}, \bar{v} = 0$ as the limit point as $\zeta \to \infty$. This is the so-called *Ekman spiral*, first employed by Ekman[5] in a discussion of the analogous problem of ocean currents produced by surface stresses.

The angle α which the wind at any height makes with the geostrophic direction is

$$\alpha = \tan^{-1} \frac{\bar{v}}{\bar{u}} = \frac{\sin \zeta}{e^{\zeta} - \cos \zeta} \quad (3.21)$$

This function is shown plotted for $0 \leq \zeta \leq \pi$ in Fig. 12. At the surface, $\alpha = \pi/4$, the effect of the stresses being to deflect the wind from the free-stream direction, so that in the surface boundary layer the wind is inclined at an angle of 45° to the isobars, in the direction of decreasing pressure. Qualitatively, this is verified by observations, but normal daytime values of α in this layer are more nearly equal to 20° in steady conditions over land.

When $\zeta = \pi$, $\alpha = 0$; this means that the wind first attains the geostrophic direction at a finite height Z, given by

$$Z = \frac{\zeta}{\sqrt{(\lambda/2K_M)}} = \frac{\pi}{\sqrt{(\lambda/2K_M)}}$$

If this height can be ascertained from pilot-balloon ascents used in conjunction with the synoptic chart, an estimate of the order of magnitude of K_M can be found from the formula

$$K_M = \frac{1}{2} \lambda \left(\frac{Z}{\pi}\right)^2 \qquad (3.22)$$

Dobson,[6] from an analysis of ascents made over Salisbury Plain, England, found that Z was between 600 and 900 m, from which Taylor[7] estimated that the order of magnitude of K_M must be at least 10^4 cm^2 sec^{-1}. This value should be contrasted with that for the kinematic viscosity of the air, which is of the order of 10^{-1} cm^2 sec^{-1}. Thus viscosity of itself is far too small to explain the observed distribution of velocity in the first kilometer above the surface, and it must be concluded that atmospheric mixing is on a scale which completely dwarfs molecular diffusion.

The preceding work is based on the assumption that K_M is independent of height, a hypothesis now regarded as untenable. The problem of the approach to the geostrophic wind for K_M variable is considered in detail in Chap. 7.

3.7. Further Development of the Molecular Analogy; Mixing-length Theories

In the kinetic theory of gases, the expression derived for the kinematic viscosity involves the product of the mean free path and the mean molecular velocity, both of which are independent of position in the field of flow. The analogy between molecular and eddy motion has been further extended by Prandtl[8] by the introduction of the *mixing length*, analogous to the free path, but variable in the field of flow. The theory may be developed in a variety of ways.

In the first place it may be supposed that, as a result of the general disorder, an "eddy," regarded as a small discrete volume of fluid, breaks away from an original level z and carries across stream momentum appropriate to the mean motion at the level z to a new level $z + l$, where the volume mixes again with the main flow. The absorption of the eddy into the motion at the new level gives rise to a fluctuation of velocity u' where

$$u' = \bar{u}(z + l) - \bar{u}(z) \simeq l\frac{d\bar{u}}{dz} \tag{3.23}$$

Since, in general, all three component fluctuations are of the same nature and of the same magnitude, similar expressions, differing at the most numerically, must hold for v' and w'. The *mixing-length hypothesis* is that the quantity l thus introduced is a unique length which characterizes the local intensity of the turbulent mixing at any level but which, unlike the mean free path, may be a function of position, of the mean velocity, etc. The Reynolds shearing stress τ, being proportional to the mean value of the product $u'w'$, is represented in this system by the equation

$$\tau = -\rho\overline{u'w'} = \rho l^2 \left(\frac{d\bar{u}}{dz}\right)\left|\frac{d\bar{u}}{dz}\right| \tag{3.24}$$

the separation of the $d\bar{u}/dz$ terms being necessary to allow τ to change sign with $d\bar{u}/dz$. From Eq. (3.16), the eddy viscosity is given by

$$K_M = -\frac{\overline{u'w'}}{d\bar{u}/dz} = l^2\frac{d\bar{u}}{dz} \tag{3.25}$$

where constants of proportionality are supposed to be absorbed in the quantity l.

The above arguments may be extended to cover the diffusion of any conservative entity by introducing a slightly different definition of the mixing length. Let $E(z)$ be an entity whose mean value, constant over any plane parallel to $z = 0$, is conserved during the passage of the eddy from the plane $z = z_1$ to $z = z_2$. The mean rate of transfer q of $E(z)$ in the z direction is

$$q = -\overline{w'[E(z_2) - E(z_1)]} \simeq -\overline{w'(z_2 - z_1)}\frac{d\bar{E}}{dz} \tag{3.26}$$

The mixing-length hypothesis is that for all such motions there exists a unique mean length l such that

$$\overline{w'(z_2 - z_1)} = l\sqrt{(\overline{w'^2})} \tag{3.27}$$

so that the flux of E caused by the turbulence is expressed by

$$q = -l\sqrt{(\overline{w'^2})}\frac{d\bar{E}}{dz} \tag{3.28}$$

This allows a virtual coefficient of diffusion K to be defined by the relation

$$K = l\sqrt{(\overline{w'^2})} \tag{3.29}$$

Putting $\bar{E} = \rho\bar{u}$, so that the problem is that of the eddy transfer of momentum in an incompressible fluid, Eq. (3.28) becomes

$$- q = \tau = \rho l \, \sqrt{(\overline{w'^2})} \, \frac{d\bar{u}}{dz} \qquad (3.30)$$

This is the same as Eq. (3.24) as regards the basic conception, but the two l's may differ in magnitude.

Either analysis is little more than a series of definitions, which of themselves give no sure ground for supposing that any such unique mixing length exists. Although this approach is obviously inspired by the successful use of the concept of the free path in the kinetic theory of gases, there are certain very important differences to be noted between the molecular and the turbulent problems. In the kinetic theory a collision is a definite event defined by a discontinuous change in the momenta of the elastic spheres. In the present problem, "mixing" cannot be defined with the same precision, and it does not seem possible to develop the theory further by constructing elaborate mechanical models of turbulent motion in which the "eddies" have properties like those of elastic spheres. The only logical approach is to use Eq. (3.24) or Eq. (3.30) as the definition of l (regarding τ, $d\bar{u}/dz$, and $\overline{w'^2}$ as known or measurable) and to ignore entirely arguments based on the supposed properties of discrete masses of fluid. The quantity l then becomes a convenient parameter, having the dimension of length, but lacking any precise physical significance.

Since the introduction of the mixing-length concept in 1925, the matter has been pursued vigorously, both theoretically and experimentally. The quantity l is not measurable directly, but the theory can be examined in two ways. The first method starts with some plausible hypothesis concerning l, say as a function of position, and ascertains how far the consequences are consistent with observation. In the second method, the mixing length is deduced from measured values of the shearing stress, velocity profile, etc., and the results examined for consistency. Both methods have been used in meteorology.

3.8. The Turbulent Boundary Layer

The detailed study of motion in the boundary layer of a flat surface, tangential to the mean velocity, at high Reynolds number, may be regarded as the idealized problem of the motion of the atmosphere over a small region of the surface of the earth.

Consider a smooth plane surface (such as a polished metal sheet) defined by $z = 0$, $x \geq 0$ (so that x is distance from the leading edge and z is the depth of the stream), and a steady two-dimensional mean motion in which the mean velocity $\bar{u}$ in any plane x is a function of x, z only. A laminar boundary layer is formed, starting at the leading edge, but for sufficiently high velocities, or sufficiently great distances downstream, the flow in the boundary layer becomes turbulent. Thus, on proceeding downstream from the leading edge, there is encountered first a laminar boundary layer, then a region of transition, and finally a fully developed turbulent boundary layer (Fig. 13). Experiments show that the breakdown of the laminar flow starts when the local Reynolds number $\bar{u}x/\nu$ attains a critical value dependent upon the amount of turbulence present

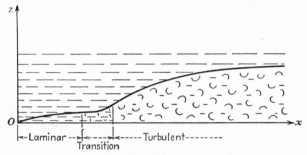

FIG. 13. The turbulent boundary layer.

in the free stream.† In meteorological problems, the leading edge is at an infinite distance upwind of the point of observation, and it may be assumed that turbulence in the earth's boundary layer is always fully developed. The application of the momentum theorem to motion near a plane surface shows that the depth of the laminar boundary layer increases as $x^{\frac{1}{2}}$ [Eq. (2.54)]. The same method can be applied to turbulent motion if the linear velocity profile assumed for laminar flow is replaced by one in which the mean velocity varies as z^m, $m > 0$. For $m = \frac{1}{7}$ [see below, Eq. (3.54)] the result is that the surface shearing stress per unit area (τ_0) and the depth of the turbulent boundary layer (δ) are given by

$$\tau_0 = 0.0228\rho\bar{u}^2 \left(\frac{\nu}{\bar{u}x}\right)^{\frac{1}{5}}$$

$$\delta = 0.366x \left(\frac{\nu}{\bar{u}x}\right)^{\frac{1}{5}}$$

respectively.‡ Thus the turbulent boundary layer over a smooth plane surface deepens with distance from the leading edge more rapidly than the laminar boundary layer.

† From results obtained at the Bureau of Standards it appears that this occurs when $\bar{u}x/\nu$ is between 10^5 and 10^6, the higher value corresponding to a free-stream turbulence of $\sqrt{(\overline{u'^2})}/\bar{u} = 5 \times 10^{-3}$ [Dryden, *J. Aeronaut. Sci.*, 1, 71, 72 (1934)].

‡ For the details of the calculation, see L. Prandtl and O. G. Tietjens "Applied Hydro- and Aeromechanics," pp. 74–76 (McGraw-Hill, 1934).

More precise consideration of the nature of the motion in a fully developed turbulent boundary layer shows, however, that the actual situation may be more complex than that indicated above. If the boundary is smooth in the ordinary sense of the word, several regions of flow can be distinguished:

1. Immediately adjacent to the surface, a very thin *laminar sublayer*, within which vertical eddy motions are practically nonexistent. Inside this layer the velocity gradient $d\bar{u}/dz$ attains very high values, and the shearing stress is effectively that caused by viscosity alone.

2. Above this, the *turbulent boundary layer* proper, characterized by strong vertical motions and a small gradient of mean velocity. In this layer the Reynolds stress is at least as great as the viscous stress and may be much greater.

3. Above the boundary layers, the *free stream*, in which the viscous stresses are negligible.

Thus, in the vicinity of a smooth plane surface, the velocity falls to zero, at first slowly and then very rapidly as the boundary is approached, so that the velocity gradient ultimately attains very large values, which in many investigations may be regarded as infinite.

The Friction Velocity. At this stage it is convenient to introduce an auxiliary reference velocity u_*. The *friction velocity (Schubspannungsgeschwindigkeit)* is defined by the relation

$$u_*{}^2 = \left| \frac{\tau}{\rho} \right| \tag{3.31}$$

In most meteorological applications the shearing stress τ may be considered to be independent of height in the shallow layer concerned (see Sec. 3.9) and thus equal to its value at the surface, τ_0, so that

$$u_* = \sqrt{\left(\left| \frac{\tau_0}{\rho} \right| \right)} = \sqrt{(|\overline{u'w'}|)} \tag{3.32}$$

The friction velocity thus depends on the nature of the surface and the magnitude of the mean velocity. The origin of this unusual reference velocity is easily seen when it is recalled that usually, in turbulent motion, the shearing stress is approximately proportional to the square of the mean velocity. [This should be compared with laminar motion, say Couette flow, Eq. (2.39), in which the shearing stress is proportional to the first power of the velocity.] The relation between the shearing stress and the square of the mean velocity is, in general, not exact,[†] and the friction velocity is the artificial but related velocity for which the square law holds exactly. From Eq. (3.32) it is obvious that u_* must be of the

† For instance, in the example of turbulent flow through a smooth pipe at moderate Reynolds numbers the relation between shearing stress and mean velocity is more accurately represented by $\tau/\rho \propto \bar{u}^{\frac{7}{4}}$.

same order of magnitude as the eddy velocities, and as a rough but useful rule in meteorological problems, it may be assumed that $u_* \simeq \bar{u}/10$.[†]

Smooth and Rough Surfaces. In everyday language, a surface is said to be "rough" if it is corrugated or covered with protuberances, usually distributed at random. In specifying the degree of roughness of different surfaces at least two lengths may be expected to enter, the height of the corrugations or protuberances and some length specifying the spacing between individual elements, such as a wavelength for regular corrugations or a mean distance apart for protuberances. The special case considered here is that in which the roughness elements are so closely distributed that, effectively, the height alone enters into consideration, and the problem is further limited by supposing that the protuberances are sufficiently similar in shape to allow a representative mean height ϵ to be defined. (This is so, for example, when the wind blows over cultivated ground, the height of the vegetation being sensibly constant over a considerable area at any given time of the year.) The definition of smooth and rough surfaces, in the aerodynamic sense, is based on a comparison of the average height ϵ with the depth of the laminar sublayer.

In general terms, a surface is called *aerodynamically smooth* if the protuberances are sufficiently small to allow the formation of a laminar sublayer, in which they are entirely submerged. An *aerodynamically rough* surface is one in which the irregularities are large enough to prevent the formation of any such layer, so that the motion is turbulent down to the surface itself. Since the depth of the laminar sublayer depends on the magnitude of the Reynolds number, the classification of a surface according to the above definitions thus involves not only the geometrical characteristics of the boundary but also the magnitude of the mean velocity, so that a surface which is "smooth" at low velocities may become "rough" as the mean velocity increases. In practice, since the laminar sublayer is always very shallow, a surface which is aerodynamically smooth at moderate Reynolds numbers must also be fairly smooth in the everyday sense of the word.

The above considerations have been made precise and quantitative by the researches of Schiller,[9] Nikuradse,[10] and Schlichting,[11] with important consequences for micrometeorology. Schiller investigated theoretically the maximum size of the irregularity which will not appreciably alter the character of laminar motion in a pipe, by finding the condition that there should not be a pronounced wake at the rear of the protuberance. His result, expressed in terms of the friction velocity, is that no change in the motion occurs when

$$\frac{u_* \epsilon}{\nu} < 5.5$$

[†] For more accurate values see Table 23.

[Assuming $u_* = 10$ cm sec^{-1} (which is probably rather low), this means that irregularities greater than about 1 mm in height will usually impair the smoothness of a surface in the aerodynamical sense.] Nikuradse's investigations, which are more significant for meteorology, dealt with turbulent flow in pipes whose interior surfaces were roughened uniformly by grains of sand. His criterion for *fully-rough flow* is based on the concept that in such circumstances the motion is virtually independent of viscosity, and he found that this occurs when

$$\frac{u_* \epsilon}{\nu} > 75 \tag{3.33}$$

At the other end of the range Nikuradse found substantial confirmation of Schiller's result. Between these two limits is a region of transition in which a surface is neither smooth nor fully rough, *i.e.*, there is evidence of an appreciable effect of viscosity. These investigations were afterward extended by Schlichting, who used surfaces roughened by obstacles of widely different size and shape. Schlichting was able to unite into one coherent theory the results for all such surfaces by the introduction of a length called the *equivalent sand roughness*, such that a uniform roughness formed by sand grains of the size and of the type used by Nikuradse would produce the same skin friction as that actually found.

In the meteorological problem, it is obviously difficult to speak with any confidence of the "average height" of the obstacles which are normally found on the surface of the earth. It is shown later that this difficulty can be overcome, and Nikuradse's test for roughness effectively applied, by the use of another length which is related to the height of the obstacles but which is found from measurement of the velocity profile. If a surface is fully rough ($u_* \epsilon / \nu$ about 100, or greater), the direct influence of viscosity is negligible and the Reynolds number does not enter into the argument. The virtual elimination of viscosity from the expression for the drag of a fully-rough surface is explained by the fact that at such a boundary the laminar sublayer does not exist, the surface effectively consisting of a dense array of small bluff bodies whose resistance is almost entirely form drag. It follows that the skin friction of such a surface is almost exactly proportional to the square of the reference velocity. It is shown later (Chap. 7) that this holds for the surface of the earth in the great majority of cases.

3.9. The Velocity Profile in the Turbulent Boundary Layer in Relation to the Mixing-length Hypothesis

Consider a steady two-dimensional mean motion in the proximity of a plane rigid surface $z = 0$. It is supposed that $\bar{u}$ is a function of z only, and the object is to determine the velocity profile $\bar{u}(z)$, in fully developed turbulence, which is consistent with a given shearing stress τ. Meteorologically, this is the problem of the variation of wind with height over an area of level ground when the temperature gradient is close to the adiabatic lapse rate, so that gravitational effects are excluded.

The equation of motion. If the x axis is in the direction of the mean wind, so that $\bar{v} = \bar{w} = 0$ throughout the layer concerned, and the Coriolis force is neglected, the equations of mean motion reduce to the single equation

$$\frac{\partial \tau}{\partial z} = \frac{\partial \bar{p}}{\partial x} \tag{3.34}$$

where $\tau = -\rho \overline{u'w'}$ and $\partial \bar{p}/\partial x$ is the pressure gradient in the direction of the mean wind. If $\partial \bar{p}/\partial x$ is supposed independent of height in the shallow layer concerned, Eq. (3.34), on integration, yields

$$\tau = \tau_0 + z \frac{\partial \bar{p}}{\partial x} \tag{3.35}$$

where τ_0 is the value of τ as $z \to 0$. In most meteorological problems the change of pressure in the direction of the mean wind is small, and provided that z is not large, say not exceeding 25 m, it is usually possible to neglect the second term on the right in Eq. (3.35) in comparison with the first.[†] The analysis is therefore restricted to the case in which $\tau = \tau_0$ throughout the layer concerned. This implies that the friction velocity $u_* = \sqrt{(|\tau_0/\rho|)}$ also is invariable with height in this layer.

Hypotheses concerning the mixing length. At this stage it is necessary to make some assumptions concerning the functional form of l before it is possible to proceed to the determination of the profile. Various possibilities exist.

HYPOTHESIS 1. It is supposed that l at any point is determined solely by distance from the boundary and the physical properties of the fluid. In general.

$$\frac{\bar{u}}{u_*} = f(l, z, \tau_0, \nu, \rho)$$

and the only nondimensional ratios which can be formed from the quantities on the right-hand side are l/z, $u_* z/\nu$. Hence

$$\frac{\bar{u}}{u_*} = f\left(\frac{l}{z}, \frac{u_* z}{\nu}\right)$$

From Eq. (3.24),

$$l^2 \left(\frac{d\bar{u}}{dz}\right)^2 = \frac{\tau_0}{\rho} = \text{constant}$$

[†] For a more detailed analysis see papers by Ertel[12] and Calder.[13]

or

$$\frac{1}{u_*}\frac{d\bar{u}}{dz} = \frac{1}{l} \tag{3.36}$$

This is the differential equation of the profile of mean velocity in the boundary layer. As a first step, it is reasonable to take $l/z = k$, where k is a constant, expressing the intuitive conception that the scale of the mixing is proportional to distance from the boundary. Equation (3.36) then becomes

$$\frac{1}{u_*}\frac{d\bar{u}}{dz} = \frac{1}{kz} \tag{3.37}$$

On integration this gives

$$\frac{\bar{u}}{u_*} = \frac{1}{k}\ln z + \text{constant}$$

which may be rearranged in the nondimensional form

$$\frac{\bar{u}}{u_*} = \frac{1}{k}\ln\left(\frac{u_* z}{\nu}\right) + \text{constant} \tag{3.38}$$

The constant of integration is to be determined by a suitable boundary condition. A characteristic feature of the behavior of real fluids near a solid boundary is the absence of any relative motion at the boundary itself. In the present problem this implies that $\bar{u} = 0$ on $z = 0$, a condition which cannot be satisfied by any finite constant of integration in Eq. (3.38). Some more restrictive boundary condition must therefore be substituted, and a corresponding limitation in the range of validity of Eq. (3.38) accepted. Such a condition, suggested by the detailed examination of the motion near a smooth surface, is that the velocity gradient increases without limit as the surface is approached. This is automatically satisfied by Eq. (3.37). For motion near smooth surfaces, Nikuradse found that

$$\frac{\bar{u}}{u_*} = \frac{1}{0.4}\ln\left(\frac{u_* z}{\nu}\right) + 5.5 \tag{3.39}$$

corresponding to $k = 0.4$. This equation may be written in a simpler approximate form

$$\frac{\bar{u}}{u_*} = \frac{1}{0.4}\ln\left(\frac{9u_* z}{\nu}\right) \tag{3.40}$$

from which it is evident that, with this formulation, the mean velocity vanishes on the plane $z = \nu/9u_*$ approximately, the equation having no meaning for smaller values of z. Even if we take u_* to be as small as 10 cm sec^{-1}, the equation is formally valid to within about 2×10^{-3} cm of the surface.

Neglecting ν in comparison with K_M, Eqs. (3.15) and (3.37) give

$$K_M = \frac{u_*{}^2}{d\bar{u}/dz} = u_* l = k u_* z \qquad (3.41)$$

so that, on the present hypothesis, the eddy viscosity increases linearly with distance from the boundary. Since k is about 4×10^{-1} and u_* is normally of the order of 10 to 20 cm sec^{-1} for winds over very smooth ground, it follows that at a height of 100 cm above the surface K_M should be of the order of 10^3 cm^2 sec^{-1}, at least, in meteorological problems. This is in agreement with estimates made in other ways and underlines an important general result, that *the mixing length is of the same order of magnitude as the height of the reference plane above the surface.* Obviously, such inferences must be restricted to shallow layers, since otherwise there would emerge the impossible result that the eddy viscosity attains unlimited values at the greater heights, *i.e.*, in regions of the atmosphere which are known to be almost free from turbulence of the type found near the ground.

HYPOTHESIS 2. An alternative expression for l, originally derived from similitude considerations, has been advanced by v. Kármán.[14] The mean velocity may be removed by taking axes moving downstream at the mean velocity appropriate to the level z under consideration, and the similitude hypothesis is that in such a system the fluctuations at all such points differ only in the scales of length and time (or velocity). This is equivalent to postulating that the mixing length must depend primarily on the distribution of mean velocity, and only indirectly on distance from the boundary. Thus, in the simple case of steady two-dimensional mean motion along the axis of x, it follows that

$$l = f\left(\frac{d\bar{u}}{dz}, \frac{d^2\bar{u}}{dz^2}, \cdots\right)$$

Disregarding derivatives higher than the second, dimensional considerations yield

$$l = k \frac{d\bar{u}/dz}{d^2\bar{u}/dz^2} \qquad (3.42)$$

where k is a constant. If τ is independent of z, for example when there is no pressure gradient in the direction of motion, Eq. (3.24) gives

$$u_*{}^2 = k^2 \frac{(d\bar{u}/dz)^4}{(d^2\bar{u}/dz^2)^2}$$

whence

$$\frac{\bar{u}}{u_*} = \frac{1}{k} \ln z + \text{constant}$$

which is identical with the profile obtained from hypothesis 1. Thus in the absence of a pressure gradient, the two hypotheses lead to identical results, and the constant k in Eq. (3.42) may be identified with that used previously, so that $l = kz$ and $k \simeq 0.4$.

The number k is called the *Kármán constant*, and it is shown later (Chap. 7) that the value 0.4 is also appropriate to motion near the surface of the earth.

3.10. Modifications of the Profile Equations for Fully-rough Surfaces

In the fully-rough regime, the influence of viscosity is negligible, so that in terms of the analysis of the preceding section, $\bar{u}/u_*$ must depend only on the lengths z, l, and ϵ. Taking, as before, $l = kz$, the profile is

$$\frac{\bar{u}}{u_*} = \frac{1}{k} \ln \left(\frac{z}{\epsilon} \right) + \text{constant} \tag{3.43}$$

which is usually written in the form

$$\frac{\bar{u}}{u_*} = \frac{1}{k} \ln \left(\frac{z}{z_0} \right) \qquad z \geq z_0 \tag{3.44}$$

where z_0 is a constant of integration known as the *roughness length*, which must be related in some way to the size of the protuberances. From measurements in pipes uniformly roughened with grains of sand it has been shown that $z_0 = \epsilon/30$ approximately. Equation (3.44) thus implies that the mean velocity vanishes at a height depending on the average height of the irregularities, the equation having no meaning below this level.

If the relation $z_0 = \epsilon/30$ be accepted, Nikuradse's tests for smooth and rough surfaces can be written

Smooth flow: $\qquad \dfrac{u_* z_0}{\nu} < 0.13$

Fully-rough flow: $\qquad \dfrac{u_* z_0}{\nu} > 2.5$

The quantity $u_* z_0$ is called the *macroviscosity* and denoted by the symbol N. Thus Nikuradse's criteria are

Smooth flow: $\qquad N < 0.13\nu \simeq 0.02 \text{ cm}^2 \text{ sec}^{-1}$

Fully-rough flow: $\qquad N > 2.5\nu \simeq 0.4 \text{ cm}^2 \text{ sec}^{-1}$ $\tag{3.45}$

The macroviscosity may be looked upon as a quantity which plays a part in fully-rough flow analogous to that exercised by the kinematic viscosity in smooth flow. The limits in (3.45) should not be accepted as exact, and they need not be so in the application of the concept to meteorology. Provided that N is, say, several orders of magnitude greater than ν (that is, $N > 10$ cm² sec⁻¹), it may be asserted with confidence that the motion is of the fully-rough type, and this is so in nearly all examples of meteorological interest (see Table 23, Chap. 7).

The Rossby Hypothesis. The problem of the mixing length and of the velocity profile in the neighborhood of a fully-rough surface has been considered by C.-G. Rossby[15] on the following lines: It is assumed that the influence of the roughness on the mixing length is virtually confined to those layers in which z and z_0 are comparable, by taking

$$l = k(z + z_0) \qquad (3.46)$$

which is indistinguishable from the usual form $l = kz$ for $z \gg z_0$. The differential equation for the profile then becomes

$$\frac{1}{u_*} \frac{d\bar{u}}{dz} = \frac{1}{k(z + z_0)} \qquad (3.47)$$

whence

$$\frac{\bar{u}}{u_*} = \frac{1}{k} \ln (z + z_0) + \text{constant}$$

It is now possible to satisfy the condition $\bar{u} = 0$ on $z = 0$, the resulting profile being

$$\frac{\bar{u}}{u_*} = \frac{1}{k} \ln \left(\frac{z + z_0}{z_0} \right) \qquad (3.48)$$

The velocity gradient remains finite as $z \to 0$ and attains the large value u_*/kz_0 on $z = 0$. Investigations based on this formulation are considered in Chap. 7.

Universal Profile. A defect in the above formulations is that neither (3.44) nor (3.48) agrees with the smooth-surface profile (3.40) for $z_0 = 0$, so that the roughness length cannot be regarded as a continuously variable parameter. The difficulty may be overcome by the use of the macro-viscosity (Sutton[16]) as follows:

Equation (3.44) may be written

$$\frac{\bar{u}}{u_*} = \frac{1}{k} \ln \left(\frac{u_* z}{N} \right) \qquad (3.49)$$

and Eq. (3.48),

$$\frac{\bar{u}}{u_*} = \frac{1}{k} \ln \left(\frac{u_* z + N}{N} \right) \qquad (3.50)$$

A universal profile, applicable to both rough and smooth surfaces, is defined by the interpolation formula

$$\frac{\bar{u}}{u_*} = \frac{1}{k} \ln \left(\frac{u_* z}{N + \nu/9} \right) \qquad (3.51)$$

corresponding to Eq. (3.44), and by

$$\frac{\bar{u}}{u_*} = \frac{1}{k} \ln \left(\frac{u_* z + N}{N + \nu/9} \right) \qquad (3.52)$$

corresponding to the Rossby formulation. The profile over an aero-dynamically smooth surface is obtained by putting $N = 0$ (since $z_0 = 0$), when both reduce to Eq. (3.40). For most meteorological problems, N is very much greater than ν, in which event Eqs. (3.51) and (3.52) are indistinguishable from Eqs. (3.44) and (3.48), respectively.

The macroviscosity, since it depends both on the configuration of the surface z_0 and the friction velocity u_*, completely specifies the aero-dynamic quality of a surface and is especially useful in the analysis of diffusion near the surface of the earth.

Alternative Expressions for the Profile.   In many meteorological problems it is often convenient to express the profile in terms of the mean velocity at a standard height, say 1 m above the surface.   Equation (3.48) is equivalent to

$$\frac{\bar{u}}{u_1} = \frac{1}{\ln (\alpha + 1)} \ln \left(\frac{\alpha z}{z_1} + 1 \right) \qquad (3.53)$$

if $\bar{u}_1$ is the mean velocity at the standard reference height z_1; $\alpha = z_1/z_0$ may be regarded as a parameter expressing the aerodynamic quality of the surface.

In many mathematical problems involving the explicit use of the velocity profile (*e.g.*, in problems of diffusion, Chap. 8), the introduction of the logarithmic profile into the differential equations raises difficulties, and it is often possible to proceed only if the logarithmic function is replaced by a simple power.   It is advantageous, for these reasons, to develop the preceding theory in terms of power laws.

As a trial hypothesis, the dependence of mixing length on height can be expressed by

$$l = l_1 z^p \qquad p \neq 1$$

where l_1 is the magnitude of the mixing length at unit height.   The profile differential equation becomes

$$\frac{1}{u_*} \frac{d\bar{u}}{dz} = \frac{1}{l_1 z^p}$$

whence

$$\frac{\bar{u}}{u_*} = \frac{1}{l_1 (1 - p)} z^{1-p} + \text{constant}$$

Provided $0 \leq p < 1$, the condition $\bar{u} = 0$ on $z = 0$ can be satisfied, giving the profile,

$$\frac{\bar{u}}{u_*} = q \left(\frac{u_* z}{\nu}\right)^{1-p} \tag{3.54}$$

where

$$q = \left(\frac{\nu}{u_*}\right)^{1-p} \frac{1}{l_1(1 - p)}$$

This formulation is applicable to a smooth surface. Observations show that for such a surface $p = \frac{6}{7}$, in which case the velocity increases as the seventh root of the distance from the boundary. For moderate values of the Reynolds number, the "seventh-root profile" gives a very fair representation of the change of velocity in the neighborhood of a smooth boundary, but for larger values of the Reynolds number, p must be increased to $\frac{7}{8}$ or $\frac{8}{9}$ to conform with the observations. The logarithmic profile, on the other hand, is in good agreement with observations over a much greater range of the Reynolds number without any adjustment of the values of the parameters.

In meteorological work it is often convenient to use a power-law profile in the form

$$\bar{u} = \bar{u}_1 \left(\frac{z}{z_1}\right)^m \qquad m \geq 0 \tag{3.55}$$

where $\bar{u}_1$ is the mean velocity at the reference height z_1. If τ is independent of height, the corresponding expression for the eddy viscosity K_M is

$$K_M = K_1 \left(\frac{z}{z_1}\right)^{1-m} \tag{3.56}$$

where K_1 is the eddy viscosity at the height z_1. Equations (3.55) and (3.56) are known in meteorology as *Schmidt's conjugate-power laws*. It is important to note that the relation between K_M and $\bar{u}$ is valid only within the relatively shallow layer in which τ may be regarded as independent of height. This restriction has not always been borne in mind in investigations on atmospheric turbulence, with results that are dubious, to say the least.

TABLE 4. SUMMARY OF FORMULAS FOR l, u, AND K_M NEAR THE SURFACE
(τ independent of z)

Hypothesis	Surface	Mixing length l	Velocity profile u/u_*	Eddy viscosity K_M
$1 \propto z$	{ Smooth	kz	$k^{-1} \ln (9u_* z/\nu)$	$ku_* z$
	Rough	kz	$k^{-1} \ln (u_* z/N)$	$ku_* z$
$1 \propto z + z_0$	Rough	$k(z + z_0)$	$k^{-1} \ln [(u_* z + N)/N]$	$k(u_* z + N)$
$1 \propto z^p$	Smooth	$l_1 z^p$	$q(u_* z/\nu)^{1-p}$	$u_* l_1 z^p$

3.11. The Validity of the Exchange-coefficient and Mixing-length Hypotheses

The exchange-coefficient hypothesis is based on the postulate that the rate of transfer of a conservative entity, in a field of flow in which the mean velocity varies in one direction only, is proportional to the gradient of the mean value of the entity. The exchange coefficient is simply the factor of proportionality. Provided that this be accepted as a definition, no objection can be raised to the exchange-coefficient theory in a mathematical sense. Physically, however, the implication is that the transfer process arises from fluctuating motions of short "period," *i.e.*, motions associated with small length scales, conventionally called *eddy diameters*. The Prandtl mixing-length hypothesis introduces two further assumptions: (1) that the exchange coefficient involves a unique representative length and a representative fluctuating velocity; (2) that the length thus introduced is proportional to the quotient of the fluctuating velocity and the gradient of mean velocity. It is possible to regard (1) as the definition of l, but (2) makes the definite assumption that the mean velocity is transferable in the sense used above, and that the ratios of $\overline{u'^2}$, $\overline{v'^2}$, $\overline{w'^2}$ are much the same at all points.†

The most obvious defect of the mixing-length theory is made evident by consideration of the magnitude of l revealed by the observations. It has been pointed out (page 81) that measurements of wind profiles near the ground indicate that l is of the same order of magnitude as the height of the observations, and therefore is not "small" in the free-path sense. Much the same conclusion is reached from laboratory measurements of wakes and jets. A particularly serious deficiency is shown in the comparison of energy distribution in a wake. In the Prandtl theory, $\overline{u'^2}$ is proportional to $l^2(d\bar{u}/dz)^2$. Hence the energy should decline to zero at the center of a wake, where $d\bar{u}/dz = 0$, unless l were infinite, which is physically unacceptable. Actually, measurements show that the eddying energy is high at the center of the wake and declines to zero only at the boundary of the disturbed flow. The conclusion reached by Dryden[18] is that not only is the mixing-length theory untenable in general but that considerable doubt is now thrown on the fundamental hypothesis that the virtual shearing stress in a boundary layer is directly related to the gradient of mean velocity. The Prandtl mixing-length theory does not take proper account of the influence of the bigger eddies.

It has been suggested, from an examination of conditions in a wake, that there may be present some transport process in turbulent flow which is independent of the gradient of the entity being transferred, *i.e.*, there

---

† G. K. Batchelor[17] has pointed out that postulate 2 is equivalent to the assumption that the turbulence has a similar structure at all points in the field and that there is no diffusion of turbulent energy.

may exist some "convective" processes as well as the usual diffusion mechanism (Batchelor[17]). The difference between a diffusion process of the type familiar in the kinetic theory of gases and other modes of transfer is discussed in Chap. 4; here it suffices to point out that it may not be possible always to formulate a consistent theory of turbulent transfer by writing simply $\overline{w'E} \propto d\bar{E}/dz$ (page 69). There may be a term, or terms, depending on $\bar{E}$ and some mean velocity.

The difficulty becomes acute in the case of heat transfer (Chap. 4), in which extraneous effects such as buoyancy enter. Momentum appears to be transferred mainly by the smaller eddies, and this may account for the initial success which attended the introduction of the mixing length.

3.12. The Vorticity-transfer Hypothesis

In formulating the mixing-length expression for the eddy shearing stress it has been assumed that momentum is a conservative transferable property in the sense indicated on page 69. This implies that the pressure fluctuations, which are by no means negligible in a turbulent fluid, do not affect the mean transfer of momentum. This is not likely to be true in general, but when the turbulence is strictly two-dimensional, one component of vorticity is conserved. This observation is the basis of the *vorticity-transfer theory* advanced by Taylor.[19]

Considering, as before, a turbulent motion in which the mean velocity is a function of z only, and in which the root mean square values of the fluctuations are constant, the equation of motion is

$$\frac{\partial u}{\partial t} = -\frac{1}{\rho}\frac{\partial p}{\partial x} - \frac{\partial}{\partial x}\left(\frac{1}{2}u^2 + \frac{1}{2}w^2\right) - w\eta$$

where η is twice the vorticity, *i.e.*,

$$\eta = \frac{\partial u}{\partial z} - \frac{\partial w}{\partial x}$$

Taking mean values,

$$\frac{\partial\bar{u}}{\partial t} = -\frac{1}{\rho}\frac{\partial\bar{p}}{\partial x} - \overline{w'\eta'}$$

where η' is twice the turbulent vorticity. Hence the rate of change of momentum per unit volume is $-\rho\overline{w'\eta'}$.

Putting $E = \rho\eta$ in Eq. (3.28), it follows that

$$-\rho\overline{w'\eta'} = \rho l \sqrt{(\overline{w'^2})}\frac{\partial\bar{\eta}}{\partial z} = \rho l \sqrt{(\overline{w'^2})}\frac{\partial^2\bar{u}}{\partial z^2}$$

since, by definition, $\bar{\eta} = \partial\bar{u}/\partial z$. Thus on the vorticity-transfer theory the rate at which momentum is communicated to unit volume of the fluid by the fluctuations is

$$\frac{1}{\rho}\frac{\partial \tau}{\partial z} = K(z)\,\frac{\partial^2 \bar{u}}{\partial z^2}$$

where, as before,

$$K(z) = l\,\sqrt{(\overline{w'^2})}.$$

This should be compared with the expression derived in the momentum-transfer theory,

$$\frac{1}{\rho}\frac{\partial \tau}{\partial z} = \frac{\partial}{\partial z}\left[K_M(z)\,\frac{\partial \bar{u}}{\partial z}\right]$$

The two expressions are identical if, and only if, the exchange coefficients are independent of z.

The vorticity-transfer theory has been further elaborated by Taylor, but the resulting equations are somewhat intractable. The matter will not be discussed further here, since the differences between the two theories are not, as yet, of prime importance for micrometeorology. The reader who wishes to pursue the discussion further should consult one of the specialized treatises on fluid dynamics.†

3.13. Statistical Theories of Turbulence

In the developments described in the previous sections, attention is focused on the distribution of mean velocity and its relation to the frictional effects of turbulence. The fluctuations or eddy velocities are dismissed from the analysis at the earliest possible stage by the introduction of exchange coefficients or by the use of the mixing-length concept. Such theories are "statistical" only in the sense that they deal with the average properties of the motion and in so far as correlation functions appear in the formulation of the virtual stress. All such theories essentially involve a large element of empiricism.

Recent experimental work has made it increasingly difficult to sustain the fundamental concepts of the mixing-length theories as originally proposed, and in the last few years the general line of attack on the turbulence problem has been along paths laid down by the so-called statistical theories. In many ways this approach is more natural, since it involves the properties of the fluctuations, which constitute turbulence, in the most direct fashion. The statistical theory, founded by Taylor in 1921, starts from the intrinsic properties and interrelations of the components of the velocity fluctuations and seeks to derive the properties of the mean flow by considering certain statistical functions of the fluctuations. The difference between the two approaches may be summed up by saying

† For example, Goldstein, "Modern Developments in Fluid Dynamics" (Oxford, 1938).

that while the empirical theories take the mean flow as established and thereafter probe its nature and its effects on other properties, the statistical theories begin with the fluctuations and seek to show how the character of the whole field, including the mean flow, arises from the properties of the fluctuations considered as a statistical assembly.

Historically, the statistical theories spring from an isolated paper on the problem of diffusion, published by Taylor[20] in 1921 in the Proceedings of the London Mathematical Society, a journal devoted mainly to problems in pure mathematics. The same decade saw the emergence of the Göttingen school and the initial successes of the mixing-length concept, and, with the exception of a few striking and highly original contributions by L. F. Richardson, the empirical theories maintained their ascendancy until 1935, when Taylor returned to the attack with a remarkable series of papers which at once placed the statistical theory in the forefront of research. Other contributions, notably by v. Kármán, followed, and the progress of the study continued to be rapid until the outbreak of the Second World War in 1939. When hostilities ceased, new developments due to A. N. Kolmogoroff became known to scientists outside Russia, and this particular extension of the theory, which has many points in common with concepts recently advanced by Heisenberg, Weiszäcker, and Onsager, is now regarded by many as the most promising yet proposed. In the field of micrometeorology, apart from the work of Richardson, which is in a class by itself, the only direct application of statistical concepts to the atmosphere during this period was made by Sutton in 1932 and 1934, again in relation to problems of diffusion.

The Random Walk and Brownian Motion. The basic concepts of the statistical theory are best introduced by considering the problem of diffusion, first in relation to molecular agitation (Brownian motion) and second in a turbulent fluid. The advantage of this procedure is that it makes clear what statistical functions are likely to be important in the development of the dynamic theory, and why.

A single molecule of a gas must follow a very irregular path in consequence of collisions with other molecules. In the simplest possible analysis it may be supposed that all the free paths are of the same length λ and are all parallel to some agreed direction, so that after a large number of collisions the molecule will have advanced in the agreed direction by a distance $\pm \lambda \pm \lambda \pm \lambda \pm \cdots$. This amounts to the problem of the "drunkard's walk"—an inebriated citizen takes a number of steps of the same length, but each is as likely to be backward as forward; what is the probability that he will have advanced a given distance at the end of n steps? It is shown in textbooks of the kinetic theory of gases that this concept, when applied to the motion of a molecule, leads to the result that the average distance traveled is proportional to the square root of the time which has elapsed since the motion started. If the motion were not random, the distance covered would be proportional to the time, and (as Jeans puts it) "travelling at random we must take four times as many steps to travel two miles as to travel one."

It is clear that a motion of this sort is something like that which affects a particle in turbulent flow, but eddy diffusion is hardly likely to be as simple as that described above, and, in particular, it is impossible to accept the notion of discontinuity, as in the molecular example. The significant fact is the idea of diffusion as a random walk.

In Brownian motion, a particle which is large compared with a molecule, but sufficiently small to respond to the effects of molecular bombardment, is supposed to experience a viscous resistance as it moves through the fluid. (This illustrates the important point that the analysis, at some stage, must take into account the intrinsic properties of the medium.) The motion of the particle will thus be influenced by (1) its inertia, (2) the viscous drag, and (3) any extraneous influences, including collisions, regarded as a statistical group of a random nature. The equation of motion in one dimension is

$$m \frac{d^2x}{dt^2} + f \frac{dx}{dt} + R_x = 0$$

where m is the mass of the particle, $f \, dx/dt$ is the viscous drag, and R_x represents the extraneous forces. It is required to find the mean rate of dispersion, or $\overline{d/dt \, (x^2)} = d/dt \, (\overline{x^2}) = S$, say, in this field. The equation of motion may be written

$$\frac{1}{2} m \frac{d^2}{dt^2} (x^2) - m \left(\frac{dx}{dt} \right)^2 + \frac{1}{2} f \frac{d}{dt} (x^2) + x R_x = 0$$

Averaging over a large number of molecules, $\overline{x R_x} = 0$, because of the random nature of the extraneous forces, and hence

$$\frac{1}{2} m \frac{dS}{dt} + \frac{1}{2} f S = m \overline{u^2}$$

since $u = dx/dt$ is the molecular velocity. If the gas is of uniform and steady temperature, $m \overline{u^2} = RT/N$, where R is the gas constant, T is the absolute temperature, and N is the number of molecules per unit volume. Integrating with respect to time,

$$S = \frac{2m}{f} \, \overline{u^2} \left[1 - \exp \left(-\frac{tf}{m} \right) \right] \tag{3.57}$$

Since $f = 6\pi\mu r$, where μ is the dynamic viscosity and r the radius of the particle, supposed spherical (Stokes' law), it follows that $f/m = 9\mu/2r^2\rho$

is, in general, large, since r must be very small for Brownian motion to be appreciable. The exponential term is thus negligible after a very short time, and another integration yields Einstein's well-known formula

$$\overline{x^2} = \frac{2m\overline{u^2}}{f} t = 2Kt \tag{3.58}$$

where K is a coefficient of diffusion whose value, in this case, depends upon the absolute temperature and viscosity of the gas and the shape of the particles. Einstein's equation has been verified experimentally.

Taylor's theorem. It was pointed out by Taylor[20] in 1921 that it is also possible to proceed as follows: From the ordinary laws of forming mean values

$$\frac{d}{dt}\overline{x^2} = 2\overline{xu} = 2\int_0^t \overline{u(t)u(t+\xi)}d\xi$$

If $\overline{u^2}$ is invariable, the correlation coefficient $R(\xi)$ between the velocity u experienced by the particle at times t and $t + \xi$ is, by definition,

$$R(\xi) = \frac{\overline{u(t)u(t+\xi)}}{\overline{u^2}} \tag{3.59}$$

Hence

$$S = \frac{d}{dt}\overline{x^2} = 2\overline{u^2}\int_0^t R(\xi)d\xi \tag{3.60}$$

Comparing Eqs. (3.57) and (3.60), it follows that, in this case,

$$R(\xi) = \exp\left(-\frac{f\xi}{m}\right)$$

so that $R(\xi)$, which is unity for $\xi = 0$, is effectively zero for large values of ξ. From Eq. (3.60)

$$\overline{x^2} = 2\overline{u^2}\int_0^t dt \int_0^t R(\xi)d\xi \tag{3.61}$$

For $R(\xi) = \exp(-\xi f/m)$ this yields

$$\overline{x^2} = 2\overline{u^2}\left[\frac{tm}{f} - \frac{m^2}{f^2}(1 - e^{-tf/m})\right]$$

and, neglecting the terms of order $(m/f)^2$ this gives

$$\overline{x^2} = \frac{2m\overline{u^2}}{f} t$$

as before. As in the simple case of the random walk, the distance covered is proportional to $\sqrt{t}$.

These considerations throw considerable light on the general problem of turbulent diffusion. As a helpful analogy, the eddies in a turbulent fluid may be compared with the molecules in a gas, in that the motion of a particle will be the result of its encounter with various eddies, but "eddy" is now merely a convenient way of describing a fluctuation of velocity associated with a certain scale of length. Taylor's theorem shows that the dispersion experienced by a group of particles in such a field is determined (1) by the over-all magnitude of the intensity of the fluctuations $\overline{u^2}$ and (2) by the nature of the correlation between the fluctuations which affect a particle at different times. This type of correlation is unlike that which enters into the expression for the shearing stress in that it involves one velocity component only.

The exponential form for $R(\xi)$ in the example of Brownian motion is explained as follows: Suppose that, like the molecules, the eddies are of the same size. The part of $u^2(t + \xi)$ due to correlation with $u(t)$ is $R^2(\xi)u^2(t)$, and the part of $u^2(t + \xi)$ independent of $u(t)$ is $[1 - R^2(\xi)]u^2(t)$. Hence, at the end of the interval, the eddying energy affecting the particle is made up of a fraction which has persisted throughout the interval plus a fraction which is due to motions which have appeared during the interval. Continuing the process during a further interval ξ, after a lapse of 2ξ sec the fraction of the eddying energy due to the original eddies is $\frac{1}{2}R^4(\xi)u^2(t)$. Hence, for this type of field, in which the eddies are all of the same size, appearing and disappearing at the same uniform rate,

$$R(2\xi) = R^2(\xi) \qquad \text{or} \qquad R(\xi) = \exp{(-a\xi)}$$

where a is a constant, depending on the size of the eddy.

Thus Brownian motion, in which the dispersion increases as the square root of the time, is the result of a very special type of disorderly motion. Since $R(\xi)$ in this case is effectively zero for all except very small values of ξ, the motion approximates closely to a series of disconnected but similar jerks. Turbulent diffusion is not of this type, and any theory which is founded on the concept of a field in which all the eddies are of the same size must be abandoned (see Sec. 8.2).

If the function $R(\xi)$, which on physical grounds must tend to zero as ξ tends to infinity, is such that $\int_0^\infty R(\xi)d\xi$ converges, it is possible to define a length l_1 by the relation

$$l_1 = \sqrt{(\overline{u^2})} \int_0^\infty R(\xi)d\xi \tag{3.62}$$

and a virtual coefficient of diffusion by

$$K = \sqrt{(\overline{u^2})}l_1 = \overline{u^2} \int_0^\infty R(\xi)d\xi \tag{3.63}$$

This should be compared with Eq. (3.29), from which it becomes clear that l_1 is analogous to the mixing length of the empirical theories, but in Taylor's treatment the concept of mixing is not essential to the argument, and the above equations have meaning when no mixing is taking place. Taylor's theorem, by extending the problem of the random walk to the case of *continuous* movement, supplies the starting point for the most far-reaching and searching investigations into the nature of the turbulent field.

Scales of Turbulence. Considering fluctuations at two points P and Q in a turbulent fluid, the correlation between $u'(P)$ and $u'(Q)$ will, in general, vary with the magnitude of the distance PQ. The expectation is that the correlation will diminish as PQ increases, and this suggests a method of defining a length which makes precise the intuitive conception of eddy "size." If $R(y)$ is the correlation coefficient between fluctuations at points separated by a distance y, that is,

$$R(y) = \frac{\overline{u'(P)u'(Q)}}{\sqrt{[\overline{u^2(P)}]}\ \sqrt{[\overline{u^2(Q)}]}}$$

—the axis of y being along PQ—a length L can be defined by the relation.

$$L = \int_0^\infty R(y)dy \tag{3.64}$$

provided that the integral converges. [This will be so, for example, if $R(y)$ is zero for y greater than some finite length.] The length L, called the *scale of turbulence*, represents the average size of the eddies or length scale of the fluctuations, but without implying any definite model of an eddy.

All turbulence, and especially that of natural winds, is a complex of motions covering a great range of length scales, varying from those associated with the fluctuations which contain most of the energy of the motion to those typical of the very small eddies which are responsible for the ultimate dissipation of the energy into heat by the action of viscosity. A relation between $R(y)$ and the length scale of the smallest eddies can be obtained as follows (Taylor[21]):

If $\overline{u'^2}$ is independent of y,

$$R(y) = \frac{\overline{u'u'_y}}{\overline{u'^2}} = \frac{1}{\overline{u'^2}}\left(\overline{u'^2} + \overline{yu'\frac{\partial u'}{\partial y}} + \frac{y^2}{2!}\overline{u'\frac{\partial^2 u'}{\partial y^2}} + \cdots\right)$$

and

$$\overline{u'\frac{\partial u'}{\partial y}} = 0, \qquad \overline{u'\frac{\partial^2 u'}{\partial y^2}} = -\overline{\left(\frac{\partial u'}{\partial y}\right)^2}$$

Hence,

$$R(y) \simeq 1 - \frac{1}{2!} \frac{y^2}{\overline{u'^2}} \overline{\left(\frac{\partial u'}{\partial y}\right)^2}$$

or

$$\overline{\left(\frac{\partial u'}{\partial y}\right)^2} = 2\overline{u'^2} \lim_{y \to 0} \left[\frac{1 - R(y)}{y^2}\right]$$

$$= \frac{2\overline{u'^2}}{\lambda^2} \tag{3.65}$$

where λ is the intercept on the axis of y of the parabola drawn to touch the $[R(y),y]$ curve at its vertex, the curvature of the $R(y)$ curve at $y = 0$ thus being a measure of $\overline{(\partial u'/\partial y)^2}$.

The length λ is called the *microscale of turbulence* and is a measure of the average "diameter" of the smallest eddies or, more accurately, of the length scale of the fluctuations which are mainly responsible for the dissipation of energy.

Isotropic Turbulence and the Dissipation of Energy. The Kármán mixing-length analysis applies to the so-called *homologous* turbulent motion in which the distributions of the fluctuations and their correlations differ only in scale at every point in the field. A simpler type of turbulent motion is one in which the average values of the velocity components or their spatial derivatives are unaltered if the axes of references are rotated in any manner, or are reflected. Such a turbulent field is said to be *isotropic* (Taylor[21]) and constitutes the simplest type of field for theoretical study. Naturally, such a field is very restricted since, by definition, changes in direction and magnitude of the fluctuations at a given point are random, and there is no correlation between the components of the fluctuations in different directions. In isotropic turbulence the normal stresses $\rho\overline{u'^2}$, $\rho\overline{v'^2}$, and $\rho\overline{w'^2}$ are equal, and the tangential stresses $-\rho\overline{u'v'}$, $-\rho\overline{v'w'}$, $-\rho\overline{u'w'}$ vanish.

Turbulent fields of this type are not found near the ground, where the motion is strongly anisotropic, but isotropy is approached in the atmosphere at heights well above the surface layers. One of the advantages of the study of isotropic turbulence is that such fields can be realized, at least approximately, in a well-designed wind tunnel, so that the theoretical work can be checked experimentally. The outstanding characteristic of isotropic turbulence is that the statistical properties of the field depend chiefly on intensity and scale, both of which can be varied easily in the laboratory.

Most of the experimental work relates to the decay of turbulence. Usually, a grid of wires is placed near the inlet end of the working section; this sets up a well-defined and fairly regular eddy system which quickly transforms into an isotropic field, whose properties can be studied at various points down wind.   Such studies have little direct application to micrometeorology but are of considerable theoretical significance.   The main points will be briefly reviewed here.

The general expression for the mean rate of dissipation in a viscous incompressible fluid is

$$\bar{W} = \mu \left[2 \overline{\left(\frac{\partial u'}{\partial x} \right)^2} + 2 \overline{\left(\frac{\partial v'}{\partial y} \right)^2} + 2 \overline{\left(\frac{\partial w'}{\partial z} \right)^2} + \overline{\left(\frac{\partial v'}{\partial x} + \frac{\partial u'}{\partial y} \right)^2} \right.$$
$$\left. + \overline{\left(\frac{\partial w'}{\partial y} + \frac{\partial v'}{\partial z} \right)^2} + \overline{\left(\frac{\partial u'}{\partial z} + \frac{\partial w'}{\partial x} \right)^2} \right]$$

In an isotropic field this reduces to

$$\bar{W} = 6\mu \left[\overline{\left(\frac{\partial u'}{\partial x} \right)^2} + \overline{\left(\frac{\partial u'}{\partial y} \right)^2} + \overline{\frac{\partial v'}{\partial x} \frac{\partial u'}{\partial y}} \right]$$

The quantities in the brackets are not independent, since the fluid is incompressible and the field is isotropic.   It can be shown† that for such fields the expression reduces to

$$\bar{W} = 7.5\mu \overline{\left(\frac{\partial u'}{\partial y} \right)^2}$$

From Eq. (3.65) it follows that

$$\bar{W} = 15\mu \frac{\overline{u'^2}}{\lambda^2} \tag{3.66}$$

On the other hand, the kinetic energy of the fluctuations per unit volume is $\frac{1}{2}\rho(\overline{u'^2} + \overline{v'^2} + \overline{w'^2})$, which for isotropic turbulence reduces to $\frac{3}{2}\rho\overline{u'^2}$. The rate of decay of turbulent energy is thus $-\frac{3}{2}\rho \, d(\overline{u'^2})/dt$. If the eddies are moving downstream at a uniform velocity $\bar{u} = dx/dt$, the rate of decay with distance x is $-\frac{3}{2}\rho\bar{u} \, d(\overline{u'^2})/dx$.   Thus

$$-\frac{3}{2}\rho\bar{u}\frac{d}{dx}(\overline{u'^2}) = 15\mu \frac{\overline{u'^2}}{\lambda^2}$$

—an equation which can be verified in a wind tunnel.

The Reynolds stresses are approximately proportional to the squares of the turbulent fluctuations, and the work done against these stresses, which in the absence of external forces must be drawn from the kinetic energy of the system, is proportional to $\rho(\overline{u'^2})^{\frac{3}{2}}/L$, where L is the scale of the turbulence [Eq. (3.64)].   Hence, when geometrically similar systems are compared on different scales and at different speeds, it follows that, at any point,

† For details, see Goldstein, *op. cit.*, Vol. 1, p. 222, or Taylor's original papers.

$$\bar{W} = \frac{15\mu\overline{u'^2}}{\lambda^2} \text{ is proportional to } \rho\,\frac{(\overline{u'^2})^{\frac{3}{2}}}{L}$$

or

$$\lambda^2 = \text{constant}\,\frac{L\nu}{\sqrt{(\overline{u'^2})}} \tag{3.67}$$

This equation shows the relation between the microscale of turbulence and the scale of turbulence in an isotropic field.

The Spectrum of Turbulence. So far the turbulent field has been analyzed in terms of the average intensity of the fluctuations and their associated length scales, rather like the kinetic theory analysis of molecular motion in a gas in terms of temperature and the free path. A fundamental problem concerns the distribution of the energy of the fluctuations among the motions of different length scales or eddy diameters.

If a sensitive and quick-response instrument (such as a hot-wire anemometer) is placed at a point in a turbulent wind and arranged to record the value of one component of the fluctuations, say u', the result will be a very irregular curve of velocity against time, without any well-marked evidence of periodic components. To borrow a phrase from radio technique, the record will have the characteristics of "noise." However (with certain restrictions which are not relevant here), any function can be expressed as a Fourier series or Fourier integral, so that $u'(t)$ at some fixed point can be resolved into a series of harmonic components, of different wavelengths or frequencies. The mean value $\overline{u'^2}$ will be made up of contributions from all frequencies, but, depending on the character of the field, fluctuations of certain frequencies will make important contributions and will thus largely determine the value of $\overline{u'^2}$, while the effects of fluctuations of other frequencies will be negligible.

The concept employed here is very similar to that which lies at the root of spectroscopic analysis. A prism placed in a beam of white light resolves the time variation of the electric intensity at a point into harmonic components and so forms a spectrum. In 1938, L. F. G. Simmons and C. Salter showed how the output from a hot-wire anemometer placed in a turbulent air stream could be resolved by electrical filters into a similar spectrum. In the familiar example of the prism, the fact that the velocity of light is the same for all wavelengths means that the time-variation analysis is exactly equivalent to a harmonic analysis of the space variation of electric intensity over the path. In the turbulence problem the same reasoning applies if the eddies are being carried past the fixed point by a constant mean velocity, and by using this concept Taylor was able to show how the spectrum of turbulence measured over an interval of time at a fixed point is related to the correlation between simultaneous values of the fluctuations measured over an interval of length in the direction of the mean wind.

The mean value $\overline{u'^2}$, which measures the average level of the turbulent energy, is built up by contributions from fluctuations of different frequencies. The *spectrum function* $F(n)$, where n is frequency (cycles per second), is defined as follows: Let $F(n)$ measure the fraction of the total energy which is associated with a particular frequency n, so that $\overline{u'^2}F(n)dn$ is the contribution to $\overline{u'^2}$ from frequencies lying between n and $n + dn$. Thus

$$\overline{u'^2} = \int_0^\infty \overline{u'^2}F(n)dn \quad \text{or} \quad \int_0^\infty F(n)dn = 1$$

The plot of $F(n)$ against n is called the spectrum curve.

The resolution of $u'(t)$ into harmonic components must now be considered. Since the representation must be over an unlimited interval, the analysis is based on the Fourier integral and not on the series. The quantities $a(n)$ and $b(n)$, defined by the relations

$$a(n) = \frac{1}{\pi} \int_{-\infty}^\infty u'(t) \cos 2\pi nt \, dt \tag{3.68}$$

$$b(n) = \frac{1}{\pi} \int_{-\infty}^\infty u'(t) \sin 2\pi nt \, dt \tag{3.69}$$

correspond, in the integral representation, to the familiar Fourier coefficients of the series. Thus the required representation, involving all frequencies, is

$$u'(t) = 2\pi \int_0^\infty [a(n) \cos 2\pi nt + b(n) \sin 2\pi nt]dn$$

To calculate the mean square $\overline{u'^2(t)}$ necessitates the integral analogue of Parseval's theorem for the series,[†] *viz.*,

$$\int_{-\infty}^\infty [u'(t)]^2 \, dt = 2\pi^2 \int_0^\infty [a^2(n) + b^2(n)]dn$$

If the range of integration is supposed to be a very long time T instead of infinity, from the ordinary rules of forming mean values it follows that

$$\overline{u'^2} = 2\pi^2 \int_0^\infty \lim_{T \to \infty} \left[\frac{a^2(n) + b^2(n)}{T} \right] dn$$

[†] Parseval's theorem is a consequence of the orthogonal property of the sine and cosine functions and is as follows: If the function $f(x)$ satisfies certain very general conditions, and $a_n \cos nx + b_n \sin nx$ is the nth term of its Fourier series,

$$\frac{1}{\pi} \int_{-\pi}^\pi f^2(x)dx = \frac{1}{2} a_0^2 + \sum_{n=1}^\infty (a_n^2 + b_n^2)$$

This shows how $\overline{u'^2}$ is made up of contributions from fluctuations of various frequencies. The contribution from fluctuations whose frequencies lie between n and $n + dn$ is $2\pi^2 \lim\limits_{T\to\infty} \left[\dfrac{a^2(n) + b^2(n)}{T} \right] dn$, and this, by definition, is $F(n)dn$. Hence

$$F(n) = 2\pi^2 \lim_{T\to\infty} \left[\frac{a^2(n) + b^2(n)}{T} \right] \tag{3.70}$$

It is now supposed that the mean velocity $\bar{u}$ which carries the turbulent field is much greater than u'† so that the sequence of changes in u' at a fixed point may be supposed to arise from an unchanging pattern of turbulent flow moving over the point. That is,

$$u'(t) = u'\left(\frac{x}{\bar{u}}\right)$$

where x is measured upstream at the time $t = 0$ from the fixed point where u' is measured. This is likely to be strictly true only when $u'/\bar{u}$ is small. The correlation coefficient $R(x)$ is defined as

$$R(x) = \frac{\overline{u'(t)u'(t + x/\bar{u})}}{\overline{u'^2}} \tag{3.71}$$

It is shown in textbooks of analysis‡ that

$$\int_{-\infty}^{\infty} u'(t)u'(t + t')dt = 2\pi^2 \int_{0}^{\infty} [a^2(n) + b^2(n)] \cos 2\pi n t' \, dn$$

Applying this to the above case, with $t' = x/\bar{u}$, using Eqs. (3.70) and (3.71), it follows that

$$R(x) = \int_{0}^{\infty} F(n) \cos \frac{2\pi n x}{\bar{u}} \, dn \tag{3.72}$$

This suggests the use of the Fourier-transform formula, *viz.*, that if $f(x)$ is an even function defined by

$$f(x) = \left(\frac{2}{\pi}\right)^{\frac{1}{2}} \int_{0}^{\infty} g(\eta) \cos \eta x \, d\eta$$

then

$$g(\eta) = \left(\frac{2}{\pi}\right)^{\frac{1}{2}} \int_{0}^{\infty} f(x) \cos \eta x \, dx$$

---

† It is generally possible to ensure this in a wind tunnel, but the assumption may not always be true in the atmosphere, *e.g.*, in the neighborhood of large obstacles, such as trees or houses. Over flat country u' is generally of the order of one-tenth of $\bar{u}$ near the ground.

‡ See, *e.g.*, N. Wiener "The Fourier Integral," p. 70 (Cambridge, 1933).

Putting

$$\eta = \frac{2\pi n}{\bar{u}}, \qquad f(x) = R(x), \qquad g(\eta) = \frac{\bar{u}F(n)}{2\sqrt{2\pi}}$$

it follows from (3.72) that

$$F(n) = \frac{4}{\bar{u}} \int_0^\infty R(x) \cos \frac{2\pi n x}{\bar{u}} \, dx \qquad (3.73)$$

This is Taylor's fundamental result: *The correlation coefficient $R(x)$ and the modified spectrum function $\bar{u}F(n)/2\sqrt{2\pi}$ are Fourier transforms of one another.* Thus, knowing $F(n)$, $R(x)$ can be deduced from (3.72); or, conversely, from a measured $R(x)$ we can deduce $F(n)$ from (3.73).

It is evident on general physical grounds that a relation must exist between $R(x)$ and $F(n)$. For large eddies, $R(x)$ will fall to zero with increasing x more slowly than when the eddies are small. Hence if the measured $R(x)$ curve has a large spread on the x axis, the spectrum will be restricted to relatively low frequencies, and vice versa. Taylor was able to compare his theory with wind-tunnel measurements made at about 2 m down wind of a turbulence-producing mesh at mean wind speeds varying from about 500 to 1000 cm sec^{-1}. Except very close to $x = 0$, $R(x)$ was found to be independent of the mean wind speed, implying that $\bar{u}F(n)$ is a function of $n/\bar{u}$. The agreement between the measured values of $R(x)$ and those calculated from Eq. (3.71), using the spectrum function $F(n)$ from the hot-wire anemometer and filter circuit, was satisfactory. The spectrum curve may also be used to estimate the value of λ, the microscale of turbulence. From the definition of λ [Eq. (3.65)]

$$\frac{1}{\lambda^2} = 2 \lim_{x \to 0} \left[\frac{1 - R(x)}{x^2} \right]$$

When n is small, $\cos 2\pi n x / \bar{u}$ in (3.73) may be replaced by $1 - 2\pi^2 x^2 n^2/\bar{u}^2$. Hence

$$\frac{1}{\lambda^2} = \frac{4\pi^2}{\bar{u}^2} \int_0^\infty n^2 F(n) \, dn \qquad (3.74)$$

In the wind-tunnel experiments, Taylor found a fair measure of agreement between λ calculated from the spectrum curves and directly from the observed energy dissipation. The values of λ were of the order of 1 cm and decreased slightly with increasing mean velocity.

3.14. The Similarity Theory of Turbulence

In 1941 A. N. Kolmogoroff[24] advanced a novel and attractive theory of turbulence, based on hypotheses about the structure of the small-scale fluctuations at very large Reynolds numbers. Because of the preoccupations of war time, these concepts were not widely examined until 1947, when G. K. Batchelor[25] published several accounts and critical discussions of the theory. Similar ideas were advanced independently by Heisenberg,[26] Onsager,[27] and Weiszäcker,[28] and in recent years wind-tunnel tests have produced much evidence in their favor. The following account is based largely on Batchelor's papers.

The fundamental concept of this work is that turbulent motion is characterized by a wide range of subsidiary motions with very different scales of length and that energy is continually passing from large to small length scales. It is customary and convenient to speak of the fluctuations as originating from eddies of different size, but nothing in the way of a definite model is implied by this usage. Any large-scale individual motion in the atmosphere cannot persist as such indefinitely; such motion is unstable to small disturbances and sooner or later must break down into motions of smaller length scales, *i.e.*, into smaller eddies. Ultimately, a limit must be reached, when the energy has been passed down to fluctuations whose Reynolds number is too low to permit the formation of yet smaller eddies. The energy is then directly absorbed into the random motion of the molecules by viscosity. Kolmogoroff suggests that as this process proceeds the direct influence of the larger eddies is gradually lost, so that the small eddies tend to have properties which are more or less their own, *i.e.*, common to all types of turbulence. As a consequence, the small-scale structures of any turbulent motion should be isotropic, and wind-tunnel tests have shown that this is likely to be true.

It cannot be asserted, however, that the average properties of the small eddies will be strictly the same for all types of turbulence; there is a kind of harness to which they must submit, provided by considerations of the conservation of energy. If the mean level of turbulent energy in the motion is constant, the small eddies must convert into heat all the energy that is passed down to them by the breakup of the larger eddies. From this arises *Kolmogoroff's first similarity hypothesis.*

The average properties of the small-scale components of any turbulent motion at large Reynolds number are determined uniquely by the kinematic viscosity of the fluid (ν) *and the average rate of dissipation of energy per unit mass of the fluid* (ϵ).

It should be noted that in this hypothesis the expression "small-scale" means that motions which contain an appreciable amount of the total turbulent energy are excluded. The large eddies represent the main storehouses of energy, and the small eddies the ultimate consumers, and it is to the latter that the first similarity hypothesis applies.

The second of Kolmogoroff's fundamental hypotheses depends directly on the circumstance that the Reynolds number involved is very large, as in the atmospheric problem. As the Reynolds number increases, the ultimate viscous dissipation will shift more and more toward the smaller and smaller eddies which are being created, and in time the largest eddies of the range covered by the first similarity hypothesis will tend to become independent of the process by which the energy is passed to the molecules (that is, independent of ν) and will be dominated solely by inertia forces. *Kolmogoroff's second similarity hypothesis* is as follows:

For sufficiently large Reynolds numbers, there is a subrange of the range of small eddies in which average properties are determined solely by the average rate of dissipation of energy per unit mass of the fluid (ϵ).

To return to the analogy of the marketing of goods, these eddies represent the "middlemen" whose characteristics are determined by the rate at which energy is passing down from the great storehouses, and not by the ultimate dissipation by the small-scale consumer. It is evident that the theory can say nothing about properties dependent on the larger scale motions but is applicable only to mean values which are markedly dependent on the small-scale components of the motion. Such mean values must then, by hypothesis, be expressable as universal functions of ϵ and ν and any time or length variables involved in their definition. The form of the universal functions can be deduced by dimensional analysis.

As an example, Batchelor considers the quantity $\overline{[u'(\mathbf{x} + \mathbf{r}) - u'(\mathbf{x})]^2}$ where $u'(\mathbf{x})$ and $u'(\mathbf{x} + \mathbf{r})$ are velocity fluctuations at two points in space with position vectors $\mathbf{x}$ and $\mathbf{x} + \mathbf{r}$, respectively. If the two points are sufficiently close, only those eddies whose length scales do not greatly exceed r (the magnitude of $\mathbf{r}$) can influence the velocity difference. Hence the similarity hypothesis can be applied. Since the smaller eddies are likely to be approximately uniformly distributed in space, the dependence of the mean value will be mainly on $\mathbf{r}$ and not on $\mathbf{x}$. Hence it is possible to write

$$\overline{[u'(\mathbf{x} + \mathbf{r}) - u'(\mathbf{x})]^2} = f(\mathbf{r}, \nu, \epsilon)$$

where f is a universal function. By dimensional analysis

$$\overline{[u'(\mathbf{x} + \mathbf{r}) - u'(\mathbf{x})]^2} = \sqrt{(\epsilon \nu)} f_1\left(\frac{r \epsilon^{\frac{1}{4}}}{\nu^{\frac{3}{4}}}\right)$$

where f_1 is another universal function. From continuity conditions and the isotropy of the small eddies, Batchelor deduces that

$$\overline{[u'(\mathbf{x} + \mathbf{r}) - u'(\mathbf{x})]^2} = \sqrt{(\epsilon \nu)} \left(f_2 + \frac{r_1^2}{2r}\frac{df_2}{dr}\right)$$

where r_1 is the component of $\mathbf{r}$ in the direction of u' and f_2 is another universal function of $(r\epsilon^{\frac{1}{4}}/\nu^{\frac{3}{4}})$. The second hypothesis is now brought in by the fact that an eddy with a length scale much less than r also will not sensibly affect $\overline{[u'(\mathbf{x}+\mathbf{r})-u'(\mathbf{x})]^2}$, so that this mean value is chiefly determined by eddy sizes in the neighborhood of r. If r is restricted by two considerations, (1) that it is far below the sizes of the energy containing eddies and (2) that it is much greater than the length $\nu^{\frac{3}{4}}/\epsilon^{\frac{1}{4}}$, that is, greater than the diameter of the viscosity-influenced eddies, the function f_2 must have a form such that ν vanishes from the whole expression. This is so when

$$f_2 = c_1 \left(\frac{r\epsilon^{\frac{1}{4}}}{\nu^{\frac{3}{4}}}\right)^{\frac{2}{3}}$$

where c_1 is an absolute constant. Hence

$$\overline{[u'(\mathbf{x}+\mathbf{r})-u'(\mathbf{x})]^2} = c_1(\epsilon r)^{\frac{2}{3}}\left(1 + \frac{r_1{}^2}{3r^2}\right)$$

for r in the range specified. This can be tested in the wind tunnel, and the evidence, according to Batchelor, is satisfactory. The same type of argument can be used to make predictions about the energy-spectrum function, also with satisfactory results.

Kolmogoroff's theory gives rise to an interesting expression for the correlation function $R(x)$. For isotropic fields behind a grid the theory predicts that

$$R(x) = 1 - \frac{1}{2}\,C\left(\frac{15\nu}{u'\lambda^2}\,x\right)^{\frac{2}{3}} = 1 - Ax^{\frac{2}{3}}$$

where A is independent of x. This expression holds, as usual, if x is much greater than λ and much less than the length scale of the largest eddies. The prediction is moderately well satisfied by observations.

The question of how far Kolmogoroff's concepts are applicable to the atmosphere has been discussed by Batchelor. The length $(\nu^3/\epsilon)^{\frac{1}{4}}$ plays much the same part in the similarity theory as the microscale of turbulence λ; it is a measure of the length scale of the motions whose energy is dissipated directly by viscosity. Brunt† estimates that the rate at which the kinetic energy of the earth's atmosphere is being dissipated by turbulence is of the order of 5 cm² sec⁻³ in the lowest 10 km. Thus, accepting this figure, $(\nu^3/\epsilon)^{\frac{1}{4}}$ is of the order of millimeters or, at the most, centimeters. Hence the viscosity-influenced eddies in the atmosphere have diameters comparable with the microscale of turbulence found in wind tunnels. On the other hand, the large-scale fluctuations of velocity in the atmosphere have periods of the order of tens of seconds, or even minutes, and are thus associated with length scales of the order of tens or

† "Physical and Dynamical Meteorology," 2d ed., p. 286 (Cambridge, 1939).

hundreds of meters. It is to be concluded that the range of atmospheric eddy sizes to which Kolmogoroff's second similarity hypothesis can be applied is very large.

A serious limitation, however, is provided by the requirement that the fluctuations to which the similarity hypotheses are to apply must be free from external influences. Kolmogoroff envisages a conservative system in that the transfer of energy is solely from the large eddies to the small eddies. If there is some external agency supplying energy to a certain range of eddies (for example, to those comparable in size with the depth of a layer in which vertical currents are caused by density differences), the similarity theory may be applied only to mean values which depend on fluctuations whose length scales are considerably less than the range in question. This may be a severe restriction for micrometeorological applications.

The position at present appears to be that while the new similarity theory has opened up fresh lines of investigation into the dynamics of turbulent motion, as yet it has not sufficiently emerged from the laboratory stage to make an effective advance in the field of meteorology. The progress of the theory should be closely watched by meteorologists, especially in applications to the problem of diffusion, which are considered in Chap. 8.

BIBLIOGRAPHY

1. W. Tollmien, Nachr. Ges. Wiss. Göttingen, Math-physik. Klasse, p. 21 (1929).
2. H. Schlichting, Nachr. Ges. Wiss. Göttingen, Math-physik. Klasse, 2, 181 (1933).
3. F. Möller, Beitr. phys. fr. Atmos., 20, 79 (1933).
4. F. J. Scrase, Geophys. Mem. 52.
5. V. W. Ekman, Nyt. Mag. Naturv., 40(1) (1902).
6. G. M. B. Dobson, Quart. J. Roy. Meteorol. Soc., 40, 123 (1914).
7. G. I. Taylor, Phil. Trans. Roy. Soc., 215, 1 (1915).
8. L. Prandtl, "The Mechanics of Viscous Fluids," W. F. Durand (ed.), Aerodynamic Theory, Vol. III, Division G (Berlin, 1934).
9. L. Schiller, "Handbuch der Experimentalphysik," 4, Part 4 (Leipzig, 1932).
10. J. Nikuradse, Verhandl. deut. Ing. Forsch., 361 (1933).
11. H. Schlichting, Ingen.-Arch., 7, 1 (1936).
12. H. Ertel, Met. Z., 50, 386 (1933).
13. K. L. Calder, Quart. J. Roy. Meteorol. Soc., 65, 537 (1939).
14. Theodore v. Kármán, Nachr. Ges. Wiss. Göttingen, Math-physik. Klasse (1930).
15. C.-G. Rossby, Mass. Inst. Technol., Meteorol. Papers 1, 4 (1932).
16. O. G. Sutton, Quart. J. Roy. Meteorol. Soc., 74, 13 (1948).
17. G. K. Batchelor, J. Aeronaut. Sci., 17, 441 (1950).
18. H. L. Dryden, Mechanics of Boundary Layer Flow, Advances in Applied Mech., 1, 2–78, (1948).
19. G. I. Taylor, Proc. Roy. Soc. (London), A135, 685 (1932).
20. G. I. Taylor, Proc. London Math. Soc., 20, 196 (1922).
21. G. I. Taylor, Proc. Roy. Soc. (London), A151, 430 (1935).

22. L. F. G. Simmons and C. Salter, Proc. Roy. Soc. (London), A165, 78 (1938).
23. G. I. Taylor, Proc. Roy. Soc. (London), 164, 476 (1938)
24. A. N. Kolmogoroff, Comptn. red. acad. sci. U.R.S.S., 30, 301 (1941); 32, 16 (1941).
25. G. K. Batchelor, Proc. Cambridge Phil. Soc., 43, 533 (1947).
26. W. Heisenberg, Proc. Roy. Soc. (London), A195, 402 (1948).
27. L. Onsager, Phys. Rev., (II), 68, 286 (1945).
28. C. F. Weiszäcker, Z. Physik, 124, 614 (1948).

CHAPTER 4

HEAT TRANSFER AND PROBLEMS OF DIFFUSION

The production and transfer of heat are widespread natural phenomena, of particular interest to the meteorologist, to whom the atmosphere often appears as a large heat engine, of peculiar complexity. The investigation of heat transfer in an ocean of air, of variable water-vapor content and bounded on one side by a solid or liquid surface of ever-changing temperature, is complex and involves many related sciences. The considerable difficulties of the subject, however, are often heightened for the micrometeorologist by the virtual impossibility of defining precise physical boundaries (for example, the exact "surface" of the earth when it is covered by vegetation) or even the temperature of the air on a day when clouds are passing in front of the sun. It is useless to expect in micrometeorology the consistency of carefully controlled laboratory experiments—as Brunt[1] puts it, "the air does not know its own temperature to that degree of accuracy." At this stage of knowledge, the most that can be expected from theory is a reasoned and mutually consistent account of the broader aspects of phenomena which take place within a few feet of the ground.

The traditional treatment of heat transfer defines three distinct processes, conduction, convection, and radiation. *Conduction*, or *diffusion of heat*, in a gas arises from the elastic impact of molecules, without any net transfer of matter, and is thus similar to the transfer of momentum by viscosity. *Convection* implies the mixing of relatively large volumes, at different temperatures, because of the motion of the fluid. *Radiation* is the transference of energy, with or without an intervening medium, by electromagnetic waves. All these processes may occur simultaneously in the atmosphere, and it is often difficult or even impossible to disentangle completely the various effects.

A further subdivision is necessary for a detailed study. Convection is called *free* or *natural* if the motion of the fluid in the gravitational field is maintained solely by differences in density caused by local temperature inequalities. *Forced convection* means that the motion of the fluid is due to an applied pressure gradient. In both instances the flow may be laminar or turbulent. On a windy day with an overcast sky, the exchange of heat between the ground and the air affords a good example of forced convection, but if the wind be low and the surface of the ground very hot,

105

the process of heat transfer will involve both types of convection. The terms "free" and "forced" can therefore be applied to atmospheric convection only in a somewhat inexact sense, indicating that in the circumstances considered one or other process is dominant, but not necessarily exclusive.

There is an obvious and fundamental relation between the transfer of momentum by viscosity and the transfer of heat by conduction in a fluid in laminar motion, and a less exact but indispensible analogy between the transfer of momentum and that of heat by forced convection in a turbulent fluid. In both processes the underlying mechanism is essentially the same. The dynamics of free convection is necessarily more complicated, since any motion started by density differences is at once modified by the action of viscosity and conduction. Thus in what appears at first sight to be the relatively simple problem of a shallow layer of fluid heated from below, vertical motion does not occur immediately, since the diffusing action of conduction and viscosity tends to smooth out differences of temperature and velocity, and it is only when the temperature gradient attains a critical value that vertical currents appear. This is easily demonstrated in the laboratory, and there is evidence that a similar state of affairs holds in the atmosphere.

4.1. Mathematical Theory of the Conduction of Heat

Solid body. The classical theory of the conduction of heat in a solid is based upon the fundamental proposition that the rate of flow of heat from one region to another is proportional to the cross-sectional area perpendicular to the direction of flow and to the temperature gradient in the direction of flow. If q be the flux of heat per unit area (in calories per square centimeter per second), T the temperature, and x the direction of the flow of heat, this is expressed by writing

$$q = -k \frac{\partial T}{\partial x}$$

The quantity k is called the *thermal conductivity* and is an intrinsic property of the conducting substance. As with viscosity, it is convenient to define a second coefficient κ, called the *thermometric conductivity* (or *thermal diffusivity*), analogous to the kinematic viscosity, by the relation

$$\kappa = \frac{k}{c\rho}$$

where c is the specific heat of the solid and ρ its density.

The equation of conduction is obtained very simply, by considering the flow of heat through a small rectangular volume of sides δx, δy, δz. Using arguments exactly similar to those in the derivation of the equation of continuity (Chap. 2), it is easily seen that the net gain of heat by the volume element from the x component of heat flow in unit time is

$$k \frac{\partial^2 T}{\partial x^2} \, \delta x \, \delta y \, \delta z \tag{4.1}$$

and there will be like contributions from the other components. The gain of heat by the volume may also be expressed as

$$c\rho \frac{\partial T}{\partial t} \, \delta x \, \delta y \, \delta z \tag{4.2}$$

Expressions (4.1) and (4.2), on being equated, yield the *equation of conduction of heat in an isotropic solid*

$$\frac{\partial T}{\partial t} = \kappa \left(\frac{\partial^2 T}{\partial x^2} + \frac{\partial^2 T}{\partial y^2} + \frac{\partial^2 T}{\partial z^2} \right) \tag{4.3}$$

Fluids. A complete discussion of the transfer of heat by conduction in a fluid is difficult since, strictly, it is necessary to take into account changes in density, heat developed in the fluid by the work done against viscosity, and the variation of conductivity and viscosity with temperature. In the simplest case, in which the fluid is regarded as incompressible and the generation of heat by friction (and consequent dissipation of energy of motion) is neglected, the equation governing the transfer of heat in a moving fluid is a straightforward generalization of that in an isotropic solid. The increase in temperature experienced by a moving particle of fluid in time δt is

$$\delta T = \frac{\partial T}{\partial t} \, \delta t + \frac{\partial T}{\partial x} \, \delta x + \frac{\partial T}{\partial y} \, \delta y + \frac{\partial T}{\partial z} \, \delta z$$

[compare Eq. (2.1)].

Dividing by δt, and making $\delta t \to 0$, gives the expression for the rate of change of temperature,

$$\frac{dT}{dt} = \frac{\partial T}{\partial t} + u \frac{\partial T}{\partial x} + v \frac{\partial T}{\partial y} + w \frac{\partial T}{\partial z}$$

with the usual notation. It has already been shown (Chap. 1) that if a quantity of heat dQ is supplied to a unit mass of air,

$$dQ = c_p \, dT - \frac{ART}{p} \, dp$$

If changes in pressure are negligible, this reduces to $dQ = c_p \, dT$ and the gain of heat by the elementary volume $\delta x \, \delta y \, \delta z$ in unit time is

$$c_p\rho \left(\frac{\partial T}{\partial t} + u \frac{\partial T}{\partial x} + v \frac{\partial T}{\partial y} + w \frac{\partial T}{\partial z} \right) \delta x \, \delta y \, \delta z$$

This must equal the gain by conduction, *i.e.*,

$$k \left(\frac{\partial^2 T}{\partial x^2} + \frac{\partial^2 T}{\partial y^2} + \frac{\partial^2 T}{\partial z^2} \right) \delta x \, \delta y \, \delta z$$

repeating the arguments of the previous section. Hence the required equation is

$$\frac{dT}{dt} = \frac{\partial T}{\partial t} + u \frac{\partial T}{\partial x} + v \frac{\partial T}{\partial y} + w \frac{\partial T}{\partial z} = \kappa \left(\frac{\partial^2 T}{\partial x^2} + \frac{\partial^2 T}{\partial y^2} + \frac{\partial^2 T}{\partial z^2} \right) \quad (4.4)$$

where $\kappa = k/c_p\rho$.

Equation (4.4) has been derived under certain restrictions. If these are removed and the general problem of the transfer of energy in a moving fluid is considered, it may be shown[†] that the equation which determines the distribution of temperature in any field of flow is

$$\rho c_v \frac{dT}{dt} + Ap \left(\frac{\partial u}{\partial x} + \frac{\partial v}{\partial y} + \frac{\partial w}{\partial z} \right) = k \left(\frac{\partial^2 T}{\partial x^2} + \frac{\partial^2 T}{\partial y^2} + \frac{\partial^2 T}{\partial z^2} \right) + A\Phi \quad (4.5)$$

where c_v is the specific heat at constant volume, A is the reciprocal of the mechanical equivalent of heat, and Φ is the dissipation function defined by

$$\Phi = \mu \left[-\frac{2}{3} \left(\frac{\partial u}{\partial x} + \frac{\partial v}{\partial y} + \frac{\partial w}{\partial z} \right)^2 + 2 \left(\frac{\partial u}{\partial x} \right)^2 + 2 \left(\frac{\partial v}{\partial y} \right)^2 + 2 \left(\frac{\partial w}{\partial z} \right)^2 \right.$$
$$\left. + \left(\frac{\partial w}{\partial y} + \frac{\partial v}{\partial z} \right)^2 + \left(\frac{\partial u}{\partial z} + \frac{\partial w}{\partial x} \right)^2 + \left(\frac{\partial v}{\partial x} + \frac{\partial u}{\partial y} \right)^2 \right]$$

For a perfect gas, Eq. (4.5) becomes

$$c_p\rho \frac{dT}{dt} - A \frac{dp}{dt} = k \left(\frac{\partial^2 T}{\partial x^2} + \frac{\partial^2 T}{\partial y^2} + \frac{\partial^2 T}{\partial z^2} \right) + A\Phi \quad (4.6)$$

The term involving Φ expresses energy dissipation by viscosity, which appears in the form of heat developed in the fluid. This term and that expressing the change of pressure are in general too small to exercise much influence in problems of micrometeorology, and it may be assumed that Eq. (4.4) gives an adequate representation of the transfer of heat in incompressible laminar motion of the atmosphere.

4.2. Simple Diffusion Processes

The equations derived above contain the Laplace operator ∇^2 defined by

$$\nabla^2 = \frac{\partial^2}{\partial x^2} + \frac{\partial^2}{\partial y^2} + \frac{\partial^2}{\partial z^2}$$

[†] See Goldstein, "Modern Developments in Fluid Dynamics," Vol. II (Oxford, 1938) for the full analysis. There is also an interesting discussion in Boussinesq, "Théorie analytique de la chaleur," Vol. II (Paris, 1903).

The appearance of this operator in so many of the equations of mathematical physics may be accounted for by an appeal to a general theorem.†
Let E be a scalar physical entity (such as temperature), and let E_0 be the value of E at the point O. The mean value $\bar{E}$ in a cube of side a around O is defined by

$$a^3\bar{E} = \int\!\!\!\int\!\!\!\int_{-a/2}^{a/2} E\,dx\,dy\,dz$$

Expanding E by Taylor's theorem,

$$E = E_0 + x\left(\frac{\partial E}{\partial x}\right)_0 + y\left(\frac{\partial E}{\partial y}\right)_0 + z\left(\frac{\partial E}{\partial z}\right)_0$$
$$+ \frac{1}{2}\left[x^2\left(\frac{\partial^2 E}{\partial x^2}\right)_0 + y^2\left(\frac{\partial^2 E}{\partial y^2}\right)_0 + z^2\left(\frac{\partial^2 E}{\partial z^2}\right)_0\right]$$
$$+ xy\left(\frac{\partial^2 E}{\partial x\,\partial y}\right)_0 + yz\left(\frac{\partial^2 E}{\partial y\,\partial z}\right)_0 + xz\left(\frac{\partial^2 E}{\partial x\,\partial z}\right)_0 + \cdots$$

On integration over the cube of side a, all integrals containing odd powers and products of the variables vanish by symmetry, and the terms which remain are only a^3E_0 and those in x^2, . . . , with

$$\int\!\!\!\int\!\!\!\int_{-a/2}^{a/2} x^2\,dx\,dy\,dz = \frac{a^5}{12}, \text{ etc.}$$

Thus, if all fourth and higher even derivatives of E are neglected,

$$a^3\bar{E} = a^3E_0 + \frac{a^5}{24}(\nabla^2 E)_0$$

or

$$\bar{E} - E_0 = \frac{a^2}{24}(\nabla^2 E)_0$$

It has thus been shown that with certain reasonable restrictions on E, the quantity $\nabla^2 E$ is proportional to the difference between the value of E at a point and its mean value in the neighborhood of the point. If the medium is one in which, because of its internal structure, a diffusion process occurs whenever there is a local divergence from the properties of the mean field, it follows that the equation describing this process will involve the Laplace operator. Thus if the medium has a "hot spot," the time rate of change of temperature at that point will be proportional to the difference $\bar{T} - T_0$, that is,

$$\left(\frac{dT}{dt}\right)_0 \propto \bar{T} - T_0 \propto (\nabla^2 T)_0$$

† Hopf, "Einfuhrung in die Differentialgleichungen der Physik" (Samm. Göschen 1933).

which is the equation of conduction. Similarly, if E represents the density of a substance in suspension, the equation of diffusion is

$$\frac{dE}{dt} = \kappa \nabla^2 E$$

where κ is the diffusivity. The same arguments may also be employed to derive the Laplace and Poisson equations in electrostatics or the equation of wave motion, etc., so that the theorem given above may be regarded as one of the basic relations of mathematical physics.†

The general form of the equation of diffusion, allowing for any spatial variations in the transfer coefficients, is

$$\frac{dE}{dt} = \frac{\partial}{\partial x}\left(\kappa_x \frac{\partial E}{\partial x}\right) + \frac{\partial}{\partial y}\left(\kappa_y \frac{\partial E}{\partial y}\right) + \frac{\partial}{\partial z}\left(\kappa_z \frac{\partial E}{\partial z}\right) \tag{4.7}$$

A *simple diffusion process* is defined as one which can be expressed completely by the above equation. If the κ's are independent of x, y, and z,

$$\frac{dE}{dt} = \kappa_x \frac{\partial^2 E}{\partial x^2} + \kappa_y \frac{\partial^2 E}{\partial y^2} + \kappa_z \frac{\partial^2 E}{\partial z^2} \tag{4.8}$$

and the diffusion is termed *Fickian*. A simple diffusion process is thus one in which the rate of transfer of the entity across a reference plane is expressed by the product of the diffusion coefficient and the spatial gradient of the entity at the level considered, *i.e.*, by

$$q = -k \frac{\partial E}{\partial z} \tag{4.9}$$

where q is the rate of transfer. Thus the transfer of momentum by viscosity or the spread of heat by conduction and the diffusion of one gas into another are simple diffusion processes. The exchange-coefficient hypothesis (Chap. 3) assumes that the transfer of the mean value of an entity by turbulence is of this type. On the other hand, the transfer of heat by free convection cannot rightly be regarded as a simple diffusion process.

The alternative approach to these problems is by the methods of the kinetic theory of gases, already outlined for viscosity in Chap. 2. For the details of the treatment the reader is referred to specialized treatises on the kinetic theory. This method brings out the fundamental characteristic of true diffusion, *viz.*, that the property is transferred from one level to another by oscillations or random motion of small length scale, acting independently of any bulk motion, in conjunction with an existing gradient.

† See Hopf, *op. cit.*, pp. 59*ff*.

At first sight it may appear that the transference of any entity may be treated as a diffusion process by using Eq. (4.9) to define the appropriate coefficient of diffusion. (This method was in considerable use in the early stages of the development of the theory of atmospheric turbulence.) It must be recognized, however, that this approach, although mathematically feasible, is artificial and unlikely to be fruitful unless the underlying physical processes are of the type envisaged in the kinetic theory. From the practical aspect, a transfer coefficient defined by Eq. (4.9) must be shown to be either constant or a simple universal function of the variables before the process under examination can be truly described as diffusion.

The molecular-diffusion coefficients are to a certain extent functions of temperature, etc. In most meteorological problems such variations may be ignored, and throughout this work molecular conduction and diffusion will be considered to be Fickian.

4.3. Boundary Conditions

The equations derived above are of themselves insufficient to solve any given problem of heat conduction. In any physical application it is necessary to bring in the particular initial and boundary conditions which make the problem determinate, and these, being as much a part of the problem as the equation itself, require careful consideration, especially in meteorological applications.

The solution of a problem in mathematical physics must satisfy three conditions:

1. The solution must *exist*.
2. The solution must be *unique*.
3. The solution must *depend continuously on the data*.

Condition 1 means simply that the mathematical statement of the solution is complete and free from inherent contradictions, but it gives no assurance that the equation can be solved in a form which will give a practicable answer to a concrete problem. Condition 2 allows the mathematician to assert that, a solution of the problem constituted by the differential equation and the conditions having been discovered, no other independent solution can be found. (It is, of course, often possible to express the same solution in two or more equivalent forms, but this is a trivial distinction.) A problem must be properly *set*, *i.e.*, have the right number and type of conditions, before the solution can be shown to be unique. Condition 3 means that the problem must be physically determinate, and if a small variation is made in the data in a region, the change in the solution in the same region must also be small.

Provided that certain reasonable restrictions are imposed on T, for example, that in the region considered the temperature and its derivatives are continuous functions of time and space, it may be shown that, with certain boundary conditions, the solutions of the equation of conduction are unique.†

The reader should note that, in general, arbitrary conditions may be imposed on T and its first-order spatial derivatives, but not on $\partial T/\partial t$ or the second-order spatial derivatives, because these are related by the differential equation.

Boundary Conditions in Meteorological Problems. The choice of the boundary conditions in a problem in mathematical physics is often a matter of difficulty. Such conditions frequently involve a limiting process, *i.e.*, it cannot be asserted that the solution will assume a prescribed value at a definite time or place, but only that the solution (or perhaps its derivatives) will behave in a certain fashion, usually as a limit. A boundary condition is a forecast of a property of the solution in certain specified conditions. An example will make this clear. In the problem of the spread of heat from hot ground to the atmosphere, the exact temperature at a great height cannot be predicted in advance, but it is quite certain that the effect of the source will decrease indefinitely with increasing height. In this example a requisite boundary condition is that $T \rightarrow 0$ as $z \rightarrow \infty$, and the problem involves finding a particular solution of the equation with exactly this property. The discovery of the solution means that henceforth a definite numerical value can be assigned to the temperature at *any* level.

Problems of meteorology are primarily concerned with the exchange of heat between the ground and the atmosphere, *i.e.*, with two infinite media of different conductivities, having a common boundary $z = 0$. The principal conditions on the common boundary are as follows:

1. *Prescribed temperature.* T may be known on $z = 0$ as a constant, a function of time, a function of position, or both. (Thus in the hours of daylight T may be given as a function of time by the first few terms of a Fourier series.)

2. *Prescribed flux.* The flow of heat across $z = 0$ is by definition

$$q_0 = -\kappa c_p \rho \left(\frac{\partial T}{\partial z} \right)_{z=0}$$

If k_a is the conductivity of the air and k_g that of the ground, the continuity of the flux of heat across $z = 0$ gives

$$k_a \left(\frac{\partial T_a}{\partial z} \right)_{z=0} = k_g \left(\frac{\partial T_g}{\partial z} \right)_{z=0} \tag{4.10}$$

† For a discussion see Carslaw and Jaeger, "Conduction of Heat in Solids" (Oxford, 1947).

as the requisite condition, T_a, T_g being temperatures in the air and in the ground, respectively.

3. *Radiation condition.* Newton's "law of cooling" states that for small temperature differences the rate of loss of heat from a body is proportional to its temperature above the ambient air. This takes into account, in an approximate fashion, conduction, natural convection, and radiation.† In this formulation, by introducing an "exterior conductivity" h the boundary condition is

$$-k\left(\frac{\partial T}{\partial z}\right)_{z=0} + h(T - T_0) = 0 \qquad (4.11)$$

where T is the temperature of the ground and T_0 that of the ambient air. If $h = 0$, this reduces to the "prescribed-flux" condition for a perfect insulator,‡ but if $h \gg k$, the condition approaches that of the "prescribed surface temperature."

4.4. The Laminar Thermal Boundary Layer

When a cool fluid moves over a hot surface, it is observed that the temperature gradient is large very near the surface and small elsewhere. This is borne out by measurements made near a closely cropped lawn on a hot day in summer; in the first half meter or so above the ground the temperature gradient may be as much as a thousand times the adiabatic lapse rate, but at heights of the order of several meters the gradient is only about one-hundredth of that observed near the ground. In a fluid of small conductivity, such as air, it is thus natural to envisage a *thermal boundary layer* of the same nature as the dynamic boundary layer described previously. Although at this stage it cannot be asserted that the two layers have much the same depth, on general physical grounds such a conclusion is very plausible.

Equation (4.4) for steady two-dimensional motion becomes

$$u\frac{\partial T}{\partial x} + w\frac{\partial T}{\partial z} = \kappa\left(\frac{\partial^2 T}{\partial x^2} + \frac{\partial^2 T}{\partial z^2}\right)$$

together with the equation of continuity

$$\frac{\partial u}{\partial x} + \frac{\partial w}{\partial z} = 0$$

---

† Strictly, the radiative loss of heat is determined by Stefan's fourth-power law; a body at absolute temperature T surrounded by a black enclosure whose walls are at absolute temperature T_0 will lose heat at the rate $\sigma e(T^4 - T_0^4)$, where σ is Stefan's constant and e is the emissivity. If $T - T_0$ is small, this is approximately

$$4\sigma e T_0^3(T - T_0) = \text{constant} (T - T_0)$$

which is Newton's law.

‡ The case $h \to 0$ needs to be handled with care. See Carslaw and Jaeger, *op. cit.*. p. **13**, footnote.

If δ_H is the depth of the thermal boundary layer and l a characteristic length of the surface in the x direction, the variables are made non-dimensional by writing, as in the treatment of the dynamic boundary layer,

$$\xi = \frac{x}{l}, \qquad \zeta = \frac{z}{\delta_H}$$

The transformed equations are

$$\frac{u}{l} \frac{\partial T}{\partial \xi} + \frac{w}{\delta_H} \frac{\partial T}{\partial \zeta} = \frac{\kappa}{l^2} \frac{\partial^2 T}{\partial \xi^2} + \frac{\kappa}{\delta_H{}^2} \frac{\partial^2 T}{\partial \zeta^2} \qquad (4.12)$$

$$\frac{1}{l} \frac{\partial u}{\partial \xi} + \frac{1}{\delta_H} \frac{\partial w}{\partial \zeta} = 0$$

The boundary layer is now defined by $0 \le \zeta \le 1$. It is supposed that

$$u, \frac{\partial T}{\partial \xi}, \frac{\partial^2 T}{\partial \xi^2}, \frac{\partial T}{\partial \zeta}, \frac{\partial^2 T}{\partial \zeta^2} = O(1)$$

It follows without difficulty that the terms on the left-hand side of Eq. (4.12) must both be $O(1)$. The term $(\kappa/l^2)(\partial^2 T/\partial \xi^2)$ on the right-hand side must be small since κ is small and l is finite. If the term

$$\left(\frac{\kappa}{\delta_H{}^2} \right) \left(\frac{\partial^2 T}{\partial \zeta^2} \right)$$

is to be of the same order of magnitude as those of the left-hand side, it follows that

$$\delta_H{}^2 = \text{constant} \, \frac{\kappa l}{u}$$

with the constant of order unity. Since u is proportional to U, the velocity outside the dynamic boundary layer, this means

$$\frac{\delta_H}{l} = \text{constant} \, \sqrt{\frac{\kappa}{lU}} \qquad (4.13)$$

which may be compared with Eq. (2.51) for the depth of the dynamic layer

$$\frac{\delta}{l} = \text{constant} \, \sqrt{\frac{\nu}{lU}}$$

Thus if Ul/κ is large, and if the ratio $\sigma = \nu/\kappa$ is not very different from unity, the distribution of temperature near a hot surface over which a fluid is streaming in laminar motion must resemble the distribution of velocity and the two boundary layers will be virtually identical. The equation governing the transfer of heat in the layer is

$$u \frac{\partial T}{\partial x} + w \frac{\partial T}{\partial z} = \kappa \frac{\partial^2 T}{\partial z^2} \tag{4.14}$$

The quantity Ul/κ is called the *Péclet number* Pé and the ratio $\sigma = \nu/\kappa$ the *Prandtl number* Pr. Obviously, Pé $= \sigma$ Re. For air near the surface of the earth $\sigma \simeq 0.7$.

The problem of the rate of loss of heat from a smooth flat plate maintained at a constant temperature in a laminar air stream flowing parallel to the plate has been considered on the above lines by Pohlhausen, whose theoretical formulas agree moderately well with the few measurements available. Of greater interest for micrometeorology is the extended problem of the removal of heat from a plane surface by a turbulent air stream, which is considered later (Sec 4.7).

4.5. Free Convection

Free convection implies that a volume of air rises in a gravitational field because of a local elevation of temperature, which causes a reduction in density and hence an upward force, or buoyancy. The magnitude of the upward force is easily determined by the principle of Archimedes. If g_z be this force, per unit volume, it follows that

$$g_z = g\rho_0 - g\rho = g\rho \left(\frac{\rho_0}{\rho} - 1 \right)$$

where ρ is the density of the heated volume and ρ_0 the density of the bulk of the fluid. The coefficient of expansion of the fluid, α, is defined by the equation

$$\frac{1}{\rho} = \frac{1}{\rho_0} [1 + \alpha(T - T_0)]$$

where T and T_0 are absolute temperatures corresponding to ρ and ρ_0, respectively. Hence the upward force due to buoyancy is

$$g_z = g\alpha\rho(T - T_0) = g\alpha\rho \, \Delta T$$

where $\Delta T = T - T_0$ is the local elevation of temperature.

For a perfect gas, $p = R\rho T$, and hence

$$\alpha = \frac{1}{T_0}$$

This means that in free convection the acceleration experienced by a heated particle is $g \, \Delta T/T_0$. The coefficient of expansion α thus appears only when multiplied by the acceleration due to gravity, *i.e.*, in the combination $g\alpha$.

The above expressions are fundamental in the theory. If T_0 be regarded as a mean value in a shallow layer near the ground, it follows that the force of buoyancy at any level is proportional to the local temperature excess.

Dimensional Analysis of Free Convection. The above considerations suggest that the rate of transfer of heat, q, by free convection in the air above unit area of a uniformly heated surface might be expressed by a relation of the type

$$q = h \, \Delta T$$

where ΔT is the difference between the temperature of the surface and that of the air in contact with it. Such an equation defines a heat-transfer coefficient h but conceals most of the real difficulties of the subject. Observation shows that the temperature of the air above a heated surface changes rapidly with elevation in the immediate neighborhood of the surface, so that ΔT cannot be defined unequivocally without further consideration. It is also found that h is far from being constant, like the conductivity, and must be further analyzed in terms of other variables before a useful system can be evolved. (The same remarks apply to the so-called "Dalton equation" of evaporation, in which an attempt is made to express the rate of removal of vapor from a moist surface by replacing ΔT by the difference between the vapor pressure at the surface and that in the ambient air and defining h to be a coefficient of mass transfer.)

It is shown in textbooks on heat transfer that, writing

$$h = f(l, \Delta T, \rho, \mu, c_p, g, k)$$

where l is a characteristic length and the other symbols have their usual meaning, and applying dimensional analysis,

$$\frac{hl}{k} = C \left(\frac{g\alpha l^3 \, \Delta T}{\nu^2} \right)^n \left(\frac{\nu}{\kappa} \right)^m$$

where C, m, and n are undetermined numbers and α is the coefficient of expansion. For a perfect gas, $\alpha = 1/T$, where T is the absolute temperature of the gas remote from the heated surface. Hence

$$\frac{hl}{k} = C \left(\frac{gl^3}{\nu^2} \frac{\Delta T}{T} \right)^n \left(\frac{\nu}{\kappa} \right)^m$$

The quantity hl/k, called the *Nusselt number* Nu, expresses the ratio of the temperature gradient at the surface to the average temperature gradient in the fluid.[†] The group $gl^3 \, \Delta T/\nu^2 T$, called the *Grashof number* Gr,

---

† See Jakob, "Heat Transfer," Vol. I (New York, 1949).

plays a part in free convection somewhat similar to that exercised by the Reynolds number in forced convection. The remaining ratio ν/κ has already been defined as the Prandtl number σ. Thus the equation of heat transfer in free convection may be written

$$\mathrm{Nu} = C \, \mathrm{Gr}^n \, \sigma^m$$

For air near the surface of the earth the Prandtl number is approximately constant ($\sigma \simeq 0.7$), and, in general, the Nusselt number is proportional to a power of the Grashof number.

The above analysis is the basis of many semiempirical investigations. In particular, Fishenden and Saunders[2] state that the rate of loss of heat from unit area of a horizontal surface is given by

$$q = 6 \times 10^{-5} \, \Delta T^{\frac{5}{4}} \qquad \text{cal cm}^{-2} \text{ sec}^{-1} \tag{4.15}$$

where $\Delta T °C$ is the difference between the temperature of the surface and that of the air well above the layer of steep temperature gradient. This relation has been examined for the atmosphere by P. K. Raman,[3] who found moderate agreement between the formula and observation when ΔT was taken to be the difference between the temperature of the ground and that of the air at 4 ft above the surface. If the Grashof number exceeds about 10^5, it appears that the index $\frac{5}{4}$ may need to be replaced by $\frac{4}{3}$, the motion then assuming a turbulent character.

Free Convection from a Vertical Wall. Consider a two-dimensional vertical surface defined by $y = 0$, $z \geq 0$, which is maintained at constant temperature T_w in an atmosphere whose temperature in regions remote from the wall is T_0. The heated air (temperature T') will be confined to a shallow layer adjacent to the wall, within which there will be a convection current, assumed slow. The problem is then one of incompressible laminar boundary-layer motion, with the force of buoyancy replacing the more usual pressure gradient, all other effects of variable density being regarded as of second order. The relevant equations are

$$w \frac{\partial w}{\partial z} + v \frac{\partial w}{\partial y} = \nu \frac{\partial^2 w}{\partial z^2} + g \left(\frac{T' - T_0}{T_0} \right) \qquad \text{(equation of motion)}$$

$$w \frac{\partial T'}{\partial z} + v \frac{\partial T'}{\partial y} = \kappa \frac{\partial^2 T'}{\partial y^2} \qquad \text{(equation of conduction)}$$

$$\frac{\partial w}{\partial z} + \frac{\partial v}{\partial y} = 0 \qquad \text{(equation of continuity)}$$

Here w is the velocity in the vertical and v the velocity normal to the wall, so that the boundary conditions are $w = v = 0$, $T' = T_w$ on $y = 0$ and $w \to 0$, $T' \to T_0$ as $y \to \infty$; it is further supposed that $T_w - T'$ is small compared with T_0.

These equations have been solved by Pohlhausen, whose solution has been shown to be in good agreement with observations by Schmidt and Beckmann. Pohlhausen's result for the vertical plate is that at a height z_0 above the lower edge of the plate

$$\mathrm{Nu} = \frac{qz_0}{k} = 0.359 \left[\frac{gz_0{}^3(T_w - T_0)}{\nu^2 T_0} \right]^{\frac{1}{4}} = 0.359 \, \mathrm{Gr}^{\frac{1}{4}}$$

where q now denotes the rate of heat transfer from unit area for unit difference of temperature. The equations given above also constitute the basis of the treatment of mountain and valley winds in Sec. 7.6.

In applying these results, care must be exercised that the Grashof number is not too large. If the thermal boundary layer becomes turbulent, it appears that the Nusselt number is proportional to $\mathrm{Gr}^{\frac{1}{3}}$, as compared with $\mathrm{Gr}^{\frac{1}{4}}$ for a laminar boundary layer.

Initiation of Free Convection above a Horizontal Surface. The analysis of free convection from a vertical surface does not present great difficulties, chiefly because the resulting motion, provided it is not turbulent, is easily defined. The problem which is of greatest interest in micrometeorology is that of free convection from a horizontal surface, but this is by no means as simple, and the intricate problem of the motion of a fluid heated from below has been the subject of considerable study since the initial mathematical investigation of Rayleigh in 1916.

The underlying physics of the process of cellular convective motion is simply described in terms of the historic experiments of Henri Bénard[4] in 1900.† If a shallow horizontal layer of fluid is uniformly heated from below, there is no immediate visible motion of the fluid and, initially, heat is transferred to the upper layers by conduction alone. This state of affairs can continue indefinitely provided that temperature differences in the fluid are kept sufficiently small, any tendency to form vertical currents being checked by viscosity. If the temperature gradient in the fluid exceeds a certain value, convective motion occurs and, if the layer is not too deep, takes regular forms. The layer divides itself up into a number of "cells," more or less identical, within which fluid is circulated from the bottom to the top and back again. In the initial stages, at least, the motion is *steady*, with none of the wild disorder typical of dynamic turbulence. Viewed from above, the fluid usually has a very distinctive appearance, the upper surface being covered by a pattern of regular polygons, usually hexagons.‡

† Bénard is invariably, and rightly, given the honor of this discovery, but James Thomson suggested some 40 years earlier that certain markings on the surface of the sea might be caused by vertical cellular currents.

‡ The reader who wishes to see this phenomenon for himself can do so quite easily by pouring a quantity of volatile fluid, such as benzene or carbon tetrachloride, into

The importance of this phenomenon for meteorology was first pointed out by Brunt and Low in 1925. Subsequently, there have been investigations by Mal, Phillips, Walker, and Chandra.† The convection-cell mechanism has also been studied in relation to the problem of the distribution of heat throughout the free atmosphere, and it is claimed that certain striking cloud patterns provide evidence that this type of motion takes place in the atmosphere on a large scale. This aspect of the problem will not be considered here.

The Mathematical Analysis of Cellular Convective Motion. In his fundamental investigation into the dynamics of Bénard cells, Rayleigh[5] discussed the geometry of the cell pattern and enunciated a criterion to decide the critical density gradient at which the motion is first established. Since then the theoretical problem has attracted considerable attention, the most notable contributions being those of Jeffreys[6,7] and of Pellew and Southwell.[8]

A full discussion of the problem involves considerable mathematical manipulation and heavy numerical work and would take too much space to be given here. The main features are as follows: Rayleigh and all the later writers regard the problem as essentially one of dynamic stability. A slow motion is assumed to start from an initial state of rest with a given temperature distribution, and the basic equations—those of viscous motion, conduction, and continuity—are examined to ascertain what relations must exist between the parameters for a convective system to be maintained indefinitely.

Suppose that initially heat is transferred by conduction only. If the fluid is at rest, the pressure varies only in the vertical according to the hydrostatic equation [Eq. (1.12)], and if the temperature is supposed steady and uniform except in the vertical, the equation of conduction reduces to

$$\kappa \frac{\partial^2 T}{\partial z^2} = 0$$

so that if $T_0(z)$ is the initial temperature,

$$T_0 = T(0) + \beta z$$

---

a shallow dish and sprinkling the surface with aluminum powder. The rapid evaporation cools the upper surface of the liquid, so that a large temperature difference is set up between the bottom and the top. Almost immediately the surface is divided into polygons, and it is easily seen that fluid is rising at the center of each polygon and descending again at the edges. Alternatively, the experiment can be done by introducing cigarette smoke into air contained between two large horizontal glass plates, the lower of which is heated.

† See Brunt, "Physical and Dynamical Meteorology," 2d ed., p. 219 (Cambridge, 1939).

where $T(0)$ is the temperature on $z = 0$ and β is the (constant) temperature gradient. Thus initially a linear temperature profile is supposed to exist throughout the entire depth of the fluid.

The equation of thermal expansion is

$$\rho = \rho_0(1 - \alpha\beta z)$$

where ρ_0 is the density corresponding to $T(0)$ and α is the coefficient of expansion. The convective motion now starts and is supposed to be so slow that squares and products of the component velocities u, v, w can be disregarded. The rise of temperature T' is also supposed small, so that writing

$$T = T_0 + T' = T(0) + \beta z + T'$$

and neglecting all second-order terms in u, v, w, T', the modified equation of conduction becomes

$$\frac{\partial T'}{\partial t} + w\beta = \kappa\nabla^2 T' \tag{4.16}$$

During the convective motion

$$\rho = \rho_0[1 - \alpha(\beta z + T')]$$

Hence the change in ρ brought about by the convective motion is a fraction $-\alpha T'/(1 - \alpha\beta z)$ of the steady value and is thus negligible when multiplied by u, v, w, or T'. Similarly, if p' is the change in pressure caused by convection, any change in density may be neglected when associated with p' and it follows that ρ may be regarded as constant throughout the motion except where it is directly related to buoyancy. This means that, as before, the expansion of the fluid by heating is supposed to have no dynamic consequences except in the one equation (for w) where it appears in the external force, *i.e.*, when α is multiplied by g.

The Navier-Stokes equations of the convective motion thus reduce to

$$\left.\begin{aligned}
\frac{\partial u}{\partial t} &= -\frac{1}{\rho}\frac{\partial p'}{\partial x} + \nu\nabla^2 u \\
\frac{\partial v}{\partial t} &= -\frac{1}{\rho}\frac{\partial p'}{\partial y} + \nu\nabla^2 v \\
\frac{\partial w}{\partial t} &= -\frac{1}{\rho}\frac{\partial p'}{\partial z} + \nu\nabla^2 w + g\alpha T'
\end{aligned}\right\} \tag{4.17}$$

in which ρ is no longer a function of z but is constant. The remaining relation is the equation of continuity for an incompressible fluid,

$$\frac{\partial u}{\partial x} + \frac{\partial v}{\partial y} + \frac{\partial w}{\partial z} = 0 \tag{4.18}$$

The result of eliminating u, v, p', and T' from Eqs. (4.16) to (4.18) is a sixth-order partial differential equation in w,

$$\left(\frac{\partial}{\partial t} - \kappa\nabla^2\right)\left(\frac{\partial}{\partial t} - \nu\nabla^2\right)\nabla^2 w + \beta g\alpha\left(\frac{\partial^2 w}{\partial x^2} + \frac{\partial^2 w}{\partial y^2}\right) = 0 \qquad (4.19)$$

which forms the basis of the subsequent analysis.

The boundary conditions need to be specified with care. The difficulty arises chiefly from the fact that certain relations already exist between the temperature and the component velocities because of the equations. At a rigid surface, $w = \partial w/\partial z = 0$, and, at a free surface, $\partial u/\partial z$ and $\partial v/\partial z$ will vanish, and thus $\partial^2 w/\partial z^2 = 0$ because of the equation of continuity; the free surface conditions are thus $w = \partial^2 w/\partial z^2 = 0$. If the temperature is maintained constant on both boundaries, $T' = 0$ on these planes.

The sixth-order partial differential equation (4.19) in w is now attacked by "separation of the variables," writing

$$w = f(x,y)F(z)e^{\sigma t} \qquad (4.20)$$

In this expression, $f(x,y)$ specifies the lateral geometry of the cells. $F(z)$ specifies the variation of w with height and therefore depends on the boundary conditions. Exact expressions for $f(x,y)$ are known for square and hexagonal cells but are not necessary for the determination of the criterion of stability. The parameter σ in the exponential term is, in general, a complex quantity, since the motion may subside (real part of σ negative), oscillate finitely (real part of σ zero), or increase indefinitely (real part of σ positive). Convection implies that the motion must not die away, and it can be shown that, in fact, convection can be sustained only when σ is wholly real. Thus instability (and hence convection) will occur when $\sigma \geq 0$, and the limiting condition is clearly given by $\sigma = 0$, in which event all time variations are zero and the problem reduces to that of steady motion. With this simplification, Eq. (4.19) becomes

$$\nabla^6 w = -\frac{\beta g\alpha}{\kappa\nu}\left(\frac{\partial^2 w}{\partial x^2} + \frac{\partial^2 w}{\partial y^2}\right)$$

The depth of the whole fluid, h, is introduced by the change of variable $\zeta = z/h$. In the transformed equation the constants are grouped in the form $-\beta g\alpha h^4/\kappa\nu$, and the analysis reduces to the purely numerical problem of finding the lowest value of $-\beta g\alpha h^4/\kappa\nu$ for which slow steady motion can occur.[†] Thus $-\beta g\alpha h^4/\kappa\nu$, called the *Rayleigh number* and denoted by Ra, is a (nondimensional) characteristic number of the problem.

[†] For details see Pellew and Southwell.[8] The numerical problem is also discussed in Jeffreys, "Methods of Mathematical Physics," pp. 413*ff.* (Cambridge, 1947).

The final result is that if Ra is below a certain critical value, equilibrium is stable and any incipient convection currents are damped out by the combined effects of viscosity and conduction. The value of the critical number depends on the physical conditions of the problem, *i.e.*, on the nature of the boundary conditions, and not on' the pattern of cells which has been assumed. The principal results obtained so far are given below.

CRITICAL VALUES OF THE RAYLEIGH NUMBER $-\beta g \alpha h^4/\kappa\nu$

Nature of boundaries	Critical value of Ra	Authority
Two free.................	$27\pi^4/4 = 657.5$	Rayleigh
One rigid, one free........	1100.7	Pellew and Southwell
Two rigid..............	1707.8	Jeffreys

Application to Micrometeorology. The physical interpretation of these results follows by writing

$$\beta = \frac{T(0) - T(h)}{h} = \frac{\Delta T}{h}$$

$$\alpha = \frac{\rho(h) - \rho(0)}{\rho(0)\,\Delta T} = \frac{\Delta\rho}{\rho(0)\,\Delta T}$$

Here $T(h)$, $\rho(h)$ and $T(0)$, $\rho(0)$ refer to the temperature and densities at the top and bottom surfaces, respectively, in the initial state. Rayleigh's result is thus that convection will commence if

$$\frac{\Delta\rho}{\rho(0)} > \mathrm{Ra}_c\,\frac{\kappa\nu}{gh^3} \tag{4.21}$$

where Ra_c is one of the critical values of the Rayleigh number given above. If h is small and derivatives of ρ higher than the first can be neglected,

$$\rho(h) = \rho(0) + h\left(\frac{d\rho}{dz}\right)_0$$

or

$$\frac{\Delta\rho}{\rho(0)} = \frac{h}{\rho(0)}\left(\frac{d\rho}{dz}\right)_0$$

For a perfect gas at rest in a gravitational field

$$\frac{1}{\rho}\frac{d\rho}{dz} = -\frac{1}{T}\left(\frac{dT}{dz} + \frac{g}{R}\right)$$

(Chap. 1). The quantity g/R is the so-called autoconvection gradient, whose value for dry air is about 3.4×10^{-4} °C cm^{-1}. The criterion may thus be expressed in the form

$$-\left(\frac{dT}{dz} + \frac{g}{R}\right) > \text{Ra}_c \, \frac{\kappa\nu}{gh^4} \, T(0)$$

Thus convection will occur when the difference between the observed gradient and the autoconvection gradient attains a certain value. Since the temperature profile is assumed linear in the initial state, the relation (4.21) may be replaced by

$$\frac{\Delta T}{T(0)} > \text{Ra}_c \, \frac{\kappa\nu}{gh^3} - \frac{hg}{RT(0)}$$

With gases such as air or carbon dioxide, if h does not exceed a few meters, the term $hg/RT(0)$ may be neglected when $T(0)$ is of the order of 300°K, that is, at normal terrestrial temperatures. The usual form of the criterion is thus

$$\frac{\Delta T}{T(0)} > \text{Ra}_c \, \frac{\kappa\nu}{gh^3} \tag{4.22}$$

Rayleigh's result in this form, with the value $\text{Ra}_c = 1708$ (Jeffreys) appropriate to a layer of gas bounded above and below by horizontal rigid surfaces, has been examined by K. Chandra[9] for air and by D. T. E. Dassanayake (unpublished) for carbon dioxide. These experiments demonstrate that, in reality, the phenomenon is more complex than is suggested by Rayleigh's analysis. Chandra and Dassanayake found that at least two modes of steady motion are possible when convection starts. If the depth of the layer exceeds a certain value, depending on the nature of the gas, the familiar cellular type of convection is initiated, for values of ΔT which agree reasonably well with the criterion (4.22). If, however, the depth of the layer is less than these critical values, another, obviously different mode of convection (called by Chandra *columnar*) is initiated, for values of ΔT much less than those required by the Rayleigh-Jeffreys criterion. Transition from the columnar to the cellular type of motion occurs when the temperature of the lower surface and the temperature difference between the boundaries are considerably increased.

The problem has recently been reexamined by Sutton,[10] who pointed out that one of the fundamental requirements of the Rayleigh analysis, the establishment of a linear temperature profile throughout the entire depth of the fluid, is unlikely to occur unless the rate of heating of the lower surface is very slow. Ramdas and Malurkar,[11] in an investigation prompted by observations on mirages near hot ground, found that in steady free convection there exists a shallow surface layer in which temperature falls very rapidly and uniformly with height, together with an overlying region of indefinite height, within which the temperature gradient is much smaller.

The region of approximately constant gradient appears to be about 1 cm or less in depth. It is thus probable that the initiation of free convection normally begins with instability in a shallow boundary layer, whose depth is unrelated to the distance between the upper and lower boundaries.

By dimensional analysis, making use of the Fishenden-Saunders equation for heat transfer in steady free convection (4.15), Sutton found that the depth of the layer is given approximately by

$$\delta = (\Delta T)^{-\frac{1}{4}}$$

where ΔT is measured in degrees centigrade. The criterion for instability in this layer should involve only the ratio of the absolute temperatures of the lower and upper surfaces. The columnar mode of convection found by Chandra occurs when the ratio $T(0)/T(h)$ attains a value between 1.02 and 1.03 (approximately) irrespective of the nature or the depth of the gas. Transition from the columnar mode to the cellular mode takes place when ΔT satisfies the equation

$$\frac{\Delta T}{T(0)} = \text{constant} \left(\frac{\kappa \nu}{gh^3} \right)^{\frac{1}{4}}$$

This investigation enables a more comprehensive view to be taken of the initiation of free convection in a layer of gas bounded by two horizontal surfaces. The Rayleigh-Jeffreys criterion indicates that $\Delta T \to \infty$ as $h \to 0$. If the layer is sufficiently deep, ΔT will attain the critical value given by the Rayleigh-Jeffreys criterion before any other. Convection then starts with the cellular mode, and it appears that once this mode is initiated, no transition to any other type of steady motion is possible. If, however, the depth of the layer is less than a certain critical value, the criterion found by Sutton is satisfied before ΔT attains the value required by the Rayleigh-Jeffreys formula and in these circumstances the columnar mode is initiated. On prolonged heating of the lower surface the linear temperature profile extends throughout the whole layer, and transition to the cellular mode takes place.

Application to the Atmosphere. The results of Rayleigh *et al.* have been quoted to explain the persistence of very large gradients of temperature in the air adjacent to bare ground on a hot day. Such theories are based on the assumption that Rayleigh's criterion, with κ and ν replaced by their eddy counterparts, is valid for air in turbulent motion. It is difficult to justify such a treatment, because the initial conditions postulated by Rayleigh and other workers are not fulfilled, and there are other difficulties associated with the variation of eddy conductivity and eddy viscosity with height.

Malurkar[12] has advanced the theory that the distribution of temperature near hot ground can be explained by taking into account radiation from successive air layers, assuming that the temperature difference between two given heights is that found by experiment. The complete problem is supposed to be divided into two main parts:

1. A study of the nature of the temperature profile consistent with a given temperature difference.

2. The determination of the maximum temperature difference over a given height interval consistent with a given temperature profile.

The temperature profile assumed by Malurkar is of the form

$$\frac{ah \sinh b(h - z)}{\sinh bh}$$

where h is the thickness of the layer and a and b are constants. Malurkar finds that the criterion of stability is very dependent on the form of the temperature profile and that much higher values of ΔT can be maintained when the profile is concave upward than when it is linear. The hyperbolic sine profile used by Malurkar is in good agreement with measurements of temperature near a heated surface if the constants a and b are chosen to give the best fit.

The problem of the onset of free convection and the maintenance of large lapse rates has not been solved satisfactorily even for the relatively simple arrangements used in laboratory work. The corresponding problem for the atmosphere is much more complex because of the presence of dynamic turbulence and the effect of ground roughness. The question of the magnitude of the temperature gradients which can exist in hot weather near the ground is far from academic and has important repercussions in studies of plant and animal life, but a satisfactory solution is hardly to be expected until the matter has been cleared at the laboratory stage.

4.6. Problems of Fickian Diffusion

The typical Fickian equation, that of conduction of heat in a solid, has attracted the attention of mathematicians for the past century, with the result that the study of this linear parabolic equation of the second order now belongs as much to pure mathematics as to applied. The techniques developed for the discovery of solutions need not be discussed here, since they are invariably given in detail in any text on mathematical physics. Instead, attention will be directed toward the meteorological interpretation of certain familiar results.†

† The most extensive account of methods of solving the Fickian equation is that given in Carslaw and Jaeger, *op. cit.* The classical solutions and practical applications of the mathematics are discussed in Ingersoll, Zobel, and Ingersoll, "Heat Conduction with Engineering and Geological Applications" (McGraw-Hill, 1948).

The account which follows is usually in terms of heat transfer, with temperature as the dependent variable. It is customary to choose some fixed temperature as zero, but this does not imply that the temperature in question is necessarily the freezing point on the centigrade scale or any other physically significant temperature. What is done is to express the variable temperature as a difference from some convenient fixed temperature in order to avoid needless complications in the expressions.

The main problems are most conveniently classified in terms of the relevant type of boundary condition.

Prescribed Surface Temperature. Semiinfinite medium with a fixed surface temperature and known initial temperature distribution. This may be regarded as the investigation of Fickian diffusion in an atmosphere bounded below by a plane surface ($z = 0$) maintained at constant (zero) temperature. The atmosphere extends to infinity with increasing z, and at time $t = 0$ the distribution of temperature is $F(z)$, where F is a known function. The problem is to find the temperature for all $z > 0$ at any time $t > 0$.

Mathematically, the problem is constituted by the equation

$$\frac{\partial T}{\partial t} = \kappa \frac{\partial^2 T}{\partial z^2}$$

with

Initial condition:

$$T = F(z) \qquad \text{when } t = 0, z > 0$$

Boundary condition:

$$T = 0 \qquad \text{on } z = 0, t > 0$$

A basic solution of the equation is

$$T = \frac{1}{\sqrt{t}} \exp\left(-\frac{z^2}{4\kappa t}\right)$$

and from this, other solutions may be constructed by making use of the fact that since the equation is linear, the sum of any number of solutions is also a solution. Thus

$$T = \frac{1}{2(\pi\kappa t)^{\frac{1}{2}}} \int_{-\infty}^{\infty} F(\zeta) \exp\left[-\frac{(z-\zeta)^2}{4\kappa t}\right] d\zeta$$

is a solution, having the property that as $t \to 0$, $T \to F(z)$. The condition that the plane $z = 0$ should remain at zero temperature is introduced by the device of supposing the medium to be continued on the negative side of the plane $z = 0$, the initial temperature at $z = -\zeta$ ($\zeta > 0$) being $-F(\zeta)$. The desired solution, which satisfies the initial condition and the boundary condition, is obtained from solutions in both half planes, *viz.*,†

$$T(z,t) = \frac{1}{(4\pi\kappa t)^{\frac{1}{2}}} \int_0^\infty F(\zeta) \left\{ \exp\left[-\frac{(z-\zeta)^2}{4\kappa t} \right] \right.$$
$$\left. - \exp\left[-\frac{(z+\zeta)^2}{4\kappa t} \right] \right\} d\zeta \quad (4.23)$$

An important special case arises when $F(z) = T_0 = $ constant. The solution then becomes

$$T = T_0 \operatorname{erf} \frac{z}{\sqrt{(4\kappa t)}} \tag{4.24}$$

Thus the distribution of temperature depends only on the nondimensional combination $z/\sqrt{(4\kappa t)}$.

As an example of the application of this solution consider the following problem: Air which has attained a definite temperature distribution in passing over heated land comes in contact with the sea, which may be regarded as a boundary of uniform (zero) temperature. It is required to determine the temperature distribution over the sea. The temperature profile in the air mass is given by (4.23) as a function of height and the time which has elapsed since it came in contact with the sea. If the wind be steady and constant with height, the time t can be replaced by x/u, where u is the wind speed and x is a new independent variable denoting distance from the shore. The equation then becomes

$$u \frac{\partial T}{\partial x} = \kappa \frac{\partial^2 T}{\partial x^2}$$

with

Initial condition:

$$T = F(z) \qquad \text{when } x = 0,\, z > 0$$

Boundary condition:

$$T = 0 \qquad \text{on } z = 0 \text{ when } x > 0$$

For $F(z) = T_0 = $ constant the solution is

$$T(x,z) = T_0 \operatorname{erf} \frac{zu^{\frac{1}{2}}}{\sqrt{(4\kappa x)}} \tag{4.25}$$

As $x \to \infty$, the error function tends to zero, expressing the fact that ultimately the whole air mass will attain the temperature of the surface of the sea. This property might have been predicted *ab initio*, but this is

† Carslaw and Jaeger, *op. cit.*, p. 40.

unnecessary, since the problem is completely specified by the initial and boundary conditions given above.

The solution (4.25) shows that theoretically the effect of the surface is felt at all heights. In practice, it is customary to consider that the effect extends to only a finite height Z defined by the convention that the effect of the surface virtually ceases when $T(x,t)/T_0 = \frac{1}{10}$. Since erf $\theta = 0.1$ when $\theta = 0.09$ approximately, it follows that the upper boundary of the layer affected by surface conditions is given by

$$Z^2 = 0.32 \frac{\kappa x}{u} \tag{4.26}$$

that is, by a parabola with the vertex at $x = z = 0$. This is illustrated in Fig. 14.

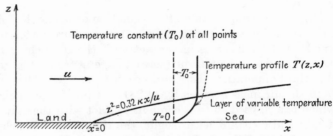

FIG. 14. Formation of inversion by offshore wind.

In reality, it is well established that the diffusion of heat in the atmosphere is mainly due not to molecular conduction but to turbulence and does not conform to the Fickian equation (see Chap. 6). Nevertheless, the above discussion yields a useful first approximation to reality if κ be replaced by a constant eddy conductivity K, several orders of magnitude greater than κ (and also a function of wind velocity). It is then possible to regard (4.26) as defining the layer within which turbulent mixing is effective in modifying the temperature profile. This is the basis of the method used by Taylor in his discussion of the vertical distribution of temperature in the air above the Grand Banks off Newfoundland.

As a further important application of this solution consider the two-dimensional problem of evaporation in a wind constant with height, with a constant coefficient of diffusivity K. The boundary condition on $z = 0$ needs to be specified with care and is not immediately obvious from physical arguments. The condition which appears to lead to results consistent with observations is that on the wetted surface the vapor concentration χ attains the saturation value χ_s.[†] If the evaporating surface is defined

† For a discussion of the boundary conditions in problems of evaporation, see Chap. 8.

by $0 \leq x \leq x_0$, $z = 0$ the equation is

$$u \frac{\partial \chi}{\partial x} = K \frac{\partial^2 \chi}{\partial z^2}$$

with the conditions

$$\chi = 0 \qquad \text{for } x = 0, z > 0$$
$$\chi = \chi_s \qquad \text{on } z = 0, 0 \leq x \leq x_0$$

The solution is

$$\chi = \chi_s \, \text{erfc} \left(z \sqrt{\frac{u}{Kx}} \right) \tag{4.27}$$

where erfc x is the complementary error function defined by

$$\text{erfc } x = 1 - \frac{2}{\sqrt{\pi}} \int_0^x e^{-\theta^2} \, d\theta$$

Equation (4.27) applies only over the wetted area, where the local rate of evaporation per unit area is

$$K\rho \left(\frac{\partial \chi}{\partial z} \right)_{z=0} = \chi_s \rho \sqrt{\frac{Ku}{x}} \tag{4.28}$$

and the total rate of evaporation from $x = 0$ to $x = x_0$ is thus proportional to $\sqrt{x_0}$. This brings out two important facts, (1) that evaporation is not simply proportional to the area of the wetted surface, and (2) that the local rate of evaporation decreases with distance from the leading edge (Jeffreys[13]). The problem is discussed at greater length in Chap. 8.

Semiinfinite medium whose surface temperature is a known periodic function of the time. Suppose that the surface temperature is given by $T(0,t) = T_1 \cos (\omega t - \epsilon)$ ($T_1 = $ constant) and that the initial temperature is zero. It may be shown that the required solution of the equation of conduction is[†]

$$T(z,t) = \frac{2T_1}{\pi^{\frac{1}{2}}} \int_{z/2 \sqrt{(\kappa t)}}^{\infty} \cos \left[\omega \left(t - \frac{z^2}{4\kappa\mu^2} \right) - \epsilon \right] e^{-\mu^2} \, d\mu$$

This solution may be expressed in the form

$$T(z,t) = \frac{2T_1}{\pi^{\frac{1}{2}}} \left[\int_0^{\infty} - \int_0^{z/2 \sqrt{(\kappa t)}} \right] \cos \left[\omega \left(t - \frac{z^2}{4\kappa\mu^2} \right) - \epsilon \right] e^{-\mu^2} \, d\mu$$

The infinite integral may be shown to be equal to

$$T_1 \exp \left(-z \sqrt{\frac{\omega}{2\kappa}} \right) \cos \left[\omega t - \left(\epsilon + z \sqrt{\frac{\omega}{2\kappa}} \right) \right] \tag{4.29}$$

[†] Carslaw and Jaeger, *op. cit.*, p. 46.

which represents a damped wave, whose amplitude and phase vary with height. The finite integral represents a transient disturbance caused by starting the temperature oscillations at the surface. If the time t is sufficiently great to make the quantity $z/2 \sqrt{(\kappa t)}$ negligibly small, the second integral effectively vanishes, the solution then being given by the expression (4.29), and this is the form usually adopted. The assumption that t can be made large without limit, however, implies that the wave is one of a succession of similar waves which has been maintained long enough to eliminate transient effects and establish a quasi-steady state. It is by no means clear that this assumption is valid for the lower atmosphere, even when applied to the temperature field observed in a long spell of fine weather, because although on such days the temperature of the surface of the earth between sunrise and sunset may be approximately represented by an expression of the type $T_1 \cos (\omega t - \epsilon)$, the same expression will not represent nocturnal surface temperatures. The application of the solution (4.29) to the atmosphere is therefore open to some doubt, and in any detailed discussion the effect of the transient term should be investigated.

If 4.29 is accepted as the required solution, it follows that:

1. The amplitude of the wave decreases with increasing height, as $\exp [-z \sqrt{(\omega/2\kappa)}]$.

2. The phase of the wave increases as $z \sqrt{(\omega/2\kappa)}$. This means that the time of maximum temperature becomes later with increasing height.

The solution (4.29) has been used by numerous workers in micrometeorology. It is obvious that if measurements of the amplitude and time of maximum temperature are made at various heights, the effective conductivity can be calculated. Taylor, Schmidt, Johnson, Best, and others have applied the solution in this way to successions of shallow layers in the atmosphere in order to deduce the order of magnitude of the eddy conductivity, supposed constant, at different heights. There is no doubt that the observed temperatures can be represented approximately by a damped wave of changing phase, but the solution fails in other respects. This problem is discussed in Chap. 6; for the time being it suffices to regard (4.29) as giving a useful qualitative picture of the variation of the diurnal temperature wave with height.

The same solution may be applied with much greater success to the problem of the penetration of the diurnal temperature wave into the ground. There is also no difficulty in extending the result to cover the case in which the temperature is represented by a Fourier series. If

$$T(0,t) = T_0 + \sum_{n=1}^{\infty} T_n \cos (n\omega t - \epsilon_n)$$

the solution is

$$T(z,t) = T_0 + \sum_{n=1}^{\infty} T_n \exp\left(-z\sqrt{\frac{n\omega}{2\kappa}}\right) \cos\left[n\omega t - \left(\epsilon_n + z\sqrt{\frac{n\omega}{2\kappa}}\right)\right]$$

This result depends on the fact that since the equation is linear, with linear boundary conditions, the sum of any number of solutions is also a solution.

Prescribed Flux. *Semiinfinite medium, with the flux across $z = 0$ constant or a given function of time, and with a given initial condition.* The heat flux across any plane z is, by definition,

$$f = -k\frac{\partial T}{\partial z}$$

This satisfies the same differential equation as T, namely,

$$\frac{\partial f}{\partial t} = \kappa\frac{\partial^2 f}{\partial z^2}$$

If the flux across $z = 0$ is constant, f_0, the required solution is a simple extension of that of (4.24), namely,

$$f = f_0 \operatorname{erfc}\frac{z}{\sqrt{(4\kappa t)}}$$

On integration it follows that

$$T(z,t) = \frac{2f_0}{k}\left[\left(\frac{\kappa t}{\pi}\right)^{\frac{1}{2}} \exp\left(-\frac{z^2}{4\kappa t}\right) - \frac{1}{2}z \operatorname{erfc}\frac{z}{\sqrt{(4\kappa t)}}\right] \qquad (4.30)$$

This solution has been used by Brunt to discuss the fall of temperature of the earth's surface on a clear calm night, when the ground loses heat at an approximately constant rate per unit area. The temperature of the surface is then given by

$$T(0,t) = \frac{2f_0}{k}\left(\frac{\kappa t}{\pi}\right)^{\frac{1}{2}} \qquad (4.31)$$

Thus the fall of temperature of the earth's surface on a clear, calm night should be represented by a parabolic curve on a temperature-time plot, provided that there is no large release of latent heat by condensation. This problem is discussed at greater length in Chap. 5.

If the temperature of the medium is supposed zero everywhere at $t = 0$ and the flux of heat across $z = 0$ is given by a known function $\phi(t)$, the subsequent temperature profile is given by†

$$T(z,t) = \frac{1}{k}\left(\frac{\kappa}{\pi}\right)^{\frac{1}{2}} \int_0^t \frac{\phi(t - t')}{\sqrt{t'}} \exp\left(-\frac{z^2}{4\kappa t'}\right) dt' \qquad (4.31a)$$

† See *ibid.*, p. 57.

Semiinfinite medium containing two layers of different thermal conductivities, surface maintained at constant temperature. On a clear night, the rapid cooling of the earth's surface by radiation to space often causes the virtual extinction of turbulence near the ground. At any time after sunset it may be supposed that there is a lower layer of cold air, in which heat is transferred by molecular conduction only, and an upper layer of warmer air, in which turbulent exchange is still active. The lower layer deepens with time, and the problem is to determine the rate at which the surface of separation, supposed at zero temperature, moves upward. For this purpose it will be assumed that the eddy transfer of heat in the warmer air can be represented by a constant coefficient of eddy conductivity.

Let T_0 be the (constant) temperature of the ground $z = 0$. If T_1, κ be the temperature and conductivity in the air from the ground to the top Z of the layer of cold air,

$$\frac{\partial T_1}{\partial t} = \kappa \frac{\partial^2 T_1}{\partial z^2} \qquad 0 < z < Z(t) \tag{4.32}$$

$$T_1 = T_0 \qquad \text{on } z = 0$$

and if T_2, K apply to the turbulent air,

$$\frac{\partial T_2}{\partial t} = K \frac{\partial^2 T_2}{\partial z^2} \qquad z \geq Z(t) \tag{4.33}$$

At great heights it is supposed that $T_2 \to T_3$ (constant). At the surface of separation

$$\left. \begin{array}{c} T_1 = T_2 = 0 \\ \kappa c_p \rho_1 \left(\dfrac{\partial T_1}{\partial z} \right) = K c_p \rho_2 \left(\dfrac{\partial T_2}{\partial z} \right) \end{array} \right\} \text{on } z = Z \tag{4.34}$$

Equation (4.32) and its boundary condition are satisfied by an expression of the type

$$T_1 = T_0 + A \operatorname{erf} \left[\frac{z}{\sqrt{(4\kappa t)}} \right]$$

where A is a constant. Also Eq. (4.33) is satisfied by

$$T_2 = T_3 + B \operatorname{erfc} \left[\frac{z}{\sqrt{(4Kt)}} \right]$$

where B is another constant. From the first condition in (4.34)

$$A \operatorname{erf} \left[\frac{Z}{\sqrt{(4\kappa t)}} \right] = -T_0$$

$$B \operatorname{erfc} \left[\frac{Z}{\sqrt{(4Kt)}} \right] = -T_3 \tag{4.35}$$

Since Eqs. (4.35) have to hold for all values of t, it follows that the arguments of the error and complementary error functions must be independent of t, that is,

$$Z = C \sqrt{t}$$

where C is a constant to be determined. The theoretical determination of C requires the use of the second condition in (4.34), leading to a transcendental equation which can only be solved approximately. In view of the drastic assumptions which have been made in respect of the conductivities in the two layers, such computations are not justified here. The main result is that the depth of the layer increases as the square root of the time. Observations by Johnson and Heywood[14] on the depth of the "inversion layer" on a clear night (a comparable phenomenon) suggest that the theoretical relation gives a moderately good approximation to the truth.

This example is of considerable economic importance. It shows how a layer of air at freezing level gradually deepens on a clear night and how the rate of growth of the layer may be estimated, provided that the constant C can be determined from observations.

The best known example of this type of problem is that of the penetration of frost into ground or the freezing of a lake. In this instance the second condition in (4.34) must be replaced by

$$\kappa_1 c_p \rho_1 \left(\frac{\partial T_1}{\partial z}\right)_z - \kappa_2 c_p \rho_2 \left(\frac{\partial T_2}{\partial z}\right)_z = L \rho_1 \frac{dZ}{dt}$$

since, if L is the latent heat of fusion, a quantity of heat $L\rho_1 \, dZ$ is released as the surface of separation moves a distance dZ. This heat is removed by conduction. The problem was solved by Neumann and also by Stefan,† whose solutions show that in this problem also the thickness of the layer of ice increases as the square root of the time.

Mathematically, this type of problem differs from the normal heat-conduction problem in that the initial condition is not given. In Neumann's problem it can be shown that the required condition is that initially the whole of the medium is at constant temperature T_3.

Method of Sources. The method of sources, originated by Kelvin, finds its natural application in meteorology in problems concerning the diffusion of matter. Fundamentally, the method is based on the existence of a solution of the equation of diffusion having the property that, as $t \to 0$, the solution is infinite at one point and zero elsewhere, and also such that the total amount of heat in the infinite medium is finite at all times. Such a solution has a simple physical interpretation as the temperature in the infinite solid due to a finite quantity of heat suddenly

† See Ingersoll, Zobell, and Ingersoll, *op. cit.*, Chap. 10.

generated at the singular point.   From this solution it is possible to form, by integration, other solutions representing continuous sources or sources distributed along lines or over areas.

The method is developed here in relation to sources of matter (such as smoke or gas) but may equally well be applied to sources of heat if concentration of matter be regarded as equivalent to temperature.

Instantaneous point source.   A quantity of matter Q g is generated at $t = 0$ and allowed to diffuse.

The differential equation is

$$\frac{\partial \chi}{\partial t} = \kappa \nabla^2 \chi = \frac{\kappa}{r^2} \frac{\partial}{\partial r} \left(r^2 \frac{\partial \chi}{\partial r} \right) \qquad \text{for spherical symmetry}$$

where χ is concentration = density of suspended matter (grams per cubic centimeter), $r^2 = x^2 + y^2 + z^2$, with the origin at the point of generation and κ is the diffusivity.

The conditions are

$$\chi \to 0 \qquad \text{as } t \to 0, \, r > 0$$
$$\chi \to 0 \qquad \text{as } t \to \infty$$

together with the continuity condition,

$$\iiint_{-\infty}^{\infty} \chi \, dx \, dy \, dz = Q$$

which expresses the fact that matter is neither created nor destroyed during the diffusion process.   The solution is

$$\chi(x,y,z,t) = \frac{Q}{8(\pi \kappa t)^{\frac{3}{2}}} \exp \left(-\frac{r^2}{4\kappa t} \right) \tag{4.36}$$

This solution has been used by Roberts[15] to represent the diffusion of a puff of smoke formed by an explosion.   It is supposed that the expansion of the puff is independent of the wind speed, the cloud being merely carried bodily forward by the wind, so that the system of axes moves with the wind.   Roberts also assumed that κ could be identified with the "eddy diffusivity" of the wind.

If the origin be at the point (x',y',z'), the solution is

$$\chi(x,y,z,t) = \frac{Q}{8(\pi \kappa t)^{\frac{3}{2}}} \exp \left[-\frac{(x - x')^2 + (y - y')^2 + (z - z')^2}{4\kappa t} \right]$$

Instantaneous infinite line and plane sources.   The solution for an instantaneous line source of strength Q g cm^{-1} parallel to the y axis and passing through the point (x',y',z') is obtained by integrating instantaneous point sources of strength $Q \, dy'$ at y' along the line. The solution is

$$\chi(x,z,t) = \frac{Q}{8(\pi\kappa t)^{\frac{3}{2}}} \int_{-\infty}^{\infty} \exp\left[-\frac{(x-x')^2 + (y-y')^2 + (z-z')^2}{4\kappa t}\right] dy'$$

$$= \frac{Q}{4\pi\kappa t} \exp\left[-\frac{(x-x')^2 + (z-z')^2}{4\kappa t}\right] \tag{4.37}$$

Similarly, by distributing line sources of strength $Q \, dx'$ over the plane $z = z'$ the solution for an instantaneous plane source, parallel to the plane $z = 0$ and passing through $(0,0,z')$, is found by integrating (4.37). The solution is

$$\chi(z,t) = \frac{Q}{\sqrt{(4\pi\kappa t)}} \exp\left[-\frac{(z-z')^2}{4\kappa t}\right] \tag{4.38}$$

The continuous point source. If the medium is at rest, the solution for a source emitting continuously from $t = 0$ to $t = t$ at the point (x',y',z') is obtained without difficulty by integrating the expression for an instantaneous point source with respect to time. Hence, writing

$$r^2 = (x-x')^2 + (y-y')^2 + (z-z')^2$$

$$\chi(x,y,z,t) = \frac{Q}{8(\pi\kappa)^{\frac{3}{2}}} \int_0^t \exp\left[-\frac{r^2}{4\kappa(t-t')}\right] \frac{dt'}{(t-t')^{\frac{3}{2}}}$$

$$= \frac{Q}{4\pi\kappa r} \operatorname{erfc} \frac{r}{\sqrt{(4\kappa t)}}$$

As $t \to \infty$, this reduces to

$$\chi(x,y,z) = \frac{Q}{4\pi\kappa r}$$

This corresponds to a source which is maintained indefinitely.

The problem of greatest interest in meteorology, because of its importance in atmospheric pollution, is that of the continuous point source in a wind. In the analysis which follows it is supposed that the wind velocity u is constant at all points and that the spread of the smoke can be represented by the Fickian equation with diffusivity K. The limitations imposed by these assumptions are considered in Chap. 8.

The solution for the continuous point source in a moving medium can be obtained from that for the instantaneous point source if the system of axes be fixed in space instead of moving down wind with the puff. The axis of x is chosen as the direction of the wind, the source of Q g sec^{-1} being placed at the origin (Fig. 15). In the fixed-axes system, the coordinates (x,y,z) of the moving system are to be replaced by $(x - ut, y, z)$. The continuous point source is equivalent to a succession of elementary instantaneous point sources, the concentration at any point being due to the integrated effect of the elementary puffs. At time t' the source emits

$Q\,dt'$ g of matter, but, because of the wind, the element of air which is at (x,y,z,t) has come from $[x - u(t - t'),\ y,\ z,\ t']$. The concentration at (x,y,z,t) due to an instantaneous puff of content $Q\,dt'$ emitted at time t' is thus, by (4.36),

$$d\chi = \frac{Q\,dt'}{8[\pi K(t - t')]^{\frac{3}{2}}} \exp\left\{-\frac{[x - u(t - t')]^2 + y^2 + z^2}{4K(t - t')}\right\} \quad (4.39)$$

The total concentration at (x,y,z,t) in the continuous-point-source cloud is the sum of all such contributions, *i.e.*, equals the integral of (4.39) with respect to t' from $t' = 0$ to $t' = t$. If the source is supposed to be maintained indefinitely, the range of integration is from $t' = 0$ to $t' = \infty$; in

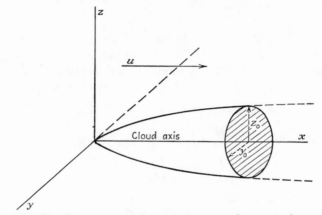

FIG. 15. Coordinate system for a continuous point source in a wind.

practice this is by far the most important case. The solution is easily seen to be, after some reduction,

$$\chi(x,y,z) = \frac{Q\exp(ux/2K)}{2K\pi^{\frac{3}{2}}r}\int_0^\infty \exp\left(-\tau^2 - \frac{u^2r^2}{16K^2\tau^2}\right)d\tau$$
$$= \frac{Q}{4\pi Kr}\exp\left[-\frac{u}{2K}(r - x)\right] \quad (4.40)$$

Observations of smoke clouds show that, unless the wind is very light, the cloud takes the form of a long, thin plume, and interest is centered on concentrations at points not too far removed from the axis of the cloud ($y = z = 0$). In most practical applications $(y^2 + z^2)/x^2$ may be regarded as a quantity whose square is negligibly small. In this case,

$$-\frac{u(r - x)}{2K} = -\frac{u}{2K}\left[x\left(1 + \frac{y^2 + z^2}{x^2}\right)^{\frac{1}{2}} - x\right]$$
$$\simeq -\frac{u(y^2 + z^2)}{4Kx}$$

Hence, for all but the lightest winds,

$$\chi(x,y,z) = \frac{Q}{4\pi K r} \exp\left[-\frac{u(y^2 + z^2)}{4Kx} \right] \tag{4.41}$$

In practice, this expression is frequently replaced by

$$\chi(x,y,z) = \frac{Q}{4\pi K x} \exp\left[-\frac{u(y^2 + z^2)}{4Kx} \right] \tag{4.42}$$

without serious error.

The solution (4.40) and the approximation (4.41) were obtained by Roberts[15] by direct solution of the differential equation

$$u\frac{\partial \chi}{\partial x} = K\nabla^2\chi$$

together with the "continuity" condition that the rate of transfer of matter across a surface enclosing the source is equal to Q.

The continuous infinite line source (across wind). If matter is emitted at the rate of Q g sec^{-1} cm^{-1} along the line $x = z = 0$, the concentration at (x,z) is

$$\chi(x,z) = \frac{Q}{4\pi K} \int_{-\infty}^{\infty} \frac{\exp\left(-\frac{u}{2K} \{[x^2 + (y - y')^2 + z^2]^{\frac{1}{2}} - x\} \right) dy'}{[x^2 + (y - y')^2 + z^2]^{\frac{1}{2}}}$$

$$= \frac{Q}{2\pi K} \exp\frac{ux}{2K} K_0\left[\frac{u(x^2 + z^2)^{\frac{1}{2}}}{2K} \right] \tag{4.43}$$

where K_0 is the modified Bessel function of the second kind. If $u(x^2 + z^2)^{\frac{1}{2}}/2K$ is sufficiently large, the asymptotic expansion for K_0 may be used, omitting all but the first term. Thus

$$K_0\left[\frac{u(x^2 + z^2)^{\frac{1}{2}}}{2K} \right] \sim \left[\frac{2\pi K}{u(x^2 + z^2)^{\frac{1}{2}}} \right]^{\frac{1}{2}} \exp\left[-\frac{u(x^2 + z^2)^{\frac{1}{2}}}{2K} \right]$$

Hence, neglecting squares and higher powers of z^2/x^2, the solution becomes

$$\chi(x,z) = \frac{Q}{[2\pi K(x^2 + z^2)^{\frac{1}{2}}]^{\frac{1}{2}}} \exp\left(-\frac{uz^2}{4Kx} \right)$$

$$\simeq \frac{Q}{\sqrt{(2\pi Kx)}} \exp\left(-\frac{uz^2}{4Kx} \right) \tag{4.44}$$

Roberts[15] also gave solutions for a system in which diffusion is anisotropic (as in the atmosphere near the ground) by defining three coefficients K_x, K_y, K_z. The solutions corresponding to (4.36), (4.42), (4.44) are

Instantaneous point source:

$$\chi(x,y,z,t) = \frac{Q}{8(\pi t)^{\frac{3}{2}}(K_x K_y K_z)^{\frac{1}{2}}} \exp\left[-\frac{1}{4t}\left(\frac{x^2}{K_x} + \frac{y^2}{K_y} + \frac{z^2}{K_z}\right)\right] \quad (4.45)$$

Continuous point source:

$$\chi(x,y,z) \simeq \frac{Q}{4\pi x (K_y K_z)^{\frac{1}{2}}} \exp\left[-\frac{u}{4x}\left(\frac{y^2}{K_y} + \frac{z^2}{K_z}\right)\right] \quad (4.46)$$

Continuous infinite line source (across wind):

$$\chi(x,z) \simeq \frac{Q}{\sqrt{(2\pi K_z x)}} \exp\left(-\frac{uz^2}{4K_z x}\right) \quad (4.47)$$

The physical meaning of these expressions is easily seen. Along the center line, or axis, of the point-source cloud ($y = z = 0$), or over the central plane of the infinite-line-source cloud ($z = 0$), concentration falls steadily with distance down wind, x, as x^{-1} in the point-source cloud, and as $x^{-\frac{1}{2}}$ in the line-source cloud. At a fixed distance from the source ($x = $ constant), the distribution of concentration follows the normal law of errors, both across wind and vertically. Theoretically, the clouds extend to infinity in all directions, and for practical work it is convenient to define finite boundaries by the convention that the concentration is effectively zero when it has fallen to some fixed fraction, say $\frac{1}{10}$, of the maximum value at that distance. If y_0 and z_0 are the semilateral and semivertical dimensions of the cloud defined in this way, it follows that

$$y_0^2 = \frac{4}{u}(\ln 10)K_y x; \qquad z_0^2 = \frac{4}{u}(\ln 10)K_z x$$

Thus the width and height of the clouds increase as $\sqrt{x}$. The *visible* outlines of the clouds cannot be found as simply, because of the necessity for introducing a theory of opacity. Details of such a theory, and of its application to diffusion, are to be found in the paper by Roberts.[15]

Although these solutions must now be regarded as no more than crude approximations for atmospheric diffusion near the ground, they constitute the basis of most of the developments which have taken place in recent years in the study of the dispersion of smoke or gas in the atmosphere. The failure of these *exact* solutions to conform to the observations produced unassailable evidence that eddy diffusion in the atmosphere cannot be represented by the Fickian equation (see Chap. 8).

Method of images. If the source of matter is on or near the surface of the earth, as in problems of atmospheric pollution, it is necessary to consider carefully the effect of the boundary. If the cloud contains particulate matter, such as grit or ash, there is usually considerable deposition near the source, caused by the falling out of the larger particles under gravity. Even with clouds of very small particles, or gas, some deposition or absorption by vegetation takes place, but in many examples the surface of the earth may be regarded, without serious error, as an impervious boundary. Mathematically, the condition for an impervious surface is $K(\partial\chi/\partial z) = 0$ on $z = 0$, but the problem is most easily solved by making use of the equation of continuity. If a continuous point source is situated at or near ground level, the condition that matter is neither lost nor created during the passage of the cloud down wind is

$$\int_{-\infty}^{\infty} \int_{0}^{\infty} u\chi(x,y,z)dz\,dy = Q \qquad (4.48)$$

for all $x > 0$. If the source is on the ground and the wind is always horizontal, the plane $z = 0$ contains the axis of symmetry of the cloud and the functional form of the solution must be the same as that in a medium extending to infinity in all directions. Hence, for a cloud generated at ground level,

$$\chi(x,y,z) = \frac{A}{4\pi Kx} \exp\left[- \frac{u(y^2 + z^2)}{4Kx} \right]$$

where A is a constant whose value is to be found in terms of the source strength, from the continuity condition. Applying (4.48), this gives $A = 2Q$, so that the effect of the impervious boundary is that the concentration at any point is twice that found in a cloud formed in an infinite medium. In this sense, the ground acts as a perfect reflector. Obviously, the same result is also true for the cloud from an infinite crosswind line source at ground level. This result has been proved for Fickian diffusion, which does not apply to the atmosphere, but the same conclusion follows for non-Fickian processes.

If the source is elevated, as with a factory stack, the effect of the impervious boundary is more complicated. If the height h of the source above ground is sufficiently great, the cloud near the source will behave as if the boundary were absent, but as distance down wind, x, increases, the influence of the boundary will be increasingly felt as the smoke diffuses to earth. The solution must therefore behave like that for an infinite medium for small x/h but for large x/h must resemble the solution for a source placed at ground level.

Problems of this type are most easily solved by the method of images. The semiinfinite medium $z > 0$ is replaced by the infinite medium $-\infty \leq z \leq \infty$, and the boundary $z = 0$ is abolished. The effect of the impervious surface is introduced by considering not only the real source at $x = y = 0$, $z = h$ but also its image in $z = 0$, that is, a source of equal strength at $x = y = 0$, $z = -h$. The required concentration at any point in the space $z > 0$ is then equal to the sum of the concentrations from the two sources,[†] since the condition of no net flux across the plane $z = 0$ is automatically satisfied because of symmetry.

The required solution is thus

$$\chi(x,y,z) = \frac{Qe^{-uy^2/4Kx}}{4\pi Kx} \left\{ \exp\left[-\frac{u(z-h)^2}{4Kx} \right] + \exp\left[-\frac{u(z+h)^2}{4Kx} \right] \right\}$$

(4.49)

based on the approximate solution (4.42) for the continuous point source.

It is easily seen that this solution possesses the desired properties. As x, $y \to 0$ and $z \to h$, the concentration becomes infinite as

$$x^{-1} \exp\left[-\frac{u(z-h)^2 + y^2}{4Kx} \right]$$

showing that near $x = y = 0$, $z = h$ the solution behaves like that for the continuous point source in an infinite medium. As x/h becomes very large, the solution is indistinguishable from that for a continuous point source at ground level ($h = 0$). Finally, the continuity condition (4.48) is satisfied for all $x > 0$.

The physical interpretation of this solution is easily seen from Fig. 16, which shows the concentration along the line $y = z = 0$, that is, directly down wind of the source. At the foot of the stack the concentration is effectively zero and remains small for some distance down wind, after which it rises steeply to a maximum and then declines to zero again, but more slowly. These features have been found in practice, but because of the assumption of Fickian diffusion the solution given above should be regarded as qualitative only for the atmosphere. The problem is discussed further in Chap. 8.

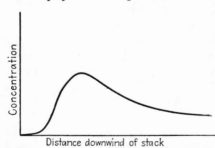

Fig. 16. Concentration at ground level from an isolated stack in a steady wind.

4.7. Heat Transfer by Turbulence

The theoretical analysis of eddy heat transfer in relation to problems of engineering or laboratory investigations, such as motion in pipes or in wakes, usually contains a number of simplifications. The most important of these are the assumptions that the profile of mean velocity and

[†] For further details of this method, and applications, see Carslaw and Jaeger, *op. cit.*, pp. 230*ff*.

the magnitude of the eddy velocities are the same as in isothermal flow and that heating caused by pressure changes and dissipation of energy by viscosity are negligible. In addition, most of the published work refers to incompressible flow.

In the meteorological problem some, at least, of the above assumptions are unacceptable, and this at once places serious obstacles in the path of the development of the theory. The main difficulty springs from the fact that the lower layers of the atmosphere are subject to diurnal variations of the density gradient which affect directly the character of the turbulence; both the profile of mean velocity and the magnitude of the velocity fluctuations are intimately related to the gradient of temperature. In addition, the great depth of the atmospheric layers makes it impossible to confine attention to incompressible flow. It follows that the transfer of heat by atmospheric turbulence is a special study in itself and that many, if not most, of the laboratory investigations have only a limited interest for meteorology.

Transfer of Heat by Turbulence in Incompressible Flow. If the fluid be regarded as incompressible, the equation of eddy heat transfer is a simple and natural extension of the equation of molecular diffusion. Neglecting dissipation by viscosity, the equation of heat transfer in an incompressible gas is

$$c_p\rho \left(\frac{\partial T}{\partial t} + u\frac{\partial T}{\partial x} + v\frac{\partial T}{\partial y} + w\frac{\partial T}{\partial z} \right) = k\nabla^2 T$$

[Eq. (4.4)].

In turbulent motion the actual temperature T may be regarded as the sum of a mean temperature $\bar{T}$ and a fluctuation of temperature T', defined by

$$T = \bar{T} + T'$$

The motion consists of the mean velocity $(\bar{u},\bar{v},\bar{w})$ and eddy velocities (u',v',w'). Taking means, and making use of the equation of continuity,

$$c_p\rho \left(\frac{\partial \bar{T}}{\partial t} + \bar{u}\frac{\partial \bar{T}}{\partial x} + \bar{v}\frac{\partial \bar{T}}{\partial y} + \bar{w}\frac{\partial \bar{T}}{\partial z} \right) = \frac{\partial}{\partial x}\left(k\frac{\partial \bar{T}}{\partial x} - c_p\rho\overline{u'T'} \right)$$
$$+ \frac{\partial}{\partial y}\left(k\frac{\partial \bar{T}}{\partial y} - c_p\rho\overline{v'T'} \right) + \frac{\partial}{\partial z}\left(k\frac{\partial \bar{T}}{\partial z} - c_p\rho\overline{w'T'} \right) \quad (4.50)$$

This equation should be compared with Eqs. (3.5) for the transfer of momentum by the velocity fluctuations. Formally, there is complete similarity. The rates of eddy heat transfer are $(-k\partial T/\partial x + c_p\rho\overline{u'T'})$, etc., so that the total rate of transfer is regarded as the sum of that arising from molecular conductivity $(-k\partial \bar{T}/\partial x)$ and that dependent on the existence of a correlation between the velocity and temperature fluctuations. Unless the gradient of mean temperature is very large, the eddy-transfer term dominates the molecular-transfer term.

If the phenomenon being investigated is of the quasi-steady type, such as the variation with height of the diurnal temperature wave, regarded as one of a succession of similar waves, it is possible to treat the mixing process as one in which conditions are constant over any horizontal plane. There is then no resultant mean wind ($\bar{u} = \bar{v} = \bar{w} = 0$), and no net flux of heat in the horizontal. The equation of heat transfer reduces to

$$c_p \rho \frac{\partial \bar{T}}{\partial t} = \frac{\partial}{\partial z} \left(k \frac{\partial \bar{T}}{\partial z} - c_p \rho \overline{w'T'} \right)$$

Neglecting molecular conductivity and any variation of density with height, this becomes

$$\frac{\partial \bar{T}}{\partial t} = - \frac{\partial}{\partial z} (\overline{w'T'}) \tag{4.51}$$

If the correlation term $\overline{w'T'}$ can be expressed as the product of an exchange coefficient and the gradient of mean temperature, *i.e.*, if

$$- \overline{w'T'} = K(z) \frac{\partial \bar{T}}{\partial z}$$

Eq. (4.51) becomes

$$\frac{\partial \bar{T}}{\partial t} = \frac{\partial}{\partial z} \left[K(z) \frac{\partial \bar{T}}{\partial z} \right] \tag{4.52}$$

If $K(z) = K = $ constant, this reduces to

$$\frac{\partial \bar{T}}{\partial t} = K \frac{\partial^2 \bar{T}}{\partial z^2}$$

—the familiar equation of conduction of heat in a solid.

Mixing-length theory. It has been shown (Sec. 3.8) that if turbulent mixing is similar to diffusion in the kinetic theory of gases, the mean rate of transfer q of an entity $E(z)$ in the z direction across unit area normal to the z axis is

$$q = - \overline{w'(z_2 - z_1)} \frac{\partial \bar{E}}{\partial z}$$

For heat transfer in an incompressible gas $E = c_p \rho T$. The mixing length l is defined by

$$\overline{w'(z - z_1)} = l \sqrt{\overline{w'^2}}$$

or, with the Prandtl hypothesis, by

$$\overline{w'(z_2 - z_1)} = l^2 \frac{d\bar{u}}{dz}$$

Hence

$$q = -c_p \rho l \sqrt{\overline{w'^2}} \frac{d\bar{T}}{dz}$$

or

$$q = -c_p \rho l^2 \left| \frac{d\bar{u}}{dz} \right| \frac{d\bar{T}}{dz}$$

This assumes that both the correlation function $\overline{w'E'}$ and the length l are the same for the transfer of heat or momentum, since basically the same mechanism of mixing is at work. Alternatively, this hypothesis may be made more general by defining a mixing length for heat, l_H, by the equation

$$T' = -l_H \frac{d\bar{T}}{dz} \tag{4.53}$$

and assuming that

$$-\overline{w'T'} = l_M \left| \frac{d\bar{u}}{dz} \right| l_H \frac{d\bar{T}}{dz}$$

where l_M is the mixing length for momentum (Sutton[16]). At this stage these equations are purely formal.

The suggestion that, in turbulent motion, momentum and heat are transferred in the same way was first put forward by Reynolds in 1874 and is generally known as the *Reynolds analogy*. For motion parallel to the x axis, with heat transfer in the z direction, this statement implies that the velocity fluctuations parallel to the mean flow should be proportional to the temperature fluctuations and that

$$\frac{\tau}{\rho} = (\nu + K) \frac{\partial \bar{u}}{\partial z}$$

$$\frac{q}{c_p \rho} = -(\kappa + K) \frac{\partial \bar{T}}{\partial z}$$

where q and τ are the rate of heat transfer and the shearing stress, respectively, per unit area and K is the exchange coefficient, supposed the same for momentum and heat. This hypothesis has been studied extensively, especially in relation to heat transfer in pipes.†

Heat Transfer by Forced Convection from a Plane Surface at Uniform Temperature. The assumption that the dynamic and thermal boundary layers are identical, and that the profiles of velocity and temperature are similar, leads to a very simple solution of the problem of heat transfer by forced (turbulent) convection from a semiinfinite plane surface at uniform temperature. The solution of this problem for laminar flow has

† See Goldstein, *op. cit.*, pp. 649*ff.*

been given on page 127, as an example of air of uniform temperature moving over a cold sea (formation of inversion by offshore wind).

Suppose that a current of air, which has attained a uniform temperature distribution in the lower layers, moves over a plane surface of constant temperature, extended infinitely across wind. It is supposed that a thermal boundary layer is formed, identical with the dynamic boundary layer, of depth δ. If x is measured down wind, starting from the upwind edge of the plane surface, and z is height, the velocity and temperature profiles may be represented by the equations

$$\bar{u} = U \left(\frac{z}{\delta}\right)^m \qquad \text{if } z \leq \delta$$
$$= U \qquad \text{if } z > \delta$$
$$T = T_0 \left(\frac{z}{\delta}\right)^m \qquad \text{if } z \leq \delta$$
$$= T_0 \qquad \text{if } z > \delta$$

where U and T_0 are the velocity and temperature, respectively, of the air before it meets the plane surface, which is defined by $x \geq 0$, $z = 0$. The surface is supposed to be at zero temperature. The boundary layer forms at the leading edge ($x = z = 0$) and develops with increasing x according to an equation of the type (Sec. 3.8)

$$\delta = ax \left(\frac{\nu}{Ux}\right)^p \qquad p > 0$$

The rate of heat transfer from the plane $x \geq 0$, $z = 0$ is now found by methods similar to those used in evaluating the skin friction of a plane surface by momentum loss (Chap. 2). Consider an elemental volume of length dx and unit width, extending from the surface to the top of the boundary layer. Heat will pass across the boundaries because of the mixing effect, and the various fluxes are as follows:

1. A flux across the plane $z = 0$; this is the quantity to be determined.
2. A net flux, equal to $(\partial/\partial x) \int_0^\delta \rho c_p \bar{u} T \, dz$, in the direction of x.
3. A flux equal to $\rho c_p T_0 (\partial/\partial x) \int_0^\delta \bar{u} \, dz$ through the upper surface.

In the steady state, these fluxes must balance. Hence, denoting the flux of heat at the surface by $q(x)$, it follows that

$$q(x) = \rho c_p T_0 \frac{\partial}{\partial x} \int_0^\delta \bar{u} \, dz - \rho c_p \frac{\partial}{\partial x} \int_0^\delta \bar{u} T \, dz$$

The integrals can be evaluated from the expressions for the profile and the boundary-layer thickness. The final result is

$$q(x) = \rho c_p U T_0 \left(\frac{\nu}{Ux}\right)^p a(1-p) \left(\frac{1}{m+1} - \frac{1}{2m+1}\right)$$

In the case of a *smooth* plane boundary, approximate values are

$$a = 0.366, \qquad m = \tfrac{1}{7}, \qquad p = \tfrac{1}{5}$$

Substitution of these values leads to Latzko's formula for the local rate of loss of heat by turbulent forced convection,

$$q(x) = 0.0285 \rho c_p U T_0 \left(\frac{\nu}{Ux}\right)^{\frac{1}{5}}$$

For micrometeorology it is usually necessary to employ other values of the constants in order to take into account the roughness of the surface, which effectively increases the value of δ.

The solution given above represents the local heat transfer between a plane surface and an air stream, provided that the surface has a definite upwind edge and is extended indefinitely across wind. It thus applies to, say, air which passes over a low-lying coast line normal to the wind direction. It should be noticed that the same solution applies equally to the problem of evaporation, when air of known uniform humidity passes over a wetted area. In this case the uniform temperature of the surface is replaced by the surface concentration of water vapor, the underlying assumption being the identity of the dynamic and mass boundary layers. The heat flux then becomes the local rate of evaporation. This problem is considered in greater detail in Chap. 8.

Heat Transfer in the Atmosphere. As yet, there is no generally accepted formulation of the problems of heat transfer by atmospheric turbulence. The principal theories are as follows:

Equalization of potential temperature. In a compressible fluid, such as the atmosphere, a volume of air which is made to change its level is bound to change its temperature because of adiabatic heating or cooling, if for no other cause. For this reason the absolute temperature of the air is not a conservative entity for large-scale mixing processes. In 1915 Taylor gave an analysis which showed that mean potential temperature θ, which remains constant during any adiabatic process, is likely to be diffused by turbulence in a manner similar to absolute temperature in a solid. The same conclusion was reached by Schmidt and Richardson.

The one-dimensional form of the equation, as employed by the above-named writers, is

$$\frac{\partial \theta}{\partial t} = \frac{\partial}{\partial z}\left[K(z)\frac{\partial \theta}{\partial z}\right] \tag{4.54}$$

where $K(z)$ is the exchange coefficient for heat, or eddy conductivity. The flow of heat across any level z is

$$q = -K(z)c_p\rho \frac{\partial \theta}{\partial z} \tag{4.55}$$

According to this theory, in an atmosphere of uniform absolute temperature there will be a net flow of heat downward, for in such an atmosphere potential temperature increases with height. The ultimate effect of eddy heat transfer is to eliminate all gradients of potential temperature.

Brunt's equation. Brunt[18] has given an equation of eddy heat transfer in the atmosphere which closely resembles Eq. (4.54). His analysis is as follows:

It is supposed that the typical eddy which crosses a level z has originated from a level $z - l$, where it possessed the mean temperature of its environment. Thus if $\bar{T}(z)$ be the mean (absolute) temperature of the air at level z, the temperature of the eddy was originally

$$\bar{T}(z - l) \simeq \bar{T}(z) - l\frac{\partial \bar{T}}{\partial z}$$

If the eddy moves from $z - l$ to z without losing or acquiring heat by mixing or conduction, its sole temperature change, owing to change of pressure, is Γl, where Γ is the adiabatic lapse rate. Hence the temperature of the eddy at level z is $\bar{T} - l\left(\frac{\partial \bar{T}}{\partial z} + \Gamma\right)$, and the heat content of the air transferred across unit horizontal surface in unit time is

$$c_p\rho w'\left[\bar{T} - l\left(\frac{\partial \bar{T}}{\partial z} + \Gamma\right)\right]$$

since $\rho w'$ is the mass rate of transfer of the air per unit area. If the surface in question is an isobaric surface, the total net transfer of air must be zero over any long period and so, by taking the mean value of the above expression over a large area and a long period of time, the net upward transfer of heat per unit area and per unit time is

$$-c_p\rho\overline{w'l}\left(\frac{\partial \bar{T}}{\partial z} + \Gamma\right)$$

The length l may now be regarded as a mixing length, and the quantity $\overline{w'l} = K(z)$, the eddy conductivity. Hence the net transfer of heat across the isobaric surface is

$$q = -K(z)c_p\rho\left(\frac{\partial \bar{T}}{\partial z} + \Gamma\right) \tag{4.56}$$

The gain of heat between the surfaces p and $p + dp$ is

$$\frac{\partial}{\partial p}\left[K(z)c_p\rho\left(\frac{\partial \bar{T}}{\partial z} + \Gamma\right)\right] dp = \frac{\partial}{\partial z}\left[K(z)c_p\rho\left(\frac{\partial \bar{T}}{\partial z} + \Gamma\right)\right] dz$$

and this must equal $c_p\rho\, dz\, d\bar{T}/dt = c_p\rho\, dz\, \partial\bar{T}/\partial t$ in the absence of mean motion. Hence the transfer of heat in the vertical over a large plane surface is given by

$$\frac{\partial \bar{T}}{\partial t} = \frac{1}{\rho}\frac{\partial}{\partial z}\left[\rho K(z)\left(\frac{\partial \bar{T}}{\partial z} + \Gamma\right)\right] \tag{4.57}$$

If the variation of ρ with height is neglected, Eq. (4.57) becomes

$$\frac{\partial \bar{T}}{\partial t} = \frac{\partial}{\partial z}\left[K(z)\left(\frac{\partial \bar{T}}{\partial z} + \Gamma\right)\right] \tag{4.58}$$

This is Brunt's equation. If $K(z) = K = $ constant, Eq. (4.58) reduces to

$$\frac{\partial \bar{T}}{\partial t} = K\frac{\partial^2 \bar{T}}{\partial z^2} \tag{4.59}$$

The difference between the two expressions for the flux of heat, $Kc_p\rho\,\partial\theta/\partial z$ and $Kc_p\rho\left(\dfrac{\partial \bar{T}}{\partial z} + \Gamma\right)$, is small in the lower layers of atmosphere (say, for $z < 100$ m), since at such heights $\theta \simeq \bar{T} + \Gamma z$. Thus for most purposes Eqs. (4.54) and (4.58) are indistinguishable, and in both theories the flux of heat is from regions of high potential temperature to regions of low potential temperature.

Modified equations. The theory as presented above gives rise to certain difficulties. According to the equations, the general effect of turbulent mixing is to reduce to zero any gradient of potential temperature so that the atmosphere, as a whole, should tend to a state of uniform potential temperature in the vertical. Observations show that, on the contrary, potential temperature usually tends to increase with height in the free atmosphere and the mean gradient is less than the adiabatic lapse rate. In the surface layers, observational difficulties arise because of the smallness of the temperature difference corresponding to the adiabatic lapse rate over limited heights, but here again there are indications that the gradients observed on overcast windy nights are less than the adiabatic, a state which could not be reached by turbulent mixing on the above theories. The analysis of the Taylor and Brunt equations is strictly applicable only to forced convection, since no attempt is made to include the effects of horizontal inhomogeneities of temperature which may give rise to buoyant motions. The vertical velocity is supposed to transfer an element of air at the mean temperature of the initial level, which amounts to assuming that the mixing process is independent of local irregularities of temperature and arises solely from dynamic instability. In the lower atmosphere there are always horizontal gradients uf temperature, and an element of air initially above or below the temperature of its surroundings may rise or fall for this reason alone.

As stated earlier in this chapter, there are good reasons for believing that atmospheric heat transfer usually involves both forced and free convection, but except in special circumstances it is extremely difficult, if not impossible, to estimate the contribution of each type of transfer to the total flux. In recent years there have been several attempts to reformulate the problem, notably by Ertel[19] and by Priestley and Swinbank.[20] Ertel concludes that the flux of heat in the atmosphere is primarily determined by the gradient of absolute temperature, as in a solid or an incompressible fluid. His arguments have been combated by Prandtl, and the question of their validity remains unsettled.

In the work of Priestley and Swinbank, which has many points of resemblance with that of Ertel, the argument is as follows: It is supposed that the typical eddy (which may cross the datum plane several times successively in opposite directions without losing its identity) was last at rest in the vertical at a level l below the datum z. This ensures that w' and l always have the same sign. When last at rest, the eddy is supposed to have an excess temperature T'' over the mean temperature $\bar{T}(z - l)$ of its level. If the eddy changes its temperature adiabatically in moving from $z - l$ to z,

$$\bar{T}(z) + T'(z) = \bar{T}(z - l) + T'' - \Gamma l$$
$$\simeq \bar{T}(z) - l \frac{\partial \bar{T}}{\partial z} + T'' - \Gamma l$$

and so

$$T'(z) = T'' - l \left(\frac{\partial \bar{T}}{\partial z} + \Gamma \right)$$

The mean flux of heat across the level z is thus, by the usual arguments,

$$q = c_p \rho \overline{w'T'} = c_p \rho \left[-\overline{w'l} \left(\frac{\partial \bar{T}}{\partial z} + \Gamma \right) + \overline{w'T''} \right]$$

The first term in this expression for the flux is that derived by Brunt and indicates a flow of heat from regions of high to regions of low potential temperature. The second term is independent of the gradient of potential temperature and represents an effect analogous to free convection, in that if there is a tendency for warmer eddies ($T'' > 0$) to rise ($w' > 0$), this term is essentially positive. Priestley and Swinbank refer to the first type of transfer as *mechanical turbulence* and to the second as *convective turbulence*.

The term $\overline{w'T''}$ cannot be measured directly, and its importance can only be inferred. However, even a small correlation between w' and T'' would make $\overline{w'T''}$ of magnitude sufficient to be comparable with, or even to dominate, the term $\overline{w'T'}$, so that on this theory a net flux of heat from regions of low to high potential temperature is possible. In this way Priestley and Swinbank account for certain phenomena of synoptic scale which are not readily explicable on the older theories, but it is difficult to judge how far the arguments may be vitiated by the neglect of radiation.

The Priestley-Swinbank dissection of the flux of heat should be regarded as a first attempt to solve the problem of heat transfer when both free and forced convection are present. The main criticism to be directed against this analysis (and, in fact, against many of the present theories) is that it involves too literal an interpretation of the word "eddy." The "mean temperature" at any level is a mathematical abstraction, dependent on the period of sampling (page 61), and the conception of an eddy as an isolated parcel of air, which moves vertically when its temperature differs from the mean temperature associated with its initial level, lacks physical reality. A parcel of air will acquire buoyant motion whenever its temperature differs by a certain finite amount from that of the surrounding air (see page 123), and the latter temperature may or may not be identical with the mean temperature which appears in the mathematical analysis. The chief value of this work lies in the fact that it calls attention to the possibility of the diffusion of heat involving, in certain circumstances, factors other than those arising from instability associated with shear of the mean motion.

4.8. Mixing-length Theory in Free Convection

Clear days in summer are frequently associated with low winds, and in these circumstances vertical currents of thermal origin exist near the surface of the earth and extend to considerable heights in the atmosphere. (Such currents are familiar to glider pilots and evidently are recognized and utilized by large birds which soar when seeking prey.) In such conditions, atmospheric heat transfer must be dominated by buoyancy effects.

It has already been pointed out that the removal of heat from a surface by free convection is not, in general, a true diffusion process. It is possible, however, to make some progress with the problem of the transfer of heat in the lower atmosphere on a hot, calm day by introducing concepts akin to those employed in normal diffusion theory (Sutton[16]).

The buoyancy of the heated masses would give rise to very large vertical velocities were it not for the continuous degradation of the kinetic energy by breakdown into smaller eddies. This fact allows the transfer of heat on a calm day to be analyzed in terms of mixing-length functions appropriate to the buoyant movements of large volumes.

The analysis may be carried out in two ways. The first method depends on the use of Taylor's expression for the dissipation of energy in isotropic turbulence in terms of the scale of turbulence [Eqs. (3.66) and (3.67)]. The intensity of the convection currents is determined by the balance between the rate of breakdown of the original mass into smaller eddies and the rate of loss of gravitational potential energy. The mean rate of loss of kinetic energy of turbulence, W, by the action of viscosity is given by

$$W = \text{constant } \frac{\rho w^3}{L} \tag{4.60}$$

where w is the mean vertical component of turbulent velocity ($w = \sqrt{\overline{w'^2}}$) and L is the scale of turbulence. When air raised to temperature ΔT above that of the surrounding atmosphere moves upward with velocity w, the rate of loss of potential energy per unit volume is

$$\rho w g \frac{\Delta T}{T} \tag{4.61}$$

where T is the mean absolute temperature of the unheated air, here supposed to be constant. If the convection currents preserve their identity over the length L, ΔT may be supposed proportional to $-L\, \partial T/\partial z$ by the usual mixing-length argument. Hence, from (4.60) and (4.61)

$$w^2 = \text{constant} \cdot \frac{gL^2}{T}\left(-\frac{\partial T}{\partial z}\right) \tag{4.62}$$

and the heat-exchange coefficient $K(z) = \overline{wL}$ may be written as

$$K(z) = \text{constant} \cdot L^2 \sqrt{\left(-\frac{g}{T}\frac{\partial T}{\partial z}\right)} \tag{4.63}$$

This expression is due to Taylor.

Alternatively, the same result follows from a "model" argument. If the heated mass has a characteristic linear dimension L, the force of buoyancy is proportional to $g\rho L^3 \Delta T/T$. In breaking through the cold air, the mass experiences a resistance proportional to $\rho L^2 w^2$. Such a rising mass would normally move at the terminal velocity appropriate to the level considered, so that the force of buoyancy may be equated to the resistance. This gives immediately Eq. (4.62) for w.

In applying the expression (4.63) to the atmosphere, Sutton replaces the gradient of absolute temperature by the difference between the observed gradient and the adiabatic lapse rate. The justification for this step is to be found in an investigation by Jeffreys,[21] who showed that, provided density differences are not too great, it is permissible in a compressible fluid to use potential temperature (or, to a sufficient degree of approximation, the deviation of temperature from the adiabatic distribution) in place of absolute temperature. A given disturbance of temperature has, to the first order of accuracy, the same effect on the motion of a compressible as on an incompressible fluid. Thus in conditions of marked free convection,

$$K(z) = \text{constant} \cdot L^2 \sqrt{\left[-\frac{g}{T}\left(\frac{\partial \bar{T}}{\partial z} + \Gamma\right) \right]}$$

As an approximation, it is supposed that this may be replaced by

$$K(z) = l_H{}^2 \sqrt{\left[-\frac{g}{T}\left(\frac{\partial \bar{T}}{\partial z} + \Gamma\right) \right]} \tag{4.64}$$

where l_H is the temperature mixing length defined by

$$l_H = -\frac{T'}{(\partial \bar{T}/\partial z) + \Gamma}$$

Relations between the Temperature Mixing Length, the Upward Velocity, and the Exchange Coefficient. If the flux of heat in the vertical, q, is independent of height, certain simple relations exist between l_H, w, $K(z)$, and T'. From (4.64)

$$K^3(z) = -\frac{g}{T} l_H{}^4 K(z)\left(\frac{\partial \bar{T}}{\partial z} + \Gamma\right)$$

The flux of heat is defined by

$$-K(z)\left(\frac{\partial \bar{T}}{\partial z} + \Gamma\right) = \frac{q}{c_p \rho} = \text{constant}$$

or

$$K(z) = \text{constant} \cdot l_H{}^{\frac{4}{3}} \tag{4.65}$$

Also

$$w = \text{constant} \cdot l_H{}^{\frac{1}{3}} \tag{4.66}$$

$$\frac{\partial \bar{T}}{\partial z} + \Gamma = \text{constant} \cdot l_H{}^{-\frac{4}{3}} \tag{4.67}$$

$$T' = \text{constant} \cdot l_H{}^{-\frac{1}{3}} \tag{4.68}$$

These relations have been employed in the analysis of free convection in the surface layers (see page 221).

4.9. The Effect of Density Gradient on Turbulence

The greatest difficulty in dealing with atmospheric turbulence arises from the fact that the density gradient in the lowest layers of the atmosphere exhibits a well-defined diurnal variation in clear weather. This is most clearly shown by the alternation of lapse and inversion conditions on clear days and nights and the corresponding rise and fall in the turbulence of the wind. It is difficult to reproduce such effects on an adequate scale in the wind tunnel, so that the observational data are, for the most part, confined to measurements made in the lower atmosphere or in the sea, with an inevitable loss of accuracy and reliability consequent upon the absence of control.

Richardson's Criterion. The fundamental investigation on the effect of gravity in suppressing turbulence in a fluid of variable density is that of L. F. Richardson.[22] Richardson's analysis is based upon the principle that, at the stage when the motion is bordering on laminar ("just-no-turbulence"), the kinetic energy of the fluctuations will increase or decrease according as the rate of supply of energy extracted from the mean motion by the Reynolds stresses exceeds or falls below the rate at which work has to be done in the gravitational field in moving masses of the fluid in the vertical.

The criterion is most simply derived as follows:[†]

A volume of air, starting from a level $z - l$, with temperature $\bar{T}(z - l) \simeq \bar{T} - l \, \partial\bar{T}/\partial z$, moves without mixing to a new level z as a result of the turbulent fluctuations. At the new level its temperature is $\bar{T} - l\left(\dfrac{\partial\bar{T}}{\partial z} + \Gamma\right)$, and its excess of density over the environment at that level is $\dfrac{l\rho}{T}\left(\dfrac{\partial\bar{T}}{\partial z} + \Gamma\right)$. The volume, being heavier than its surroundings, will experience a downward force equal to

$$\frac{gl\rho}{\bar{T}}\left(\frac{\partial\bar{T}}{\partial z} + \Gamma\right)$$

per unit volume. The rate of upward flow of fluid per unit area is w', and so the mean rate of working against gravity per unit volume is

$$g\rho \, \frac{\overline{w'l}}{\bar{T}}\left(\frac{\partial\bar{T}}{\partial z} + \Gamma\right)$$

In this expression the quantity $\overline{w'l}$ may be identified as the eddy conductivity K_H.

The work done by the Reynolds stress, per unit volume, is

$$\tau \frac{\partial\bar{u}}{\partial z} = K_M\rho\left(\frac{\partial\bar{u}}{\partial z}\right)^2$$

where τ is the eddy shearing stress per unit area, K_M is the eddy viscosity, and $\bar{u}$ is the mean velocity normal to the axis of z. Applying

[†] Brunt, *op. cit.*, p. 237.

Richardson's principle, if $\rho \bar{E}(z,t)$ is the mean turbulent energy per unit volume at height z,

$$\frac{\partial \bar{E}(z,t)}{\partial t} = K_M \left(\frac{\partial \bar{u}}{\partial z}\right)^2 - K_H \frac{g}{T}\left(\frac{\partial \bar{T}}{\partial z} + \Gamma\right)$$

$$= K_H \left(\frac{\partial \bar{u}}{\partial z}\right)^2 \left[\frac{K_M}{K_H} - \frac{g}{T}\frac{(\partial \bar{T}/\partial z) + \Gamma}{(\partial \bar{u}/\partial z)^2}\right]$$

Since $K_H(\partial \bar{u}/\partial z)^2$ is essentially positive and different from zero (except in the trivial case $\bar{u} = $ constant), the sign of $\partial \bar{E}/\partial t$ depends on whether the nondimensional quantity

$$\text{Ri} = \frac{g}{T}\frac{(\partial \bar{T}/\partial z) + \Gamma}{(\partial \bar{u}/\partial z)^2} = \frac{g(\partial \theta/\partial z)}{\theta(\partial \bar{u}/\partial z)^2}$$

($\theta = $ potential temperature), called the *Richardson number* Ri, is greater or less than the ratio K_M/K_H. In his original discussion Richardson assumed $K_M = K_H$ and asserted that a motion which is slightly turbulent (E just different from zero) will remain turbulent if $\text{Ri} < 1$ and will subside into laminar motion if $\text{Ri} > 1$. This implies that there exists a critical value Ri_c of the Richardson number, in this case unity.

It follows from the above analysis that a necessary condition for the suppression of turbulence by a density gradient is that the potential temperature must increase with height ($\partial \theta/\partial z > 0$), but the condition is not sufficient. Turbulence can be maintained in the presence of an inversion of potential temperature if $\partial \bar{u}/\partial z$ is large enough. It is a familiar fact of meteorology that on a clear night the wind velocity in the layers adjacent to the ground is usually very low, whereas the wind at the higher levels remains strong. The sharp decrease of density with height allows a large velocity gradient to be maintained, and this is possible only when turbulent mixing falls to a low level or is extinguished in the bottom layers.

The physical interpretation of Richardson's criterion is also clearly seen from the following crude derivation. The vertical velocity w_c of air masses of characteristic linear dimension l_H moving at their terminal velocity is

$$w_c = \text{constant} \cdot l_H \sqrt{\left(\frac{g}{\theta}\frac{\partial \theta}{\partial z}\right)} \qquad \frac{\partial \theta}{\partial z} > 0$$

[Eq. (4.62)]. The energy of this motion is, per unit volume,

$$\rho w_c^2 = \text{constant} \cdot \rho l_H^2 \frac{g}{\theta}\frac{\partial \theta}{\partial z}$$

The energy of the vertical component of the turbulent velocities, arising from instability associated with shear of the mean velocity is, per unit volume,

$$\rho w_M{}^2 = \rho l_M{}^2 \left(\frac{\partial \bar{u}}{\partial z}\right)^2$$

where l_M is the momentum mixing length as defined by Prandtl. The ratio of these energies is

$$\frac{\rho w_c{}^2}{\rho w_M{}^2} = \text{constant} \cdot \left(\frac{l_H}{l_M}\right)^2 \text{Ri} \qquad (4.69)$$

Richardson's criterion is now obtained by supposing that the "constant" in Equation (4.69) is unity and that $l_H = l_M$. If the energy associated with the density gradient, $\rho w_c{}^2$, which in this case tends to stabilize, is greater than that available from the instability of the mean motion, $\rho w_M{}^2$, so that $\text{Ri} > 1$, the turbulence will subside, and if the reverse holds ($\text{Ri} < 1$), the turbulence will be maintained.

The problem of the stability of motion in the presence of a density gradient has received considerable attention from mathematicians. In 1931 Taylor[23] published an account of some earlier investigations on this subject and obtained a definite result for an infinite fluid in which density varies in the vertical according to the law $\rho = \rho_0 \exp(-\beta z)$ and velocity according to $u = u_0 + \alpha z$, where $z = 0$ is some plane of reference (not a rigid boundary) so that $\beta = -(1/\rho)(d\rho/dz)$ and $\alpha = du/dz$. In such a fluid motion progressive internal waves can exist if

$$\frac{g\beta}{\alpha^2} = -\frac{(g/\rho)(d\rho/dz)}{(du/dz)^2} < \frac{1}{4}$$

but no waves, either progressive or exponentially unstable, can exist indefinitely if $g\beta/\alpha^2 > \frac{1}{4}$.

This result applies only to a fluid of infinite extent. Stability of motion near a rigid boundary in the presence of a density gradient has been examined by Schlichting[24] in a long and difficult extension of the investigations of Tollmien on the stability of a boundary layer in an isothermal viscous incompressible fluid (see Chap. 3). In this case the critical value of $g\beta/\alpha^2$ was found to depend on both the Reynolds number $\bar{u}\delta/\nu$ and the Froude number $\bar{u}/\sqrt{(\delta g)}$ (δ = boundary-layer thickness). For large Reynolds number and small Froude number (corresponding to conditions in the atmosphere, where δ is large), Schlichting found that $g\beta/\alpha^2$ must not exceed 0.0409 if turbulence is to be maintained.

The most recent investigation is that of Calder,[25] who has reexamined Richardson's original method, in which certain terms were omitted (a fact recognized by Richardson) on the assumption that these are negligibly small in a state bordering on laminar motion. Calder's equation is

$$\bar{\rho}\,\frac{d\bar{E}}{dt} = \bar{\rho}K_M\left(\frac{\partial\bar{u}}{\partial z}\right)^2 - \frac{\bar{\rho}g}{\bar{T}}\,K_H\left(\frac{\partial\bar{T}}{\partial z}+\Gamma\right) - \Phi - \frac{\partial}{\partial z}\left[\,\overline{w'\left(p'+\frac{1}{2}\,\bar{\rho}\overline{w'^2}\right)}\,\right]$$

where Φ represents the dissipation of energy by viscosity. This differs from Richardson's equation chiefly with regard to the final term, which represents the rate of working of the fluctuating gradients of static pressure on the eddying motion. In an atmosphere possessing the adiabatic distribution of temperature, and when conditions are steady ($\partial\bar{E}/\partial t = 0$), Calder concludes that the terms omitted by Richardson exactly balance the rate of transformation of the energy of the mean motion into eddying energy. It follows that if $K_M = K_H$, the criterion should take the form that turbulence will decay when

$$\mathrm{Ri} > 1 - a$$

where a is some positive quantity whose value has not been determined in general.

Attempts to verify Richardson's criterion for the lower atmosphere have not been entirely successful, and there is some doubt whether a unique value, applicable to all types of surface, can be said to exist (see Chap. 7 for an account of the experimental work). It is possible that some of this variation arises from the nature of the surface over which the wind is blowing.

Some light is thrown on this matter by a dissection of the Richardson number in a shallow layer adjacent to the surface. On a clear night the temperature inversion builds up from the ground, so that in the early stages of the suppression of turbulence, a motion bordering on laminar is established in a shallow layer of relatively dense air near the ground. Within such a layer, the gradients of velocity and temperature may be supposed invariable with height without serious error, so that the differential coefficients may be replaced by finite differences divided by the depth of the layer (δ). Thus, in the layer $(0,\delta)$,

$$\mathrm{Ri} \simeq \left(\frac{\Delta T}{T}\frac{g\delta^3}{\nu^2}\right)\left(\frac{\nu}{\bar{u}\delta}\right)^2 \tag{4.70}$$

In laminar motion

$$\frac{\nu\bar{u}}{\delta} = \nu\left(\frac{\partial\bar{u}}{\partial z}\right)_0 = u_*{}^2$$

and

$$\left(\frac{\nu}{\bar{u}\delta}\right)^2 = \left(\frac{u_*}{\bar{u}}\right)^4 = \frac{1}{4}\,C_D{}^2$$

where C_D is the skin-friction coefficient of the surface, defined by the relation

$$\tau_0 = \tfrac{1}{2} C_D \rho \bar{u}^2$$

The first group of terms in the expression (4.70) is a Grashof number, and thus in near-laminar motion adjacent to the surface

$$\text{Ri} \simeq \tfrac{1}{4} \text{Gr } C_D^2$$

Measurements of the skin-friction coefficient of the ground show that, in general, C_D is independent of the magnitude of the reference velocity but greatly influenced by the nature of the surface (see Chap. 7). On general physical grounds, it is to be expected that turbulence is more easily suppressed over a relatively smooth surface than over one covered with large obstacles. It is therefore plausible, but not established, that the critical value of Ri varies with the roughness of the ground. Schlicting and Reichardt's result for motion near a smooth laboratory surface does not necessarily contradict Richardson's conclusion that turbulence in the vicinity of trees is quenched when $\text{Ri} > 1$, but the whole question is one which needs much deeper investigation before a detailed picture can be formed of the process of suppression of turbulence by a density gradient.

On the theoretical side, as yet there is no completely reliable investigation of the effects of density gradient on the mean velocity profile and the eddy fluctuations. From observations made near the ground it is well established that as the inversion builds up, the velocity gradient steepens and approaches a constant value (linear velocity profile), but no theoretical expression has yet been found which relates the velocity profile to the temperature profile. In the inversion period the magnitude of the velocity fluctuations is considerably reduced, sometimes to vanishing point, but here again there is no theoretical relation to guide the experimenter.

Problems of diffusion in varying lapse rate are usually investigated on lines initiated by Sutton, in which the velocity profile is expressed by a power law of height, the exponent being regarded as a function of the temperature gradient. Near the ground the mean velocity may be expressed approximately in the form

$$\bar{u} = \bar{u}_1 \left(\frac{z}{z_1} \right)^m$$

where $\bar{u}_1$ is the velocity on the fixed reference plane $z = z_1$. In large lapse rates m is small, and in large inversions m increases toward unity. Such changes in the form of the profile of mean velocity indicate the effects of density gradient on the transfer of momentum and it may be supposed that other transferrable entities, such as concentration of mat-

ter, are similarly affected. In this fashion it is possible to obtain an approximation to the effects of density gradient on diffusion. The problem is considered in detail in Chap. 8.

BIBLIOGRAPHY

1. D. BRUNT, "Physical and Dynamical Meteorology" (Cambridge, 1938).
2. M. FISHENDEN and O. A. SAUNDERS, "The Calculation of Heat Transmission" (London, 1932).
3. P. K. RAMAN, Proc. Indian Acad. Sci., 3, 89 (1936).
4. H. BÉNARD, Rev. gén. sci., 12, 1261, 1309 (1900).
5. LORD RAYLEIGH, Phil. Mag., 32, 529 (1916).
6. H. JEFFREYS, Phil. Mag., 2, 833 (1926).
7. H. JEFFREYS, Proc. Roy. Soc. (London), A118, 195 (1928).
8. A. PELLEW and R. V. SOUTHWELL, Proc. Roy. Soc. (London), 176, 312 (1940).
9. K. CHANDRA, Proc. Roy. Soc. (London), 164, 231 (1938).
10. O. G. SUTTON, Proc. Roy. Soc. (London), 204, 297 (1950).
11. L. A. RAMDAS and S. L. MALURKAR, Indian J. Phys., 7, 1 (1932).
12. S. L. MALURKAR, Gerlands Beitr. Geophys., 51, 270 (1937).
13. H. JEFFREYS, Phil. Mag., 35, 270 (1918).
14. N. K. JOHNSON and G. S. P. HEYWOOD, Geophys. Mem. 77.
15. O. F. T. ROBERTS, Proc. Roy. Soc. (London), A104, 640 (1923).
16. O. G. SUTTON, Quart. J. Roy. Meteorol. Soc., 74, 13 (1948).
17. G. I. TAYLOR, Phil. Trans. Roy. Soc., A25, 1 (1915).
18. D. BRUNT, Proc. Roy. Soc. (London), A124, 201 (1924).   See also (1).
19. H. ERTEL, Meteorol. Z., 59, 250 (1942); 60, 246 (1943); 61, 8 (1944); 61, 207 (1944).
20. C. H. B. PRIESTLEY and W. C. SWINBANK, Proc. Roy. Soc. (London), A189, 543 (1937).
21. H. JEFFREYS, Proc. Cambridge Phil. Soc., 26, 170 (1930).
22. L. F. RICHARDSON, Phil. Mag., 49, 81 (1925).
23. G. I. TAYLOR, Proc. Roy. Soc. (London), 132, 499 (1931).
24. H. SCHLICHTING, Z. angew. Math. u. Mech., 15, 313 (1935).
25. K. L. CALDER, Quart. J. Roy. Meteorol. Soc., 75, 71 (1949).

CHAPTER 5

RADIATION

The earth receives its heat from the sun, the other heavenly bodies contributing a negligible amount. A theoretical analysis of the temperature of the surface of the earth, and of the atmosphere immediately above it, must thus involve a detailed study of solar radiation, but this is only a partial aspect of the problem. The surface of the earth, in turn, radiates to the atmosphere and to space, and it happens that the gas water vapor, a normal constituent of the atmosphere, is able to absorb and emit strongly for certain wavelengths prominent in the spectrum of terrestrial radiation. In addition, the solar beam is subject to diffuse scattering by air molecules and suspended particles, resulting in the so-called sky radiation, while a considerable amount of reflection arises from clouds, snow, and water surfaces. The atmosphere is thus crossed by a complex of beams, some of which pass through with little absorption but are subject to considerable scattering and reflection; others, notably those comprising the so-called long-wave, or dark, radiation, are continually being absorbed and reemitted. An exact mathematical treatment of this highly complicated field can hardly be contemplated, since the state of the atmosphere, as regards radiation, fluctuates with such irregularly variable quantities as cloud amount, water-vapor content, and atmospheric pollution.

Radiation passing through the atmosphere affects meteorological conditions by virtue of its power to transmit energy to the air and the earth. Such energy is manifested in the first instance as heat. The complexity of the meteorological problem arises partly from the fact that the radiation is not monochromatic, and absorption by the atmosphere varies considerably with wavelength, and partly because of inevitable variations in the medium. An analysis of the different effects must therefore take into consideration such factors as the spectrum of the primary and secondary radiation in the atmosphere and the selective transmission and absorption of the rays by the various constituents of the atmosphere and of the surface of the earth.

5.1. Fundamental Relations

The fundamental laws of radiation are briefly recapitulated here for reference. They will not be discussed in detail, and for further information the reader is referred to textbooks on this subject.

1. *Units*. The *intensity of radiation* is defined in terms of the amount of energy received in unit time on unit surface and so can be expressed as erg cm^{-2} sec^{-1}. In meteorology it is customary to express the intensity as the number of calories per square centimeter per minute, and the following relations hold:

$$1 \text{ g cal cm}^{-2} \text{min}^{-1} = 4.19 \times 10^7 \text{ erg cm}^{-2} \text{min}^{-1} = 6.97 \times 10^{-2} \text{ watt cm}^{-2}$$

2. *Definition of a Black Body*. The intensity of the radiation emitted by a body is a function of the wavelength of the radiation, the absolute temperature of the body, and the area of the emitting surface. For given temperature, wavelength, and surface area, the intensity has an upper bound. A body which emits for every wavelength the maximum intensity of radiation is termed a *full radiator* or *black body*. It should be noted that the latter term has no reference to the normal color of the body.

3. *Kirchhoff's Law*. The ratio of the emissive power (intensity of radiation emitted) and the absorptivity (fraction of radiation absorbed) of a body is a universal function of the wavelength and the absolute temperature. For a black body, this ratio is equal to the emissive power. It follows that every body absorbs radiation of exactly those wavelengths which it is capable of emitting at the same temperature. The nature and intensity of the radiation from a black body depend only on the absolute temperature of the body.

4. *Stefan's Law*. A black body at absolute temperature T_1 placed in an enclosure at absolute temperature T_2 gains or loses energy at a rate given by

$$\sigma(T_1{}^4 - T_2{}^4) \tag{5.1}$$

where σ is an absolute constant whose value is 5.77×10^{-5} erg cm^{-2} sec^{-1}.

5. *Planck's Radiation Formula*. The radiation $E(\lambda,T)d\lambda$, of wavelength lying between λ and $\lambda + d\lambda$, emitted by unit surface of a black body at absolute temperature T, is given by

$$E(\lambda,T)d\lambda = c_1\lambda^{-5}\left(\exp\frac{c_2}{\lambda T} - 1\right)^{-1} d\lambda \qquad \text{erg sec}^{-1} \tag{5.2}$$

where c_1 and c_2 are constants.

6. *Wien's Displacement Law*. It follows from Planck's formula that

$$T^{-5}E(\lambda,T) = f(\lambda T) \tag{5.3}$$

The function $f(\lambda T)$ vanishes for $\lambda = 0$ and as $\lambda \to \infty$ and reaches a maximum at a wavelength $\lambda_{\max}$ given by Wien's relation ·

$$\lambda_{\max} T = 2940 \tag{5.4}$$

where λ is measured in $\mu = 10^{-4}$ cm and T in °K.

Short-wave and Long-wave Radiation. The sun may be regarded as a black body whose surface radiates at about 6000°K. It follows from the laws of Planck and Wien that the maximum intensity in sunbeams occurs at about 0.5μ, and almost the whole solar emission is contained between 0.15 and 4μ. The surface of the earth is approximately a black body at 300°K, and the maximum intensity is in radiation of wavelength about 10μ, the limits of the spectrum for most practical purposes being set at 3 and 80μ. The virtual nonoverlapping of the two spectra enable an effective distinction to be made between *short-wave solar radiation* and *long-wave terrestrial radiation.*

Radiation Balance. Since the earth, both surface and atmosphere, is neither gaining nor losing heat at an appreciable rate, the amount of radiation received must balance that emitted. The details of this balance sheet have been differently estimated by various workers, and the question is one for the climatologist rather than the micrometeorologist. The following figures are those of Bauer and Phillipps,[1] modified by Möller.[2] About 43 per cent of the incoming solar radiation reaches the surface, either directly (27 per cent) or as diffused sky radiation (16 per cent). About 42 per cent is lost to space, mainly by direct reflection from clouds and the surface, and about 15 per cent is absorbed by the atmosphere. Thus 58 per cent of the original incoming energy must be reemitted by the surface of the earth and the atmosphere as long-wave radiation, if the balance is to be maintained.

The net outgoing radiation from the earth is about one-quarter of the incoming radiation, but the total intensity of the surface emission is about 120 per cent of the original solar beam. From this must be subtracted the back radiation from the atmosphere to the surface, amounting to about 96 per cent of the incoming radiation. The difference is 24 per cent, of which about two-thirds is reabsorbed by the atmosphere and one-third lost to space.

Radiation alone does not account for the heat balance of the surface, since there is an internal transport of energy by turbulent mixing, and a transfer of heat from the surface to the atmosphere by evaporation and subsequent condensation at higher levels. On the whole, the surface of the earth loses about equal amounts of energy by radiation and water-vapor transport, and this loss is almost entirely made up by incoming radiation, direct and diffuse. The amount of heat gained by turbulent mixing is small, probably less than one-twentieth of the original incoming radiation from the sun.

5.2. Short-wave Radiation

Solar Constant. Measurements of solar radiation are often expressed in terms of the solar constant, defined as the intensity of radiation from the sun at the mean distance of the earth, the atmosphere being supposed absent. In practice, the solar constant is regarded as the intensity of sunbeams at the outer limit of the earth's atmosphere and is obtained by extrapolation from measurements made at high-altitude stations. The accepted value of the solar constant is

$$I_0 = 1.94 \text{ cal cm}^{-2} \text{ min}^{-1} \tag{5.5}$$

The Solar Spectrum. Observation shows that the bulk of the solar spectrum is restricted to wavelengths lying between 0.3 and 2μ. Radiation of wavelength below 0.36μ is usually referred to as *ultraviolet*, while that of wavelength greater than 0.76μ is termed *infrared*.

The spectrum of the sun's light shows many absorption lines, some caused by the constituents of the solar atmosphere itself, but others are due to absorption by the earth's atmosphere. The almost complete absence of radiation of wavelength less than 0.3μ is attributed to the presence of ozone, which has a marked absorption band between 0.2 and 0.32μ, and to oxygen, in the upper atmosphere. Of the remaining constituents of the atmosphere, carbon dioxide has two small absorption bands from 2.3 to 3.0μ and 4.2 to 4.4μ and consequently has little effect on the beam as a whole. Oxygen absorbs also at 0.69 and 0.76μ, but these bands are narrow and represent little loss. The principal absorption is due to water vapor, with bands at 0.72, 0.81, 0.93, 1.13, 1.37, 1.89μ and wider bands centered at 1.91 and 2.03μ.

Table 5, for Davos, shows the percentage distribution of solar energy by wavelengths for various months of the year.

TABLE 5. PERCENTAGE DISTRIBUTION OF ENERGY IN SOLAR RADIATION BY WAVELENGTHS, NOON

Month	Ultra-violet, $0.295-$ 0.40μ	Violet, $0.40-$ 0.47μ	Blue-green, $0.47-$ 0.56μ	Yellow, $0.56-$ 0.63μ	Red, $0.63-$ 0.76μ	Infrared, $> 0.76\mu$	Total radiation, g cal cm^{-2} min^{-1}
March.........	0.6	10.0	16.1	11.7	17.9	43.6	1.49
June..........	1.0	11.4	16.7	11.9	17.7	41.2	1.45
September.....	0.8	10.2	16.4	11.8	17.9	42.9	1.45
December......	0.2	8.7	14.8	11.7	17.1	48.5	1.35

Thus about half the energy received from the sun is in the form of visible light, but a very considerable fraction, over 40 per cent, is in the infrared region of the spectrum.

Beer's Law. The relation between the solar constant and the intensity of the radiation actually received at the earth's surface is given by Beer's law. If $I_0 q$ be the intensity after transmission through a layer of

unit thickness, the intensity after transmission through a similar layer
m units thick is

$$I = I_0 q^m$$

The quantity q is called the *transmission coefficient*. The introduction of
the *extinction coefficient* a defined by the equation

$$a = -\ln q \tag{5.6}$$

gives Beer's law

$$I = I_0 \exp(-am) \tag{5.7}$$

The air mass through which the beam passes must be taken relative to
some fixed standard, and the usual convention is that $m = 1$ when the
sun is in the zenith and the point of observation is at sea level. For
other solar elevations m is proportional to the secant of the zenith
distance.

Beer's law is strictly valid only for a monochromatic beam; for radiation covering a wide range of wavelengths, the extinction coefficient
decreases with increasing air mass. The extinction coefficient may be
expressed in the form

$$a = a_g + s a_s + w a_w$$

where a_g is the scattering coefficient for the air molecules, a_s that for
dry particles, and a_w the absorption coefficient for water vapor; w and s
denote the relative water-vapor and dust contents, respectively.

The value of a_g is given by Rayleigh's well-known expression

$$a_g = \frac{32\pi^3(n-1)^2}{3N\lambda^4}$$

where N is the Loschmidt number, n the refractive index for dry air,
and λ the wavelength. This formula may also be applied to air containing discrete particles, provided that these have diameters less than
the wavelength of the incident light.

Turbidity. The amount of radiation falling on unit area of the earth's
surface depends upon a number of astronomical factors such as the solar
constant, the latitude of the place, and the time of day and year. All
of these can be allowed for by fairly simple calculations. The factor
which remains is the transparency of the atmosphere, and this is much
more troublesome. Linke has proposed to express the variation of transparency with water vapor and dust content by the introduction of the
so-called "turbidity factor" (*Trübungsfaktor*) T, which denotes the ratio
of the total (observed) extinction coefficient to that for molecular scattering alone, as calculated by Rayleigh's formula. Thus

$$T = \frac{a}{a_g} = 1 + \frac{wa_w}{a_g} + \frac{sa_s}{a_s}$$

Combining the above definition with Beer's law gives the relation

$$I_m = I_0 \exp\left(-a_g Tm\right)$$

or

$$T = \frac{2.303}{ma_g} \log \frac{I_0}{I_m}$$

An analogous quantity, the *turbidity coefficient*, has been defined by Ångström.

The turbidity factor, as might be expected, shows marked variations with time and place. There is usually a pronounced annual variation with a maximum in the summer and a minimum in the winter, but the greatest changes are those which arise from atmospheric pollution. The clear mountain air above the Zugspitze (2962 m) shows a small annual variation from $T = 1.8$ to $T = 2.1$, whereas at Kew, near London, the turbidity factor is as high as 4.1 in winter and rises to 5.1 in summer.

The Local Intensity of Solar Radiation. If parallel radiation inclined at an angle h to the horizontal has an intensity I on a surface normal to the rays, the intensity on the horizontal surface will be given by

$$I' = I \sin h$$

The intensity of the sun's radiation, for a small range of wavelengths passing through a clear atmosphere, thus varies as the sine of the sun's elevation. Expressing the elevation of the sun in terms of the declination δ and hour angle τ of the sun, and of the latitude ϕ of the place, we have

$$I' = I(\sin \delta \sin \phi + \cos \delta \cos \phi \cos \tau)$$

This simple relation, however, is distorted by the fact that the absorption of radiation by the constituents of the atmosphere depends upon the wavelength of the radiation. In terms of Beer's law, q^m is a function of λ, the wavelength. The general character of the results is that, for low elevations of the sun, the shorter waves suffer much greater loss than the long waves.

It is estimated that for ultraviolet light ($\lambda \leq 0.35\mu$) about 38 per cent reaches the ground from a zenith sun but only a negligible amount (about 0.04 per cent) is received when the elevation of the sun is 7°. The variation is much less at the red end of the spectrum.[†]

The length of the path of the sun's rays through the atmosphere is not, however, the only factor affecting the annual and diurnal variations. At Davos (1600 m) the spring radiation exceeds the autumn with the

† Hann-Sürung, "Lehrbuch der Meteorologie," 5th ed., p. 51 (Leipzig, 1937).

same solar altitude, and a midsummer falling off of the maximum radiation for the day is also manifested. On the other hand, at Naples radiation is most intense in the autumn, while Java reveals an increase in November following the dry season, June to September.† Such differences are probably associated with the increase in the dust content of the atmosphere in dry weather. These considerations show that no single law can be expected to express the magnitude and diurnal variation of solar radiation at any place and at any time. Sunshine is very much a "local" phenomenon.

Sky Radiation. The earth receives heat, not only from the direct sunbeams, but also from the short-wave radiation scattered by the air and the constituents of the atmosphere. Such diffuse radiation forms a very important source of heat for the earth's surface, particularly in the higher latitudes, where the intensity of solar radiation is considerably diminished in the winter months. In the middle latitudes King[3] and Trabert[4] estimate the diffuse radiation to be about 30 to 40 per cent of the direct solar intensity. Ångström[5] gives the figures in Table 6 for the distribution of the total radiation (sun and sky) into solar radiation and sky radiation at Stockholm (1905 to 1926).

TABLE 6. DISTRIBUTION OF INCOMING SHORT-WAVE RADIATION AT STOCKHOLM, 1905–1926, EXPRESSED AS PERCENTAGES

Radiation	Jan.	Feb.	Mar.	Apr.	May	June	July	Aug.	Sept.	Oct.	Nov.	Dec.
Solar....	37	44	57	73	77	76	81	74	66	48	23	13
Sky.....	63	56	43	27	23	24	19	26	34	52	77	87

These figures show clearly the importance of the diffuse sky radiation in the maintenance of the earth's surface temperature during the winter months.

Ångström has proposed an empirical formula to express the dependence of the sky radiation on the amount of cloud present,

$$Q_w = Q_0 \left(0.235 + \frac{0.765n}{N} \right)$$

where Q_w is the total incoming short-wave radiation during the period
Q_0 is the total radiation for cloudless skies
n is the total period of bright sunshine
N is the maximum possible period of bright sunshine
For $n = 0$ we have the case of a completely cloudy sky, when

$$Q_w = 0.235Q_0$$

† Shaw, "Manual of Meteorology," Vol. II (Cambridge, 1930).

Thus with overcast skies, incoming short-wave radiation is, on the average, about a quarter of that received on a cloudless day.

Reflection of Short-wave Radiation. Albedo. A considerable amount of short-wave radiation is diffused by reflection and scattering and is lost to space. The most effective reflecting surfaces are clouds and sheets of snow, ice, and water, but contributions arise also from surfaces of sand, soil, and vegetation.

On striking a small element of rough surface a beam of sunlight is subjected to diffuse reflection, parts of the incident energy being scattered in all directions. For an ideal rough surface, the amount reflected is independent of the direction of the primary beam, but for natural surfaces, the intensity of the reflected beam is a function of its direction and of the incidence of the impinging beam. In dealing with a large plane surface, we imagine a small horizontal test surface to be placed a short distance above it; the *albedo* of the ground (the large surface) is then defined as the ratio r/i, where i is the intensity of the radiation passing the test surface in the downward direction and r is the intensity of the upward beam, it being supposed that the surfaces do not send out any radiation of their own. In practice this condition is realized by employing an instrument which is sensitive to short-wave radiation but which is unaffected by radiation of wavelength greater than 4μ. The instrument is pointed to the sky and the ground in turn, and the readings compared.

Ångström[6] has given the results of investigation with such an instrument (the pyranometer), and other values have been obtained by Luneland[7] and Stucktey and Wegener.[8] Some values obtained by Ångström are given in Table 7.

TABLE 7. ALBEDO OF VARIOUS NATURAL SURFACES, AFTER ÅNGSTRÖM

Flat ground, grass covered	0.25–0.33
Flat ground, rock	0.12–0.15
Sand	0.18
Dry black mold	0.14
Snow	0.70–0.18

Ångström's measurements, unlike these of Stucktey and Wegener, include the near-infrared radiation present in sunlight, and from his measurements the result emerges that the reflection from the longer waves is much greater than for the total radiation, which includes the shorter waves. This conclusion may have some biological significance, for nocturnal radiation is entirely composed of long waves, and Ångström suggests that the emissive power of living plants for nocturnal radiation is small, resulting in a natural safeguard against night frosts. Ångström's measurements also show that wet ground has only about half the reflecting power of dry ground. This difference is partly due to the absorption of the red end of the spectrum in the thin water films, but the greater part of the effect arises from internal total reflection in the water films.

Clouds are very efficient reflecting surfaces; for cloud amount n Ångström gives the expression

$$\text{Albedo} = 0.70 + 0.17(1 - n)$$

showing that some 70 per cent of the incoming short-wave radiation is reflected back to space by an overcast sky. For water surfaces, despite the disturbances due to wind, Ångström concludes that the Fresnel formula for plane surfaces and unpolarized light,

$$R = \frac{1}{2}\left[\frac{\sin^2 (i - r)}{\sin^2 (i + r)} + \frac{\tan^2 (i - r)}{\tan^2 (i + r)}\right]$$

(i = angle of incidence, r = angle between the normal and the reflected beam) is satisfactory for solar elevations exceeding 15°. It follows that in this case the albedo varies considerably with the direction of the incident beam.

Depletion of Short-wave Radiation by Vegetation. Ångström[6] gives the figures in Table 8 concerning the transformation of incoming short-wave radiation by green leaves.

TABLE 8. EFFECT OF VEGETATION ON INCOMING RADIATION

	Early summer— leaves with high water content, per cent	Late, dry summer— leaves with low water content, per cent
Reflection	19	29
Absorption	55.5	38
Transmission	25.5	33

The general effect of trees on incoming radiation is shown by the following figures:

Incoming short-wave radiation	g cal cm^{-2} min^{-1}
In the open	0.99
Thin woods	0.04–0.07
Thick woods	0.007–0.01

The effect of high grass is shown by the following example:

Incoming short-wave radiation	g cal cm^{-2} min^{-1}
At top of grass 1 m high	1.08
50 cm above ground	1.04
10 cm above ground	0.28
Surface of ground	0.19

It is evident from the above figures that in regions covered with dense vegetation, the soil receives only a small fraction of the sun and sky radiation, even on a cloudless day. Much of the heat obtained by the soil in this case must be due to the downward flow of heat caused by conduction and turbulent mixing. In dealing with observations made over grassland it cannot be assumed that the surface of the earth itself is subject to the full effect of the diurnal variation of solar radiation, as measured by a recording instrument placed several feet above the surface. Neglect of this fact may lead to serious errors in the treatment of the heat distribution in the lower atmosphere.

5.3. Long-wave Radiation

In the problem of emission and absorption of radiation proceeding from the surface of the earth and its atmosphere, the part played by water present in the atmosphere, either as vapor or as liquid, is decisive. Radiation produced by matter at terrestrial temperature is entirely in the far infrared $(\lambda > 4\mu)$, and for such radiation the only atmospheric gases which need be considered are carbon dioxide and water vapor, the latter being by far the more important. The great complexity of the problem resides almost entirely in the fact that water vapor absorbs selectively over the whole spectrum. Radiation of certain wavelengths is able to pass through deep layers of the atmosphere with little or no hindrance, but radiation of other wavelengths is partially or completely absorbed and reemitted. Any detailed study of the temperature changes in the atmosphere must make use of laboratory measurements of absorption, but these need to be extended by theoretical arguments, because of the enormous path lengths involved and the fact that the absorbing gas is at variable pressure.

Band Spectra. It was early recognized that the absorption spectra of gases consisting of single atoms differed widely from those made up of polyatomic molecules, such as H_2O. The former, known as line spectra, contain clearly marked discrete lines, whereas polyatomic gases yield spectra characterized by structures of fluted appearance, known as *bands*. With instruments of high resolving power, the bands are seen to be made up of large numbers of lines.

The phenomenon of band spectra depends essentially on the fact that a polyatomic molecule may gain or lose (1) electronic energy, (2) energy of rotation, and (3) energy of vibration. Thus in a simple diatomic molecule (such as HCl) the total internal energy arises partly from the motion of the electrons, partly from the mutual vibrations of the nuclei, and partly from the rotation of the whole molecule about an axis through its center of gravity. There is virtually no interaction between these three motions, and the respective energies are "quantized," so that there are three kinds of molecular spectra, electronic, vibrational, and rotational. The theory of molecular spectra is complex and as yet only partially developed, even for such seemingly simple molecules as H_2O, and cannot be considered here. For present purposes it is sufficient to state that electronic spectra are confined almost entirely to the ultraviolet and visible ends of the spectrum, the vibrational spectra to the region 1 to 30μ, and the pure rotational spectra from 15μ upward. Thus the meteorologist is mainly interested (as far as terrestrial radiation is concerned) in the vibrational, vibrational-rotational, and rotational bands of the water-vapor spectrum.

The Water-vapor Absorption Spectrum in the Far Infrared. The water-vapor molecule is an example of what is called in spectroscopic work an *asymmetric top molecule, i.e.,* one possessing three unequal moments of inertia. The principal investigations on the infrared absorption spectrum of water vapor are those of Hettner,[9] Rubens,[10] Weber and Randall,[11] and finally (and most completely) Randall, Dennison, Ginsburg, and Weber.[12] A fairly detailed account of Hettner's results and subsequent modifications by Weber and Randall is given in the second edition of Brunt's "Physical and Dynamical Meteorology."

Hettner's original work is of considerable importance in meteorology, since it forms the basis of memorable investigations by Simpson and by Brunt. Except in regions of great opacity, Hettner employed a column of steam at 127°C; where the absorption was found to be very great, a mixture of air and steam was used. His main discoveries can be summarized as follows:

1. Absorption bands centered at 1.37, 1.84, and 2.66μ
2. A region of almost complete transparency from 3.5 to 4.5μ
3. Intense absorption in a band centered at 6.26μ
4. Virtual transparency from 8.5 to 9.5μ
5. A wide band, starting at 9.5μ and proceeding with increasing absorption to the limit of the observations at about 34μ

A particularly interesting feature of the above results is the existence of the two "windows" at 4μ and 9μ, respectively. Of these, the window at 9μ is of great importance, for, by Wien's law, radiation from a black body at 300°K is most intense at about 10μ.

The later measurements of Weber and Randall confirm the general trend of Hettner's results, but with the important difference that the coefficients of absorption are in general smaller than those given by Hettner. One important result of the later work is to widen the window around 10μ.

The only other normal constituent of the atmosphere which need be considered is carbon dioxide, which has one narrow but intense absorption band centered at about 15μ.

The broad picture presented by the above investigations is summed up by saying that the atmosphere is partly opaque and partly transparent to long-wave radiation. The most notable attempts to discuss the transference of energy by radiation in such an atmosphere are those of Simpson[13] and Elsasser,[14] which will now be considered.

Simpson's Treatment of Long-wave Radiation. Prior to Simpson's work, much of the theory of atmospheric radiation had been based upon the concept of a "gray" atmosphere, defined as one in which the emission of radiation, for all wavelengths, is some fixed fraction of black-body radiation at the same temperature. Such an assumption is very far removed from the truth when a moist atmosphere is crossed by beams of long-wave radiation, but since some simplification has to be made in all radiation problems arising in meteorology, there is at least a prima-facie case for the assumption of a gray atmosphere as a useful approximation. Simpson's analysis of the problem, however, leaves little doubt that this scheme is quite unacceptable.

The case for a gray atmosphere is considered in the first of Simpson's three memoirs. Three major difficulties arise when this hypothesis is used. First, it appears that the outgoing radiation is virtually independent of latitude, a circumstance which makes the problem of the stratosphere (the region of radiative equilibrium) in a gray atmosphere difficult on account of the variation of stratosphere temperature with latitude. Second, there is an excess of outgoing radiation over incoming. Finally, the scheme does not allow of changes in insolation, if such occur. We shall not consider here the details of this work, but it may be accepted that the completeness of the discussion excludes the assumption that water vapor radiates as a gray body from any realistic analysis.

In his second memoir Simpson starts with a discussion of the absorption coefficients of water vapor and carbon dioxide, based on the measurements of Hettner for water vapor and on Rubens and Aschkinass'[15] work on carbon dioxide. From these results Simpson gives a chart showing the absorption by air containing 0.3 mm of precipitable water and 0.06 g of carbon dioxide. Since Hettner's data are for steam at high temperatures, and in view of the fact that Fowle's measurements on water vapor under atmospheric conditions show everywhere a smaller absorption, Simpson adopted the compromise of assuming complete transparency in the region $8\frac{1}{2}$ to 11μ. Combining the water-vapor and carbon dioxide features, the essential facts concerning absorption of long waves by a column of air containing 0.3 mm of precipitable water are as follows:

1. Complete absorption from $5\frac{1}{2}$ to 7μ and from 14μ onward
2. Complete transparency below 4μ and between $8\frac{1}{2}$ and 11μ
3. Incomplete absorption from 7 to $8\frac{1}{2}\mu$ and from 11 to 14μ

The simplicity and effectiveness of Simpson's analysis are well shown by his treatment of the problem of the outgoing radiation from the middle latitudes. This is based on two statements equivalent to Kirchhoff's law:

1. A layer of gas at a uniform temperature T which completely absorbs radiation of wavelength λ will emit radiation of this wavelength exactly as if it were a black body at temperature T.

2. If a layer of gas rests on a black surface of infinite extent at temperature T, and if the temperature within the gas decreases from the surface outward, so that at its outer boundary the temperature of the gas is T_1, the outward flux of radiation of any wavelength cannot be greater than that of a black body at temperature T or less than that of a black body at temperature T_1.

The second statement simply expresses the fact that a moist atmosphere is absorbing and reemitting radiation continually, and because the temperature decreases upward, so must the radiation current.

These laws, and Simpson's interpretation of the absorption spectrum, enable the net outgoing radiation to be computed by simple planimeter measurements.† The earth's surface is regarded as a black body at 280°K, and the stratosphere temperature as 218°K, the sky being supposed clear. From the first principle there is outgoing radiation, originating in the stratosphere, from the opaque bands $5\frac{1}{2}$ to 7μ and beyond 14μ. Terrestrial radiation in the transparent band $8\frac{1}{2}$ to 11μ escapes to space. There remain the bands of incomplete absorption, 7 to $8\frac{1}{2}\mu$ and 11 to 14μ, and Simpson, from his second principle, assumes that their effect will be represented by some intermediate areas on the diagram, but as he points out, there is very little latitude allowed the draftsman, and any reasonable curve will give much the same result. The final result of the planimeter measurements is as shown in the accompanying table.

Wavelengths μ	Origin of radiation	Intensity, g cal cm^{-2} min^{-1}
$5\frac{1}{2}$–7	Stratosphere	0.003
7–$8\frac{1}{2}$	Mean of surface and stratosphere	$\frac{1}{2}(0.041 + 0.007) = 0.024$
$8\frac{1}{2}$–11	Surface	0.079
11–14	Mean of surface and stratosphere	$\frac{1}{2}(0.091 + 0.028) = 0.059$
> 14	Stratosphere	0.128
Total		0.293

The data in the table apply to clear skies; for cloudy skies the temperature of the surface of the earth must be replaced by the average temperature of the upper surface of the cloud sheet. When this is done

† For the details, see Simpson's memoir.[13] The diagram is also reproduced in Brunt, "Physical and Dynamical Meteorology," 2d ed., p. 156 (1939).

and a mean cloud amount assumed, the net outgoing radiation agrees very closely with the estimate of incoming radiation obtained from the solar constant and Aldrich's mean value of the albedo. The problem of the heat balance thus seems to be satisfactorily solved.

It should be noted that Simpson's analysis makes no direct use of the actual values of the absorption coefficients given by Hettner. All that is done is to specify the bands of transparency and opacity, and certain intermediate bands where even rough estimates will give reasonably accurate results. Only the limits of the bands have to be fixed with precision, and this circumstance adds importance to the results of later investigations, that the interval of transparency is broader than Simpson estimated.

The later work of Randall *et al.* throws some doubt on the accuracy of Simpson's deductions in another way. Their coefficients of absorption of water vapor are much smaller than those given by Hettner, with the result that considerably more water vapor is needed for complete absorption. Instead of 0.3 mm of precipitable water, an amount of the order of 1 mm appears to be necessary. Abbot has also pointed out that it is uncertain that the stratosphere contains 0.3 mm of precipitable water, so that if this figure has to be increased to allow for the lower absorption coefficient, the validity of Simpson's method becomes questionable.

Elsasser's Radiation—Flux Diagram. Laboratory measurements of water-vapor absorption, made with instruments of high resolving power subsequent to Hettner's work, have shown that the curve of absorption coefficient versus wavelength is even more complicated than had been suggested by the earlier results. In Simpson's treatment this highly irregular variation is effectively eliminated by the use of a scheme in which the absorption coefficient is deemed constant, or slowly variable, over certain wavelength intervals. Elsasser[14] has elaborated this principle and has constructed a diagram which allows the rapid estimation of radiant flux at any level (including the surface) if the humidity and temperature profiles are known. The main features of Elsasser's scheme are as follows:

1. The atmosphere is supposed transparent except for water vapor and carbon dioxide.

2. Carbon dioxide is regarded as transparent except for radiation centered about $\lambda = 15\mu$. In this band the absorption is so intense that the layer concerned may be supposed to be of negligible depth.

3. The problem of water-vapor absorption and emission is made tractable by a smoothing process resulting in the definition of a generalized absorption coefficient of relatively simple form.

Considering (3), it is convenient to write Beer's law in the form

$$I(\lambda) = I_0(\lambda) \exp (-k_\lambda u)$$

where k_λ is the absorption coefficient and u is the optical thickness, equal to the mass of absorbing matter in a vertical column of unit cross-sectional area between the levels considered.   If the total range of wavelength is divided into a number of subintervals, smoothing of the irregularities in absorption may be carried out by replacing the function $\exp(-k_\lambda u)$ by mean values over the subintervals.   In effect, this substitutes for Beer's

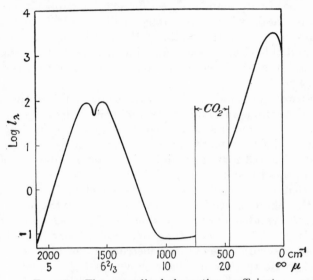

Fig. 17.   The generalized absorption coefficient.

law, which strictly is valid only for single wavelengths, a more general and less explicit relation

$$I = I_0 \tau_I(u)$$

where τ_I is a generalized transmission function, valid over a finite wavelength interval.   Elsasser shows that this function is approximately represented by

$$\tau_I = \operatorname{erfc}\,\sqrt{(\tfrac{1}{2}l_\lambda u)}$$

where l_λ is a generalized absorption coefficient, shown graphically in Fig. 17.   It is clear that much of the irregularity of the true absorption coefficient k_λ has been removed by the smoothing.   The value of Elsasser's work largely depends on the smoothing being just right—it must be severe to give a workable curve and yet not so drastic that the real character of the absorption spectrum is lost.

Absorption also depends on pressure and temperature, and these cannot be ignored a priori in view of the long path lengths involved.   However, the temperature effect need not be considered except for very accurate work. It appears reasonably certain that l_λ is proportional to the square root of the pressure, and since pressure varies throughout the column, it is necessary to introduce a corrected optical depth u', defined by

$$u' = \int \left(\frac{p}{p_s}\right)^{\frac{1}{2}} du$$

where p_s is a fixed reference pressure.

The essential details of the Elsasser chart are shown in Fig. 18. It consists of a wedge-shaped area crossed by isotherms (vertical lines) and isopleths of corrected optical depth (sloping lines), the latter intersecting at a point (off the chart) at which the absolute temperature is zero. The horizontal base of the chart is formed by the line $u' = \infty$. Carbon

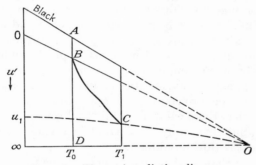

Fig. 18. Elsasser's radiation diagram.

dioxide radiation, by Elsasser's hypothesis, is a function of temperature only and is therefore expressed on the diagram by the introduction of the line marked "Black" above the moisture isopleths, such that the area between this line, $u' = 0$, and to the right of an isotherm is equal to the carbon dioxide flux at the given temperature (about 18 per cent of black-body radiation for tropospheric temperatures).

The flux of radiation from the base of a layer is very simply determined by planimeter measurement. Suppose that T_0 is the temperature at the base and T_1 the temperature at the top of the layer. These temperatures define two points, $B(u' = 0, T = T_0)$ and $C(u' = u_1, T = T_1)$, where u_1 corresponds to the top of the layer. The area $OBCO$ represents the flux of radiation from the water vapor in the layer. The flux associated with carbon dioxide is simply the area $OABO$, where A is the point on the "Black" line on the T_0 isotherm. This is in accordance with Elsasser's assumption 2. The total radiative flux from the layer is thus the area $OABCO$. The flux from a full radiator (such as the ground) is equivalent to that from a column of infinite optical depth and is thus given by an area such as $OBDO$.

For a detailed description of the construction of the chart the reader is referred to Elsasser's original papers or to the account given in the "Handbook of Meteorology," pages 301 to 303 (New York, 1945), which also contains a reproduction of the standard working chart (second edition, revised).   A critical examination of the accuracy of the Elsasser chart has been made by G. D. Robinson,[16] who compares the radiative flux computed from the chart with measurements made at Kew Observatory, England.   The results show that in general the chart overestimates atmospheric radiation, more especially when the observed intensity of radiation is low.   The errors are of the order of $+6$ per cent to $+14$ per cent when the observed radiation is between 0.3 and 0.35 g cal cm^{-2} min^{-1} but decreases to ± 3 per cent when the observed radiation is 0.4 g cal cm^{-2} min^{-1} or higher.   High values of radiation may arise from high temperatures or high humidities, but Robinson shows that the excess persists when the difference between the computed and measured radiation is plotted against radiating path length (total atmospheric moisture corrected for pressure) expressed in terms of precipitable water.   Thus the divergence between computation and observation may be explained in two ways: (1) that the emissivities assumed by Elsasser are too great for relatively low moisture content but approximately correct for greater amounts or (2) that there exists an additional source of radiation which is usually, but not invariably, associated in greater measure with the longer optical paths (low humidity).

Robinson shows that by the use of a method due to F. A. Brooks[17] it is possible to produce a corrected curve of the isothermal emissivity for unidirectional radiation of a given path length of water vapor, the contribution from CO_2 being allowed for by adding 18.5 per cent of blackbody radiation at screen temperature.   This composite curve gives results which are in better agreement with the observations than those computed from Elsasser's chart.   Robinson also states that such a process has been used to construct an empirical radiation chart, which has been tried at Kew with good results.   Essentially, the Kew chart is based on the measurements of Elsasser and Brooks, made in isothermal conditions, up to an optical path length equivalent to 0.25 cm of precipitable water, plus certain Kew measurements, reduced for longer paths by Brooks' method.   The Kew chart may thus be looked upon as a corrected and extended version of the original Elsasser chart.

Nocturnal Radiation.   In the meteorology of the lower atmosphere a reasonably accurate estimate of the loss of heat by radiation from bodies at terrestrial temperatures is essential.   It is a matter of common observation that severe ground frosts can occur on clear nights when the air temperature a few feet above the ground is well above the freezing point.   The economic importance of such low temperature is obvious; a "killing" frost may destroy the major part of a valuable crop in one night. The frost problem is considered in greater detail later; in the present section it will be shown how Simpson's method of computing the flux of long-wave radiation is capable of giving very simply the limits of such radiation.

In problems of terrestrial radiation, it is usually assumed that the surface of the earth, whether bare soil, ground covered with vegetation, a sheet of water, or a snow surface, is effectively a full radiator. It is somewhat difficult to estimate the real accuracy of this assumption. The measurement of the true surface temperature of any object is difficult, and especially so when the ''surface'' consists of a mass of vegetation. In such cases the radiation summed by the receiving instrument, and recorded as "surface radiation," actually proceeds from both soil and leaves. Since temperature changes rapidly with height in the first few centimeters above the ground, it is almost impossible to assign a definite temperature to a natural radiating surface.

Robinson,[16] in the course of the investigation referred to above, makes a point of considerable practical importance. During the experiments the temperature shown by a standard "grass-minimum" type of thermometer (with colorless liquid) lying directly on the close-cut grass was noted and compared with the radiative temperature of the lawn as recorded by the radiometers. As a result of 95 comparisons Robinson found that the surface behaved like a black body radiating at the temperature shown by the exposed thermometer, with a mean deviation of about $\pm\frac{1}{2}°C$. The readings were obtained with dry, wet, and snow-covered ground, both by day and by night, and include some with a low-altitude sun shining directly on the thermometer and the grass. If this result be accepted, it appears that it is unnecessary to investigate the actual temperature of the leaves and that a thermometer exposed in this way enables the equivalent black-body radiation to be calculated with an error not exceeding $\pm 7 \times 10^{-3}$ g cal cm^{-2} min^{-1}.

The difference between black-body radiation at the surface and the long-wave back radiation from the atmosphere is called the *net outgoing radiation* or *nocturnal radiation* of the surface. The latter term is misleading, because the net outgoing radiation is much the same by day as by night, but is easier to measure after sunset. On the black-body hypothesis, radiation from the surface is determined immediately by Stefan's formula (5.1), and the determination of nocturnal radiation thus reduces to the estimation of the intensity of downward radiation (*Gegenstrahlung*) from the atmosphere.

An essential preliminary for the application of Simpson's method is the calculation of the depths of the air masses concerned. Simpson's basic hypothesis is that a column of air containing 0.3 mm of precipitable water is capable of absorbing completely radiation of certain wavelengths. The length l of such a column is easily calculated if water vapor is treated as a perfect gas. If e be the vapor pressure in millibars, ρ_w the density of water vapor, and R_w the gas constant for water vapor ($R_w = 4.62 \times 10^3$), the equations are

$$e = R_w \rho_w T$$
$$l \rho_w = 0.03$$

whence

$$l = \frac{139T}{e} \quad \text{cm}$$

For $T = 288°\text{K}$ ($15°\text{C}$), the saturation value of e is about 17 mb, giving $l = 24$ m. If the air is unsaturated, say $e = 10$ mb (relative humidity about 60 per cent), the length of the column is increased to about 40 m. Thus on Simpson's original hypothesis, the layers of air concerned are relatively shallow near the ground. Within such layers the temperature and the water-vapor content may be represented by mean values with little error.

Simpson's method of estimating the radiation received from the atmosphere is as follows: Absorption is complete in the bands $5\frac{1}{2}$ to 7μ and for wavelengths greater than 14μ in the layer of air extending from the surface to about 50 m, the actual depth of the air mass depending on the water-vapor content. This relatively thin layer of air may be assumed to be at a uniform temperature. The surface receives from the atmosphere full black-body radiation in these bands. For wavelengths between $8\frac{1}{2}$ and 11μ the air is transparent, and hence no radiation is received by the surface from a clear sky. In the partially transparent bands, the radiation flux will depend on the water-vapor content, but it is possible to make a reasonable estimate owing to the shape of the areas in the radiation diagram. Simpson gives the results shown in Table 9 for the limits of nocturnal radiation at stations where the surface vapor pressure exceeds 1 mb.

TABLE 9. LIMITS OF NOCTURNAL RADIATION, AFTER SIMPSON

Temperature, °K	Nocturnal radiation (g cal cm^{-2} min^{-1})		
	Maximum	Minimum	Mean
261	0.146	0.055	0.100
271	0.176	0.066	0.121
280	0.211	0.079	0.145
292	0.262	0.100	0.181
299	0.293	0.115	0.204

Simpson compares the figures of Table 9 with the results of observations made by W. H. Dines at Benson and shows that the results lie within the limits shown in the table. Other observations are given in Table 10.

TABLE 10. NOCTURNAL RADIATION TO CLEAR SKIES

Observer	Place	Temperature near surface, °K	Mean nocturnal radiation, g cal cm^{-2} min^{-1}	Black-body radiation, g cal cm^{-2} min^{-1}	Nocturnal radiation expressed as percentage of black-body radiation
Maurer.........	Zurich	288–291	0.128	0.568–0.592	22
Pernter..........	Sonnblock	265	0.201	0.407	49
K. Ångström.....	Upsala	273–283	0.155	0.459–0.530	34–29
Lo Surdo........	Naples	293–303	0.182	0.609–0.696	29–26
A. Ångström.....	Algeria	293	0.174	0.609	29

So far the discussion has been limited to clear skies. A cloud layer may be regarded as a black body at the temperature of its lower surface, from which the surface will receive radiation in the transparent bands. Low clouds may thus be expected to be very effective in preventing loss of heat by the surface, and in certain cases, where a temperature inversion exists, the surface will actually receive from the atmosphere more radiation than its emits.

In general terms, the situation on a clear night is that the resultant outward flow of energy is about one-third of black-body radiation at the air temperature when the vapor pressure is in the region of 10 mb. If the ground be cooled about 5°C below air temperature, the loss is reduced to about 25 per cent of black-body radiation. As a rough average, this means that the surface of the earth loses between 0.1 and 0.2 g cal cm^{-2} min^{-1}, or a total of the order of 10^2 g cal cm^{-2} during a clear night of low wind ("radiation night"). Such a loss is greatly reduced by low, thick cloud but is hardly affected by thin, high cloud. Brunt[18] concludes that, on the average, the net loss of heat from the ground is only about one-seventh of that observed with clear skies. Ångström[19] has proposed an empirical formula relating the ratio of the loss of radiation when n tenths of the sky are covered by cloud, R_n, to that which would be observed in the same conditions of temperature and humidity with a clear sky, R_0, namely,

$$\frac{R_n}{R_0} = 1 - 0.09n$$

but, as Brunt remarks, this must be of limited application since it does not differentiate between the highly effective low, thick clouds and ineffective high, thin clouds.

The effect of dust particles in reducing long-wave radiative loss is less clear. Veryard[20] has recorded the fact that occasions when the night minimum temperature remained unexpectedly high at Peshawar, India, were often marked by heavy dust haze; Robinson[16] considers that suspended particles may affect downward radiation by a few per cent, but the general opinion appears to be that the effect is not of the first order for most localities. The question may be of importance in the problem of frost protection by smoke clouds.

5.4. Prediction of Night Minimum Temperatures

The precise determination of the rate of loss of heat by the surface of the earth during the night is a matter of considerable economic importance. The connection with frost damage is obvious, but the problem also appears in the field of synoptic meteorology, because of the formation of "radiation fog." It is thus not surprising that many attempts have been made to find some simple rule which would facilitate the forecasting of night minimum temperatures. In the main such relations are empirical; a few formulas have considerable theoretical foundation but are not necessarily more successful. A full discussion of the problem is outside the scope of this book, and attention will be directed here only to those aspects which bear on the micrometeorology of the lower atmosphere.

Formulas for Nocturnal Radiation with Clear Skies. From the discussion of the previous sections it is obvious that low night minimum temperatures are likely to be found with (1) relatively dry air; (2) clear skies or only high cloud; (3) low wind or calms. The net outgoing radiation with clear skies is mainly the difference between that of a full radiator (the surface) to space and the radiation from water vapor in the lower air layers, and is usually about one-third of the surface radiation. This suggests the possibility of devising an approximate expression for the downward radiation R in the form

$$R = f(e)(\sigma T^4) \tag{5.8}$$

where $f(e)$ is some function of the vapor pressure e in the lower atmosphere and T is the "surface" temperature. Two such formulas have gained prominence:

1. Ångström:[21]

$$f(e) = A - B10^{-\gamma e} \qquad (A,B,\gamma \text{ constants}) \tag{5.9}$$

2. Brunt:[22]

$$f(e) = a + b \sqrt{e} \qquad (a,b \text{ constants}) \qquad (5.10)$$

Neither expression compares in accuracy with individual estimates made with the aid of a radiation-flux chart and accurately determined profiles of humidity and temperature, and it would be unreasonable to expect formulas of this type to do so. Both the Ångström and Brunt expressions are statistical summaries of the results of series of observations. For any one series, it is possible to find values of the constants which yield a high correlation between formulas and measurement, but there is usually considerable scatter of individual points about the theoretical line, and the "constants" differ from series to series and from place to place. Mean values are

Ångström:

$$A = 0.25, \qquad B = 0.32, \qquad \gamma = 0.052$$

Brunt:

$$a = 0.44, \qquad b = 0.080$$

when the vapor pressure e is measured in millibars.

There is some theoretical justification for both equations.† Neither expression takes into account radiation from CO_2, and both formulas are unreliable for very small values of e. The expressions are noticeable for the implications that the downward radiation at any given locality is largely determined by surface conditions (temperature and water-vapor content) and that a considerable part of the radiation must originate in sources other than water vapor. Robinson,[16] who took both water vapor and CO_2 radiation into account, also found that up to 8 per cent of black-body radiation at tropospheric temperatures remained to be accounted for. The origin of the additional radiation is still not settled.

Brunt's Parabolic Formula for Nocturnal Surface Temperatures. Nocturnal radiation on a clear night depends on the temperature of the surface (a full radiator) and on the temperature and water-vapor content of the adjacent air layers. The radiative flux is thus independent of the nature of the lower boundary, but the temperature which the surface attains on a clear, calm night must involve the flow of heat from layers beneath the surface and thus depends, *inter alia*, on the conductivity of the material which forms the lower boundary. This may be soil, soil covered with vegetation, rock, sand, water, snow, or ice, with very different thermal constants; in addition, the conductivity of soil is very dependent on its water content. The fall of temperature on a clear, calm night is thus likely to be mainly determined by two factors, the humidity of the air and the nature and state of the surface.

† See Brunt, *op. cit.*, p. 137.

Brunt[18] has given a theoretical analysis of the variation of surface temperature on a clear, calm night which brings out the precise effect of these factors. The absolute humidity of the lower atmosphere, expressed either by the vapor density or by the vapor pressure (Chap. 1), usually shows only small changes throughout the night.† The change in temperature is a small fraction of the *absolute* temperature of the surface, and hence R_N, the net outgoing radiation, given by

$$R_N = \sigma T^4 - \sigma T^4 (a + b \sqrt{e}) \tag{5.11}$$

(T = surface temperature in degrees Kelvin), as a first approximation, may be assumed constant during a clear night. Heating of the surface by conduction from the air or by condensation of water vapor is neglected. The validity of these assumptions is considered later.

The essential feature of Brunt's analysis is that, with these simplifications, the atmosphere is effectively eliminated from the argument, the surface temperature being determined by heat transfer in the upper layers of the ground. The mathematical formulation of the problem requires, in addition, an initial condition. The condition adopted by Brunt is that at the zero of time (say, sunset) the layers of soil considered are at uniform temperature $[T(z,t) = T_0 = $ constant, at $t = 0]$, so that temperature has to be determined in a semiinfinite solid, initially at fixed temperature, having a constant flux of heat across the surface $z = 0$. The solution of this problem is given in Eqs. (4.30) and (4.31) (page 131). In the present notation the temperature of the surface is

$$T(0,t) = T_0 - \frac{2R_N}{\rho_1 c_1 \kappa_1^{\frac{1}{2}}} \left(\frac{t}{\pi}\right)^{\frac{1}{2}} \tag{5.12}$$

where ρ_1, c_1, and κ_1 are the density, specific heat, and thermometric conductivity, respectively, of the upper layers of the ground.

Brunt has compared this expression with observations by Johnson on the fall of air temperature near the ground during clear nights in Southern England. In summer, when the ground was dry, the agreement was good, the predicted decrease of temperature being 11°C compared with an observed fall of 9°C. For winter conditions the value of $\rho_1 c_1 \kappa_1^{\frac{1}{2}}$ has to be increased fivefold to allow for the increased water content of the soil, and with this value the predicted fall was 3.3°C, compared with 2.9°C observed. For conditions at Ismailia, Egypt, Flower[23] found excellent agreement between the formula and observations in winter but a significant discrepancy in summer. Thus, on the whole, Brunt's formula is in reasonable accord with the facts, but it should be noted

† The relative humidity, of course, exhibits considerable changes throughout a period of 24 hr; very roughly, the diurnal variation of relative humidity is the "mirror image" of the diurnal curve of temperature.

that in each case the comparison is with screen minima (4 ft above ground) and not with true surface temperatures. The drop in temperature may have been somewhat greater at ground level, but there is no precise information on this point.

Extensions of Brunt's Formula. The energy balance at the surface of the earth may be put concisely in the form

$$-\kappa_1\rho_1 c_1 \left(\frac{\partial T}{\partial z}\right)_0 = R_N - A - C \qquad (5.13)$$

expressing the fact that conduction of heat into the ground is balanced by the net radiative flux R_N, the conduction flux per unit area from the air, either molecular or turbulent, A, and the heat flux C arising from condensation or evaporation of water at the surface; A and C are positive when the flux is toward the surface. In Brunt's analysis A and C are neglected, and R_N is supposed to be a constant whose value is chiefly determined by the average state (temperature and water-vapor content) of the lowest layers of the atmosphere throughout the night. In later work some of these conditions have been relaxed. Phillipps[24] and Jaeger[25] have both considered the problem when R_N is constant, $C = 0$, but $A > 0$, that is, when there is an additional transfer of heat by conduction from the air to the ground. Groen[26] has dealt with the problem when $A = C = 0$ but R_N is a function of time, for an initial isothermal state of the ground and also for a variable initial ground temperature.

If heat transfer in the air is entirely due to molecular processes, the problem considered by Phillipps and Jaeger is that of finding the temperature of the surface separating two media of different conductivities, with a given initial condition, and is thus easily solved by classical methods. The result is that Brunt's solution is modified by the substitution of $(\rho_1 c_1 \kappa_1^{\frac{1}{2}} + \rho c_p \kappa^{\frac{1}{2}})$ for $\rho_1 c_1 \kappa_1^{\frac{1}{2}}$, where ρ, c_p, and κ refer to the air. A representative value for dry soil is $\rho_1 c_1 \kappa_1^{\frac{1}{2}} = 4 \times 10^{-2}$ in cgs units; for air, taking $\kappa = 0.2$ cm^2 sec^{-1}, the value of $\rho c_p \kappa^{\frac{1}{2}}$ is about 10^{-4} in the same units. Thus, in general, the inclusion of a term representing heat transfer from stagnant air near the ground makes little difference to Brunt's result.

When a wind is blowing, the possibility of enhanced conduction owing to eddy motion arises. This problem has been considered by Jaeger,[25] who identifies the eddy conductivity of the air with the eddy viscosity (a doubtful procedure; see Chap. 6), the transfer coefficient being assumed to vary as a constant power of height above the ground. The problem is again one of media of different conductivities, but rendered more difficult because the equation of conduction of heat in the air now has the form

$$\frac{\partial T}{\partial t} = \frac{\partial}{\partial z}\left(az^p \frac{\partial T}{\partial z}\right) \qquad p > 0$$

while the temperature in the soil satisfies the Fickian equation. Jaeger's solution, obtained concisely by the method of the Laplace transform, is complicated, consisting of a term in $t^{\frac{1}{2}}$ (as in Brunt's solution), together with an infinite series of terms involving other powers of the time. The difficulty of finding reliable values of the parameters expressing the eddy conduction of heat in an unsteady air stream of varying degree of turbulence probably makes this expression of little practical value in the problem of forecasting night temperatures.

In Groen's analysis, attention is focused on the term R_N, A and C being neglected. Writing

$$R_N = \sigma T^4 - R' \tag{5.14}$$

where R' is back radiation from the atmosphere, Groen remarks that Brunt's hypothesis that R_N is sensibly constant during the night is too restrictive, since it implies, among other things, that the thermal structure of the lower atmosphere remains qualitatively of the same type throughout the night, which very rarely happens. From a study of radiation-flux charts of the Elsasser type in a typical case, Groen concludes that R_N may decrease from 0.15 to 0.09 g cal cm^{-2} min^{-1} in the course of a night when the surface temperature falls 12°C. This change in R_N is too large to be ignored a priori.

If R_N were known explicitly as a function of time, the solution of the problem would be that given in Eq. (4.31a). In general, such a formulation is not feasible, since the variation of R_N is intimately related to the change of surface temperature with time, the quantity which is to be determined. Groen overcomes this difficulty by considering R_N as a function of the dependent variable T, which thus enters into the boundary condition. Approximately, using the Taylor expansion,

$$R_N(T) = R_0 + (T - T_0) \frac{dR}{dT} \tag{5.15}$$

where R_0 is the value of R_N and T_0 that of T, at $t = 0$. In the subsequent analysis dR/dT is supposed constant. This amounts to ignoring any variation of R_N with changes in wind speed and water-vapor content of the air throughout the night and concentrating attention on the variation with absolute temperature only. In the example quoted, Groen finds that $dR/dT = 0.005$ g cal cm^{-2} min^{-1} deg^{-1}, corresponding to the formation of a fairly large inversion.

Introducing an auxiliary temperature $T_1 = T_0 - R/(dR/dT)$, for which R_N is zero according to Eq. (5.15), the boundary condition on $z = 0$ becomes

$$-\kappa_1 c_1 \rho_1 \left(\frac{\partial T}{\partial z}\right)_0 = \left(\frac{dR}{dT}\right)(T - T_1) \tag{5.16}$$

the initial condition, as before, being

$$T(z,0) = T_0 \qquad \text{for } z \leq 0$$

The boundary condition is thus of the "radiation" type [see Eq. (4.11)], involving an expression similar to Newton's law of cooling, and the problem is soluble by classical methods.† The temperature T at the surface is given by

$$T = T_0 + \frac{R_0}{f} \left\{ \exp\left[\frac{f^2 t}{(\rho_1 c_1)^2 \kappa_1}\right] \text{erfc} \frac{t^{\frac{1}{2}}}{\rho_1 c_1 \kappa_1^{\frac{1}{2}}} - 1 \right\} \qquad (5.17)$$

where f is written for dR/dT. On expansion this becomes

$$T = T_0 - \frac{R_0}{f}\left[\frac{2f}{\rho_1 c_1 \kappa_1^{\frac{1}{2}}}\left(\frac{t}{\pi}\right)^{\frac{1}{2}} - \left(\frac{ft^{\frac{1}{2}}}{\rho_1 c_1 \kappa_1^{\frac{1}{2}}}\right)^2 + \frac{4}{3\pi^{\frac{1}{2}}}\left(\frac{ft^{\frac{1}{2}}}{\rho_1 c_1 \kappa_1^{\frac{1}{2}}}\right)^3 - \cdots \right] \qquad (5.18)$$

Brunt's formula is obtained by putting $f = 0$, $R_N = R_0$, when all terms involving t vanish except the first. The solution may be written in a convenient nondimensional form by taking $u = R_0/f$ as the unit of temperature and $\tau = (\rho_1 c_1 \kappa_1^{\frac{1}{2}}/f)^2$ as the unit of time. Equation (5.17), in these units, becomes

$$\frac{T - T_0}{u} = \exp\left(\frac{t}{\tau}\right) \text{erfc} \sqrt{\left(\frac{t}{\tau}\right)} - 1 \qquad (5.19)$$

Figure 19, reproduced from Groen's paper, shows the comparison between Eqs. (5.12) and (5.19).

For small values of t/τ (< 0.02) the two expressions are in close agreement but diverge considerably for larger values of t and differ fundamentally as $t \to \infty$, when, according to Groen's expression, $T \to T_1$ at a rate proportional to $t^{-\frac{1}{2}}$.

The divergence shown in Fig. 19 is, however, more apparent than real. Taking Groen's values ($R_0 = 0.15$ g cal cm^{-2} min^{-1}, $dR/dT = 5 \times 10^{-3}$ g cal cm^{-2} min^{-1} deg^{-1}, $\rho_1 c_1 \kappa_1^{\frac{1}{2}} = 0.15$ cal cm^{-2} min$^{-\frac{1}{2}}$ deg^{-1}), the unit of temperature u is 30°C, and the unit

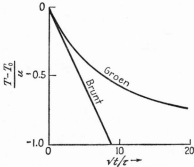

Fig. 19. Comparison of Brunt and Groen solutions for nocturnal cooling. [*J. Meteorol.* 4 (1947).]

of time τ is 100 hr. Both the temperature and time scales of the graph are thus very condensed, and the difference between the Brunt and Groen

† The details are given in Groen's papers.[26]

formulas is not likely to be large for periods of the order of a night in middle and lower latitudes. This is well illustrated in the example given by Groen, who, using the above values, calculated a temperature fall of 8°C in 9 hr. Brunt's formula for the same conditions gives a fall of 10°C. On the other hand, during a long polar night the divergence between the two expressions would be considerable, more especially because the low conductivity of snow would tend to reduce the value of κ_1.

In continuation of this work Groen considers the effects of relaxing other conditions. A solution is easily obtained in which the initial condition of an isothermal ground is replaced by

$$T(z,0) = T_0 + mz$$

i.e., a linear profile of temperature in the layers beneath the surface. This, as Groen shows, has the effect of replacing the real radiation R by an "apparent radiation" $R + \rho_1 c_1 \kappa_1 m$. The effect of conduction from the air has already been dealt with. There remains the problem of condensation, for which Groen appeals to some measurements of Franssila,[27] which show that a linear law of the type

$$C = C_0 + f'(T_0 - T)$$

holds, where $T_0 - T$ is the temperature fall during the night. Thus the principal modification introduced by the inclusion of the condensation term C is the substitution of $f + f'$ for $f(= dR/dT)$ in the formulas. In all, Groen concludes that expression (5.19) is still valid, provided that u and τ are defined by

$$u = \frac{R_0 + \rho_1 c_1 \kappa_1 m + C_0}{f + f'}, \qquad \tau = \left(\frac{1 + r}{f + f'}\right)^2 (\rho_1 c_1)^2 \kappa_1$$

where r is a quantity arising from the conductivity of the air and defined, according to the Phillipps-Jaeger solution, by

$$r = \frac{\rho c_p \kappa^{\frac{1}{2}}}{\rho_1 c_1 \kappa_1^{\frac{1}{2}}}$$

As a numerical example, Groen considers observations made by Franssila[27] in a short grass meadow on a summer night. The values of the constants are

$m = 0.125°C \text{ cm}^{-1}$ $\qquad\qquad$ $R_0 = 0.15 \text{ g cal cm}^{-2} \text{ min}^{-1}$

$f = \dfrac{dR}{dT} = 5 \times 10^{-3} \text{ g cal cm}^{-2} \text{ min}^{-1} \text{ deg}^{-1}$

$\qquad\qquad\qquad\qquad\qquad\qquad\qquad$ $\rho_1 c_1 = 0.59 \text{ g cal cm}^{-3} \text{ deg}^{-1}$

$f' = 2.5 \times 10^{-3} \text{ g cal cm}^{-2} \text{ min}^{-1} \text{ deg}^{-1}$ $\qquad$ $\kappa_1 = 3.3 \times 10^{-3} \text{ cm}^{-2} \text{ sec}^{-1}$

$r = 0.32$ $\qquad\qquad\qquad\qquad\qquad\qquad\qquad\qquad$ $C_0 = 0$

From these values it follows that in this particular example

$$u = 22°C, \qquad \tau = 37 \text{ hr}$$

Groen compares the computed curve with Franssila's measurements, taking the initial temperature to be that measured at sunset. There is close agreement throughout the whole night.

An outstanding feature of this work is the importance of the thermal constants of the surface layers in formulas of the Brunt-Groen type. The conduction of heat in soil is discussed more fully in Chap. 6, where it is shown that the relevant physical constants vary considerably with the nature and state of the surface layers, especially as regards moisture content. (Brunt has pointed out that the circumstance that the value of $\rho_1 c_1 \kappa_1^{\frac{1}{2}}$ for snow is only about one-tenth of that for dry soil must imply, on the basis of his expression, very large variations in temperature at the surface of a snow field. This is borne out by observations made in polar regions.) The dependence on soil constants seriously limits the practical application of theoretical formulas of the type discussed above, since it is improbable that accurately determined values of soil density, specific heat, and conductivity will be available to the meteorologist on all occasions. Average values of the constants are of little use in this connection because of the large changes in conductivity which are brought about by relatively small variations in water content, amount of vegetation, and so on. Groen gives some discussion of the practical use of the formulas, but at the present time the strictly mathematical approach to the problem of forecasting night minimum temperatures tends to be somewhat discredited by practical meteorologists, who more often rely upon empirical formulas with little or no theoretical basis.

Empirical Forecasting Formulas for Night Minimum Temperature. The importance of providing adequate warning of radiation fog at airfields has led to much attention being paid in routine forecasting to the adjoint problem of the prediction of night minimum temperatures. In this method of forecasting fog the meteorologist concentrates attention on the night minimum temperature and the fog point—if the former is the lower, fog is entered in the forecast together with an estimate of the time of onset, the latter necessitating some additional information on the rate at which the surface air is cooling. The initial step is the estimation of the probable night minimum temperature from observations made earlier in the period.

Relation between surface and air minima. Pick and Paton,[28] and later Pick,[29] have studied the relation between screen minima (4 ft above ground) and the grass-minimum readings at Cranwell, an airfield in England. They found a fairly well defined relation of the form

$$T_a = aT_s + b$$

where T_a is the minimum temperature recorded in the screen and T_s the temperature recorded by an exposed grass-minimum thermometer, in degrees Fahrenheit. For "radiation nights," defined as those in which the mean cloud amount did not exceed $\frac{4}{10}$, the values of the constants were as shown in the accompanying table.

Mean wind speed at 13 m, mps	Winter		Summer	
	a	b, °F	a	b, °F
< 3.6	0.84	11	0.96	8
3.6 to 6.7	0.89	8	0.97	6.6
> 6.7	0.94	5	1.05	3.2

Such expressions must be regarded as useful general guides, the "constants" being valid only for the chosen site. In the present instance, the value of the formula resides chiefly in the fact that, according to Robinson, the reading of a freely exposed grass-minimum thermometer is almost exactly equal to the radiative temperature of the surface, regarded as a black body. Data for screen-minimum temperatures are more plentiful than any other, and empirical equations of this type are often useful in filling gaps in information.

Formulas for forecasting screen minimum temperatures. Considerable attention has been given to the problem of estimating the minimum temperature at screen level in terms of other meteorological entities measured at some previous time. Among the earlier rules is that of Kammermann, that the minimum temperature is obtained by subtracting a constant number of degrees from the wet-bulb reading at a certain time before. For clear nights Ångström concludes that such a rule is fairly successful when applied to the wet-bulb reading at sunset but that, in general, a better relation can be derived involving both the dry- and wet-bulb readings and factors depending on the cloudiness.

There are many such formulas, the entities usually considered being the dry-bulb temperature T, the wet-bulb temperature T_w, the dew point T_d, wind speed v, and cloud amount n. Some typical equations are given in the accompanying table.

Authority	Site investigated	Type of equation
Ångström[30]	Upsala, Sweden	$T_{min} = T_w(t) - aT(t) - b$
Pick[31]	Cranwell, England	$T_{min} = T_d(t) - a$
Flower and Davies[32]	Ismailia, Egypt	$T_{min} = aT(t) + bT_d(t) + c$
Peatfield[33]	Aldergrove, England	$T_{min} = aT(t) + bT_d(t)$
MacDonald[34]	Habbaniya	$T_{min} = aT(t) + bT_d(t) + c$
Boyden[35]	Various sites in British Isles	$T_{min} = \frac{1}{2}[T_w(\text{max}) + T_d(\text{max})] + c$
McKenzie	British Isles	$T_{min} = \frac{1}{2}T_w(\text{max}) + T_d(\text{max})] + f(v,n)$

In the table $T_d(t)$, etc., denotes the value of the entity at some arbitrary time t (usually 1500 or 1800 hr on the same day); $T_w(\text{max})$ and $T_d(\text{max})$ indicate the maximum values of the wet-bulb temperature and dew point, respectively, on the same day. In McKenzie's formula $f(v,n)$ is a quantity depending on wind speed and cloud amount but independent of temperature. Pick's formula is the same as Kammermann's except that the quantity a is mainly dependent on wind speed.

Forecasting of Night Frosts in Fruit-growing Areas. The damage to fruit and other crops caused by nocturnal frosts in the Pacific Coast valleys of North America has prompted detailed studies of local forecasting formulas derived by statistical procedures from the data. A collection of papers dealing with such methods is available as Supplement 16 of the *Monthly Weather Review* (1920).

The occurrence of low night minima in valleys is a complicated phenomenon, depending not only on the radiative loss of heat by the ground but also on the incidence of local drifts of cold air into the valley because of gravitational effects. The dynamics of such winds is discussed in Chap. 7, the physical process being that, on occasion, cold, and therefore dense, air slides down the valley sides to form a pool on the floor of the valley. The forecasting formulas which have been derived from the data are usually elaborations of Kammermann's rule quoted above and rely mainly on the effect of the humidity of the air in controlling the radiative loss of heat. This is only a partial aspect of the problem, and it is therefore to be expected that other important effects, such as drainage of cold air into the orchards, must be allowed for by adjustment of the constants to meet local conditions.

Most of the methods are based on the observation that if the difference between the screen-minimum temperature of the night, $T_{\min}$, and the evening dew point $T_d(t)$ is plotted against the evening relative humidity f, the points form a scatter diagram of the type illustrated in Fig. 20. It is evident that there is a fairly high correlation between the variables, and as would be anticipated on physical grounds, the difference of temperature is greatest when the air is very dry. The forecasting method advocated by Warren Smith consists in placing a mean curve through the points by means of the parabolic formula

$$T_{\min} - T_d(t) = a + bf + cf^2$$

where a, b, and c are constants which must be determined by statistical procedures (such as the method of least squares) from the data for a particular site. If temperatures are expressed in degrees Fahrenheit, a is generally of the order of 40, b about 2, and c about 0.01 but there are considerable variations from one locality to another. Kammermann's rule amounts to taking $b = c = 0$, and the extremely approximate nature of this formula can be seen by reference to Fig. 20. Another type of expression has been used by F. D. Young in California, *viz.*,

$$T_{\min} - T_d(t) = V + V' - \frac{f - a}{4}$$

where V and V' are variable quantities depending on the evening dew point and relative humidity, respectively, and a is a "constant of locality," which also depends on the state of the sky.

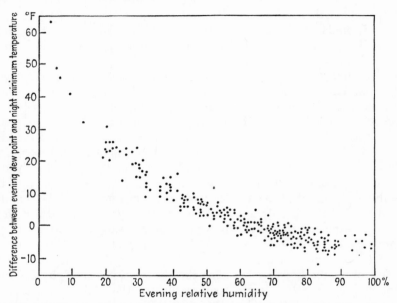

Fig. 20. Relation between night minimum temperature, evening dew point, and evening relative humidity for a station in California.

Equations of the above types are often reasonably successful when used by experienced meteorologists with considerable knowledge of local conditions. They are, however, essentially empirical, and their theoretical significance is necessarily very slight. The parabolic formula of Warren Smith amounts to a convenient statistical summary of the data given by the dot diagram, and it is possible that equally good results would be obtained by a simple freehand curve or by the use of other mathematical forms, such as exponential functions or fractional powers of the variable. In such expressions theory does little more than to provide guidance by indicating the most significant variables, and the final closure of the formulas (the determination of the constants) depends on an appeal to past experience. If the main features of the landscape remain unaltered over long periods, this procedure is probably as valuable as any other when, as at present, a complete theoretical solution is not in sight.

BIBLIOGRAPHY

1. F. BAUER and H. PHILLIPPS, Gerlands Beitr. Geophys., 45, 82 (1935); 47, 218 (1936).
2. F. MÖLLER, Gerlands Beitr. Geophys., 47, 215 (1936).
3. L. V. KING, Phil. Trans. Roy. Soc., 22, (1912).
4. W. TRABERT, Z. Meteorol., 337 (1907).
5. A. ÅNGSTRÖM, Medd. Stat. Meteor. Hydr. Anstalt 4, No. 3 (1928).
6. A. ÅNGSTRÖM, Geogr. Ann., 4, 331 (1925).
7. H. LUNELAND, Soc. Sci. Fennica, Commentations Phys.-Math, III, 5 (1926); IV, 2 (1927).
8. K. STUCKTEY and A. WEGENER, Nachr. Ges. Wiss. Göttingen, Math.-physik. Klasse, 229 (1911).
9. G. HETTNER, Ann. Physik, 55, 476 (1918).
10. H. RUBENS, Sitzber Akad. Wiss. Berlin, 167 (1916).
11. R. L. WEBER and H. M. RANDALL, Phys. Rev., 40, 835 (1932).
12. H. M. RANDALL, D. M. DENNISON, N. GINSBURG, and R. L. WEBER, Phys. Rev., 52, 160 (1937).
13. G. C. SIMPSON, Mem. Roy. Meteorol. Soc., 2, 16 (1927); 3, 21 (1928); 3, 23 (1929).
14. W. M. ELSASSER, Quart. J. Roy. Meteorol. Soc., 66 Suppl. 41 (1940), and Harvard Meteorol. Study 6 (1942).
15. H. RUBENS and E. ASCHKINASS, Ann. Physik u. Chem., 64, 584 (1898).
16. G. D. ROBINSON, Quart. J. Roy. Meteorol. Soc., 73, 127 (1947).
17. F. A. BROOKS, Inst. Papers Phys. Oceanog. Meteorol., 8, No. 2.
18. D. BRUNT, "Physical and Dynamical Meteorology," 2d ed. (1939).
19. A. ÅNGSTRÖM, Beitr. Phys. fr. Atmos., 14 (1928).
20. R. S. VERYARD, Meteorol. Mag., 71, 69 (1936).
21. A. ÅNGSTRÖM, Geogr. Ann., 2, 253 (1920).
22. D. BRUNT, Quart. J. Roy. Meteorol. Soc., 58, 389 (1932).
23. W. D. FLOWER, Geophys. Mem. 71.
24. H. PHILLIPPS, Gerlands Beitr. Geophys., 56, 229 (1940).
25. J. C. JAEGER, Quart. J. Roy. Meteorol. Soc., 71, 388 (1945).
26. P. GROEN, Koninkl. Nederland. Meteorol. Inst. de Bilt, No. 125, Ser. B, D. 1. No. 9 (1947); J. Meteorol., 4, 63 (1947).
27. M. FRANSSILA, Mitt. Meteorol. Zentral. Helsinki, No. 20 (1936).
28. W. H. PICK and J. PATON, Meteorol. Mag., 62, 260 (1927).
29. W. H. PICK, Meteorol. Mag., 63, 211 (1928).
30. A. ÅNGSTRÖM, Geogr. Ann., I–III (1920, 1921, 1923).
31. W. H. PICK, Meteorol. Mag., 63, 20 (1928).
32. W. D. FLOWER and E. LL. DAVIES, Meteorol. Mag., 69, 231 (1934).
33. W. F. PEATFIELD, Meteorol. Mag., 72, 190 (1937).
34. C. G. MACDONALD, Meteorol. Mag., 74, 234 (1939).
35. C. J. BOYDEN, Quart. J. Roy. Meteorol. Soc., 63, 383 (1937).

CHAPTER 6

THE TEMPERATURE FIELD IN THE LOWEST LAYERS OF THE ATMOSPHERE

In this chapter the detailed structure of the atmospheric temperature field is examined from the surface to a height of about 100 m. Over land, this layer is generally accessible to direct observation by fixed instruments. Over large stretches of water, data are not as easily obtained and usually are less reliable. As a result of numerous investigations, the position reached today is that the main features of this field have been accurately mapped, but the theoretical analysis of the processes of heat transfer in these layers still leaves much to be explained.

6.1. General Features

The diurnal variation of temperature in the lowest layers of the atmosphere is a commonplace feature of daily life. In clear weather the temperature profile in the first hundred meters also exhibits a marked diurnal variation whose character is best revealed by an examination of the gradient of temperature in the vertical, dT/dz. During the hours of daylight, from shortly after dawn to about an hour before sunset, temperature decreases with height, rapidly in the lowest layers and more slowly at the greater heights. At night, temperature increases with height, the gradient again being greatest in the lowest layers. The clear-weather oscillation of the temperature profile over land is clearly shown in Fig. 21, which refers to conditions over undulating pasture land at Leafield[1] (Southern England) in spring, between heights of 1.2 and 87.7 m. There is one brief period (0800 to 0900 hr) shortly after dawn, when the layer is approximately isothermal, and a similar period (1500 to 1600 hr) of small temperature gradient before sunset. Curvature of the profile is most pronounced in the lowest layer (1.2 to 12.4 m), and it is clear that between these heights, at least, the average gradient is numerically considerably greater than the adiabatic lapse rate.

In overcast conditions, the diurnal variation of the temperature profile almost entirely disappears, the gradient being small at all heights.

The above description is based mainly on records obtained in open, cultivated country in a temperate zone, but the same type of variation is found over deserts and in tropical lands. As might be expected, the magnitude of the gradients shows some variation with local conditions.

190

In England, average gradients at Porton[2,3] (chalky soil) were found to be significantly greater than those at Leafield[1] (loam) less than 100 miles away, but the extreme values of the gradient at Porton are much the same as at Ismailia, Egypt.[4] In general, daytime values of the temperature gradient in tropical countries are considerably in excess of the summer gradients in temperate climates. In hilly country or in thickly wooded areas, the temperature profiles are often very irregular because of shielding from insolation during the day and the formation of pools of cold air during the night.

Curves of the frequency of occurrence of temperature gradients of different magnitudes show that at all levels the mode gradient is not far removed from the adiabatic lapse rate. At the lowest levels the distribution is wide, but at greater heights the observations tend to be grouped closely around the mode. The curves usually show strong asymmetry, the largest gradients at all levels being associated with inversions $(dT/dz > 0)$. Superadiabatic lapse rates and inversion gradients numerically many times the adiabatic lapse rate are thus essentially persistent features of the temperature field in the first hundred meters above the ground.

Much less information is available concerning temperature profiles over the oceans, and the results must be stated less emphatically. In general, the observed gradients are smaller than those measured in the same layers over land, a result which is to be expected from the relatively small effects of incoming and outgoing radiation on the temperature of the sea surface and the large amount of vertical mixing which takes place in the surface layers. Diurnal effects have been observed over shallow, landlocked stretches of water but are difficult to detect in areas of the ocean far from land. Superadiabatic gradients certainly exist over water but are usually confined to relatively shallow layers near the surface.

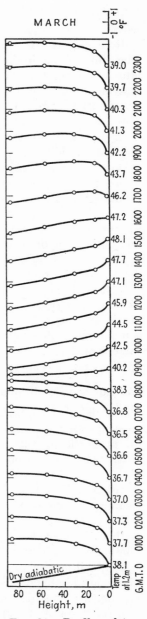

Fig. 21. Profiles of temperature between 1.2 and 87.7 m at Leafield, Southern England, in spring. (*Geophys. Mem.* 77.)

The diurnal variation of temperature is well in evidence at all heights within the first hundred meters above the ground on clear days, especially in summer, the amplitude of the variation decreasing with height. The time of maximum temperature also varies with height, becoming later with height above the ground. These facts are summed up by the statement that the diurnal variation of temperature may be regarded as a wave whose amplitude and phase vary with height as well as with season, locality, and state of sky.

In clear weather, the mean gradient of temperature in the lower layers increases rapidly during the early part of the morning but remains fairly steady for some hours around midday. The maximum value is attained at local noon. In the afternoon the gradient declines in magnitude, becoming zero some time before sunset, usually when the elevation of the sun is some 10° to 15° above the horizon in open country. In clear weather both temperature and temperature gradient show rapid random fluctuations in daytime, but these oscillations die out as the gradient approaches the adiabatic lapse rate. On completely overcast, windy days both the temperature and temperature-gradient records are very steady, with no large high-frequency oscillations. During a clear night (inversion period) the gradient in the lower layers is rarely steady but is subject to large long-period variations, usually a slow increase to a maximum value followed by a quick fall to a low value, after which there is another slow increase, and so on. On windy, overcast nights the gradient remains small and steady, as in daytime.

6.2. Surface Conditions

Any detailed study of the temperature field in the lower atmosphere must necessarily consider conditions at the surface itself, beginning with the properties of the ground, regarded as a medium for the transfer of heat. The conduction of heat through soil is a subject outside the scope of this book, and for detailed information on this matter the reader must be referred to one of the specialized treatises on the subject.† A brief résumé only will be given here.

Soil Constants. The *density* of the material forming the surface of the earth varies considerably with locality and with the state of the soil, *e.g.*, whether wet or dry, undisturbed or freshly dug, etc. When examined *in situ*, soil is seen to consist of matter in the form of rock or particles, with considerable voids, which may or may not be filled with water. The density thus depends on the specific gravity of the rocks or particles, the ratio of the volume of the voids to that of the solids, and the moisture content (defined as the ratio of the weight of water to the weight

† For example, Keen, "The Physical Properties of the Soil" (London, 1931) or Keränen.[21]

of solid matter and expressed as a percentage). Some typical values (necessarily approximate) are as follows:

	g cm^{-3}
Dry, loose loam	1
Wet loam	1.8
Clay	2
Sandy loam	1.5
Sand, loose, fine	0.7
Sand, compact, wet	1.8
Light soil containing grass roots	0.3 to 0.5

The *specific heat* of soil is likewise very variable. Wedmore[5] gives values ranging from 0.8 for clay to 0.27 for sandy loam. The specific heat also depends markedly on the water content, and, in general, wet soils have a higher specific heat than dry soils.

On general physical grounds, the *conductivity* of soil must be variable and, in particular, very dependent on water content. The latter aspect has been investigated by Patten,[6] who found that the thermal conductivity of sandy loam rises rapidly with increasing water content but that the thermometric conductivity (temperature diffusivity) increases to a maximum when the water content is about 12 per cent and then decreases. Despite these complexities, however, it is possible to state with something approaching certainty that the average thermometric conductivities of most soils lie between 10^{-2} and 10^{-3} cm^2 sec^{-1}. The seems to be true even for such very different media as clay ($\rho_1 = 1.8$ g cm^{-3}, $c_1 = 0.8$, $\kappa_1 = 2 \times 10^{-3}$ cm^2 sec^{-1}) and light soil containing grass roots ($\rho_1 = 0.3$ g cm^{-3}, $c_1 = 0.3$, $\kappa_1 = 3 \times 10^{-3}$ cm^2 sec^{-1}) (Wedmore,[5] Rider and Robinson[7]).   On the other hand, the short-period changes which can take place in the thermometric conductivity of soil at the same locality are well illustrated in the results of Callendar and McLeod,[8] who found in Canada a low value ($\kappa_1 = 1.6 \times 10^{-3}$ cm^2 sec^{-1}) for frozen soil under snow but a much higher value ($\kappa_1 = 0.3$ cm^2 sec^{-1}) when water was able to percolate into the same soil in large amounts. (The latter value probably indicates convection of heat by the downward movement of water, rather than true conduction.)

Penetration of Heat into the Ground. The above results show that in general the thermometric conductivity of soil is small, being much less than that of air at rest ($\kappa = 0.2$ cm^2 sec^{-1}). It is thus to be expected that the diurnal wave of temperature will be well in evidence at the surface but will be rapidly extinguished with depth. This is well borne out by the observations, the amplitude of the diurnal wave being negligible at depths greater than (about) 50 to 60 cm. Vujevic's[9] observations in Belgrade in July show that a diurnal surface variation of 29°C (15 to 44°C) is reduced to 11°C (19.5 to 31.5°C) at a depth of 1 cm, to 2.5°C

(22.5 to 25°C) at 20 cm, and could not be detected at 50 cm below the surface. Keränen[21] has given a tabular statement of the first three harmonics of the diurnal wave in (1) granite rocks, (2) a sandy soil, thinly covered with grass and brambles, and (3) moorland, covered with grass and moss, based on Homén's[10] observations in Finland. These show that in summer there is very little change of mean temperature with depth in granite and dry sandy soil, and also below 5 cm in the moist moor'and. The highest mean temperature was found in the granite and was some 6°C above the mean air temperature at the normal height of observation. In both sandy soil and moorland the amplitudes of the harmonics fell rapidly with increasing depth, becoming negligible at 40 cm (sandy soil) and at 20 cm (moorland). In the rock strata the decrease was much slower. These differences are primarily associated with the water content of the media; for moorland, and to a lesser extent for sand, much heat is used up in the process of evaporation.

The annual variation penetrates to much greater depths. If waves of temperature were propagated through soil strictly according to the theory of heat conduction in a solid, the depth at which the annual wave is extinguished should be $\sqrt{365} \simeq 19$ times as great as the depth to which the diurnal wave penetrates, being as the square root of the ratio of the periods (see Chap. 4). This is approximately verified by the observations.[†]

In the Northern Hemisphere, the minimum temperature of the upper layers occurs in February, and in winter and early spring there is an upward flow of heat. In March the upper layers begin to warm up, with the lower layers still cooling, but in April a downward flow of heat commences, arresting the cooling of the lower layers and raising the temperature of the soil as a whole. A maximum is reached in August, after which the upper layers begin to cool, giving in November an upward flow of heat which continues until February, when the whole cycle begins once more.

The rapid decline of the amplitude of the diurnal wave with depth means that very large temperature gradients can be found in the uppermost layers of the ground at certain times of the day. A well-known example of extremely large gradients is that given by Sinclair[11] for desert soil at Tucson, Arizona. On June 21, the maximum and minimum temperatures shown in the table on page 195 were recorded.

The temperature of the true surface can only be conjectured; its maximum value must have been in excess of 71.5°C (161°F). The matters of greatest interest to the micrometeorologist are the very large gradients (> 6°C cm^{-1}) which can exist near the surface, especially at the time of maximum surface temperature, and the enormous amplitude (56.5°C) of

[†] Keränen,[21] pp. 212–214.

the diurnal variation of temperature in the uppermost layer of soil in a desert during the season of maximum temperature.

The Tucson data furnish an extreme example of the large changes in temperature which are a normal feature of conditions very near the surface of the earth. Changes of smaller amplitude, but still large compared with temperature variations in the air at the normal height of observation, are found in the upper layers of the ground even in temperate climates. This fact is of considerable significance in biological studies.

Depth below surface, cm	Maximum temperature, °C	Time of maximum	Minimum temperature, °C	Time of minimum
0.4	71.5	1300	15.0	0400–0500
2	62.1	1400	22.0	0500
4	48.1	1530	23.5	0530
7	44.1	1630	25.2	0600

Surface Temperatures. It is difficult to define the "surface" of the earth for the purpose of temperature investigations, except when vegetation is absent. The matter of prime interest to the meteorologist is the locality of the "seat" of the temperature variations, and this may be either the ground itself or the leaves of the plants. Even when the boundary may be defined uniquivocally as in the case of bare ground, the measurement, and especially the recording, of true surface temperature is difficult.

Studies of the life history of plants and minute animal life often demand a knowledge of the amplitude of the variation of surface temperature. This involves the measurement of surface temperatures in all conditions, including those of intense insolation or strong outgoing radiation. Ideally, the method adopted should allow radiation to pass freely to and from the soil when the measurement is being made, the instrument itself being shielded from direct radiation. These conditions are not easy to satisfy in practice, particularly when autographic records are desired.

Various expedients, none of them completely satisfactory, have been adopted to overcome these difficulties. Some experimenters have placed the thermometer with the element half in air and half in soil; others have been content to place the instrument in a slight depression in the ground, with the element covered by a thin sprinkling of soil. Instantaneous measurements of surface temperature can be made with the commercial type of "surface thermometer" (usually a thermocouple embedded in a strip of springy metal), the instrument being moved rapidly from place to place and a mean value adopted as the true surface temperature. The problem has been discussed by Wild, Vujevic, Keränen, and others, but no really satisfactory method for the continuous recording of the exact temperature of the surface seems to have emerged. In view of these difficulties the results quoted below must be regarded as approximate and not necessarily mutually consistent.

The *annual variation of surface temperature* is fairly easily defined. In the Northern Hemisphere the maximum values are attained in July and August and the minimum in January and February. Variation with position is very pronounced, the greatest amplitudes being found in the lower latitudes (*e.g.*, Pavlovsk, 59°N, has an annual variation of about 19°C, whereas at Lahore, 31°N, the variation is 40°C, the ground being bare in both examples).

The matter of greatest interest to the micrometeorologist is the *diurnal variation*, and particularly the maximum temperature attained in conditions of high insolation. A useful upper limit for surface temperature has been suggested by Johnson and Davies,[15] that in the hottest areas of the globe, when the air temperature in the screen (4 ft above ground) reaches values in the neighborhood of 57°C (135°F), the surface temperature of bare soil is unlikely to exceed 93°C (200°F). There is no direct evidence of any natural surface temperature as high as this, but the example of Tucson, Arizona, quoted on page 194 makes it clear that in this locality surface temperatures must have been considerably in excess of 71.5°C, and Field[12] measured 69°C (156°F) at Agra, India. In America (Riverside, Illinois) Eaton[13] measured 51°C (124°F) at the surface of an asphalt road on a day when the air temperature over a nearby lawn did not exceed 37°C (99°F). Further examples of high surface temperatures have been given by Geiger.[14]

The nature of the material forming the surface layers exercises a marked influence. Johnson and Davies[15] investigated temperatures in layers 15 cm deep of (1) tar macadam (road-making material), (2) bare earth, (3) grass-covered soil, (4) sand, (5) rubble, and (6) bare clay. They avoided the problems inherent in the direct measurement of surface temperatures by extrapolating the observed diurnal wave at 1 cm depth to the surface, using the classical solution of the equation of conduction (Chap. 4). For conditions at Porton, Southern England, they found that the highest temperatures were reached in the tar-macadam layer, whose surface was estimated to attain 60°C (140°F) on the hottest days. The corresponding maximum for sand was 55°C (130°F) and for the grass-covered surface, 44°C (111°F).

The *amplitude of the surface diurnal variation* varies considerably with latitude, season, nature of surface, and state of sky. Sinclair's data for Tucson show that the maximum value can exceed 56.5°C in deserts.

In Finland, Homén found amplitudes of 34.5°C (sandy heath), 21.4°C (moorland), and 20.3°C (granite) during the same period in August.   For clear days and a bare or nearly bare surface, a fairly representative value for the diurnal oscillation in the season of maximum temperature outside the tropics is 25°C.   On the other hand, the diurnal variation can be reduced almost to vanishing point in a period of heavily overcast skies and high winds.

The *time of maximum surface temperature* is of interest in the theoretical analysis of heat transfer in the lower atmosphere.   Best,[3] in the course of an investigation on air temperature near the ground at Porton, Southern England, made a special study of this matter and concluded that on clear days the surface attains its maximum temperature at 1317 GMT, about 1 hr after the time of maximum solar radiation.   Schreiber's[16] measurements during a clear June day in Dresden (sandy soil) show that the curve of temperature reaches a maximum about 1300 hr but there is little variation from 1200 to 1400 hr.   The observations of Wild and Vujevic[9] also imply that the maximum surface temperature is observed about 1 hr after local noon.   The minimum temperature of the surface during clear weather is determined chiefly by the balance between outgoing radiation and conduction of heat in the soil and usually occurs shortly before dawn.   This problem has already been discussed in Chap. 5.

The maximum temperature of the surface is reached when the flow of heat into the soil exactly balances the flow outward and so depends not only on the incoming radiation but also on heat transfer in the soil and in the air above the surface.   Thus it is not surprising that the incidence of maximum temperature of the surface is some considerable time after local noon.   At night the surface usually continues to cool until the fall of temperature is checked by the appearance of solar radiation at dawn, when the curve of temperature takes an abrupt upward turn.

Effects of Surface Cover.   The above considerations apply to soil either bare or covered by sparse or low vegetation.   If the vegetation is dense or deep, the temperature of the soil surface cannot be expressed by a few simple rules.   In such cases the leaves themselves form the true meteorological surface, reducing the incoming radiation by absorption and reflection, and acting as the primary source of radiation during the night. The general effect is that the soil surface is subject to much less violent temperature oscillations than when bare.

Wild's[17] observations at Pavlovsk show that soil under grass is on the average 2 to 3°C cooler than bare soil from May to August.   Luboslawsky's[18] measurements at Leningrad are of considerable interest in that they illustrate clearly the way in which a snow cover protects the soil from extremes of cold.   The observations were made in bare sand and in a neighboring area of vegetation (mainly grass) which in winter was covered with snow. From December to March the uppermost layer of snow covered soil was about 6°C warmer than that under the bare surface, while in the summer (May to August) the soil under vegetation was from 2 to 4°C cooler than the bare sand.

The above examples illustrate the general tendency of the vegetation cover to reduce the amplitude of the temperature oscillations. For a more detailed examination, the reader is referred to the many examples given in Geiger's[14] treatise on microclimatology.

Heat Exchange in the Surface Layers of the Soil. In many problems of micrometeorology (for example, evaporation) it is necessary to evaluate as precisely as possible the various terms in the equation of heat balance. The heat flux through the surface, q_0, is given by

$$q_0 = -\kappa_1 c_1 \rho_1 \left(\frac{\partial T}{\partial z}\right)_{z=0}$$

where κ_1, c_1, and ρ_1 refer, as usual, to the soil. From a detailed study of heat transfer in sandy soil at Dresden, Schreiber[16] has given the first few terms of the solution which expresses the temperature at any time throughout the year for depths up to 2.5 m. From such an expression q_0 may be calculated, provided that κ_1, c_1, and ρ_1 are known. The results, referred to the middle day of each month, are given in the accompanying table.

Month	Jan.	Feb.	Mar.	Apr.	May	June	July	Aug.	Sept.	Oct.	Nov.	Dec.
Surface temperature, °C	−1.5	0.9	5.5	11.5	17.1	20.9	21.7	19.4	14.5	8.5	2.9	−0.7
Solar radiation, g cal cm^{-2} day^{-1}	10	34	105	236	330	408	372	308	172	69	34	7
Heat flux, g cal cm^{-2} day^{-1}	−7.8	−4.4	2.5	12.9	18.3	14.6	7.3	1.3	−5.5	−12.9	−15.6	−12.1

This example shows that on a typical day in June, when the solar radiation is at its maximum, only a small fraction (less than 4 per cent) of the incoming energy penetrates into the soil. During the winter months the amount of heat given up by the earth (negative sign) approaches and sometimes exceeds (December) that received from the sun.

A similar examination by Schreiber of the diurnal variation reveals some interesting features. The data in the accompanying table are for a clear day in June at Dresden.

Time	0	2	4	6	8	10	12	14	16	18	20	22	24
Surface temperature, °C	15.1	15.1	16.7	19.3	22.5	25.1	26.7	26.7	25.1	22.5	19.3	16.7	15.1
Heat flux, g cal cm^{-2} min^{-1}	−0.07	−0.04	0.01	0.06	0.09	0.11	0.09	0.06	0.01	−0.04	−0.07	−0.08	−0.07

According to this analysis, the flow of heat into the soil attains its maximum value (0.1 g cal cm^{-2} min^{-1}) between 0900 and 1100 hr. The outward flow of heat is greatest (0.08 g cal cm^{-2} min^{-1}) just before midnight. Schreiber expresses this variation by

$$q_0 = 0.01 + 0.097 \sin (\phi + 300°) \qquad \text{g cal cm}^{-2} \text{ min}^{-1}$$

where $\phi = 360°t/24$, t being the time in hours after midnight.

The above data reveal the general character of the heat fluxes at the surface. The actual heat exchange (*Wärmeaustausch*) has been studied by Bezold.[19] In Fig. 22 let AB and CD be the temperature profiles $T = T(z,t_1)$ and $T = T(z,t_2)$, at times t_1 and t_2, respectively. The area between these profiles and the lines $z = 0$, $z = z_1$ indicates the amount of heat stored in the soil in the period t_1 to t_2. In symbols

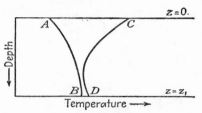

Fig. 22. Evaluation of heat exchange.

$$H = c_1\rho_1 \int_0^{z_1} [T(z,t_2) - T(z,t_1)]dz$$

In circumstances in which there are no latent heat effects (completely dry soil, or temperatures above freezing point), the annual or daily heat exchange ΔH is defined as the difference between the highest and lowest values of H in the period in question. The extended problem in which latent heat sources are considered has been treated by Keränen. Kühl[20] has dealt with the problem of the variation of heat content in a slightly different and somewhat more practical fashion by the use of the "temperature integral"

$$V = \int_0^\infty (T - \bar{T})dz$$

where $\bar{T}$ is the spatial mean temperature of the layers of soil. The heat exchange is given by

$$\Delta H = c_1\rho_1 \Delta V$$

where ΔV is the difference between the extreme values of V. When T is known as an explicit function of z and t, V (and hence ΔH) is easily determined.

Some typical daily values of ΔH, based on information collected by Keränen,[21] are shown in Table 11.

The range of ΔH is thus very large, nearly 10 to 1. Kühl has also given an extensive list of yearly values of V and ΔH for various latitudes

TABLE 11. DAILY VALUES OF THE VARIATION OF HEAT CONTENT OF THE SURFACE
LAYERS OF THE SOIL

Type of country	ΔH, g cal cm^{-2}
Woods, sandy or moorland soil	15–24
Moorland meadow	33–43
Sandy soil, bare (summer)	95–105
Sandy soil, bare (fall)	27–42
Sandy soil, grass-covered	52–67
Rock (granite)	128

and widely different types of soil. For details of this, and other data, the reader is referred to Keränen's article or to the original papers.

Heat balance. A full account of the heat balance at the surface is difficult, mainly because of the complications arising from evaporation and condensation. Pasquill[22] has made a detailed examination for a few selected occasions. This work is of considerable importance because of the care taken to obtain direct measurements of the various heat streams concerned, but the conclusions are, naturally, lacking in generality. The data of Table 12 summarize the magnitudes of the various heat fluxes found by Pasquill on a clear day in March for clay-land pasture near

TABLE 12. HEAT FLUXES FOR A CLEAR SPRING DAY, CLAY-LAND PASTURE, AFTER
PASQUILL
(In °C and g. cal cm^{-2} min^{-1})

Time, GMT	1033	1230	1530	1730	1930
Surface temperature	16.3	17.9	13.4	7.3	5.7
Solar radiation, incoming	0.715	0.770	0.336	0.031	Nil
Solar radiation, reflected	0.123	0.128	0.073	0.008	Nil
Net outward radiation (long waves)	0.191	0.196	0.153	0.116	0.109
Heat absorbed in soil	0.057	0.105	0.017	−0.048	−0.063
Heat used in evaporation	0.120	0.126	0.097	0.029	0.023
Heat removed by turbulence	0.224	0.215	−0.004	−0.074	−0.069

TABLE 13. ESTIMATES OF HEAT BALANCE AT THE SURFACE, AFTER HOMÉN
(Average fluxes over period in g cal cm^{-2} min^{-1})

Month	Period	Radiation		Heat								
				Absorbed in ground			Used in evaporation			Given to atmosphere		
		Solar	Out-going	Rock	Sandy heath	Mead-ow	Rock	Sandy heath	Mead-ow	Rock	Sandy heath	Mead-ow
Aug	0550–1770	0.72	0.18	0.30	0.13	0.07	Nil	0.12	0.35	0.24	0.29	0.13
Sept	0550–1630	0.64	0.16	0.23	0.11	0.05	Nil	0.18	0.22	0.24	0.19	0.19
Oct	0730–1500	0.41	0.10	0.18	0.12	0.03	Nil	0.06	0.08	0.13	0.13	0.20

Cambridge, England. The surface temperature was measured by a spirit thermometer lying on the ground; most of the values quoted are from direct measurement, but the turbulent flux was assessed by differences.

These results may be compared with those given by Homén[10] for a site in Finland (Table 13).

A further set of values has been given (in graphical form) by Lettau,[23] based on Haude's observations in the Gobi Desert during the Sven Hedin expedition of 1931. One such set, averaged over 6 days in June, is shown in Table 14.

TABLE 14. HEAT FLUXES IN THE GOBI DESERT, BASED ON LETTAU'S REDUCTION OF HAUDE'S OBSERVATIONS

(In °C, g cal cm^{-2} min^{-1}, and cm sec^{-1})

Time	0	2	4	6	8	10	12	14	16	18	20	22
Surface temperature	12	8	7	15	25	39	43	41	37	28	19	15
Net radiation	−0.12	−0.11	−0.08	0.07	0.32	0.56	0.64	0.53	0.28	0.01	−0.14	−0.13
Used in evaporation	0.0	0.0	0.0	0.0	0.03	0.08	0.11	0.10	0.06	0.02	0.01	0.0
Absorbed in soil	−0.07	−0.06	−0.02	0.06	0.14	0.14	0.18	0.17	0.10	−0.04	−0.09	−0.08
Removed by turbulence	−0.05	−0.05	−0.06	0.01	0.15	0.30	0.36	0.33	0.20	0.01	−0.06	−0.05
Wind at 6 m	?	?	?	400	510	580	500	430	300	260	?	?

In this summary, the term "Net radiation" includes direct and indirect incoming radiation, less that reflected from the surface and the amount returned to space as long-wave radiation. The net radiation is balanced by the sum of the heat used in evaporation, absorbed in the soil, and removed by turbulence.

These three examples show a general degree of resemblance, despite the fact that they refer to very different types of soil and climatic conditions. Although Homén's data are given as averages over many hours, it is clear that the results quoted are of the same general order as those of Pasquill and Haude.

Comparison of these measurements with laboratory data is difficult, but one result may be quoted here. The Fishenden-Saunders expression for free convection from a heated horizontal surface is

$$q = 3.6 \times 10^{-3}(\Delta T)^{\frac{4}{3}} \qquad \text{g cal cm}^{-2} \text{ min}^{-1}$$

[Eq. (4.15), page 117]. This gives

$$q = 0.15 \text{ g cal cm}^{-2} \text{ min}^{-1} \qquad \text{for } \Delta T = 20°C$$
$$= 0.2 \text{ g cal cm}^{-2} \text{ min}^{-1} \qquad \text{for } \Delta T = 25°C$$

On a clear day in summer the surface, provided it is bare or covered at the most with sparse or close-cut vegetation, may be 20 to 25°C above the air temperature at the normal height of observation (say, 1 m). Thus the data are fairly consistent with laboratory measurements of free convection.

6.3. Temperature Profiles

The account of the temperature field in the lower atmosphere (0 to 100 m) given in this section is based mainly on the observations of Johnson[2] and Best[3] at Porton, England, Johnson and Heywood[1] at Leafield, England, and Flower[4] at Ismailia, Egypt. The Porton records refer to conditions in open downland on Salisbury Plain, where the subsoil is chalk covered with a thin layer of turf. Leafield lies to the north of Salisbury Plain, in the Cotswolds, a region of hilly pasture and arable land. Ismailia may be considered to be representative of conditions at the edge of a desert.

A comprehensive review of existing information on temperature profiles near the ground in all climates is impossible on the scale of the present book. Attention is therefore confined, in the main, to features revealed by the above investigations. This must involve some loss of generality, but this is probably more than compensated by the fact that these particular studies are based on systematic continuous investigations of the detailed structure of the temperature field, carried out solely for the purposes of micrometeorology. In addition, all four investigators used virtually the same type of instrumentation, screened and aspirated electrical thermometers mounted on towers in open country. The results are thus reliable and comparable.

Magnitudes of Temperature Gradient. Best measured temperature differences over height intervals of 2.5 to 30 cm and 30 to 120 cm at the same site as that used by Johnson for investigations over the intervals 120 to 710 cm and 710 to 1710 cm. At Leafield the height intervals were 120 to 1240 cm, 1240 to 3050 cm, 3050 to 5740 cm, and 5740 to 8770 cm and at Ismailia 110 to 1620 cm, 1620 to 4640 cm, and 4640 to 6100 cm.

Figure 23 shows the diurnal variation of temperature differences at Porton for the months of January and June. Table 15 gives the mean midday temperature differences, expressed as gradients in terms of the adiabatic lapse rate Γ for heights up to 1710 cm (Porton).

TABLE 15. MEAN NOON TEMPERATURE GRADIENTS OVER GRASS AT PORTON, SOUTHERN ENGLAND, AFTER BEST

Layer, cm	Temperature gradients	
	January	June
2.5–30	100Γ	625Γ
30–120	11Γ	78Γ
120–710	2Γ	14Γ
710–1710	1Γ	5Γ

The outstanding features are the large gradients observed in the lower layers, even in winter, and the rapid fall of temperature gradient with height in the first meter or so above the ground. Superadiabatic gra-

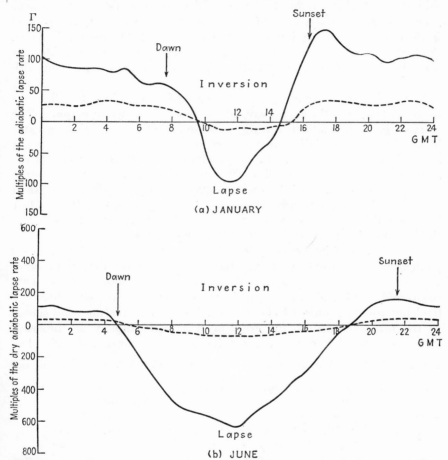

FIG. 23. Mean diurnal variation of temperature differences between heights of 2.5 and 30.5 cm (full line) and 30.5 and 120 cm (dotted line) over short grass in (a) winter and (b) summer at Porton (Southern England). The differences are shown as multiples of the dry adiabatic lapse rate. (*After Best.*)

dients must thus be regarded as permanent features of the lowest parts of the temperature field during the hours around noon.

These values are not absolute maxima, and higher gradients are frequently reached during brief periods. The highest hourly value recorded by Best during the course of his investigations was a difference of 9.7°C over the layer 2.5 to 30 cm, equivalent to a mean gradient of 1800Γ.

Best compared this result with Brunt's theoretical deduction that if I is the incoming radiation in gram calories per square centimeter per minute and e the vapor pressure in millibars, the gradient near the surface cannot exceed $100eI\Gamma$. Records of solar radiation at Kew Observatory, near London, indicate that a value of $I = 1.5$ g cal cm^{-2} min^{-1} may be attained in clear country air (maximum value at Kew, $I = 1.39$ g cal cm^{-2} min^{-1}). With this value of I and the measured value of $e = 11.7$ mb, Brunt's formula gives $(\partial T/\partial z)_{max} = 1755\Gamma$, which is in excellent agreement with observation.

In winter, the inversion predominates during a period of 24 hr. In summer, lapse conditions prevail during most of the same period. The magnitude of the gradients during the lapse periods is many times greater in summer than in winter, but the nocturnal inversion shows a somewhat smaller seasonal variation. In winter months, the greatest values of the nocturnal inversion over the layer 2.5 to 30 cm are usually found before midnight, numerically of the order of 1000Γ and generally greater than the maximum lapse rates over the same interval. In summer the greatest inversion differences usually occur after midnight but are numerically less than the maximum lapse rates over the same interval.

The effect of wind velocity on the magnitude of the temperature gradients is somewhat complex. Best's records show that in the lapse period the gradient decreases with increasing wind above 400 cm sec^{-1} (measured at 13 m above ground) but that below this velocity there is a tendency for the gradient to become smaller with decreasing wind speed. In the inversion period, the gradient falls fairly rapidly as the wind increases from calm to 200 cm sec^{-1}, but above this, increasing wind has

TABLE 16. DIURNAL VARIATION OF TEMPERATURE ON CLEAR DAYS AT PORTON AND LEAFIELD

Porton			Leafield		
Month	Height, cm	Diurnal variation, °C	Month	Height, cm	Diurnal variation, °C
December....	2.5	3.7	December....	120	3.2
	30	3.3		1240	2.2
	120	3.1		3050	1.6
	710	2.7		5740	1.2
	1710	2.4		8770	0.9
June.........	2.5	11.8	June....	120	10.8
	30	10.2		1240	8.8
	120	9.4		3050	8.1
	710	8.3		5740	7.4
	1710	7.7		8770	7.0

but little effect.   These results are not easy to explain, since it is to be expected that the enhanced mixing caused by increasing wind speed would invariably lead to a reduction of temperature gradient.

Diurnal Variation.   Table 16 gives the diurnal variation of temperature on clear days at Porton and Leafield.

The diurnal variation has also been expressed in the form of a Fourier series by Best for Porton and by Flower for Ismailia.   The results are given in Table 17.

TABLE 17. COEFFICIENTS IN THE FIRST TWO HARMONICS OF THE DIURNAL TEMPERATURE WAVE

Porton					
Month	Height, cm	c_1, °C	ϕ_1	c_2, °C	ϕ_2
December.......	2.5	1.37	244°	0.84	59°
(all days)	30	1.23	238°	0.72	55°
	120	1.16	233°	0.64	52°
	710	1.03	225°	0.54	45°
	1710	0.93	218°	0.46	40°
June............	2.5	5.78	246°	0.48	108°
(all days)	30	5.14	238°	0.29	107°
	120	4.72	235°	0.25	110°
	710	4.10	228°	0.28	107°
	1710	3.76	223°	0.31	103°
Ismailia					
December.......	110	6.40	228°	1.97	61°
(clear days)	1620	4.06	219°	1.32	42°
	4640	2.49	209°	0.98	28°
	6100	1.94	204°	0.92	27°
August..........	110	6.56	225°	1.41	50°
(clear days)	1620	5.28	219°	1.30	42°
	4640	4.82	218°	1.41	31°
	6100	4.69	219°	1.41	28°

Temperature inequality (difference from mean) $= c_1 \sin (t + \phi_1) + c_2 \sin (2t + \phi_2)$. $t =$ time from midnight, measured in degrees; $\pi/12 = 15° = 1$ hr.

These results have some interesting features.   At Porton in December, the amplitude of the second harmonic c_2 is comparable in magnitude with the amplitude of the first harmonic c_1.   Thus in winter, the diurnal temperature curve cannot be represented as a simple sine wave with much accuracy.   In summer the second harmonic is of less importance, and the diurnal temperature curve can be assumed to follow a simple sinusoidal variation throughout the whole 24 hr without serious error.　There is also a large variation in the magnitudes of the amplitudes of the harmonics from winter to summer.　In Egypt, the amplitudes of the second harmonic are always fairly large fractions of the amplitudes of the first harmonic, especially at the greater heights, and the seasonal variation is marked only above the surface layers.

The variation of the time of maximum temperature with height is of importance in the theoretical analysis.　Table 18 gives data for Porton, Leafield, and Ismailia.

TABLE 18. TIMES OF MAXIMUM TEMPERATURE AT VARIOUS HEIGHTS

Porton

Height, cm..........................	0	2.5	30	120	710	1710
Time, GMT, of maximum temperature						
Clear days in March, 1932.........	....	1403	1424	1445	1518	1533
Clear days in March, 1933.........	1317	1348	1405	1430	1445(?)	1500

Leafield

Height, cm......................	120	1240	3050	5740	8770
Time, GMT, of maximum temperature					
Clear days in December.........	1330	1342	1400	1438(?)	1514(?)
Clear days in June.............	1545	1635	1700	1714	1724

Ismailia

Height, cm...............................	110	1620	4640	6100
(Zone) time of maximum temperature				
Clear days in December.................	1447	1524	1603	1623
Clear days in August...................	1459	1522	1525	1525

6.4. Analysis of Observations of Temperature near the Surface

The data of the preceding section may be analyzed in two ways, (1) by following the lead of a theory which has undergone sufficient mathematical development to make possible detailed comparison with measurement or (2) by the investigation of empirical relations which may serve subsequently as the foundation of a rational theory.　Historically the sequence has been that indicated above; here the second approach will be followed in the first instance, leading naturally to the consideration of the various theories which have been advanced to account for the observations.

Empirical Relations.　Profiles.　The variability of the temperature field near the ground makes it difficult to envisage any simple mathematical expression for the profile which will be valid at all times, and it would be unreasonable to expect that any such expression exists, because the physical factors which predominate during the lapse period are quite different from those prevailing during inversions. A more promising approach is to isolate certain periods of the day when conditions are quasi-steady and the temperature profile may be expected to have a relatively simple form. The hours around noon constitute one such period, and Best,[3] by analyzing profiles for clear June days from 1000 to 1400 hr, found that temperature is approximately a linear function of log z (z = height) between 30 and 1710 cm. A similar law holds in the middle of the inversion period. Sheppard[24] states that in the layer 0 to 100 m temperature decreases roughly proportional to the logarithm of the height during daylight hours but gives no precise law.

The above conclusions refer to the actual temperature at different levels. Sutton,[25] from an examination of June clear-day profiles at Leafield, concluded that in the hours around noon $\partial T/\partial z + \Gamma$ decreases as $z^{-1.75}$ for z between 7 and 45 m. This statement implies that potential temperature decreases approximately as $z^{-0.75}$ between the heights considered in the period of maximum lapse rate. A rapid decrease of potential temperature in the lowest layers is implied by the observation that the temperature gradient approaches the adiabatic lapse rate as height increases, and the two laws, for actual and potential temperature, respectively, are not necessarily inconsistent. It should be noted that the expressions do not hold very near the surface.

In a recent investigation E. L. Deacon[26] states that the profiles of potential temperature in the lower layers of the atmosphere satisfy the relation

$$\frac{d\theta}{dz} = \text{constant} \cdot z^{-\delta} \tag{6.1}$$

where δ is positive and greater than unity in the lapse period and positive and numerically less than unity in the inversion period. No observations are given to support this statement, and no actual values of δ are quoted. It should be observed that for lapse periods this relation is virtually of the same type as that derived by Sutton for clear days at Leafield.

If heat and momentum were transferred in precisely the same way, the profiles of temperature and velocity would be similar in any period in which conditions are steady and in which all variations except those in the vertical are supposed negligible. The boundary conditions may be made identical by measuring all temperatures as differences from the surface temperature, and in such circumstances the equation of transfer is

$$\frac{\partial}{\partial z}\left[K(z)\,\frac{\partial \bar{E}}{\partial z}\right] = 0 \tag{6.2}$$

where E stands either for temperature or velocity. The variation of velocity with height in the surface layers is slow in the lapse periods, and the velocity profile may be represented by the logarithm, or a small power, of the height. Thus it is not surprising that the temperature profile also is expressible by the logarithm of the height, but the problem is too complex and the data too uncertain for the conclusion to be reached immediately that there is complete similarity between the transfer of heat and momentum in all conditions, and some of the evidence points to the opposite conclusion.

Diurnal variation. Logarithmic and power laws for the decrease of the amplitude of the diurnal variation with height have been given by Best[3] for clear days in March and June and for the complete months of December, March, and June. In all cases the range of temperature, R, was found to be a linear function of log z for 2.5 cm $\leq z \leq$ 1710 cm. Best also found that a power law of the type

$$R = \text{constant} \cdot z^s \tag{6.3}$$

could be fitted to the observations from $z = 2.5$ to 120 cm. The values of s vary from -0.04 to -0.07.

These laws must be regarded as entirely empirical; as yet no theory has been advanced which requires the diurnal variation to vary either as log z or as z^s. On the other hand, most theories require the phase of the diurnal wave to increase as a power of the height, and this appears to be well satisfied by most of the observations. Best found that the time of maximum temperature at Porton increases as $z^{0.19}$. This relation was found independently of any assumption regarding the time of maximum temperature at the surface, but the empirical law indicates that the surface maximum should be reached at 1318 GMT, which agrees almost exactly with the time obtained by other means, namely, 1317 GMT. The variation of time of maximum temperature with height for clear June days at Leafield[1] also conforms to a simple power law if the time of surface maximum temperature is assumed to be 1315 GMT, but the index, although of the same magnitude as that found by Best, is less, about 0.1. The Ismailia[4] observations fail to give a well-defined power law, but for clear days in December the lag of the incidence of maximum temperature behind that of the surface, assumed to be 75 min after local noon, may be approximately represented by a power of the height with an index of 0.13. The conclusion is that on clear days the phase of the diurnal wave usually increases as a small power of the height, the exponent lying between 0.1 and 0.2, and in view of the difficulty of fixing the precise time of maximum temperature from the observations (especially at the greater heights, where the temperature-time curve tends to be flat), it would be unwise to attempt to define the exponent with greater precision.

Time of zero gradient. During any period of 24 hr of clear weather, the temperature gradient changes sign twice, shortly after sunrise and before sunset. Best[3] found that the evening transition occurs at much the same time before sunset throughout the year but that the time of morning transition varies considerably from winter to summer. His results are given in Table 19.

TABLE 19. TIMES OF CHANGE OF SIGN OF $\partial T/\partial z$, AFTER BEST

Season	Morning transition, min after sunrise		Evening transition, min before sunset	
	2.5–30 cm.	30–120 cm.	2.5–30 cm.	30–120 cm.
Winter...........	91	96	115	111
Summer..........	35	78	107	98

From the Ismailia observations, Flower[4] found a much greater variability in the time of the evening transition than in that of the morning. In view of the importance of radiation cooling in the establishment of the nocturnal inversion, Flower examined the data with reference to humidity and suggested for the evening transition a relation of the form

$$\frac{T}{e}(t + av + b) = c + d \log \boldsymbol{v}$$

where t = time in minutes from sunset, v = wind speed, e = vapor pressure, a, b, c, d = constants. For a given T and v the time of zero gradient becomes later as e increases. This is to be expected, because the greater the humidity of the lower atmosphere, the smaller is the net loss of heat from the ground. There appears to be no similar relation for the morning transition.

Temperature fluctuations. There is little reliable information on the magnitude and distribution of the fluctuations T' which arise as a result of the turbulence. Schmidt[27] has given curves showing the diurnal variation of T' at a fixed level compared with simultaneous records of solar radiation and the gustiness of the wind. All three entities exhibit much the same type of variation, each reaching a maximum in the hours around noon.

Temperature fluctuations are strongly correlated with the gradient of temperature and tend to vanish as the gradient becomes small. From a single set of observations relating to a clear summer day at Leafield,

Sutton[25] found that the temperature mixing length l_H, defined by the equation

$$l_H = - \frac{T'}{(\partial T / \partial z) + \Gamma} \tag{6.4}$$

satisfied the equation

$$l_H = \text{constant} \cdot z^{1.35} \qquad 7 \text{ m} \le z \le 45 \text{ m} \tag{6.5}$$

The same investigation showed that $\partial T / \partial z + \Gamma$ decreases as $z^{-1.75}$ (see page 207) so that

$$T' = \text{constant} \cdot z^{-0.4} \tag{6.6}$$

Too great reliance should not be placed on this isolated result, especially in view of the fact that the values of T' given by Johnson and Heywood[1] include an instrumental error of uncertain magnitude which may or may not have repercussions on the deduced variation of T' with height.

Diurnal variation of $\partial T / \partial t$. Values of $\partial T / \partial t$ throughout 24 hr of clear June weather have been obtained by Sutton[25] from the Leafield data for heights from 1.2 to 87.7 m. The largest values are found in the early morning and evening and are summarized in Table 20.

TABLE 20. MAXIMUM RATES OF CHANGE OF TEMPERATURE WITH TIME, CLEAR JUNE
DAYS, AFTER SUTTON
(Times given to nearest half hour)

Height (cm)	Lapse period		Inversion period	
	Time (GMT)	$10^4 \, \partial T / \partial t,$ °C sec^{-1}	Time (GMT)	$10^4 \, \partial T / \partial t,$ °C sec^{-1}
120	0630	5.93	1930	−6.78
1240	0630	4.20	2030	−4.57
3050	0730	3.43	2030	−3.83
8770	0730	2.47	2030	−3.42

During the hours around noon, 1030 to 1330, $\partial T / \partial t$ is very nearly constant with respect to height and time. The mean value over these hours and from 1.2 to 87.7 m is

$$\frac{\partial T}{\partial t} = 1.83 \times 10^{-4} \text{ °C sec}^{-1} \qquad 1.2 \text{ m} \le z \le 87.7 \text{ m} \tag{6.7}$$

There is a tendency for $\partial T / \partial t$ to become independent of height for a brief period before midnight, the numerical value being much the same as that found in the noon period.

An interesting and well-marked feature is that $\partial T / \partial t$ becomes zero almost simultaneously at all levels in the morning, but in the evening $\partial T / \partial t$ changes sign first at the lowest level and much later at the greater heights. At dawn, the temperature rise starts at all levels up to 100 m within a short space of time, but in the evening, cooling of the atmosphere starts at the lowest level and slowly ascends to the greater heights. A similar feature has been noticed by Johnson at Porton and by Chapman in the Eiffel Tower data.

Temperature Profiles over Water. The few observations which relate to the temperature field over the sea have been summarized by P. A. Sheppard,[24] who shows that some representative mean profiles conform fairly closely to a linear variation of $T - T_0$ (T_0 = surface temperature) with log z over the interval 0 to 38 m (Wust,[28] Johnson,[29] Montgomery[30]). The general character of the field differs significantly from that over land, chiefly because of the different behavior of the surface as regards radiation. Sheppard concludes that the sign and magnitude of the temperature gradient over the sea are mainly determined by the character of the atmospheric circulation and ocean currents. The profiles are strongly influenced by the past history of the air masses, especially in the vicinity of the mainland. Diurnal effects are usually very slight compared with those over land.

6.5. Theoretical Treatment of Heat Transfer in the Lower Layers

The Classical K Theory. In Taylor's treatment of eddy conduction the basic hypothesis is that the transfer of heat across any level z is expressed by $-K_H c_p \rho \; \partial\theta/\partial z$, where θ is mean potential temperature and K_H is a virtual coefficient of conduction. In the layers near the ground this is very nearly the same as Brunt's expression for the flux

$$-K_H c_p \rho \left(\frac{\partial T}{\partial z} + \Gamma \right)$$

where T is the mean temperature at height z. If variations in density are neglected, these expressions lead to the following equations (see Sec. 4.7):

$$\frac{\partial\theta}{\partial t} = \frac{\partial}{\partial z}\left(K_H \frac{\partial\theta}{\partial z} \right) \qquad \text{(Taylor)} \qquad (6.8)$$

$$\frac{\partial T}{\partial t} = \frac{\partial}{\partial z}\left[K_H \left(\frac{\partial T}{\partial z} + \Gamma \right) \right] \qquad \text{(Brunt)} \qquad (6.9)$$

As a first approximation K_H may be supposed independent of height, in which case the above equations become

$$\frac{\partial\theta}{\partial t} = K_H \frac{\partial^2\theta}{\partial z^2} \qquad (6.10)$$

and

$$\frac{\partial T}{\partial t} = K_H \frac{\partial^2 T}{\partial z^2} \qquad (6.11)$$

respectively.

Two types of problems have been treated on this basis. These are

1. The vertical propagation of heat in an atmosphere with a given initial temperature distribution, and a constant temperature on the lower boundary

2. The propagation of the diurnal temperature wave through the atmosphere

The classical example of the first of these problems is Taylor's[31] analysis of the vertical distribution of temperature above the Grand Banks of Newfoundland. During the foggy weather typical of these seas, observations show a pronounced inversion in the lower layers, caused by the passage of warm winds over the cold sea. Mathematically this is the problem of air whose temperature profile at $t = 0$ is given by $T = T_0 - \beta z$ (β = constant) passing over a surface whose temperature is $T_1 < T_0$. The solution is given in Chap. 4 and in the present notation is

$$T(z,t) = T_0 - \beta z + (T_1 - T_0) \, \text{erfc} \, \frac{z}{\sqrt{(4K_H t)}}$$

Theoretically, the effect of the cold surface extends to infinity for all $t > 0$, but in practice it is sufficiently accurate to assume that the depth of the layer influenced by the surface is given by $z^2/4K_H t = 1$. From measurements of the height of the inversion top, together with an estimate of the time t during which the air had been moving over the cold sea, Taylor found that K_H is roughly proportional to the force of the wind and is of the order of 10^3 cm^2 sec^{-1}.

This type of investigation serves to establish the order of magnitude of the eddy conductivity and to suggest a simple dependence of K_H on wind speed but does not allow the premises of the theory to be tested adequately. A more searching test is afforded by a discussion of the propagation of the diurnal wave of temperature in clear weather.

The temperature of the surface of the earth during a spell of clear weather may be represented to any desired degree of accuracy by a finite number of terms of a Fourier series. In clear summer weather it appears that the surface diurnal variation can be closely approximated by a single sine term, but in general at least two harmonics are required. The problem is thus that of an atmosphere with a given initial condition whose boundary experiences a variation of temperature expressed by a trigonometric polynomial function of the time.

This problem has been discussed mathematically in Chap. 4. If the initial condition is that of zero temperature everywhere, the complete solution involves a transient term plus an expression of the damped-wave type. If the surface changes have been of the same type for a number of days (as in a spell of fine weather), the transient term may be eliminated by taking the origin of time to be very remote. In these circumstances, if the surface temperature be given by

$$T(0,t) = T_0 + \sum_{n=1}^{N} T_n \cos (n\omega t - \epsilon_n) \tag{6.12}$$

the required solution is

$$T(z,t) = T_0 + \sum_{n=1}^{N} T_n \exp\left(-z\sqrt{\frac{n\omega}{2K_H}}\right) \cos\left[n\omega t - \left(\epsilon_n + z\sqrt{\frac{n\omega}{2K_H}}\right)\right] \tag{6.13}$$

Applications of this solution, usually with $N = 1$ or 2, have been made by Schmidt,[27] Taylor,[32] Johnson,[2] Best,[3] and Johnson and Heywood.[1] The method generally employed has been to evaluate K_H in different layers, whose depth is usually dictated by the placing of the thermometers.

Before considering the detailed results, it is advisable to examine the premises with some care. In the first place, it has been assumed that conditions are typical of a medium which has experienced a long succession of very similar temperature waves, so that the transient term may be safely ignored. Second, the successful application of the method requires that the characteristics of the diurnal wave can be easily evaluated at the heights considered, and last, the height intervals should not be too great if any variability of K_H with height is suspected.

The first two requirements mean, in practice, that consistent results can be expected only for temperature fields measured in a spell of warm, clear weather, so that a large diurnal variation is assured. Such conditions are frequently associated with low winds or calms, and the question immediately arises whether the process of heat transfer on such days can be adequately represented by a diffusion equation or whether free convection should be considered to play an equally important part or even to predominate.

The results obtained by Best[3] (for Porton) and by Johnson and Heywood[1] (for Leafield) are typical of this type of study. Best used two harmonics (see Table 17) and deduced values of K_H by the following methods: (1) from the observed times of maximum temperature; (2) from the diurnal range of temperature; (3) from the amplitudes and phases of the two harmonics separately. His data covered groups of clear days in March and June and the whole months of December, March, and June. The methods of computation can be seen by considering a single term of the solution (6.13) corresponding to the first harmonic. This is of the form

$$T_1 \exp\left(-z\sqrt{\frac{\omega}{2K_H}}\right) \cos\left[\omega t - \left(\epsilon_1 + z\sqrt{\frac{\omega}{2K_H}}\right)\right] \tag{6.14}$$

The ratio of the amplitudes at heights z_1 and z_2 is

$$\exp\left[\sqrt{\left(\frac{\omega}{2K_H}\right)}(z_2 - z_1)\right] \tag{6.15}$$

and if t_1 and t_2 are the times of maximum temperature at heights z_1 and z_2, respectively,

$$\omega(t_2 - t_1) = (z_2 - z_1)\sqrt{\frac{\omega}{2K_H}} \tag{6.16}$$

Hence values of K_H appropriate to the height interval $z_2 - z_1$ may be calculated if the form of the diurnal wave is known at these heights, without making any assumptions concerning the exact form of the diurnal wave on $z = 0$, except that it can be represented by the basic trigonometric polynomial.

Best's results for the six methods of calculation adopted show some internal discrepancies but on the whole form a fairly consistent set. The means for all methods and selected months are given in Table 21.

TABLE 21. VALUES OF K_H DERIVED FROM ANALYSIS OF THE DIURNAL TEMPERATURE
WAVE, AFTER BEST
(In $cm^2 sec^{-1}$)

Period	2.5–30 cm	30–120 cm	120–710 cm	710–1710 cm
March, clear days	2.7	29	1310	6800
June, clear days	1.0	39	510	4100
December, all days	3.8	106	1015	4700
June, all days	1.3	48	750	4950
Mean, all estimations	2.2	43	917	4940

Results obtained by other workers using the same methods are similar in trend but show individual differences. The values given in Table 21 should be looked upon as significant in order of magnitude only.

These and other results show clearly that the assumption $K_H = $ constant is not consistent with the data, and the very rapid increase of K_H with height above ground indicates that the hypothesis of a constant virtual conductivity is unacceptable except as an extremely crude approximation. The statement frequently found in meteorological literature that the eddy conductivity of the atmosphere is of the order of 10^3 or 10^4 $cm^2 sec^{-1}$ is a dangerous oversimplification and, if applied very near the ground, is certain to give results which are very far removed from the truth.

There is a tendency to explain results such as these in terms of a "model" theory of turbulence, by interpreting the increase of K_H with height as an indication that the average "size" of eddy increases with distance from the boundary. While this is true in a certain sense, it is easily seen that such an explanation will not suffice in the present instance. The assumption that K_H is independent of height implies, for example, that the phase of the diurnal wave should increase in direct proportion to the height. No such rapid change of phase has been observed, the actual result being an increase of phase angle proportional to a very small power of the height. Thus the functional form of the solution (6.13) does not agree with the observed facts and must lead to contradictions and inconsistences when fitted to the observations.

The Leafield data have been subjected to a searching examination by Cowling and White,[33] with the object of testing the validity of the concept of virtual conductivity and especially the possibility of using K_H = constant as a first approximation. They show conclusively that methods of analysis based on this assumption, even when applied to shallow layers, must lead to inconsistent results. Cowling and White lay particular emphasis on the diurnal variation of K_H, which may be large, and in addition state that certain features of the potential temperature-height curves cannot be explained by the concept of eddy conduction as presented in the classical theories and that some other factor, possibly radiation, must play a significant part in atmospheric heat transfer.

Later Developments; K_H Variable. Best[3] has employed the mean values of K_H given in Table 21 to investigate the probable form of K_H as a function of height. The mean values satisfy an empirical law

$$K_H = \text{constant} \cdot z^p \tag{6.17}$$

with $p = 1.8$, to a satisfactory degree of accuracy. Much the same conclusion follows from the data of Homén and Rossi, analyzed by Best. Johnson and Heywood[1] also found an apparent power-law variation of K_H with height and gave the values of p shown in the accompanying table.

	6–21 m	21–72 m
Clear June days................	$p = 2.3$	$p = 1.9$
Clear December days..........	$p = 0.9$	Not determined

These results imply that, in clear, warm weather, values of K_H deduced from solution (6.13) increase upward approximately as the square of the height, but in winter, when temperature gradients are much smaller than in summer, the apparent increase of K_H is in rough proportion to the height within the lowest 20 m.

The regularity of the variation of K_H with height noted by Best and other workers suggests the desirability of finding the solution of the problem constituted by the equation of conduction and the usual boundary conditions with the constant K_H replaced by a power of the height. Taking Brunt's formulation of the eddy flux of heat, the equation to be solved is

$$\frac{\partial T}{\partial t} = \frac{\partial}{\partial z}\left[K_1 z^p \left(\frac{\partial T}{\partial z} + \Gamma\right)\right] \tag{6.18}$$

where $K_H = K_1 z^p$, K_1 = constant.   Introducing the approximate potential temperature $\theta = T + \Gamma z$, this equation reduces to

$$\frac{\partial \theta}{\partial t} = \frac{\partial}{\partial z}\left(K_1 z^p \frac{\partial \theta}{\partial z}\right) \tag{6.19}$$

which is Taylor's equation with K_H variable.

The theory of this equation has been considered by Köhler,[34] who has constructed a general solution satisfying the initial condition $\theta = f(z)$ when $t = 0$ and the boundary condition $\theta = g(t)$ when $z = 0$.   The solution for a periodic source can be derived from Köhler's expression by taking $g(t)$ to be the appropriate trigonometric function and $f(z) = 0$. The same solution will be obtained here by the method of sources.

The solution of Eq. (6.19), which represents an instantaneous plane source of heat, Q, at $t = 0$ over the plane $z = 0$, is easily found as a simple generalization of the solution of the same problem in the classical theory of conduction of heat in a solid, *viz.*,

$$\theta = \frac{Q}{2(\pi \kappa t)^{\frac{1}{2}}} \exp\left(-\frac{z^2}{4\kappa t}\right)$$

(Chap. 4).   For $K = K_1 z^p$, $p \geq 0$, the corresponding solution of the generalized equation is

$$\theta = \frac{Q}{q^{2/q} K_1^{1/q} \Gamma(1/q) t^{1/q}} \exp\left(-\frac{z^q}{q^2 K_1 t}\right)$$

where $q = 2 - p$.   This expression is valid for $0 \leq p < 2$.

The solution for a periodic source $Q_0 \sin \omega t$ is obtained by replacing Q by $Q_0 e^{\Omega t}$, where Ω is the complex frequency $\omega \sqrt{-1}$, integrating and resolving the result into real and imaginary parts.   It is assumed that the temperature wave being investigated is part of a long succession of similar waves, so that the situation is quasi-steady, with the origin of time infinitely remote.   This removes from the solution the transient term representing the effect of starting the oscillations in an atmosphere of uniform temperature (page 130).   With this proviso, the solution for the periodic source becomes

$$\theta = \text{const} \int_{-\infty}^{t} \exp\left[\Omega t' - \frac{(2/q)^2 z^q}{4K_1(t - t')} \right] \frac{dt'}{(t - t')^{1/q}}$$

If a change of variable is made by writing $t - t' = \phi/\Omega$, this becomes

$$\theta = \text{const} \cdot e^{\Omega t} \int_{0}^{\infty} \exp\left[-\phi - \frac{\Omega(2/q)^2 z^q}{4K_1\phi} \right] \frac{d\phi}{\phi^{1/q}}$$

This integral may be expressed in terms of the modified Bessel function of the second kind, $K_\nu(x)$, by using the identity†

$$K_\nu(x) = \frac{1}{2}\left(\frac{1}{2}x\right)^\nu \int_{0}^{\infty} \exp\left(-\phi - \frac{x^2}{4\phi}\right) \frac{d\phi}{\phi^{\nu+1}}$$

The required solution thus takes the form

$$\theta = \text{const} \cdot e^{\Omega t} \left[\left(\frac{\Omega}{K_1}\right)^{\frac{1}{2}} \left(\frac{2}{q}\right) z^{\frac{1}{2}q} \right]^{(q-1)/q} K_{(q-1)/q}\left[\left(\frac{\Omega}{K_1}\right)^{\frac{1}{2}} \left(\frac{2}{q}\right) z^{\frac{1}{2}q} \right] \quad (6.20)$$

So far the analysis has been formal, and it remains to be ascertained whether or not the above expression for θ can be made to satisfy the boundary conditions. These are $\theta \to 0$ as $z \to \infty$, and θ to remain finite (equal to $Q_0 e^{\Omega t}$) as $z \to 0$. For very large and very small values of z the solution is effectively

$$\theta = z^{\frac{1}{2}(q-1)} K_{(q-1)/q}(z^{\frac{1}{2}q}) = z^{\frac{1}{2}(1-p)} K_{(1-p)/(2-p)}(z^{1-\frac{1}{2}p})$$

As $z \to \infty$, $\theta \to 0$ for $0 \le p < 2$, but as $z \to 0$, the value of θ can remain finite if, and only if, $p \le 1$. Negative values of p are without physical significance in the present problem, so that the condition is effectively $0 \le p \le 1$.‡ The final solution, satisfying both boundary conditions, is

$$\theta = \frac{2Q_0 e^{i\omega t}}{\left(\dfrac{1-p}{2-p}\right)} \left[\left(\frac{i\omega}{K_1}\right)^{\frac{1}{2}} \left(\frac{2}{2-p}\right) z^{1-\frac{1}{2}p} \right]^{(1-p)/(2-p)}$$

$$\times K_{(1-p)/(2-p)}\left[\left(\frac{i\omega}{K_1}\right)^{\frac{1}{2}} \left(\frac{2}{2-p}\right) z^{1-\frac{1}{2}p} \right] \quad (6.21)$$

provided that $0 \le p \le 1$.

† See G. N. Watson, "A Treatise on the Theory of Bessel Functions," 2d ed., p. 183 (Cambridge, 1944).

‡ This restriction on p has been given by E. Knighting in *Quart. J. Mech. Applied Math.* 5 (1952). Köhler's treatment also is restricted to values of p lying between 0 and 1.

The physical meaning of this expression is easily seen by considering the form of the solution for large values of z. For large $|x|$ and $-\frac{3}{2}\pi \le \arg x \le \frac{3}{2}\pi$, the asymptotic expansion of the Bessel function is

$$K_\nu(x) \sim \left(\frac{\pi}{2x}\right)^{\frac{1}{2}} e^{-x} \left(1 - \frac{4\nu^2 - 1}{8x} + \cdots\right)$$

$$\simeq \left(\frac{\pi}{2x}\right)^{\frac{1}{2}} e^{-x}$$

if terms in $1/x$ and higher powers are neglected. For sufficiently large values of z the imaginary part of (6.21) yields

$$\theta \sim \text{const} \cdot z^{-\frac{1}{4}p} \exp\left[-\left(\frac{\omega}{2K_1}\right)^{\frac{1}{2}}\left(\frac{2}{2-p}\right)z^{1-\frac{1}{2}p}\right]$$

$$\sin\left[\omega t - \left(\frac{2}{2-p}\right)\left(\frac{\omega}{2K_1}\right)^{\frac{1}{2}}z^{1-\frac{1}{2}p}\right] \quad (6.22)$$

This expression reduces to the classical solution for $K_H = \text{constant}$ when $p = 0$. Thus at sufficiently great heights the solution is recognizable as a damped wave whose phase increases as $z^{1-\frac{1}{2}p}$. Observations show that for heights up to 100 m, the phase of the diurnal temperature wave increases as $z^{0.1}$ or $z^{0.2}$ (page 208). To secure agreement with the theoretical solution for large z necessitates taking $p = 1.8$ or 1.6, values outside the range of validity of the present solution but which agree with those suggested by the inexact method of assuming K_H to be invariable with height in a succession of shallow layers (page 215). On the other hand, if $p \le 1$, the increase of phase with height in the asymptotic form of the solution cannot be slower than $\sqrt{z}$, but all observations on the time of maximum temperature in the lower layers indicate a shift of phase much less rapid than this. It thus appears that the solution which satisfies both boundary conditions cannot be made to agree with the observations, but the analysis is not conclusive, since the neglect of the transient term has not been justified and it has not been shown that the asymptotic form of the Bessel function is valid in the range of height to which the empirical law of phase shift applies. In the problem of momentum transfer, reasonably good agreement with observation can be secured by taking the eddy viscosity to increase as z^p, $0 \le p \le 1$ but in heat transfer the position reached at the present time is that there is no unassailable evidence that a similar assumption for the eddy conductivity can provide a significantly better representation of the facts than is possible with the assumption of a constant K_H.

The case $p = 1$ is of considerable interest, since observations on wind profiles suggest a linear variation of the exchange coefficient with height.

Haurwitz[35] has made a detailed examination of this problem, using the law

$$K_H(z) = K(0) + K_1 z$$

where $K(0)$ is the conductivity on $z = 0$ and K_1 is a constant. The solution obtained by Haurwitz has the form

$$\theta = a(y) \cos [\omega t - \delta(y)] \qquad (6.23)$$

where

$$a(y) = a_0 \left[\frac{(\text{kei } y)^2 + (\text{ker } y)^2}{(\text{kei } y_0)^2 + (\text{ker } y_0)^2} \right]^{\frac{1}{2}}$$

$$\tan \delta = - \frac{\text{kei } y \ \text{ker } y_0 + \text{ker } y \ \text{kei } y_0}{\text{ker } y \ \text{ker } y_0 + \text{kei } y \ \text{kei } y_0}$$

and

$$y^2 = \frac{4}{K_1{}^2} K_H(z)$$

The functions ker y and kei y are the real and imaginary parts of the modified Bessel function of the second kind and zero order, K_0. These

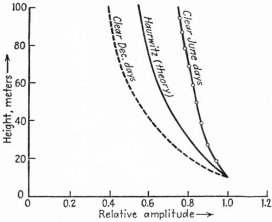

FIG. 24. Variation of amplitude of the diurnal temperature wave with height.

functions have been tabulated, so that a detailed examination of a particular case is possible. As a numerical example, Haurwitz assumes that the exchange coefficient $A = K_H \rho$ increases from 10 to 100 g cm^{-1} sec^{-1} from the surface to 100 m, so that in the present notation

$$K(0) = 8 \times 10^3 \text{ cm}^2 \text{ sec}^{-1} \qquad K_1 = 7.2 \text{ cm sec}^{-1}$$

(These values of the constants are significant only as regards order of magnitude.) Table 22 and Fig. 24 show how the amplitudes computed by Haurwitz compare with values for clear days in June and December at Leafield. For convenience, all results have been given relative to the amplitude at 10 m, the observed values being interpolated and extrapolated (from 87.7 to 100 m.) from the data of Table 16.

TABLE 22. CHANGE OF AMPLITUDE OF THE DIURNAL WAVE (a) FOR CLEAR JUNE DAYS, (b) FOR CLEAR DECEMBER DAYS, AT LEAFIELD, AND (c) COMPUTED FOR $K_H = 8.3 \times 10^3 + 0.72z$ CM^2 SEC^{-1} (HAURWITZ)

Height, m..........	0	10	25	50	75	100
Relative amplitudes						
(a) June	?	1.00	0.90	0.84	0.79	0.77
(b) December	?	1.00	0.74	0.54	0.44	0.40
(c) Theory	1.20	1.00	0.845	0.701	0.614	0.552

With these particular values of the constants, the theoretical solution lies between the two sets of observed values. In part, this is doubtless due to the choice of constants, but it is clear that the theoretical solution implies that the amplitude decreases much more rapidly than is observed in summer. There is, however, some parallelism between the theoretical curve and the winter observations at the greater heights, which suggests that these two curves might be made to approach each other by a suitable choice of constants in the definition of K_H. It is difficult to see how this could be done for the summer data.

The above comparison is qualitative rather than quantitative but suggests forcibly that if the concept of eddy conductivity is to be retained, some variation in the functional form of K_H must take place between winter and summer. This suggestion is reinforced by a comparison of the theoretical results and the observations relating to change of phase with height. In the theoretical solution, the phase increases approximately as $z^{0.6}$ over the height interval considered (the asymptotic value, for large z, is as $z^{\frac{1}{2}}$), and this cannot be made to agree with the observations for the summer month. The winter observations of time of maximum temperature are too meager and uncertain to enable a definite comparison to be made.

The relatively small change of amplitude of the diurnal wave above 10 m in summer compared with that in winter indicates that a more effective mechanism for the upward transfer of heat is at work in the summer than in the winter. The implications of the theoretical study are that such a change cannot be accounted for by a simple increase in the magnitude of K_H from winter to summer. It appears that to provide a sufficiently large upward flow of heat in these layers, it is necessary to make K_H increase with height much more rapidly in summer than in winter. This suggests that some additional form of heat transfer appears in summer, and this in turn directs attention toward the part played by buoyancy, or free convection, as opposed to heat transfer brought about by dynamic instability associated with shear of the mean motion.

Before considering in detail theories which take explicit account of buoyancy, attention must be drawn to one of the many uncertainties which beset this problem. The Leafield data indicate that there is a significant difference between the way in which heat is transferred upward in clear weather in summer and winter, but it would be difficult to draw the same conclusion from an examination of the Porton results. In the layer 2.5 to 1710 cm (Table 16, Porton), the rate of decrease of amplitude with height is not very different in December and June, as is shown by Best's empirical law [Eq. (6.3)]. Whether this is to be attributed to some variation in local conditions, such as topography, or whether the seasonal change is not so well marked in the lowest layers, is unknown, and the question can be resolved only by systematic observations at other sites.

Effects of Buoyancy on Heat Transfer. The hypothesis that the properties of the temperature field observed in clear summer weather in the layers between 10 and 100 m are mainly the result of penetrative convection has been considered by Sutton.[25] The basis of the method has already been given in Chap. 4, where it is shown that free convection may be approximately represented by the introduction of a characteristic length l_H defined by

$$l_H = - \frac{T'}{(\partial \bar{T}/\partial z) + \Gamma}$$

called the temperature mixing length, and a virtual coefficient of conduction K_H defined by

$$K_H = \text{constant} \cdot l_H{}^2 \sqrt{- \frac{g}{T} \left(\frac{\partial \bar{T}}{\partial z} + \Gamma \right)} \qquad (6.24)$$

In the subsequent analysis the "constant" in the definition of K_H is supposed to be unity. It is further supposed that the flux of heat q across a level z caused by the convection can be represented by the usual equation

$$q = -K_H c_p \rho \left(\frac{\partial \bar{T}}{\partial z} + \Gamma \right) \qquad (6.25)$$

so that the equation of conduction may be written

$$c_p \rho \frac{\partial \bar{T}}{\partial t} = - \frac{\partial q}{\partial z}$$

This gives, on integration,

$$\frac{q}{q_0} = 1 - \frac{c_p \rho}{q_0} \int_0^z \left(\frac{\partial \bar{T}}{\partial t} \right) dz$$

where q_0 is the flux of heat across $z = 0$.

In the hours around noon on a clear day in summer $\partial \bar{T}/\partial t$ is very nearly constant with height and time between 1.2 and 87.7 m, with the mean value

$$\frac{\partial \bar{T}}{\partial t} = 1.83 \times 10^{-4} \text{ °C sec}^{-1}$$

Thus for this period, and between these levels,

$$\frac{q}{q_0} = 1 - \frac{c_p \rho}{q_0} \left(\frac{\partial \bar{T}}{\partial t} \right) z$$
$$\simeq 1 - \frac{5.4 \times 10^{-8}}{q_0} z \tag{6.26}$$

taking representative values of c_p and ρ, z being measured in centimeters. The value of q_0 must be estimated, but since all that is required is the order of magnitude, no serious error can arise if q_0 is supposed to lie between 0.1 and 0.3 g cal cm^{-2} min^{-1}, a range of values supported by Tables 12 to 14.   Hence

$$\frac{q}{q_0} = 1 - 1.8 \times 10^{-5} z \tag{6.27}$$

approximately, so that the upward flux of heat on a clear summer day in Southern England is virtually independent of height between 120 and 10^4 cm.

When q is independent of height, the analysis of Chap. 4 shows that the quantities $K_H(z)$, $(\partial \bar{T}/\partial z) + \Gamma$, T' and the upward velocity $w' = \sqrt{\overline{w'^2}}$ may all be expressed as simple powers of l_H.   From the data Sutton shows that

$$l_H = \text{constant} \cdot z^{1.35} \tag{6.28}$$

Hence, using Eqs. (4.65) to (4.68), it follows that

$$w' = \text{constant} \cdot z^{0.45} \tag{6.29}$$
$$\frac{\partial \bar{T}}{\partial z} + \Gamma = \text{constant} \cdot z^{-1.8} \tag{6.30}$$
$$K_H(z) = \text{constant} \cdot z^{1.8} \tag{6.31}$$

An examination of the records shows that these deductions can be verified independently.   In the layer 7 m $< z <$ 45 m, it is found that

$$\frac{\partial \bar{T}}{\partial z} + \Gamma = \text{constant} \cdot z^{-1.75} \tag{6.32}$$

which is in close agreement with Eq. (6.30).   From this result and Eq. (6.25), using the assumed value of q_0, it follows that $K_H(z)$ varies from 10^4 to 5×10^5 cm^2 sec^{-1} between 7 and 60 m.   These estimates also agree, in order of magnitude, with those obtained from Eq. (6.24) using values of l_H deduced from the observations, together with observed values of the temperature gradient.

The analysis given above assumes that heat transfer in warm clear weather arises mainly from the motion of discrete "bubbles" of heated air rising because of buoyancy, and a mathematical model of convection, based on this concept, has been given by Sutton in the same paper. There is good evidence to show that in certain circumstances (hot surface, low wind) penetrative convection of this type actually occurs. Johnson and Heywood[1] found that, in conditions of strong insolation, the records show well-defined isolated fluctuations of temperature, occurring about once every minute, which they attribute to the formation of layers of heated air near the ground which eventually become unstable and move upward. Similar fluctuations have been found by Swinbank, using more sensitive apparatus.† Thus there seems little doubt that, in warm weather, isolated masses of heated air break away from the surface and ascend into the cooler air above. The integrated effect of such bubbles over a large horizontal area resembles that produced by a regular succession of instantaneous plane sources of heat generated at ground level, with the resulting volumes of warm air growing vertically, by entrainment of cooler air, as they rise. The typical convection eddy may thus be regarded as resembling a puff of smoke, initially of great horizontal area but relatively shallow, which ascends into the atmosphere because of buoyancy. As it rises, the eddy grows in the vertical direction and reduces its excess temperature exactly as the smoke cloud becomes attenuated, by drawing in cool air at its boundaries and, at the same time, cooling by adiabatic expansion. The flux of heat arising from buoyancy is thus caused by the bodily rise of the heated air as modified by the entrainment process, and the mean temperature field is the time mean effect of the passage of these heated masses across the various levels. Using this concept, Sutton found that the temperature distribution observed at Leafield on clear summer days could be explained by the generation of instantaneous plane sources of heat, of strength about 5×10^{-2} g cal cm^{-2}, at the rate of about four per minute, the average rate of ascent at 2 m being about 25 cm sec^{-1}.

The introduction of buoyancy into the process of atmospheric heat transfer thus serves to explain, in part, why the coefficient of eddy conduction increases more rapidly with height in summer than in winter. When the temperature of the surface of the earth is only slightly above

---

† Swinbank describes these fluctuations as follows: "On clear days there is an overriding short period fluctuation of temperature and this stands out very clearly in the traces. . . . The frequency is a few to a minute. . . . Superimposed on this main oscillation is . . . a finer structure which the present instrument and recording apparatus are not able to register adequately." (Quoted by Sutton.[25])

that of the air, as in winter, or when the wind is high, the transfer of heat must be due, almost entirely, to frictional turbulence. This is the ordinary case of forced convection. Atmospheric heat transfer should thus be regarded, in general, as a mixture of forced and free convection whose proportions vary according to the general weather situation.

This is the fundamental concept in the theory advanced by C. H. B. Priestley and W. C. Swinbank,[36] the theoretical basis of which has already been discussed briefly in Chap. 4. The heat flux is resolved into two terms, one of which originates in "mechanical turbulence" (or turbulence primarily associated with shear of the mean motion) and the other in "convective turbulence," otherwise, free convection, or motion associated with buoyancy. Thus the flux is written as

$$q = c_p\rho \left[-\overline{w'l}\left(\frac{\partial \bar{T}}{\partial z} + \Gamma\right) + \overline{w'T''} \right]$$

(see page 148). The difficulty in examining this theory resides mainly in the fact that the temperature anomaly T'' is not an observable quantity.[†] Priestley and Swinbank assume that T'' must be of the same magnitude as T', the variation of temperature at a fixed level. By adopting a model eddy of spherical shape they find that the fluctuations observed at a height of $4\frac{1}{2}$ ft in June cannot be accounted for by purely mechanical turbulence. On the other hand, by assigning reasonable magnitudes to the constituents of the various terms in the expression for the flux, they indicate that only a small correlation between w' and T'' will produce a buoyancy flux somewhat greater than the flux associated with mechanical turbulence. This conclusion is significant because the mechanical flux of heat is from regions of high to regions of low potential temperature, but the buoyancy flux is independent of the sign of $\partial\theta/\partial z$. If the whole flux be written in the form

$$q = -c_p\rho\, \overline{w'(l - l')}\left(\frac{\partial \bar{T}}{\partial z} + \Gamma\right)$$

where l' is a "buoyancy length" defined by

$$l' = \frac{T''}{(\partial \bar{T}/\partial z) + \Gamma}$$

it follows that a virtual conductivity K_H' may be defined by

$$K_H' = \overline{w'(l - l')}$$

[†] See p. 149. T'' is the difference between the temperature of the eddy and the mean temperature of the level at which the eddy originates.

Unlike the ordinary eddy conductivity, K_H' is not necessarily positive. Thus the direction of the flux of heat in the atmosphere is not necessarily determined by the sign of the gradient of potential temperature. The magnitude of K_H' will be largely determined by the amplitude of the temperature fluctuations at the level considered.

In Ertel's[37] analysis of the same problem, which preceded that of Priestley and Swinbank, the conclusion is reached that the flux of heat is mainly determined by the gradient of temperature $\partial \bar{T}/\partial z$, and not by the gradient of potential temperature $\partial \theta/\partial z$ or by the difference between the gradient of temperature and the adiabatic lapse rate $(\partial \bar{T}/\partial z) + \Gamma$. Ertel's arguments have been challenged by Prandtl, and the status of the theory is still obscure.

In general it appears that for high winds and small temperature differences, atmospheric heat transfer follows the normal laws of forced convection and is very similar to the transfer of momentum. In such conditions, buoyancy effects can be neglected without serious error. In other conditions, and especially when the wind is very low, it would be unwise, to say the least, to ignore the effects of buoyancy. The typical meteorological problem is characteristic of the transitional zone between forced and free convection and therefore difficult to analyze mathematically. For reasons which are obvious from an inspection of typical records, there has been a tendency to concentrate attention on data obtained in clear, warm weather, when the gradients are large enough to be measured accurately. This has tended inevitably to give undue weight to conditions in which buoyancy effects are prominent. The transfer of heat in conditions of high wind is a somewhat simpler problem, but one in which it is more difficult to compare theory with observation because of the generally uniform nature of the temperature field.

A further examination of the heat-transfer problem in the atmosphere requires an examination of the velocity field. This is dealt with in Chap. 7.

Radiative Transfer of Heat. The discussions given above are incomplete since no account is taken of possible effects of radiation on the distribution of temperature. This problem, one of the most difficult in meteorology, is considered at length in Brunt's "Physical and Dynamical Meteorology" (Chap. VI), and the discussion given below follows much the same lines.

The temperature of the air is affected by radiation which is absorbed or emitted by constituents of the atmosphere. From the analysis of Chap. 5 it follows that only long-wave radiation ($\lambda > 4\mu$) need be considered, since short-wave radiation passes through the lower atmosphere, when clear, with negligible absorption. Similarly, the only constituent of the atmosphere which is effective in this problem is water vapor. The difficulties of the analysis arise from three main causes: (1) the radiation is not truly parallel but is made up of beams of different intensities inclined at various angles to the earth's surface; (2) the distribution of humidity with height needs to be known very accurately; (3) the absorption coefficient for water vapor in the far infrared is a complicated function of wavelength, not expressible by any concise mathematical formula. Long-wave radiation emitted by the surface of the earth is partly absorbed by the atmosphere and partly transmitted through the various "windows" in the absorption spectrum with little loss, and in addition, the water vapor present in the air radiates on its own to any body or region of space at lower temperature.

Brunt has suggested that some of these difficulties can be overcome by assuming the beams to be vertical and adopting Simpson's method of simplifying the absorption spectrum of water vapor for long waves, the main feature of which is that a column of air containing 0.3 mm of precipitable water as vapor completely absorbs all radiation of wavelength between 5.5 and 7μ and greater than 14μ but is otherwise transparent (page 169).   For the lower atmosphere, in conditions of normal humidity, this implies complete absorption of radiation in these wavelengths by layers of air whose depth is of the order of 50 m.   By dividing the atmosphere into layers of this order of depth, Brunt shows that the radiative transfer of heat in the vertical is a simple diffusion process, conforming to the equation

$$\frac{\partial T}{\partial t} = K_R \frac{\partial^2 T}{\partial z^2}$$

where K_R is an exchange coefficient called the *radiative diffusivity*.   This equation implies that, to a first approximation, the radiative transfer of heat in the lower atmosphere resembles the conduction of heat by molecular agitation in a solid.   Brunt finds that K_R is given by

$$K_R = \frac{139T}{60\rho c_p e} \frac{\partial E}{\partial T}$$

where E is the intensity of radiation in the opaque bands of the water-vapor absorption spectrum, e is the vapor pressure in millibars, and the other symbols have their usual meaning.   Simpson's data show that $\partial E/\partial T$ varies very slowly for the range of values of T of interest, and Brunt concludes that K_R is effectively constant in the lower atmosphere, with a value about 10^3 cm^2 sec^{-1}.   On the basis of this argument, the radiative diffusivity is much greater than the molecular thermometric conductivity of air and is of the order of magnitude usually assigned to the eddy conductivity at a few meters above the surface.   Brunt afterward applies the equation of diffusion to show that, from the records of temperature obtained on the Eiffel Tower, Paris, radiation has a negligible effect on the diurnal variation of temperature at a height of 300 m.

In considering the validity of these results, it should be borne in mind that the analysis is directly dependent on Hettner's values of the absorption coefficients, which have now been superseded by those of Randall *et al.* (page 168). The later values indicate a much greater depth of the stratum of air required for complete absorption and underline Brunt's statement that the method gives no information about the lowest layers of the atmosphere, say below 50 m. The concept of radiative diffusivity provides a fairly satisfactory proof that, at heights of the order of several hundred meters, radiation cannot exercise a first-order effect on the diurnal temperature wave. At these heights the observed field can be accounted for only by mixing, *i.e.*, by dynamic turbulence or free convection.

The matter will not be pursued further here, since at present there is no wholly satisfactory treatment of radiative transfer in the lowest layers and it is not possible to state with confidence how far the observed distribution of temperature near the ground is directly influenced by radiation. This lack of progress is partly due to the absence of reliable continuous records of water-vapor concentration in the first 100 m above the surface, but mainly to the great mathematical complexity of the complete problem. At the present time the radiative transfer of heat from the surface to the adjacent air layers, and vice versa, must be considered as an unsolved problem of micrometeorology.

BIBLIOGRAPHY

1. N. K. JOHNSON and G. S. P. HEYWOOD, Geophys. Mem. 77.
2. N. K. JOHNSON, Geophys. Mem. 46.
3. A. C. BEST, Geophys. Mem. 65.
4. W. D. FLOWER, Geophys. Mem. 71.
5. F. B. WEDMORE, Quart. J. Roy. Meteorol. Soc., 67, 38 (1941).
6. H. E. PATTEN, U.S. Dept. Agr. Bur. Soils Bull. 59 (1909).
7. N. E. RIDER and G. D. ROBINSON, London Meteorol. Office M.R.P. (unpublished).
8. H. L. CALLENDAR and C. H. McLEOD, Proc. Roy. Soc. Canada, (2) 3, 31 (1897).
9. P. VUJEVIC, Z. Meteorol., 29, 570 (1912).
10. TH. HOMÉN, "Der tägliche Warmeumsatz in Boden usw" (Leipzig, 1897).
11. J. G. SINCLAIR, Monthly Weather Rev., 50, 142 (1922).
12. J. H. FIELD, Mem. Indian Meteorol. Dept., 24, 38.
13. G. S. EATON, Monthly Weather Rev., 47, 861 (1919).
14. R. GEIGER, "Das Klima der bodennahen Luftschicht," 3d ed. (Brunswick, 1950).
15. N. K. JOHNSON and E. LL. DAVIES, Quart. J. Roy. Meteorol. Soc., 53, 45 (1927).
16. P. SCHREIBER, Jahrb. K. Sächs Landes-Wetterwarte, 29 (1910, 1912).
17. H. WILD, Mem. Pétersb. S. VIII Physik. math. Klasse, 5, No. 8.
18. G. LUBOSLAWSKY, Mitt. d. k. Forstinst. St. Petersburg, 19 (1909).
19. W. V. BEZOLD, Sitzber. preuss. Akad. Wiss. Physik.-math Klasse, 1139 (1892).
20. W. KÜHL, Gerlands Beitr. Geophys., 8, 519.
21. J. KERÄNEN, "Einfuhrung in die Geophysik," Vol. II (Berlin, 1929).

22. F. Pasquill, Proc. Roy. Soc. (London) A198, 116 (1949).
23. H. Lettau, Geophys. Research Papers 1 (1949).
24. P. A. Sheppard, "Meteorological Factors in Radio Wave Propagation," The Physical Society (London) (1947).
25. O. G. Sutton, Quart. J. Roy. Meteorol. Soc., 74, 13 (1948).
26. E. L. Deacon, Quart. J. Roy. Meteorol. Soc., 75, 89 (1949).
27. W. Schmidt, "Der Massenaustausch in freier Luft" (Hamburg, 1925).
28. G. Wust, Meteorol. Z., 54, 4 (1937).
29. N. K. Johnson, Quart. J. Roy. Meteorol. Soc., 53, 59 (1927).
30. R. B. Montgomery, Papers Phys. Oceanog. Meteorol., Mass. Inst. Technol. and Woods Hole Oceanog. Inst., 7, No. 4 (1940).
31. G. I. Taylor, Phil. Trans. Roy. Soc. A215, 1 (1915).
32. G. T. Taylor, Proc. Roy. Soc. (London), A94, 137, (1918).
33. T. G. Cowling and A. White, Quart. J. Roy. Meteorol. Soc., 75, 71 (1949).
34. H. Köhler, Kgl. Svenska Vetenskansakad. Handl., 13, No. 1; Beitr. Phys. fr. Atmos., 19, 91 (1932).
35. B. Haurwitz, Trans. Roy. Soc. Canada, 3d ser., III, 30, 1 (1936).
36. C. H. B. Priestley and W. C. Swinbank, Proc. Roy. Soc. (London), A189, 543 (1947).
37. H. Ertel, Meteorol. Z., 59, 250 (1942); 60, 246 (1943); 60, 289 (1943); 61, 8 (1944); 61, 207 (1944).

CHAPTER 7

PROBLEMS OF WIND STRUCTURE NEAR THE SURFACE

The maintenance of many forms of life, and particularly that of civilized man, is largely dependent on the existence of a vigorous exchange of air masses near the surface. It is difficult to visualize a world in which the atmosphere either is devoid of motion or else moves only as a laminar stream, but we may be sure that in such circumstances living matter would have to take forms very different from those of the present time. The basic fact of micrometeorology is not only that the atmosphere is in constant motion but that the motion is normally turbulent, resulting in a continuous diffusion of properties from one region to another. Problems of wind structure in the lowest layers are thus fundamental, and much energy has been spent, and ingenuity exercised, in investigating this aspect of the subject.

7.1. General Features of the Surface Velocity Field

The motion of the air in the middle regions of the troposphere derives directly from the gradients of the macroscopic pressure field and the effects of the rotation of the earth. At sufficiently great heights (say, in excess of 500 m over level country) the steady motion usually approximates fairly closely to that given by the geostrophic balance (see Chap. 2). In the lower layers the motion is inevitably more complicated because of the disturbing effects of the surface. In this region the wind is subjected to a frictional force whose magnitude varies with the nature of the surface and with the prevailing density distribution in the vertical, factors whose effects are not easily expressed by exact mathematical analysis. Additional complications arise from the appearance of local air currents unrelated to the main pressure field, especially at night in undulating or hilly country.

There is a well-defined diurnal variation of wind. At an inland site, the wind in the lowest layers reaches its maximum speed in the daytime, usually with a somewhat ill-defined peak about noon. At heights of the order of 100 to 300 m, the reverse variation is observed, a maximum at night and a minimum value during the day. At intermediate heights the variation is more complex. Thus Hellmann's[1] observations in a flat meadow at Nauen, where anemometers were installed at heights of 2, 16, and 32 m above ground, indicate that, in the upper levels, two maxima may occur, one about noon and one about midnight, and two minima, in the early morning and afternoon. Brunt[2] concludes that with light winds the reversal of the diurnal variation takes place below 40 m, but with strong winds the reversal occurs at some height above 40 m. The general character of these results is confirmed by Heywood's[3] analysis of the winds at Leafield, Southern England. There is relatively little information available concerning the diurnal variation of wind over large stretches of water, and the evidence obtained so far suggests that the amplitude is much less than that found over land. On the coast the normal diurnal variation tends to be masked by land and sea breezes.

The direction of the wind also shows a diurnal variation, the usual tendency being for the wind to veer during the day and to back by night. The regularity of such changes is, however, always liable to be upset by local influences, especially at night.

In the theoretical study of atmospheric turbulence, accurate determinations of the wind profile near the ground are essential, and considerable attention has been paid by meteorologists to this matter. The earlier investigators expressed their results in the form $\bar{u} = \bar{u}_1 z^p$, $p > 0$, or $\bar{u} = a \log z + b$, and with the relatively crude observations of this period, the choice appeared to be dictated mainly by taste or convenience. It was soon realized, however, that not only did the accurate determination of the profile demand specially designed sensitive anemometers, capable of working in both light and strong winds, but attention must also be given to the effects of density gradient and the roughness of the surface. In 1932 Sutton[4] showed that the index p in the power law $\bar{u} = \bar{u}_1 z^p$ is subject to a pronounced diurnal variation in clear weather, changing from about $\frac{1}{6}$ in large inversions to about $\frac{1}{14}$ in large lapse rates. Similar changes were found by other investigators. Scrase,[5] by confining attention to periods of very small temperature gradient, found that the wind profile between heights of 3 and 13 m over level downland could be adequately represented by the law $\bar{u} = \bar{u}_1 z^{0.13}$. This is of particular interest in the theory of atmospheric turbulence because this is virtually the same profile as the well-known "seventh-root law" of variation of wind speed with height in the turbulent boundary layer of a flat plate. Other investigators, notably Best and Paeschke, found good evidence to support the logarithmic profile.

In general terms, it is clear that these results express the fact that the turbulent transfer of momentum from one level to another is either promoted or hindered by the prevailing density gradient. In conditions of superadiabatic lapse rate, the turbulence of the wind is at its highest level, and there is a free flow of momentum from the unretarded stream at the greater heights to replace that used up in overcoming the friction of the surface. In such conditions velocity tends to become nearly uniform with height, except in the immediate vicinity of the surface. When turbulence is being suppressed by an inversion, the vertical exchange of momentum is reduced and the velocity near the ground sinks to a much lower level, resulting in a more sharply curved velocity profile. This explains the low values ascribed to the index p in the middle of the day and the rise of p at night.

The situation regarding the functional form of the velocity profile near the ground has been clarified by the researches of Thornthwaite and Kaser[6] and, more recently, of E. L. Deacon.[7] Thornthwaite and Kaser made accurate observations of the profile between 1 and 28 ft (0.3 to 8.5 m) during a June day at New Philadelphia, Ohio. In conditions of small temperature gradient they found that the $\bar{u}$, log z plot was accurately linear over the range of height considered, but in other conditions the plot diverged significantly from a straight line. In periods of superadiabatic lapse rates the $\bar{u}$, log z plot was convex to the axis of $\bar{u}$ and, in inversion periods, concave to the same axis (see Fig. 25). Thus the logarithmic law of variation of wind with height is valid only when the air stream is homogeneous, or nearly so. Deacon, from an examination of carefully measured profiles over downland between heights of 0.5 and 4 m (and possibly up to 13 m), enunciated the general law

$$\frac{d\bar{u}}{dz} = az^{-\beta}$$

(a independent of z), with $\beta = 1$ for small or adiabatic temperature gradients, $\beta > 1$ for superadiabatic lapse rates, and $\beta < 1$ for inversions. The value $\beta = 1$ leads to the logarithmic profile, but in other conditions the profile expression involves powers of the height.

Measurements of the magnitude and frequency of occurrence of the eddy velocities u' (along wind), v' (across wind), and w' (vertical) have been made by several workers, notably Scrase[5] and Best.[8] In such work the period over which mean values are taken must be specified with care, because of the wide range of frequencies found in the oscillations of a natural wind. For "intermediate-scale turbulence" (mean values over periods of the order of a few minutes) the data show that, in conditions of small temperature gradient, all three components are approximately proportional to the mean wind speed, but the lateral component v' is about 50 per cent greater than the vertical component w' at a height of 2 m, over level country. The asymmetry declines with height, and at levels in excess of 25 m, over downland, all three components are approximately equal. Thus there is equipartition of eddying energy in the upper reaches of the surface layers, but not near the ground. This fact is of considerable importance in problems of diffusion. The frequency distribution of eddy velocities follows the normal Maxwell law and thus closely resembles the distribution of molecular velocities in a gas. In conditions of high lapse rate, the eddy velocities are considerably greater (for the same mean wind speed) than those observed in adiabatic or near-adiabatic conditions, and the reverse holds in large inversions, when the fluctuations tend to die away.

These matters will now be considered in greater detail.

7.2. Wind Profiles

In the analysis of wind structure in the lowest layers of the atmosphere, it is advantageous to regard the air at these levels as part of a fully developed turbulent boundary layer, in which both the Coriolis force and changes in the gradient of pressure in the direction of the mean wind are negligible. This implies that for steady motion the eddy shearing stress is invariable with height, so that the analysis is restricted to motion in a layer of depth not exceeding a few tens of meters [see Eqs. (3.34) and (3.35)]. The change of wind direction with height in such a layer is also small, so that a system of fixed axes may be defined, in which x is measured in the direction of the mean wind, y across wind, and z vertically. In such a system

$$\bar{u} = \bar{u}(z), \qquad \bar{v} = \bar{w} = 0$$

Neutral Stability. If the temperature gradient is small throughout the layer, so that virtually the air is of uniform density, the motion should resemble that found in laboratory experiments on flow over a plane surface. From the analysis of Secs. 3.9 and 3.10 it follows that the velocity profiles would be expected to conform to one or another of the equations:

Smooth flow:
$$\frac{\bar{u}}{u_*} = \frac{1}{k} \ln\left(\frac{u_* z}{\nu}\right) + \text{constant} \tag{7.1}$$

Fully-rough flow:
$$\frac{\bar{u}}{u_*} = \frac{1}{k} \ln \frac{z}{z_0} \tag{7.2}$$

or
$$\frac{\bar{u}}{u_*} = \frac{1}{k} \ln\left(\frac{z + z_0}{z_0}\right) \tag{7.3}$$

where $u_* = \sqrt{(\tau_0/\rho)}$ is the friction velocity and z_0 the roughness length. It is convenient to introduce here the drag coefficient of the surface, C_D, defined by

$$C_D = \frac{\tau_0}{\frac{1}{2}\rho \bar{u}^2} = 2\left(\frac{u_*}{\bar{u}}\right)^2 \tag{7.4}$$

The suggestion that the profile of the natural wind should conform to the above equations in conditions of neutral stability ($\partial\theta/\partial z = 0$) appears to have originated with Prandtl in 1932. Since that date accurate observations by Best,[8] Sverdrup,[9] Paeschke,[10] Thornthwaite and Kaser,[6] E. L. Deacon,[7] and others have established this beyond reasonable doubt and have enabled the basic parameters u_* and z_0 to be determined for a wide range of natural surfaces. An extensive collection of values of z_0 has been prepared by Deacon.[7] Table 23 shows values of z_0, u_*, and the macroviscosity $N = u_* z_0$ (see Chap. 3) given by Sutton from data published by P. A. Sheppard.[11] These values should be regarded as a general guide only.

TABLE 23. REPRESENTATIVE VALUES OF z_0 AND u_* FOR NATURAL SURFACES
(Neutral stability; values of u_* corresponding to $\bar{u} = 500$ cm sec^{-1} at 200 cm)

Type of surface	z_0, cm	u_*, cm sec^{-1}	N, cm^2 sec^{-1}
Very smooth (mud flats, ice)...............	0.001	16	0.016
Lawn, grass up to 1 cm high...............	0.1	26	2.6
Downland, thin grass up to 10 cm high.....	0.7	36	26
Thick grass, up to 10 cm high..............	2.3	45	104
Thin grass, up to 50 cm high..............	5	55	275
Thick grass, up to 50 cm high..............	9	63	560

In most cases z_0 is substantially independent of $\bar{u}$, but Deacon has shown that with long grass z_0 decreases with increasing mean wind speed, an effect which is ascribed to the bending of the stems of the plants in the wind, thus producing a flatter and smoother surface. Lettau[12] has shown that Paeschke's observations over a wide variety of surfaces (snow, grassland, root crops) indicate that $u_*/\bar{u}$ is constant for any given surface, for $\bar{u}$ (measured at 500 cm above the ground) varying from about 20 to 500 cm sec^{-1}.

The values of u_* vary from about 3 to 12 per cent of the mean wind speed, the lower values being associated with surfaces which have a smooth appearance. The values of N, however, show that only an exceptional natural surface can be smooth in the aerodynamical sense. Nikuradse's criterion for fully-rough flow is that N should exceed 0.4 cm^2 sec^{-1}, and smooth flow requires that N should be less than 0.02 cm^2 sec^{-1}, taking $\nu = 0.15$ cm^2 sec^{-1} in each case (see Chap. 3). Thus for a mean wind of 500 cm sec^{-1} at 200 cm, only a surface of the type of mud flats or a large sheet of ice could be called smooth. A closely cut and well-rolled lawn would be aerodynamically smooth for winds (at 200 cm) below 100 cm sec^{-1} but is rough at more normal speeds.

The conclusion that nearly all natural surfaces are aerodynamically rough is of the greatest importance in problems of diffusion. For meteorological work the profile which is most appropriate appears to be that suggested by Rossby [Eq. (7.3)]. Theoretically, this is valid down to $z = 0$, but it must be recognized that this cannot be true when the vegetation is dense and high. In a field of corn, for example, it is clear that the movement of air among the stalks must be very restricted and

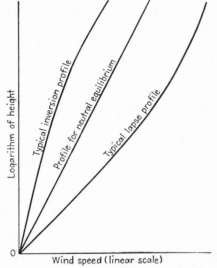

of a totally different character from that found above the tops of the plants. The profile equations represent the integrated effect of the fluctuations on the transfer of momentum and therefore must be applied only in those regions in which such transfer is taking place. It is shown later that a modified form of the profile equation for fully-rough flow may be used above dense vegetation.

FIG. 25. Thornthwaite and Kaser's observations on wind profiles during 24 hr of summer weather.

Stable and Unstable Atmospheres. Figure 25 shows some of the observations of Thornthwaite and Kaser,[6] which make it clear that the logarithmic profile represents a transition between the types of profiles found in the presence of marked density gradients. The matter has been further examined

by Deacon,[7] who introduces the Richardson number as the basic parameter. In general,

$$\frac{\bar{u}}{u_*} = f(\mathrm{Re}, \mathrm{Ri}, z_0)$$

If the motion is of the fully-rough type, the influence of viscosity, and hence of the Reynolds number, is negligible, and if the observations are always made over the same surface, the roughness may be regarded as constant, so that, with these assumptions, $\bar{u}/u_*$ should depend only on Ri, which thus may be expected to play much the same part as that exercised by the Reynolds number in the motion of a homogeneous air stream. If the temperature gradient is superadiabatic, Ri < 0, and in inversions of potential temperature Ri > 0; the case Ri = 0 implies $\partial T/\partial z = -\Gamma$.

Figure 26, taken from Deacon's paper, shows the ratio of the mean wind velocity at $z = 4.5$ m to that at $z = 0.5$ m, plotted against the mean value of Ri for the same layer, the surface being an area of short grass on level open downland. To a good approximation, the wind gradient is a function of the Richardson number alone, the surface roughness being constant. Figure 27 shows a further development of this concept. In these diagrams the velocity profiles are classified according to the sign and magnitude of Ri, and it is clear that the u, log z profiles are convex to the u axis for Ri < 0 and concave to the same axis when Ri > 0. This is the same type of variation as that found by Thornthwaite and Kaser.

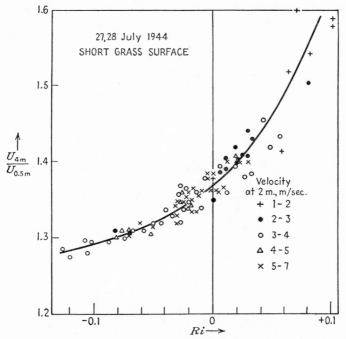

FIG. 26. The 4:0.5 m wind ratio related to the Richardson number. (*After Deacon.*)

Deacon states that for such groups the relation

$$\frac{d\bar{u}}{dz} = az^{-\beta} \tag{7.5}$$

(a independent of z) satisfies the data "quite closely," with

$$\beta > 1 \quad \text{for Ri} < 0$$
$$\beta = 1 \quad \text{for Ri} = 0$$
$$\beta < 1 \quad \text{for Ri} > 0$$

The variation of β with Ri is shown in Fig. 28, which is based on more than 600 observations of 15 min duration. The range is approximately $0.75 \leq \beta \leq 1.2$; there are indications that when Ri > 0.1 the relationship becomes very uncertain.

Integrating Eq. (7.5) for the condition $\bar{u} = 0$ on $z = z_0$, Deacon finds

$$\frac{\bar{u}}{u_*} = \frac{1}{k(1-\beta)} \left[\left(\frac{z}{z_0}\right)^{1-\beta} - 1 \right] \tag{7.6}$$

the constant a in Eq. (7.5) being put equal to $u_*/kz_0^{1-\beta}$ to allow the transition to the usual logarithmic profile [Eq. (7.2)] to be effected.

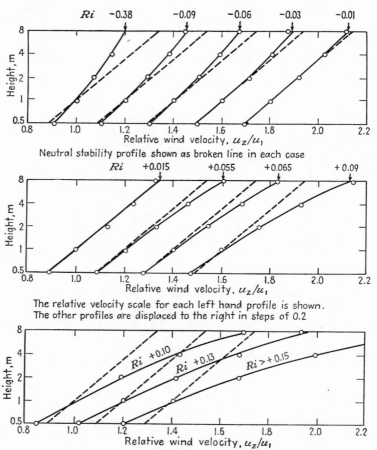

Neutral stability profile shown as broken line in each case

The relative velocity scale for each left hand profile is shown.
The other profiles are displaced to the right in steps of 0.2

FIG. 27. Variation of velocity profiles with stability. (*After Deacon.*)

Expanding the right-hand side of Eq. (7.6), the profile expression becomes

$$\frac{\bar{u}}{u_*} = \frac{1}{k} \left[\ln\left(\frac{z}{z_0}\right) + \frac{1-\beta}{2!} \ln^2\left(\frac{z}{z_0}\right) + \cdots \right]$$

which yields Eq. (7.2) as $\beta \to 1$.

In considering the validity of this analysis, it should be noted that the roughness length z_0 is supposed to be constant for a given terrain and that the same value of z_0 is appropriate for all conditions of stability. In the derivation of the equations, z_0 is merely a constant of integration, the assumption being that the velocity vanishes on the plane $z = z_0$, whose height above the ground is determined solely by the average height of the irregularities, supposed uniformly scattered over the surface. The connection between z_0 and the size of the irregularities has been

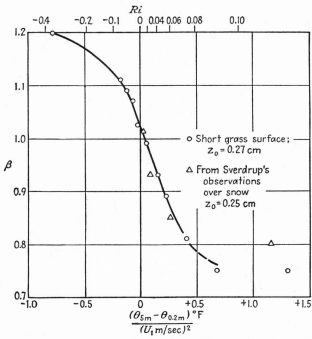

FIG. 28. The variation of β with stability. (*After Deacon.*)

established only for the motion of a homogeneous air stream (see Chap. 3), and it is by no means clear at this stage that the criteria for "fully-rough" and "smooth" flow can be assumed to hold with equal validity in all conditions of density gradient. It was shown by Sutton, and later confirmed by Sheppard,[11] that if the logarithmic profile be supposed to hold for all gradients, a variation of z_0 with temperature gradient necessarily follows. The later investigations, which have established beyond doubt that the logarithmic profile does not hold in conditions of marked density gradients, make it possible to regard z_0 as independent of the thermal stratification, as Deacon[7] does, with a resulting gain in simplicity. The question is one which is in need of detailed investigation.

As the matter stands at present, there is some evidence in favor of Deacon's profiles for conditions other than adiabatic, but the point is by no means completely established. Deacon states that β is not completely independent of height in unstable conditions, but this may be due, in part, to the incursion of large disturbances from the rough downland which surrounded the area of 200 yd square of closely cut grass on which the anemometers were erected. Here again, no final verdict can be given at this stage.

The above profiles were measured in a shallow layer near the ground. Deeper layers, 5 to 400 ft (1.5 to 122 m) and 4 to 1000 ft (1.2 to 305 m), have been investigated by R. Frost,[13] using instruments suspended from a captive balloon over the airfield at Cardington, Southern England. His results indicate that in these layers the profile can be represented by power laws in all conditions of temperature gradient. Using the relation

$$\bar{u} = \bar{u}_1 \left(\frac{z}{z_1}\right)^p \tag{7.7}$$

where $\bar{u}_1$ is the mean velocity at a fixed reference height z_1, the values of Table 24 were found for p in terms of the temperature differences between 400 and 5 ft.

TABLE 24. VALUES OF p IN THE EQUATION $\bar{u} = \bar{u}_1(z/z_1)^p$ RELATED TO THE TEMPERATURE DIFFERENCE $\Delta T = T_{400'} - T_{5'}$ IN THE LAYER 5–400 FT, AFTER FROST
(Temperature difference over layer corresponding to adiabatic lapse rate is $\Delta T = -2.15°F$)

ΔT, °F	−4 to −2	−2.5 to −1.5	−2 to 0	−1 to 1	0 to 2	2 to 4	4 to 6	6 to 8	8 to 10	10 to 12
p	0.145	0.17	0.25	0.29	0.32	0.44	0.59	0.63	0.62	0.77

From a further examination of extended profiles from 4 to 1000 ft, Frost concludes that the value of p in conditions of adiabatic lapse rate is 0.149, which is very close to the value $\frac{1}{7}$ ($= 0.142$) occurring in the generally accepted power-law profile for the turbulent boundary layer of a flat plate in a wind tunnel. There can be little doubt that in conditions of neutral stability the power-law form of the profile is not as accurate as the logarithmic form, especially near the surface, but Frost's result is in good agreement with that of Scrase,[5] who found $p = 0.13$ to be appropriate for conditions of small temperature gradient in the layer 3 to 13 m, and the seventh-root formula is probably a satisfactory approximation to the profile in a fairly deep layer, when neutral stability is judged by the value of the temperature difference over the whole layer.

Most attempts to fit power laws to the observed profiles employ Eq. (7.7), and it is invariably found that $0 < p < 1$. The greatest range of *observed* values of p so far published is that given by Barkat Ali,[14] namely,

$0.02 \leq p \leq 0.87$, but the upper limit is somewhat uncertain because of the failure of the bottom anemometer to register on certain occasions of high stability. The largest published value of p which is completely reliable is $p = 0.85$, obtained by Best[8] in the shallow layer 10 to 110 cm, in conditions of exceptional stability. The power law proposed by Deacon [Eq. (7.6)] is totally different from that given by Eq. (7.7), since it consists of a term independent of height plus a term involving a power of the height, and the values of p given above are not simply related to the index $1 - \beta$ in Deacon's expression.

The case $p = 0$ represents the limiting case of an atmosphere in which the turbulence is sufficiently active to ensure a uniform velocity throughout the layer concerned. The observations of Barkat Ali, and the data given by Giblett et al.[15] for Cardington, Southern England, suggest that this state is very nearly reached on certain occasions of very large lapse rate.† The upper limit $p = 1$ implies the Couette profile found in laminar motion over a plane surface in the absence of a pressure gradient (see Chap. 2). The near-linear profiles observed by Barkat Ali and Best thus imply a close approach to laminar motion in the lowest layers in conditions of great stability.

Extension to Very Rough Surfaces. The preceding account is restricted to surfaces which are either bare or covered with very short vegetation, of height not exceeding a few centimeters. A great portion of the ground, however, is covered with high vegetation, such as tall grass, cereal crops, or trees, and in these conditions the velocity profile is bound to become more complex and, in certain cases, hardly capable of mathematical representation.

Some progress can be made, however, by an empirical modification of the profile equation if the roughness elements are sufficiently uniform in height and distribution. If the logarithmic profile be written empirically in the form

$$\frac{\bar{u}}{u_*} = \frac{1}{k} \ln \left(\frac{z - d}{z_0} \right) \tag{7.8}$$

where d is a *zero-plane displacement*, it is possible to extend some of the above work to layers of air above ground covered by tall vegetation. The length d is to be regarded as a datum level above which the normal turbulent exchange takes place, and Eq. (7.8) has a meaning only if $z \geq d + z_0$. If d and z_0 are regarded as independent arbitrary constants, Eq. (7.8) cannot be derived from the original differential equation (3.36), for Eq. (3.36) is of the first order, whose solution must involve not more than one arbitrary constant.

† Giblett et al. state in very large superadiabatic lapse rates, the ratio of the wind at 150 ft to that at 50 ft was 1.01, but there is some doubt concerning the exposure of the anemometers (see Frost[13]).

The profile (7.8) has been used by many investigators. Paeschke, who dealt with both smooth and very rough surfaces, takes d to be a length equal to the average of the measured heights of the roughness elements. E. L. Deacon concludes that in conditions of small temperature gradient the logarithmic law can represent the profile between heights of 1 and 13 m, over surfaces covered with grass of varying length, with very great accuracy, provided that d and z_0 are chosen independently to give the best fit. Calder,[16] in a study of diffusion of smoke over downland (see Chap. 8), gives the following values for the constants in Eq. (7.8):

Short grass (1–3 cm):

$$u_* = 33 \text{ cm sec}^{-1}$$
$$z_0 = 0.5 \text{ cm}, \qquad d = 0$$

Long grass (60–70 cm):

$$u_* = 50 \text{ cm sec}^{-1}$$
$$z_0 = 3 \text{ cm}, \qquad d = 30 \text{ cm}$$

where $\bar{u} = 500$ cm sec^{-1} at $z = 200$ cm, above ground. The problem of the representation of the profile over long grass in nonadiabatic conditions has not been studied in sufficient detail to allow definite conclusions to be reached.

Profiles over Water. The problem of the distribution of velocity over large stretches of water is essentially different from that over land, chiefly because of wave formation. Because of the much reduced range of temperature gradient, stability effects are not as marked, but the fact that the surface "roughness" is now a function of the strength of the wind complicates the problem very seriously. In addition, the purely experimental difficulties of making reliable measurements of wind structure at sea makes some of the published work of doubtful value.

Rossby and Montgomery[17] have considered conditions at the junction of the water and air and conclude that interaction takes place through both tangential and normal stresses, the latter being of importance only in the stronger winds. For light winds, it is considered that Eq. (7.1) is appropriate to motion in the lowest layers. For moderate and strong winds the surface becomes aerodynamically rough, and Rossby and Montgomery suggest that in these conditions there is a discontinuity in the stress pattern near the wave tops, the profile below this level being of the smooth flow type. For winds below 600 to 700 cm sec^{-1}, the sea surface is regarded as aerodynamically smooth. For stronger winds, the surface is rough, the appropriate value of z_0 being 0.6 cm. Munk's[18] work supports Rossby and Montgomery's conclusions concerning the magnitude of the critical wind speed at which the sea becomes aerodynamically rough.

Model,[19] from an analysis of Bruch's observations over the Baltic and an inland lake, concludes that the best representation of the wind profile over the sea is given by Eq. (7.8) with $d = 4$ cm, $z_0 = 0.03$ cm. The value of z_0 is considerably smaller than that derived by Rossby and Montgomery, but the two expressions for the profile are not strictly comparable because of the introduction of the zero-plane displacement.

It will be seen from the above that the evidence gathered so far is not entirely consistent and that a satisfactory account of air motion over the ocean has yet to emerge. It is clear, however, that the broad picture does not differ essentially from that of wind structure over land, if due allowance is made for the disturbing effects of waves. The question is partly oceanographic and partly meteorological and involves problems which are not yet completely solved in either science.

7.3. The Approach to the Geostrophic Wind

The discussion of the preceding section is limited to conditions in shallow layers near the surface, usually of depth not exceeding 100 m. The problem about to be considered is that of the variation of wind in a deeper layer, extending from the surface to about 500 to 1000 m (depending on the latitude), the upper level being the height at which there is no systematic deviation from the motion implied by the principle of the geostrophic balance. This deeper layer has been called the *planetary boundary layer* by Lettau,[12] to distinguish it from the surface boundary layer discussed previously.

The geostrophic balance does not involve friction of any type, and thus the upper limit of the planetary boundary layer may be regarded as the level at which the motion of the air conforms to the Eulerian equations of an inviscid fluid (see Chap. 2). Mathematically, this is conveniently expressed by the statement that the eddy shearing stresses are zero for $z \geq H$, where H is the depth of the planetary boundary layer. For $z < H$, the factors which determine the distribution of velocity are: (1) the prevailing pressure gradient; (2) the Coriolis force of the earth's rotation; (3) the friction of the surface; (4) gravitational forces. In the discussion which follows, the pressure gradient will be assumed to be independent of height in magnitude and direction throughout the layer. The mean motion will be supposed two-dimensional, with horizontal components $\bar{u}$, $\bar{v}$, so that the Coriolis force has components $\rho \lambda \bar{v}$, $-\rho \lambda \bar{u}$ in the x and y directions, respectively, where

$$\lambda = 2\omega \sin \phi \simeq 1.458 \times 10^{-4} \sin \phi \ \sec^{-1}$$

ω being the angular velocity of rotation of the earth and ϕ the latitude of the site of observation. In addition, the variation of density with height will be supposed negligible for $0 \leq z \leq H$.

General Features of the Problem.   In conditions in which the pressure field is steady or only slowly changing, observation shows that the mean motion of the air above a certain level $z = H$ conforms to the theoretical geostrophic wind and thus is parallel to the isobars.   At lower levels, the wind not only is reduced in velocity by the friction of the surface but blows at an angle to the isobars.   A general explanation of these features is afforded by the Ekman spiral (see Chap. 3), but a closer examination is needed to account for the details of the velocity distribution for $0 \leq z < H$.   This necessitates making allowance for the decay of turbulence with height, and it has already been shown that better agreement with observations can be obtained by assuming that the eddy viscosity depends on height (Chap. 3).

The setting of the mathematical problem requires care.   The planetary boundary layer may be thought of as two layers, the surface boundary layer and an overlying zone of transition to the frictionless motion of the free atmosphere.   Within the lower layer, the motion is greatly influenced by the state of the surface, but in the upper zone, surface roughness must be of negligible importance.   The effects of temperature gradient, whether stabilizing or destabilizing, are not as easily delimited and in the first instance, at least, must be presumed to influence the motion at all levels.   In the surface layer, the shearing stress is virtually independent of height, and in this region, existing theories of turbulence require the eddy viscosity to increase indefinitely with height.   Turbulent transfer of momentum is negligible at the level of the geostrophic wind, so that the shearing stress must decrease to zero at an appreciable rate in the transition zone.   This is not necessarily mathematically inconsistent with the assumption that the eddy viscosity increases with height everywhere, provided that the velocity gradient tends to zero sufficiently rapidly to make the product $K_M dV/dz$ (V = wind in the region $0 \leq z \leq H$) vanish or become negligibly small for $z \geq H$, but on physical grounds it may be objected that it is unreasonable to suppose that $K_M(z)$ can be large at a level where turbulence is vanishingly small.   Such an objection can be met by assuming that the eddy viscosity follows the normal increase with height throughout the surface layer and afterward decreases steadily to zero, or some small value, on $z = H$, so that $K_M(z)$ attains a maximum value at some level between the surface and the height at which frictional effects are no longer appreciable.

A distribution of this type must not be taken to imply that the turbulent exchange reaches a maximum at some level (of the order of 100 m) above the surface.   Apart from a complex variation in a shallow layer near the ground, turbulence, as measured by the rms value of the amplitude of the oscillations over periods of the order of a few minutes, decreases steadily from the surface upward.   Physically, the outstanding facts are that the eddy shearing stress and the gradient of mean velocity decrease with height throughout the planetary boundary layer, but the variation in shearing stress is sufficiently small to be neglected within the layer influenced by surface roughness. The increase of $K_M(z)$ with height inside this layer reflects simply the decrease of dV/dz with z. In the deeper transition layer, the ultimate vanishing of $K_M(z)$ is a consequence of the disappearance of the turbulent stresses at the geostrophic wind level, and the peculiar variation postulated for $K_M(z)$ is a consequence of the mathematical method adopted and has no particular physical significance.

There are thus two possible approaches to the problem of wind structure in the earth's boundary layer. One is to assume that $K_M(z)$ increases monotonically throughout the entire planetary boundary layer and to seek a solution of the equation of mean motion which satisfies the requisite boundary conditions on $z = 0$ and as $z \to \infty$. This is the method initiated by Prandtl and Tollmien[20] in 1923 and later extended by Köhler[21] in an important memoir published in 1933. In this approach, variations in surface roughness are not taken into account in an explicit fashion. The second method, due to Rossby and Montgomery,[22,17] follows the lines indicated in the preceding paragraph, the effects of surface irregularities being allowed for in the relatively shallow surface layer and disregarded in the transition layer. This is more in accordance with physical concepts, since it is clear that surface roughness of the type considered in the previous section cannot influence significantly the structure of the wind except near the surface.

Solution for $K_M = K_1 z^m$ *throughout Layer.* The coordinate system employed is that of Sec. 3.6, in which the x axis lies along parallel straight isobars, so that by the principle of the geostrophic balance, $\partial p/\partial x = 0$ and $\partial p/\partial y = -\rho \lambda G$, where $\mathbf{G}$ is the geostrophic wind. By a simple extension of the analysis of Sec. 3.6, it is easily seen that the equations of steady two-dimensional motion reduce to

$$\frac{\partial}{\partial z}\left[K_M(z)\,\frac{\partial \mathbf{V}}{\partial z}\right] = i\lambda(\mathbf{V} - \mathbf{G}) \tag{7.9}$$

where $\mathbf{V} = \bar{u} + i\bar{v}$ is the resultant wind. The boundary conditions adopted are, as before,

$$\begin{array}{ll} \mathbf{V} = 0 & \text{on } z = 0 \\ \lim_{z \to \infty} \mathbf{V} = \mathbf{G} \end{array} \tag{7.10}$$

In the Prandtl-Tollmien analysis, K_M is supposed proportional to $z^{0.343}$, corresponding to the profile $\bar{u} = \bar{u}_1 z^{0.157}$ in the layer of constant shearing stress, a formulation suggested by the velocity profile observed in the boundary layer of a pipe.   The solution of Eq. (7.9) with the conditions (7.10) is then obtained as an infinite series.   Köhler considers the more general case

$$K_M(z) = K_1 z^m \qquad 0 \leq m < 1 \tag{7.11}$$

where K_1 is the value of $K_M(z)$ for $z = 1$.   This expression allows the effects of both surface roughness and stability to be taken into account implicitly by varying K_1 and m to suit the prevailing conditions.

Equation (7.9) thus becomes

$$\frac{\partial}{\partial z}\left(K_1 z^m \frac{\partial \mathbf{V}}{\partial z}\right) = i\lambda(\mathbf{V} - \mathbf{G}) \tag{7.12}$$

To reduce Eq. 7.12 to a more familiar form, Köhler substitutes

$$\zeta = \frac{1}{K_1(1 - m)} z^{1-m} \tag{7.13}$$

and writes

$$\mathbf{V} - \mathbf{G} = \mathbf{W}$$

Since $m < 1$, it follows that $\zeta \to 0$ as $z \to 0$ and $\zeta \to \infty$ as $z \to \infty$.   The transformed equation and boundary conditions are

$$\frac{\partial^2 \mathbf{W}}{\partial \zeta^2} = ia^2 \zeta^{m/(1-m)} \mathbf{W} \tag{7.14}$$

$$\mathbf{W} = -\mathbf{G} \qquad \text{on } \zeta = 0$$
$$\lim_{\zeta \to \infty} \mathbf{W} = 0 \tag{7.15}$$

where $a^2 = K_1^{1/(1-m)}(1 - m)^{m/(1-m)}$.

Equation (7.14) is of the Bessel type.   A solution tending to zero as $\zeta \to \infty$, which does not vanish identically for $\zeta = 0$, is

$$\mathbf{W} = A\zeta^{\frac{1}{2}}K_{(1-m)/(2-m)}\left[\frac{2(1 - m)}{2 - m} a \sqrt{i} \, \zeta^{(2-m)/2(1-m)}\right] \tag{7.16}$$

where $K_\nu(x)$ is the modified Bessel function of the second kind of order ν[†] and A is a constant found by using the power-series expansion of $K_\nu(x)$ and the condition that $\mathbf{W} = -\mathbf{G}$ on $\zeta = 0$.   The explicit expression for A, which is somewhat complicated, can be found in Köhler's memoir, together with tables of the values of other constants in the expression for $\mathbf{V}$, for $m = \frac{1}{2}, \frac{2}{3}, \frac{3}{4}, \frac{4}{5}, \frac{5}{6}, \frac{6}{7}, \frac{7}{8}, \frac{8}{9}$, $\lambda = 1.3 \times 10^{-4} \sec^{-1}$ (corresponding to latitude 60°), $|K_1| = 15.4$ cgs units.[‡]

[†] G. N. Watson, "A Treatise on Bessel Functions," 2d ed., Chap. VII (Cambridge, 1944). $K_\nu(x)$ should not be confused with the eddy viscosity $K_M(z)$.

[‡] Köhler,[21] pp. 12–14.   The reader should note that the notation used by Köhler is not identical with that given above.

Köhler's analysis thus indicates that the wind in the planetary boundary layer can be represented by an expression of the type

$$V(z) = G + Cz^{\frac{1}{2}(1-m)}K_{(1-m)/(2-m)}(Dz^{1-\frac{1}{2}m}) \tag{7.17}$$

where G is the geostrophic wind and C and D are complex quantities depending on λ, m, K_1, and G. For $m = 0$ $[K_M(z) = $ constant$]$ the solution can be expressed in terms of elementary functions, by making use of the familiar result in the theory of Bessel functions,

$$K_{\frac{1}{2}}(x) = \left(\frac{\pi}{2x}\right)^{\frac{1}{2}}e^{-x}$$

The expression obtained in this way is identical with Eq. (3.20), the analytical representation of the Ekman spiral.

The principal results of Köhler's investigation are as follows:

1. In the layers of air very near the ground, the profile of the resultant wind approximates closely to a simple power law of the type $V = V_1z^{1-m}$, where V_1 is a quantity depending upon λ, m, K_1, and G and is thus independent of height. This is exactly the profile predicted by Schmidt's conjugate-power-law theorem and implies the familiar result that the resultant shearing stress $\tau = \rho K_M \, dV/dz$ is invariable with height in these layers. From an examination of the order of magnitude of the various constants, Köhler concludes that this approximation is valid for $z \leq 10$ m, which agrees with observations in the surface layer.

2. The angle α between the surface and geostrophic winds is given by

$$\alpha = \frac{1-m}{2(2-m)}\pi \tag{7.18}$$

Table 25 gives values of α for the range of values of m employed by Köhler.

TABLE 25. ANGLE α BETWEEN THE SURFACE AND GEOSTROPHIC WINDS AS A FUNCTION OF m IN THE RELATION $K_M(z) = K_1z^m$

m	$\frac{1}{2}$	$\frac{2}{3}$	$\frac{3}{4}$	$\frac{4}{5}$	$\frac{5}{6}$	$\frac{6}{7}$	$\frac{7}{8}$	$\frac{8}{9}$
α	30°	28°30′	18°	15°	12°48′	11°15′	10°	9°

Equation (7.18) indicates that α depends only on the exponent m (that is, mainly on the stability of the motion) and is independent of the Coriolis parameter λ, and consequently of the latitude. There is good evidence to support both this deduction and the values of α given in Table 25. Åkerblom[24] has recorded measurements of α in the North Atlantic, between latitude 9° and 60°; his results range from $\alpha = 22°$ to $\alpha = 12°$, with a mean value of 18°, and show no systematic variation with latitude. Jeffreys,[25] in a survey of 600 observations over the North Sea, found that α exhibited a skew frequency distribution with the mean value 16° and mode 11°. Westwater,[26] using data from naval aircraft carriers, found a mean angle of veer of 8° between 30 and 3000 ft (9 to 900 m). These results suggest that for winds over the ocean, m lies between $\frac{3}{4}$ and $\frac{8}{9}$, implying that, over sea, the surface wind increases as $z^{\frac{1}{7}}$ to $z^{\frac{1}{9}}$. It is significant that the mode value given by Jeffreys, $\alpha = 11°$, corresponds to a profile of the form $V = V_1 z^{\frac{1}{7}}$, typical of neutral stability. This is consistent with the observations, which indicate that on the majority of occasions the atmosphere over extratropical seas shows only relatively small deviations from the adiabatic lapse rate in the lower layers.

The above comparisons refer to wind over the sea. Over land, the average value of α appears to be about 20°, which implies that m is about $\frac{3}{4}$ and hence that the average profile near the ground should be represented by $V = V_1 z^{\frac{1}{7}}$, which indicates a somewhat steeper velocity gradient than that found over sea. Such a result can be accounted for by the greater roughness of the land and the increased effects of temperature gradient.

3. The nature of the wind structure for large values of z may be seen by employing the asymptotic expansion of $K_\nu(x)$. Retaining only the leading term, it follows that for large values of $|Dz^{1-\frac{1}{2}m}|$

$$V(z) \simeq G + A' z^{-\frac{1}{4}m} \exp(-Dz^{1-\frac{1}{2}m}) \tag{7.19}$$

where A' is a constant, from which it is easily seen that both dV/dz and $K_M(z)dV/dz$ tend to zero as $z \to \infty$. Thus the eddy shearing stress vanishes at great heights, despite the fact that $K_M(z)$ increases indefinitely with z, and the system is physically possible.

The conclusion reached from an examination of Köhler's work is that it provides a convincing explanation of most of the features of wind structure observed in the planetary boundary layer. Variations in surface conditions can be taken into account in a limited fashion by selecting appropriate values of K_1, but this is not altogether satisfactory since it implies that the effects of surface irregularities are felt equally at all heights up to the geostrophic wind level, and in any practical application K_1 must be regarded as a mean value which gives the best fit to the observations throughout the whole layer of frictional influence. Certain other aspects of Köhler's exposition, and in particular his analysis of the three-dimensional character of atmospheric turbulence, are more speculative and will not be considered here, but the whole of this lengthy memoir deserves close study as an example of the successful application of power laws to problems of atmospheric turbulence.

Depth of the Planetary Boundary Layer. In the preceding work the planetary boundary layer is supposed, theoretically, to extend upward to infinity. From the solution for $K_M =$ constant, a rough estimate can be made of the depth of the layer. From Eq. (3.20), following Brunt,[2] the vectorial effect of surface friction on the wind is measured by

$$\sqrt{2}\, \mathbf{G} \sin \alpha \exp\left(- z \sqrt{\frac{\lambda}{2K_M}}\right)$$

Taking $K_M = 10^5$ cm^2 sec^{-1}, the height at which the exponential term is 0.1 is $z = 10^5$ cm for $\phi = 60°$. Thus the effects of surface friction are confined to a layer not exceeding about 1 km in depth, and for many practical purposes it is sufficient to consider a much smaller depth, say 500 m. For a given K_M, the depth of the layer varies as $1/\sqrt{\sin \phi}$, which is large in low latitudes. Thus, theoretically, eddy friction should affect the wind at much greater heights in the tropics than in the temperate zones, but in view of the decreasing importance of the Coriolis component as the equator is approached, and of the restrictive nature of the assumption that the motion is strictly two-dimensional at all heights, such deductions from the equations given above cannot be regarded as very reliable.

The Rossby-Montgomery Two-layer Solution. The treatment of the problem proposed by Rossby and Montgomery is contained in two memoirs, the first (1932) by Rossby[22] and the second (1935) by Rossby and Montgomery.[17] In the lower layer ($0 \leq z \leq h$), the shearing stress is supposed invariable with height, the mixing length being given by

$$l = k(z + z_0)$$

which leads to the familiar logarithmic profile (7.3). In the upper layer, extending from $z = h$ to $z = H$, where H is the height at which the wind attains the geostrophic value, it is assumed that the pressure gradient is constant at all points and that the frictional drag is parallel to the wind on $z = h$. In the earlier memoir Rossby shows that this implies that the mixing length is given by

$$l = \frac{0.065}{\sqrt{2}} (H - z)$$

so that l vanishes on $z = H$. If τ_0 is the shearing stress on $z = h$, it is deduced that

$$\tau_0 = \frac{\rho \lambda^2 H^2}{9(0.065)^2}$$

and the resultant wind on $z = h$ is

$$V(h) = G\left(\cos \alpha - \frac{1}{\sqrt{2}} \sin \alpha\right)$$

The eddy viscosity is given by

$$K_M = \frac{\lambda}{3\sqrt{2}} (H - z)^2$$

so that K_M vanishes at the level of the geostrophic wind.

The solutions for the upper and lower layers are formed by ensuring continuity in mixing length, shearing stress, wind velocity, and wind direction at the level $z = h$. From the condition of continuity of mixing length,

$$k(h + z_0) = \frac{0.065}{\sqrt{2}} H$$

or since z_0 is small compared with h and H,

$$h = 0.12H$$

Thus the mixing length and eddy viscosity reach maximum values at a level which is about one-eighth of the depth of the planetary layer (that is, $h = 50$ to 100 m).

The conditions of continuity in shearing stress and wind speed give the relation

$$\frac{h + z_0}{z_0} = \exp\left[\frac{2k}{3(0.065)}\left(\cot \alpha - \frac{1}{\sqrt{2}}\right)\right]$$

from which may be derived the equation

$$\frac{G}{\lambda z_0} = \frac{2\sqrt{2k}}{9(0.065)^3} \operatorname{cosec} \alpha \exp\left[\frac{2k}{3(0.065)}\left(\cot \alpha - \frac{1}{\sqrt{2}}\right)\right]$$

The nondimensional parameter $G/\lambda z_0$, which depends only on the initial conditions (magnitude of geostrophic wind speed, latitude, and roughness of the ground), enables the angle α to be evaluated easily. It is found that α is almost independent of G and λ but increases from about 15° for $z_0 = 0.1$ cm to about 21° for $z_0 = 10$ cm. These results apply only to conditions of neutral stability because of the use of the logarithmic profile in the lower layer, and it may be concluded that, in such conditions, increasing surface roughness produces a small but measurable increase of α.

The ratio between the wind speed as measured by an anemometer in the lower layer and the geostrophic wind velocity is found to be

$$\frac{V(z_1)}{G} = \frac{3(0.065)}{2k} \sin \alpha \ln\left(\frac{z_1 + z_0}{z_0}\right) \qquad (z_1 < h)$$

For Taylor's example of strong winds over Salisbury Plain [$G = 1560$ cm sec^{-1}, $\alpha = 20°$, $z_0 = 3.2$ cm (estimated)] it follows that $V(z_1)/G = 0.595$, in excellent agreement with the measured ratio 0.61. For hilly country Rossby and Montgomery take $z_0 = 320$ cm and find, for other values the same as before, $V(z_1)/G = 0.29$, but this is perhaps extending the rough surface theory beyond the point of legitimate application.

In an extension of this work, Rossby and Montgomery remove the restriction that eddy motion vanishes completely on $z = H$ and assume instead that at these levels there exists a "residual turbulence" corresponding to a constant value of the exchange coefficient,

$$A_M = K_M \rho = 50 \text{ g cm}^{-1} \text{ sec}^{-1}$$

This assumption causes a radical change in the relation between $G/\lambda z_0$ and α. In the first solution, corresponding to $K_M = 0$ at $z = H$, α increases steadily with $G/\lambda z_0$, but in the second solution, α is roughly constant (about 20°) over a wide range of values of $G/\lambda z_0$. The observations are not sufficiently consistent to allow a judgment to be given in favor of either supposition.

In a further extension, the effects of variations in stability are included. The assumptions upon which this analysis is based are somewhat questionable and are considered below (page 265).

7.4. Detailed Study of Wind near the Surface

Velocity Fluctuations. An irregular variation of wind speed is a characteristic feature of the record produced by an instrument such as the pressure-tube anemometer, and similar oscillations are found in the direction trace. On a close time scale, the traces appear as "ribbons" whose width is roughly proportional to the average speed of the wind. The *gustiness* of the wind, defined as the ratio of the average width of the velocity trace to the mean velocity, is commonly used as a rough measure of the degree of turbulence at a site. Shaw,[27] in a review of wind characteristics at various localities, some in open country or on the coast and others in settled areas, gives values of gustiness ranging from 0.25 to 1. These values are typical of the records produced by the Dines pressure-tube anemometer, when the head is some 30 or 40 ft above the ground. Some information on the fluctuations of upper winds was given by J. S. Dines[28] in 1911, based on measurements of the changes in the pull of a kite, but the modern systematic investigation of wind fluctuations, or eddy velocities, begins with Taylor's[29] study of the partition of eddy energy near the ground.

If the end point of the vector representing the instantaneous speed of the wind moves inside a circle, it follows that

$$\frac{V_{\max} - V_{\min}}{V_{\max} + V_{\min}} = \sin \frac{1}{2}\theta$$

where θ is the angular width of the trace of wind direction. From an examination of records obtained at the top of an isolated stack, Taylor was able to show that this relationship is confirmed in practice and that consequently the average magnitude of the component of eddy velocity in the direction of the mean wind is equal to the average magnitude of the cross-wind component. This result was extended to include the vertical component by an examination of the oscillations of a tethered balloon, and it is to be concluded that at moderate heights eddying energy is equally divided along all three axes. On the other hand, Taylor demonstrated, by the use of the bidirectional vane,† that the cross-wind component of eddy velocity was much greater than the vertical component at levels within a few feet of the ground.

The extension of this work to cover the wide range of conditions encountered in micrometeorology requires precise definitions of the system of axes and of certain functions of velocity. Let the surface of the earth be the plane $z = 0$, over which a wind V is blowing. In general, V changes rapidly from point to point and from instant to instant of time, but if observations are made at a fixed point, it is possible to define a mean wind $\bar{V}$ by the relation

$$\bar{V} = \frac{1}{T} \int_{t-\frac{1}{2}T}^{t+\frac{1}{2}T} V \, dt$$

where T is the period of sampling, centered at the instant t. It is supposed that conditions are uniform over any horizontal plane, so that $\bar{V}$ depends only on the height z, the time t, and the period of sampling T. The direction of $\bar{V}$ is taken as that of the axis of x, assumed horizontal, so that, with the usual notation, the velocity components are defined as in the accompanying tabulation.

Axes	x	y	z
Instantaneous velocity............	u	v	w
Mean velocity....................	$\bar{u}$	0	0
Eddy velocities (fluctuations)......	u'	v'	w'

Since conditions do not vary in the horizontal, the velocities are functions of z, t, and T only. By definition, $\overline{u'} = \overline{v'} = \overline{w'} = 0$, and the *average magnitude of the eddy velocities* may be defined either as $\overline{|u'|}$, $\overline{|v'|}$, and $\overline{|w'|}$ or by their rms values $\sqrt{\overline{w'^2}}$, $\sqrt{\overline{v'^2}}$, $\sqrt{\overline{w'^2}}$. The *components of gustiness*, longitudinal (g_x), lateral (g_y), and vertical (g_z), are defined as the ratios of the average magnitudes of the component fluctuations to the mean wind

† A vane arranged so that it is free to move across wind and vertically. See A. C. Best, *Geophys. Mem.* 65, for a full description.

velocity. Like the eddy velocities, the gustiness components are functions of z, t, and T.

The time t which enters into the above expressions may be effectively eliminated from further consideration by the assumption (usually satisfied in practice) that conditions are sufficiently steady during the period of observation to ensure that the particular instant about which the period of sampling is centered is of no consequence. On the other hand, the specification of the period of sampling is essential in all work dealing with the fluctuations of the natural wind, because of the wide range of frequency of oscillations in the eddy spectrum. Scrase,[5] in an analysis of eddy velocities over downland, divided his results into those typical of *large-scale turbulence* ($T \simeq 1$ hr), *intermediate-scale turbulence* ($T = 2$ to 3 min), and *small-scale turbulence* (T a few seconds). Such a subdivision is arbitrary and mainly dictated by the characteristics of the instruments and methods of analysis employed, but it serves to bring out clearly the wide range of periods found in the fluctuations of wind near the surface.

Scrase examined the fine structure of the wind (small-scale turbulence) by means of ciné photographs (16 frames per second) of a swinging plate and a light bidirectional vane, with results that show the important part played by fluctuations of periods of the order of seconds. The analysis suggests that at least two-thirds of the eddying energy is associated with fluctuations lasting less than 5 sec, and there is some evidence that a significant increase in eddying energy can be detected when the period of sampling is reduced from 0.2 to 0.06 sec. If these results are typical, it follows that important contributions to the eddying energy of the natural wind must arise from oscillations whose frequency is as high as 10 to 20 cycles/sec. At the other end of the scale, it is evident from an inspection of anemometer records that large oscillations, lasting for minutes, are not uncommon.

Some of the most important results obtained by Scrase relate to the partition of eddying energy very near the ground. For intermediate-scale turbulence analyzed by the bidirectional vane in conditions of small temperature gradient, Scrase confirmed the result previously obtained by Taylor that, at heights of the order of 2 m, the lateral eddy velocity v' is about 50 per cent greater than the vertical component w' so that $\overline{v'^2}$ is more than twice $\overline{w'^2}$. At greater heights above ground, the asymmetry is reduced and tends to vanish above 20 m, in agreement with Taylor's balloon observations quoted above. This unequal partition of eddy energy in the surface air layers is of importance in problems of diffusion (see Chap. 8). Scrase was able to confirm that in conditions of small temperature gradient u', v', and w' are approximately proportional to the mean velocity (gustiness independent of mean wind speed), except perhaps for very low winds.

Scrase's work was confined in the main to periods of small temperature gradient. A more detailed examination of the structure of turbulence near the ground, covering a wide range of temperature gradient, was made by Best,[8] using a hot-wire anemometer and the bidirectional vane. The accurate measurement of wind fluctuations necessitates the use of a sensitive instrument of quick response, and in any realistic study of atmospheric turbulence the characteristics of the measuring instrument cannot be ignored. Best has shown that a hot-wire anemometer consisting of a short length (about 1 cm) of fine platinum wire, arranged with the element vertical and facing the mean wind, measures not u but

$$u + \frac{v'^2}{2\bar{u}}$$

Hence, as measured by such an instrument,

$$\frac{\text{Instantaneous mean velocity}}{\bar{u}} = \frac{u'}{\bar{u}} + \left[\frac{v'^2}{2\bar{u}^2} - \left(\overline{\frac{v'^2}{2\bar{u}^2}} \right) \right] \quad (7.20)$$

Best concludes that the term in brackets in Eq. (7.20) is usually small enough to allow the arrangement to be regarded as one which measures, to a moderate degree of approximation, velocities along the x axis only. During runs of 3 min total duration, the left-hand side of Eq. (7.20) was evaluated at 10-sec intervals, and the 19 readings so obtained were averaged to give g_x. The observations were made over a level sports field with grass 1 to 2 cm high, for the conditions given in the accompanying tabulation.

Range of height z, cm.................................... 2.5 to 200
Range of mean velocity (measured at $z = 200$ cm), cm sec^{-1}..... 50 to 800
Range of temperature gradient (10 to 110 cm), °C cm^{-1}........ -0.015 to $+0.01$

The results may be summarized as follows:
1. Nearly all values of g_x lie between 0.1 and 0.2.
2. g_x shows no well-defined variation with height for $2.5 \leq z \leq 200$ cm.
3. g_x is virtually independent of temperature gradient for $2.5 \leq z \leq 10$ cm but decreases with the change from lapse to inversion for $z \geq 25$ cm.
4. The variation of g_x with mean velocity is irregular, but, regarding the results as a whole, the longitudinal component of gustiness is independent of mean velocity to a moderate degree of approximation.
Since $g_x = \overline{|u'|}/\bar{u}$ does not vary appreciably with height, it follows that, over the interval considered, u' increases with height at much the same rate as $\bar{u}$. Best gives the equation

$$\overline{|u'|} = 0.15 \log (z - 1) + c$$

where z is measured in centimeters. It is clear that the increase of u' with height must be confined to a shallow layer.

The frequency distribution of eddy velocities has been examined by Hesselberg and Bjorkdal,[30] Wagner,[31] and Best.[8] The analogy between the kinetic theory of gases and the older theories of turbulence suggests that the familiar Maxwellian distribution should hold equally well for the velocity fluctuations. This is supported by the observations. Best has expressed the results in the form

$$f = f_0 \exp\,(-kg_x{}^2) \qquad\qquad (7.21)$$

where f is the number of fluctuations, expressed as a percentage of the total number examined, per unit range of $100g_x$ (that is, of gustiness expressed as a percentage). The results show close agreement with the Maxwell law (7.21). The values of k lie between 9.8 and 25.4 according as the mean wind velocity is above or below 400 cm sec^{-1} at $z = 200$ cm; there is also some evidence of an effect of temperature gradient.

The above results refer to fluctuations in the direction of the mean wind. The lateral and vertical fluctuations have also been examined by Best,[8] who followed Taylor and Scrase in using the bidirectional vane. This instrument is arranged so that movements in the (x,y) and (x,z) planes are recorded as a confused area of lines and loops. These areas are either oval or circular, and it is easily seen that the horizontal and vertical diameters of the areas measure g_y and g_z, respectively. A difficulty arises, however, in analyzing the records. It is fairly easy, as Best shows, to draw consistent ovals which enclose nearly all the loops made by the pen, and the diameters of these curves may be regarded as "extreme" values of g_y and g_z. It is more difficult to construct objectively curves which represent the mean excursions of the pen, and thus the data given for "mean" g_y and g_z are less certain. Despite these difficulties, the bidirectional vane must be regarded as a valuable asset in the study of the structure of a turbulent wind, and the conclusions drawn from a study of its records are, on the whole, reliable.

The main results are as follows:

At a fixed height of 200 cm above grassland:

1. Extreme lateral and vertical gustiness are practically independent of the magnitude of the mean wind velocity in lapse conditions ($\partial T/\partial z < 0$), but both components increase sharply with increasing wind speed in inversion conditions ($\partial T/\partial z > 0$).

2. Extreme lateral and vertical gustiness decrease as the temperature gradient changes from lapse to inversion (mean velocity constant).

3. The ratio of extreme values of g_y to extreme values of g_z is about 1.8, irrespective of mean wind speed and temperature gradient.

4. Mean values of g_y and g_z increase with mean velocity during lapses and inversions.

Over the height interval 25 to 506 cm:

1. The ratio of extreme g_y to extreme g_z at various heights is shown in the accompanying tabulation.

Height, cm..........	25	49	100	200	506
Ratio..............	2.93	2.58	2.13	1.81	1.40

The asymmetry is very strongly marked at 25 cm, where the lateral eddying energy $\rho v'^2$ can be nearly nine times greater than the vertical eddying energy $\rho w'^2$. There is a steady approach to equipartition with increasing height, and by extrapolation Best estimates that the lateral and vertical components should be about equal at heights greater than 25 m. Perhaps the most interesting fact revealed by this investigation is that while the lateral component of extreme gustiness decreases with height between 25 and 500 cm, the vertical component increases with height over the same interval.

Best gives the empirical laws

$$\text{Extreme lateral component } g_y \propto z^{-0.062} \qquad (7.22)$$
$$\text{Extreme vertical component } g_z \propto z^{0.175} \qquad (7.23)$$

Thus the vertical component of extreme gustiness increases with height at much the same rate as the mean velocity, in the layer 25 to 500 cm over grass.

2. The variation of eddy velocities with height (mean values) is shown by Table 26.

TABLE 26. VARIATION OF COMPONENTS OF EDDY VELOCITY, WITH HEIGHT, FOR ZERO
TEMPERATURE GRADIENT OVER GRASSLAND, AFTER BEST

z, cm	$\bar{u}$	u'	v'	w', cm sec^{-1}
25	262	41	86	24
49	299	44	96	29
100	331	..	103	37
200	370	52	111	50
506	405	..	109	64

It is clear from Table 26 that the variation is complex. There is a suggestion that the lateral component v' attains a maximum value between 200 and 500 cm, whereas the vertical component w' increases throughout the interval. This is somewhat different from the result previously obtained by Scrase, who found that both v' and w' have well-defined maxima about $1\frac{1}{2}$ m above ground. Best suggests that the empirical laws

$$v' = \text{constant} \cdot z^{0.11} \qquad (7.24)$$
$$w' = \text{constant} \cdot z^{0.34} \qquad (7.25)$$

hold for $25 \leq z \leq 500$ cm and zero temperature gradient. These results resemble those found by Fage and Townsend[32] for motion near the wall of a pipe, where much the same type of variation of u', v', and w' was found.

Very little exact information is available concerning the effect of roughness on the gustiness components. Some general information may be gathered from Table 27 (page 258), which shows values of the skin-friction coefficient C_D for various surfaces. Since $C_D = 2(u_*/\bar{u})^2$ and u_* is much the same, numerically, as u', it follows that there is a close correlation between C_D and $g_x{}^2$. It is also known that surface roughness affects the partition of eddying energy near the ground; over a very smooth surface, such as snow, equipartition is attained at a much lower level than over a rough surface. A complete explanation of this feature is lacking.

One further result may be quoted, because of its importance in problems of diffusion (Chap. 8). The size of the area covered by the pen of the bidirectional vane increases rapidly in the first minute, and only very slowly afterward. This may be interpreted as an effect caused by the intermingling of large and small eddies in the natural wind.

The above summary shows that the exploration of the fine structure of wind near the ground is far from complete and that a clear and self-consistent picture of the velocity field has yet to emerge. In certain respects the results gained so far throw doubt on some of the assumptions commonly made in the mathematical analysis of atmospheric turbulence, *e.g.*, it is usually assumed that the eddy velocities are virtually independent of height near the ground, whereas the observations indicate a variation with height of the same order as that of the mean velocity [compare Eqs. (7.22) to (7.25)]. It is also doubtful that the data obtained by the use of totally different instruments, such as the hot-wire anemometer and the bidirectional vane, are strictly comparable. These, and other uncertainties, can be resolved only by systematic observations of the microstructure of surface air currents, and as yet very few such surveys have been attempted.

Surface Friction and Shearing Stress. Estimations of the surface friction of the earth have been made (1) from observations on the approach to the geostrophic wind, (2) from wind profiles in the lower layers, (3) by direct measurement, using "drag plates." Method 1 yields the average value of the surface friction over a large area, and the results belong more to the realm of normal climatology than micrometeorology. Method 2 usually gives values typical of areas of the order of a few thousand square meters, while 3 may be looked upon as the nearest approach yet devised to the determination of friction at a point on the earth's surface.

1. The evaluation of surface friction from the wind profile in the

planetary boundary layer is usually included in textbooks of dynamic meteorology† and will be given here only in outline. The resultant shearing stress at any level is, by definition,

$$\tau_{zx} + i\tau_{zy} = K_M\rho \frac{\partial}{\partial z}(u + iv)$$

with the usual notation and system of axes. For the determination of the order of magnitude of the stress at the surface, τ_0, it is sufficient to consider the profile for $K_M = $ constant (Chap. 3). From this

$$\tau_{zx} + i\tau_{zy} = K_M\rho G(1 + i)\left(\frac{\lambda}{2K_M}\right)^{\frac{1}{2}} \exp\left[-(1 + i)\left(\frac{\lambda}{2K_M}\right)^{\frac{1}{2}}z\right]$$

If Z is the height at which the geostrophic direction is attained, it follows that the shearing stress at the surface is given by

$$\tau_0 = \frac{\lambda\rho ZG}{\pi\sqrt{2}}$$

From Dobson's observations of Z over Salisbury Plain the values shown in the accompanying table have been derived.

G, cm sec^{-1}	460	910	1560
τ_0, dynes cm^{-2}	0.8	2.2	4.2

It is customary to express the surface friction by means of the skin-friction coefficient C_D, defined by the equation

$$\tau_0 = \tfrac{1}{2}C_D\rho\bar{u}_s{}^2$$

where $\bar{u}_s$ is the wind velocity "near" the surface, *i.e.*, at some convenient height for continuous observations. In his analysis of Dobson's observations, Taylor[33] took $\bar{u}_s$ to be the wind at 30 m and found C_D to be about 0.005.‡ From Taylor's work it is clear that τ_0 is roughly proportional to $\bar{u}_s{}^2$, that is, C_D is approximately independent of the magnitude of the wind speed.

Taylor's original investigation has been followed by others. Sutcliffe,[34] using a somewhat different method, found C_D to be about 0.01 for land, using the wind at 10 m as the reference velocity. For the ocean, Sutcliffe gives the average value as 0.0008, and Durst[35] suggests that there is a

---

† See, *e.g.*, Brunt, "Physical and Dynamical Meteorology," 2d ed., pp. 259–260 (Cambridge, 1939); or Berry, Bollay, and Beers, "Handbook of Meteorology," pp. 454–455 (McGraw-Hill, 1945).

‡ The reader should take note that there is a lack of uniformity in the definition of the skin-friction coefficient. Some writers omit the factor $\tfrac{1}{2}$ and use $\tau = \kappa\rho u^2$, instead of $\tau = \tfrac{1}{2}C_D\,\rho u^2$. Taylor's results were originally given in terms of κ, which is one-half of C_D as defined in this book.

significant difference between polar and equatorial air, the greater value for equatorial air ($C_D \simeq 0.0014$ as compared with $C_D \simeq 0.0006$ for polar air) being ascribed to the fact that equatorial air is more stable than polar air. Durst finds that, for the oceans, C_D varies directly as the wind speed and that K_M is proportional to the fourth power of the surface wind velocity.

The outstanding fact which emerges from the above summary is that the values of C_D derived in this way are of the same order of magnitude as those employed in aerodynamics. For large Reynolds numbers ($10^5 \leq \text{Re} \leq 10^8$) the skin-friction coefficient for artificial surfaces such as wings and struts, flat plates, and airship hulls lies between 0.001 and 0.007 (Piercey[36]), a range which includes most of the values found for land. The remarkable nature of this result becomes clear on comparing the scales of length of the two sets of determinations, kilometers in the meteorological problem and centimeters in wind-tunnel work. The very small values found for the oceans are doubtless caused mainly by the special conditions which prevail at the water-air interface.

2. The derivation of values of τ_0 or C_D from profiles of wind near the surface is of more direct interest in micrometeorology. In conditions of neutral equilibrium, or small departures therefrom, Eqs. (7.1) to (7.3) are valid for smooth and fully-rough surfaces, respectively, provided that the vegetation cover is not too high. By definition

$$C_D = \frac{2\tau_0}{\rho \bar{u}^2} = 2\left(\frac{u_*}{\bar{u}}\right)^2 \tag{7.4}$$

Hence the profile equations may be written

$$\sqrt{\frac{2}{C_D}} = \frac{1}{k} \ln\left(\frac{u_* z}{\nu}\right) + \text{constant} \qquad \text{(smooth surface)}$$

or

$$\left. \begin{aligned} \sqrt{\frac{2}{C_D}} &= \frac{1}{k} \ln \frac{z}{z_0} \\[2mm] \sqrt{\frac{2}{C_D}} &= \frac{1}{k} \ln\left(\frac{z + z_0}{z_0}\right) \end{aligned} \right\} \text{(fully-rough surface)}$$

The expressions for fully-rough surfaces indicate that the skin-friction coefficient of the earth's surface should be independent of the magnitude of the reference velocity but dependent on the height z_1 at which the reference velocity is measured. Using the Rossby profile (7.3), it follows that

$$C_D = \frac{2k^2}{\left(\ln \dfrac{z_1 + z_0}{z_0}\right)^2}$$

where z_1 is some convenient height (usually 100 or 200 cm).

The statement that C_D for a fully-rough surface is independent of the magnitude of the reference velocity at a fixed height is well supported by observations, except for surfaces whose geometrical form changes with wind speed, such as a field of tall grass or a sheet of water. In all cases the values of C_D derived from the profiles reflect, to a greater or less degree, the immediate past history of the wind and are typical of the surface over which the air moves before reaching the anemometers. From studies of smoke clouds generated at ground level in conditions of neutral stability (see Chap. 8), an anemometer at height h will be influenced by the nature of the surface some $10h$ to $20h$ upwind, provided that the irregularities are not more than a few tens of centimeters high. Larger obstacles, such as trees, houses, and small hills, will affect profiles in their lee for much greater distances.

Table 27 shows values of C_D deduced by the use of Eq. (7.4) from the values of u_* given in Table 23 (page 233), taking the reference velocity $\bar{u}$ to be 500 cm sec^{-1} at $z = 200$ cm.

TABLE 27. VALUES OF THE SKIN-FRICTION COEFFICIENT C_D FOR NATURAL SURFACES
(Neutral equilibrium: reference velocity $\bar{u} = 500$ cm sec^{-1} at $z = 200$ cm)

Type of surface	C_D
Very smooth (mud flats, ice)	0.002
Lawn, grass up to 1 cm high	0.005
Downland, thin grass up to 10 cm high	0.010
Thick grass up to 10 cm high	0.016
Thin grass, up to 50 cm high	0.023
Thick grass, up to 50 cm high	0.032
Sea	0.002

For a field of long grass, C_D decreases with increasing wind speed, owing to the reduction of surface drag by the bending of the grass blades in the wind. Otherwise, the above values do not show any marked dependence on wind velocity. The value for sea is that given by Model[19] from an examination of Bruch's profiles and is the same as that for very smooth land, a result probably due to the motion of the water induced by the wind. Model's value of C_D for sea is somewhat greater than those found from a study of the slowing down of the geostrophic wind over the oceans, but apart from this the analysis of wind profiles in the surface boundary layer may be said to confirm the results given by the large-scale method 1.

The above values of C_D are valid for conditions of neutral stability. The question of possible variations of C_D with stability is discussed below (page 261).

3. A method for the direct measurement of surface friction at a point has been devised by Sheppard and extended by Pasquill.[37] Essentially, Sheppard's method consists in replacing a small portion of the earth's surface by a horizontal plate floating in oil, and under torsional control,

so that the plate is deflected from its original position by the pull of the wind. From measurements of the deflection it is possible to find the net horizontal force acting on the plate and hence the surface shearing stress. Sheppard used a smooth flat plate in the center of a wide faired surround and placed the whole apparatus near the down-wind edge of a horizontal circular area of concrete about 160 m in diameter, located on a ridge in Salisbury Plain. The results are therefore typical of a very smooth surface. Pasquill's apparatus followed the same general pattern, except that the smooth drag plate was replaced by a shallow pan containing a close-fitting sample of the grassland on which the experiments were conducted. Pasquill's results are thus typical of level pasture, with grass from 1 to 15 cm high. The principal results are given in Table 28.

TABLE 28. VALUES OF SURFACE FRICTION τ_0 AND DRAG COEFFICIENT C_D MEASURED BY DRAG PLATES

Smooth concrete surface, after Sheppard			
Wind speed at 100 cm, cm sec^{-1}	τ_0, dynes cm^{-2}	C_D†	Temperature difference, °C, 710–120 cm
480	0.310	0.0020	−0.44
377	0.206	0.0021	−0.44
356	0.193	0.0023	−0.56

Grassland, after Pasquill				
Wind speed at 100 cm, cm sec^{-1}	τ_0, dynes cm^{-2}	C_D‡	Temperature difference, °C, 150–37.5 cm	Grass length, cm
403	0.90	0.009	−0.40	1–5
478	1.44	0.011	−0.47	
483	1.53	0.011	−0.34	5–10
513	1.53	0.010	−0.18	
429	1.38	0.013	+0.41	10–15
440	1.59	0.014	+0.40	

† Relative to $\bar{u}$ measured at $z = 200$ cm.
‡ Relative to $\bar{u}$ measured at $z = 100$ cm.

These results are in satisfactory agreement with values deduced from wind structure.

Determinations of Kármán's Constant k and Mixing Length l. Sheppard, in the same paper,[11] has also discussed the direct determination of k and l near the ground. In aerodynamic problems it is customary to take

$k = 0.4$, a value also used in most investigations in atmospheric turbulence. For neutral stability, k can be found directly by the use of one or another of Eqs. (7.1) to (7.3). Sheppard assumed that the logarithmic form is a sufficiently good approximation to the velocity profile in the layer $0 \leq z \leq 200$ cm, for all temperature gradients, and deduced the values of k shown in the accompanying table from Best's profiles over

Temperature difference, °C, 110–10 cm...............	$-.167$	0.0	$+0.56$
k.......................	0.61	0.40	0.22

short grass. Pasquill found that the mean profile over grass agreed with the theoretical equation

$$\frac{\bar{u}(z)}{\bar{u}(100)} = \frac{\log_{10} e}{k} \left[\frac{u_*}{\bar{u}(100)} \right] \log_{10} \frac{z - d}{z_0}$$

if $z_0 = 0.66$ cm and $\dfrac{\log_{10} e}{k} \left[\dfrac{u_*}{\bar{u}(100)} \right] = 0.466$. The mean value of $u_*/\bar{u}(100)$ in Pasquill's experiments was 0.075, with little variation with temperature gradient. This gives $k = 0.37$, a value in good agreement with that obtained in laboratory investigations.

Variations in k are thus intimately related to changes in $C_D = 2(u_*/\bar{u})^2$, and it is difficult to separate the two in the present state of knowledge. If k is regarded simply as a constant in the profile equation, any extension to nonadiabatic gradients is of doubtful validity because of the breakdown of the logarithmic profile in large lapse rates and large inversions. If k is defined by the equations

$$l = k \frac{\partial \bar{u}/\partial z}{\partial^2 \bar{u}/\partial z^2}$$

$$w' = l \frac{\partial \bar{u}}{\partial z}$$

[Eq. (3.42)], it follows that

$$k = \frac{w' \, \partial^2 \bar{u}/\partial z^2}{(\partial \bar{u}/\partial z)^2} \tag{7.26}$$

and this definition may be adopted for all conditions of stability. Applying this to a simple power-law profile

$$\bar{u}(z) = \bar{u}(z_1) \left(\frac{z}{z_1} \right)^p \qquad p > 0$$

it follows that

$$\frac{|w'|}{\bar{u}} = g_z = k \left| \frac{p}{p - 1} \right| \tag{7.27}$$

Sheppard uses this equation, and Best's values for g_z, to confirm that k decreases with the change from unstable to stable conditions.

If k is allowed to vary in the manner quoted above, the fitting of the logarithmic profile to Best's observations of wind velocities over grass requires the additional complication that z_0 must also depend on stability, being small for unstable profiles and relatively large for stable conditions. With these assumptions, C_D remains approximately constant in the range of stability covered by Best's work. These views conflict with the opinion expressed by Deacon, that z_0 may be regarded as a parameter which is virtually independent of the thermal stratification. The values of z_0 and k in Deacon's power-law profile for nonadiabatic conditions are identical with those employed in the logarithmic profile for neutral stability.

It does not seem possible, at the present time, to carry the examination of the various theories further with profit, and the ultimate resolution of the problem must await further experimental work. It seems fairly clear, however, from the work of Sheppard and Pasquill that for a given surface, variations in C_D cannot be large for any but the largest departures from neutral stability.

Sheppard[11] has computed the mixing length l as a function of height from the equation

$$l = \frac{u_*}{(\partial \bar{u}/\partial z)}$$

For the temperature gradients given in Table 28 (lapse conditions), Sheppard finds that the points fit the line

$$l = 0.45z$$

for $20 \leq z \leq 100$ cm but that for $z > 100$ cm, l increases more rapidly than the height. The value 0.45 of the slope of the linear portion of the plot is in good agreement with the value of k obtained above. The whole (l,z) curve is well represented by

$$l = 0.25z^{1.15}$$

for $20 \leq z \leq 200$ cm. From the general result that the u, log z curve is convex to the u axis in lapse conditions and concave to the same axis in inversion conditions (Fig. 25) it follows that if the variation of l with height can be represented by a power law

$$l = l_1 z^q$$

in all conditions, it would be expected that $q > 1$ in unstable conditions, $q = 1$ for neutral stability, and $q < 1$ for stable conditions. In lapse conditions the mixing length increases more rapidly than the height and in inversion conditions less rapidly than the height.

Direct Measurements of the Reynolds Stress.   Scrase[5] has evaluated the Reynolds stress

$$\tau = -\rho\overline{u'w'}$$

directly from ciné records of the movements of light vanes at heights of 1.5 and 19 m, above downland in conditions of neutral stability.   This involved finding directly the correlation between u' and w'.   As originally published, Scrase's values indicated a large increase (roughly 4 to 1) of τ with height over this interval, a conclusion which is in striking contradiction to the familiar assumption that τ is invariable with height, to a high degree of approximation, for $z \leq 25$ m (page 79).   Scrase later corrected this result, giving the ratio $\tau_{19}/\tau_{1.5} = 2.5$.   This is still too large to remove the discrepancy noted above, and the anomaly has yet to be explained.   Pasquill suggests that the stress at 1.5 m, being primarily dependent on the nature of the surface within a few tens of meters upwind of the anemometer, is not strictly comparable with that at 19 m, since the latter is influenced by surface conditions at much greater distances upwind, but if this were so, the profiles observed in these layers would not be expected to conform so closely to those predicted by theory.   The absolute value obtained by Scrase ($\tau = 0.9$ dynes cm^{-2} for $\bar{u} = 468$ cm sec^{-1} at $z = 150$ cm) agrees reasonably well with the values obtained by Pasquill for a not dissimilar surface.

Scrase's work on the direct determination of $\overline{u'w'}$ is of fundamental importance, since the whole theory of atmospheric turbulence is founded on the conception of the Reynolds stress, and it is essential that additional observations should be made over a wide range of different conditions. Rossby[38] has given some values of

$$r = \frac{\overline{u'w'}}{\overline{u'^2}} = -\frac{\tau}{\rho\overline{u'^2}}$$

at seven different heights between 0.5 and 7.7 m, in the neighborhood of sand dunes on the eastern shore of Lake Michigan.   His results are as given in the accompanying table.

Height, cm......	50	100	200	400	500	600	770
r..............	0.51	0.31	0.28	0.23	0.27	0.23	0.22

These values agree well with those found by Wattendorf,[39] working in a rectangular channel, namely, $r = 0.32$ from 0.3 of the distance from the channel center to the wall and up to the immediate vicinity of the wall. Reichardt[40] in Göttingen found $r = 0.23$.   Rossby does not give the value of $\rho\overline{u'^2}$, so that a direct comparison with values of τ obtained by other workers is not possible, and in view of the uncertain nature of the variation of u' with height it would be unwise to make any detailed deduction concerning changes of τ, but it appears that any variation with height is not likely to be as large as that found by Scrase.

Correlations. The statistical theory of turbulence involves the study of correlations between velocity fluctuations. Such correlations may be in time, *e.g.*, the autocorrelation between the velocity at a fixed point at successive instants of time, or in space, *e.g.*, the correlation between velocities at a fixed time at different points.

Measurements of the autocorrelation coefficient (correlation of a speed with itself) have been published by Giblett *et al.*[15] for the airfield at Cardington, England. One such example is given in the accompanying tabulation, based on records taken by a pressure-tube anemometer at 50 ft above the ground.

Time, sec..............	0	5	10	20	30	40	50	60
Correlation coefficient.....	1.0	0.69	0.50	0.11	−0.08	−0.19	−0.42	−0.38

This may be interpreted as showing the existence of a pattern which tends to repeat itself in about 100 sec which, with a mean wind of about 17 m sec^{-1}, indicates an eddy structure of dimension about 1700 meters.

The autocorrelation coefficient $R(\xi)$ which occurs in Taylor's theory (Chap. 3) is defined as the correlation between velocity fluctuations which affect a particle at an instant t and at a time $t + \xi$ later. Measurements of a similar quantity were made by P. A. Sheppard in 1936 with the aid of a hot-wire anemometer and quoted by Sutton[40] in 1949. The data are given in the adjoining table.

ξ, sec...........	0	0.05	0.1	0.2	0.5	1	2	3	4	5	10
$R(\xi)$.............	1.0	0.907	0.885	0.788	0.680	0.572	0.456	0.431	0.358	0.281	0.034

Height of observations: 200 cm.
Terrain: Downland, grass up to 30 cm high.
Correlations between u', where $\overline{u'^2} = 6.51 \times 10^3$ cm^2 sec^{-2}.

Sutton has shown that the variation given in this table is moderately well expressed by the formula

$$R(\xi) = \left(\frac{N}{N + \overline{u'^2}\xi}\right)^n \tag{7.28}$$

where $N = u_* z_0 = 100$ cm^2 sec^{-1} and $n = 0.15$. This form is of importance in problems of diffusion (Chap. 8).

The eddy viscosity K_M is given by

$$K_M = \overline{u'^2} \int_0^{t_0} R(\xi)d\xi \qquad (7.29)$$

where t_0 is the time taken for a disturbance to travel a distance down wind before mixing again with the main body of the turbulent fluid. This distance must be of the same order of magnitude as the vertical mixing length l, and therefore is about 100 cm at a height of 200 cm above the ground. Thus $t_0 \simeq l/\sqrt{(\overline{u'^2})}$ does not exceed 2 sec. The value of $\int_0^2 R(\xi)d\xi$ is about 1.32 sec, so that

$$K_M = 6.51 \times 10^3 \times 1.32 = 8.6 \times 10^3 \text{ cm}^2 \text{ sec}^{-1}$$

This estimate agrees with those obtained by other methods.

7.5. Effects of Stabilizing Density Gradients

The typical nocturnal inversion of the lower atmosphere is rarely steady throughout a clear night but usually shows a succession of increases to large values, followed by relatively rapid falls to zero, or some low value. The build-up of the temperature gradient is generally accompanied by a steepening of the velocity gradient and a pronounced decrease in the gustiness of the wind. In general terms, it appears that the stabilizing density gradient brings about a close approach to laminar flow, but with such large velocity differences between adjacent layers of fluid, the motion is highly susceptible to the effects of finite random disturbances and sooner or later breaks down into turbulence. The subsequent mixing causes a rapid fall in the gradients of temperature and velocity. A well-defined instance of this process has been given by Durst[41] in an examination of wind structure over the airfield at Cardington, England, and this example has been used to deduce the critical value of the Richardson number (Sec. 4.9). At the time when $(\partial \bar{u}/\partial z)^2$ was approximately equal to $g(\partial \ln \theta/\partial z)$, the pressure-tube anemometers indicated perfectly steady motion, but this state lasted only for a short period and was quickly followed by the reappearance of gusts, with simultaneous rapid falls in $\partial \bar{u}/\partial z$ and $\partial \theta/\partial z$. From these observations Durst concludes that turbulence is extinguished when $\text{Ri} = g(\partial \theta/\partial z)/\theta(\partial \bar{u}/\partial z)^2 = 1$. This agrees with Richardson's original deduction.

Other meteorological investigations have produced a wide range of values for Ri_c. Some of this scatter is due to the absence of a clear-cut definition of turbulence, and there is also a marked tendency for the conclusion to be affected by the type of anemometer used. Paeschke[10] has compared his results for winds near the surface with Schlichting's theoretical criterion $\text{Ri}_c = \frac{1}{24}$, but no very definite conclusion emerges, except that the magnitude of the oscillations decreases as Ri increases. Other evidence, suggesting values of Ri_c between $\frac{1}{2}$ and 1, has been summarized by Sutton.[42] The possible effect of surface roughness has been noted in Chap. 4, and the evidence available so far lends weight to the view that a unique value of Ri_c may not exist.

Some fairly weighty evidence against this suggestion has been assembled by Deacon[7] in an examination of the work of Rossby and Montgomery[17] and of Holzman[43] on velocity profiles in thermally stratified flow. Rossby and Montgomery consider that the chief effect of a stabilizing gradient is to reduce the mixing length from its value in neutral equilibrium, l, to a value $l_s < l$. If $\partial\bar{u}/\partial z$ is the velocity gradient for neutral equilibrium and $(\partial\bar{u}/\partial z)_s$ that for stable equilibrium, the corresponding turbulent kinetic energies are proportional to $l^2(\partial\bar{u}/\partial z)^2$ and $l_s^2(\partial\bar{u}/\partial z)_s^2$, respectively. The decrease in the kinetic energy of the fluctuations is proportional to the work done against gravity in the vertical displacement of eddies in the stable state. Rossby and Montgomery express this by the equation

$$l^2 \left(\frac{\partial\bar{u}}{\partial z}\right)_s^2 - l_s^2 \left(\frac{\partial\bar{u}}{\partial z}\right)_s^2 = \beta \frac{g}{\theta} l_s^2 \frac{\partial\theta}{\partial z}$$

where β is supposed to be an absolute constant and differences between velocity gradients are neglected. Hence

$$l_s = \frac{l}{\sqrt{(1 + \beta\,\text{Ri})}} = \frac{kz}{\sqrt{(1 + \beta\,\text{Ri})}} \tag{7.30}$$

and the velocity profile should therefore satisfy the differential equation

$$\frac{d\bar{u}}{dz} = \frac{u_*}{l_s} = \frac{u_*}{kz} \sqrt{(1 + \beta\,\text{Ri})} \tag{7.31}$$

in all conditions. This equation reduces to the usual form (3.36) in neutral equilibrium (Ri = 0), and in this respect the Rossby-Montgomery equation is consistent with previous work, but the assumption that there exists a unique constant β is arbitrary and can be justified only by an appeal to observations. Sverdrup, in the course of an extensive analysis of wind profiles over snow (usually with Ri > 0), found support for this theory and deduced the value $\beta = 11$, but Deacon, using profiles measured over short grass and in a desert, found that β increases systematically as the stability increases.

In laminar flow, mixing is characterized by the infinitesimal molecular free path, and the vanishing of the turbulent mixing length therefore indicates the extinction of turbulence. The Rossby-Montgomery expression for l_s tends to zero rather slowly with increasing Ri and does not vanish for any finite value of the Richardson number, a property which is con-

trary to most of the observations.   Holzman suggested, entirely empirically, that a more reasonable form for l_s is

$$l_s = l \sqrt{(1 - \sigma \text{ Ri})} = kz \sqrt{(1 - \sigma \text{ Ri})} \tag{7.32}$$

where σ is another (positive) constant.   This makes $l_s = 0$ when $\text{Ri} = 1/\sigma$,
a finite value.   The differential equation for the profile is

$$\frac{d\bar{u}}{dz} = \frac{u_*}{kz \sqrt{(1 - \sigma \text{ Ri})}} \tag{7.33}$$

provided that $\sigma \text{ Ri} < 1$.   Holzman's conjecture may be tested in two
ways, first, by finding whether or not σ shows any systematic variation
with surface roughness and stability and, second, by examining the prediction that turbulence is extinguished when $\text{Ri} = 1/\sigma$.   These tests have
been carried out by Deacon for a moderately wide range of conditions,
using, in the first place, profiles measured over grassland and desert
$(0.03 \leq z_0 \leq 0.4; -0.4 \leq \text{Ri} \leq 0.3)$ and, for the second test, records
from bidirectional vanes and a Dines pressure-tube anemometer (head
13 m above downland), with very satisfactory results.   Values of σ
obtained from the wind profiles show no systematic variation with either
z_0 or Ri but are grouped in a random fashion about the mean value $\sigma = 7$,
the range of individual values being 4 to 11.   In the second test, both
the bidirectional vane and the anemometer indicated a complete absence
of gustiness when $\text{Ri} \geq 0.15$.   This agrees very well with the value
$1/\sigma = 1/7 \simeq 0.14$ obtained from the profiles.

When Ri is very small, Holzman's expression for l_s is almost identical
with that proposed by Rossby and Montgomery, but, apart from this,
Eq. (7.32) has no theoretical basis.   Deacon's result that $\text{Ri}_c = 0.15$
appears to be based on better evidence than most of the earlier results,
but the investigation needs to be extended to a variety of surfaces before
the conclusion can be accepted as final.   The most encouraging feature
of this work is that it indicates a possible link between the turbulent and
laminar states.   In the present state of the development of the theory of
atmospheric turbulence it is difficult to predict diffusion processes in
extremes of temperature gradient with confidence, and any advance on
these lines is to be welcomed.   The general problem of the transition
from turbulent to laminar flow still remains, however, one of the most
difficult and obscure in meteorology.

7.6. Winds of Local Origin

The preceding discussions are concerned with winds which form part of
large-scale dynamic systems, but there exist near the surface of the earth
air movements of purely local origin, only indirectly related to the main

pressure field. Such winds usually last only a few hours and extend, at the most, over a few tens of kilometers of the earth's surface. Very often, they have important effects on agriculture and other forms of human activity.

Land and Sea Breezes. The most familiar example of a local wind is found in coastal areas. In strong sunshine, the surface of the earth becomes warmer than that of the adjacent ocean, and, as a result, pressure falls less rapidly over the land than over the sea. At the junction of land and sea, the isobaric and isoteric (equal density) surfaces slope in different directions, intersecting over the coast line. This condition, as Brunt[2] shows, sets up a circulation about the intersections of the surfaces, and a wind blows from sea to land during the day. Physically, the cold air from the sea pushes underneath the warm air over the land. At night, when the land is colder than the surface of the sea, the drift of air is from land to sea.

Observations of the sea breeze on the coast of New England have been made by Willett,[44] who finds that the current is shallow, usually from 250 to 400 m in depth. The effects are noticeable as much as 30 miles (50 km) inland and out to sea. In the late afternoon the sea breeze tends to become parallel to the coast.

Haurwitz[23] has considered the general theory of the sea breeze and finds that the Coriolis term exercises a significant influence. The term equivalent to the pressure gradient in the circulation theorem is proportional to the difference in temperature over the land and sea. W. J. Pierson[45] has recently extended this work to include the effects of eddy friction, but the complete mathematical expression for the velocity is extremely long and complicated and will not be given here. The results agree qualitatively with Willett's data for New England and show some measure of general quantitative agreement with observations at Boston, Massachusetts, but there are discrepancies in detail.

Mountain and Valley Winds. The phenomenon of mountain and valley winds, which is of considerable importance in the economics of agriculture in hilly country, has been investigated by Wagner, Defant, and others. Observation shows that well-defined local circulations are found in valleys leading into mountain ranges from a plain. Such circulations show a marked diurnal variation in conditions where the main pressure field is fairly steady. An idealized description of valley winds, given by F. Defant[46] on the basis of Wagner's work, runs as follows: Before sunrise there is a steady movement of air down the valley into the plain, the so-called mountain wind (*Bergwind*). As the sun rises, the sloping sides of the valley are warmed and buoyant air begins to move up the slopes, to descend again in the center of the valley. This upslope wind (*Hangaufwinde*) prevails until about noon, when it is joined by a wind blowing up the valley from the plain.   In the late afternoon the valley wind dominates, and the upslope wind weakens and disappears. In the evening, the cooling of the air in contact with the upper parts of the sloping sides starts a downslope, or katabatic, wind (*Hangabwinde*), which ultimately produces a typical circulation in which air rolls down the slopes and is pushed up in the center of the valley.   Late at night the katabatic circulation is replaced by the mountain wind, and a steady drift of air from the head of the valley into the plain continues until dawn.

Mathematical analysis of slope winds.   The kinematics of air motion in undulating country has been discussed in Chap. 2 as an example of irrotational motion of a perfect fluid.   Prandtl[47] has given a simple solution of the problem of convective motion on a slope, taking friction into account.   Considering the case of upslope winds (the analysis needs only

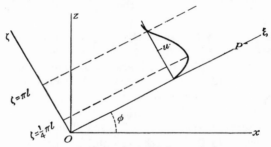

Fig. 29.   Analysis of slope winds.

slight modification for downslope currents), let OP be a section of a plane inclined at an angle ϕ to the horizontal, and let ξ, ζ be coordinates measured along and normal to the slope.   If z is height above the horizontal plane Ox,

$$z = \xi \sin \phi + \zeta \cos \phi \qquad (7.34)$$

During the night the atmosphere is in stable equilibrium, with potential temperature θ increasing upward.   At dawn, the sun's rays heat the surface, and heat is conducted to the air, causing a deviation θ' from the initial state.   It is assumed that during the night there is a linear increase of potential temperature with height.   Soon after dawn

$$\theta = A + Bz + \theta'(\zeta) \qquad (7.35)$$

where A and B are constants.   The acceleration of the air in the vertical, due to buoyancy, is $g\alpha\theta'$, where α is the coefficient of thermal expansion (Chap. 4).   Resolving parallel to the slope, the equation of motion of the upslope wind u is

$$\frac{du}{dt} = g\alpha\theta' \sin \phi + K_M \frac{\partial^2 u}{\partial \zeta^2} \qquad (7.36)$$

and it is supposed that u is a function of ζ only, and always parallel to the slope, so that $du/dt = \partial u/\partial t$; K_M is the eddy viscosity, assumed constant. The equation of conduction of heat is

$$\frac{d\theta}{dt} = K_H \left(\frac{\partial^2 \theta}{\partial \xi^2} + \frac{\partial^2 \theta}{\partial \zeta^2} \right) \tag{7.37}$$

where K_H is the eddy conductivity, also assumed constant. It is supposed that $K_M \neq K_H$.

The steady state, defined by $\partial u/\partial t = 0$, implies that $d\theta/dt = u\partial\theta/\partial\xi$, and it is further assumed that $\partial^2\theta/\partial\xi^2$ is vanishingly small compared with $\partial^2\theta/\partial\zeta^2$. Equations (7.36) and (7.37) reduce to

$$0 = g\alpha\theta' \cdot \sin\phi + K_M \frac{\partial^2 u}{\partial\xi^2} \tag{7.38}$$

$$u \frac{\partial\theta}{\partial\xi} = K_H \frac{\partial^2\theta}{\partial\zeta^2} \tag{7.39}$$

Transforming the coordinates by (7.34), it follows that

$$uB \sin\phi = K_H \frac{\partial^2\theta'}{\partial\zeta^2} \tag{7.40}$$

Differentiating Eq. (7.40) twice with respect to ζ and substituting for $\partial^2 u/\partial\zeta^2$ in Eq. (7.38) results in the fourth-order equation

$$\frac{\partial^4\theta'}{\partial\zeta^4} + \left(\frac{g\alpha}{K_M K_H} \right) B \sin^2\phi \cdot \theta' = 0$$

The solution of this equation, which is finite on $\zeta = 0$ and vanishes as $\zeta \to \infty$, is

$$\theta'(\zeta) = \theta_0' \cos\frac{\zeta}{l} \exp\left(-\frac{\zeta}{l} \right) \tag{7.41}$$

where θ_0' is the temperature rise on the surface of the slope ($\zeta = 0$) and l is a constant length defined by the equation

$$l^4 = 4 \left(\frac{K_M K_H}{g\alpha} \right) \frac{\operatorname{cosec}^2\phi}{B}$$

The velocity profile of the slope wind in the direction of the normal to the slope is given by

$$u = \theta_0' \left(\frac{g\alpha K_M}{B K_H} \right)^{\frac{1}{2}} \sin\frac{\zeta}{l} \exp\left(-\frac{\zeta}{l} \right) \tag{7.42}$$

This profile is in the form of a damped oscillation about $u = 0$, the amplitude decreasing with distance normal to the slope. The velocity vanishes and changes sign on $\zeta = 0$, πl, $2\pi l$, . . . , but in practice the wind is effectively confined to the layer $(0,\pi l)$ because of the rapid decrease of the factor exp $(-\zeta/l)$ as ζ becomes large (Fig. 29). The velocity gradient normal to the slope is given by

$$\frac{\partial u}{\partial \zeta} = \theta_0' \left(\frac{g\alpha K_H}{BK_M}\right)^{\frac{1}{2}} \exp\left(-\frac{\zeta}{l}\right)\left(\cos\frac{\zeta}{l} - \sin\frac{\zeta}{l}\right)$$

Thus the wind reaches its first and absolute maximum at a distance normal to the slope given by

$$\zeta = \tfrac{1}{4}\,\pi l \tag{7.43}$$

Observations on slope winds. F. Defant has given the results of observations made with pilot balloons on a steep slope ($\phi = 42°$) in the Innsbruck range. These are reproduced in Table 29.

TABLE 29. UP- AND DOWNSLOPE WINDS FOR A STEEP HILL ($\phi = 42°$), AFTER F. DEFANT

Upslope winds											
Distance normal to slope (ζ), m	5	10	15	20	25	30	35	40	50	100	120	130
Velocity (u), cm sec^{-1}	229	291	339	370	386	386	380	367	339	242	226	238

Downslope winds											
Distance normal to slope (ζ), m	5	10	15	20	25	30	35	40	50	100	110
Velocity ($\bar{u}$), cm sec^{-1}	96	150	195	222	234	235	227	215	191	23	−2

It is noticeable that although both currents reach fairly well-defined maxima about $\zeta = 27$ m, the upslope wind shows no appreciable decline at $\zeta = 130$ m, whereas the downslope wind vanishes at about $\zeta = 100$ m.

From Eq. (7.48) and the recorded position of maximum velocity on the plane $\zeta = 27$ m, it follows that

$$l = 34.4 \text{ m}$$

Hence both the upslope and downslope winds should be shallow currents, effectively confined to the layer $0 \leq \zeta \leq \pi l = 108$ m. This is in excellent agreement with observations on the downslope winds but is contradicted by measurements of the upslope current. For the determination of the actual velocities which, for a given l, depend only on the ratio K_H/K_M, it is assumed that the eddy conductivity is 50 per cent greater than the eddy viscosity, a conclusion based on wind-tunnel observations by Elias and Lorenz. The results show reasonably good agreement with the absolute magnitudes obtained from the pilot-balloon studies, except for the discrepancy, noted above, between the theoretical and observed upslope winds for values of ζ in the neighborhood of 100 m.

F. Defant has also extended Prandtl's solution to the nonsteady case, for the details of which the reader is referred to the original paper. Prandtl's simple analysis thus gives results which are in good agreement with the observations, despite the somewhat drastic nature of the assumptions, and the solution may be regarded as a successful first attack on a problem of considerable importance. The drainage of cold air into a valley may have serious consequences on crops, or even on human welfare if a source of pollution is involved, and the problem merits deeper study if only for these reasons.

BIBLIOGRAPHY

1. G. Hellmann, Meteorol. Z., 32, 1 (1915).
2. D. Brunt, "Physical and Dynamical Meteorology" (Cambridge, 1939).
3. G. S. P. Heywood, Quart. J. Roy. Meteorol. Soc., 57, 433 (1931).
4. O. G. Sutton, Quart. J. Roy. Meteorol. Soc., 58, 74 (1932).
5. F. J. Scrase, Geophys. Mem. 52.
6. C. W. Thornthwaite and P. Kaser, Trans. Am. Geophys. Union, 1, 166 (1943).
7. E. L. Deacon, Quart. J. Roy. Meteorol. Soc., 75, 89 (1949).
8. A. C. Best, Geophys. Mem. 65.
9. H. U. Sverdrup, Geophys. Pub., 11, 7 (1936).
10. W. Paeschke, Beitr. Phys. fr. Atmos., 24, 163 (1937).
11. P. A. Sheppard, Proc. Roy. Soc. (London), A188, 208 (1947).
12. H. Lettau, "Atmosphärische Turbulenz" (Leipzig, 1939).
13. R. Frost, Meteorol. Mag., 76, 14 (1947).
14. Barkat Ali, Quart. J. Roy. Meteorol. Soc., 58, 285 (1932).
15. M. A. Giblett et al., Geophys. Mem. 54.
16. K. L. Calder, Quart. J. Mech. Applied Math., 2, 153 (1949).
17. C.-G. Rossby and R. B. Montgomery, Papers Phys. Oceanog. Meteorol., Mass. Inst. Technol. and Woods Hole Oceaneog. Inst., 3, No. 3 (1935).
18. W. H. Munk, J. Maritime Research, VI, 203 (1947).
19. F. Model, Beitr. Angew. Geophys., 59, 102, (1942).
20. L. Prandtl and W. Tollmien, Z. Geophys., 1, 47 (1923).
21. H. Köhler, Kgl. Svenska Vetenskansakad. Handl., 13, 1 (1933).
22. C.-G. Rossby, Mass. Inst. Technol., Meteorol. Papers, 1, 4 (1932).
23. B. Haurwitz, J. Meteorol, 4, 1 (1947).
24. F. Åkerblom, Arkiv Mat. Astron. Fysih, 11, No. 18 (1916).
25. H. Jeffreys, Proc. Roy. Soc. (London), A96, 233 (1920).
26. F. L. Westwater, Quart. J. Roy. Meteorol. Soc., 69, 207 (1943).
27. Sir Napier Shaw, "Manual of Meteorology," Vol. IV (Cambridge, 1930).
28. J. S. Dines, Aeronaut. Research Committee, R. and M., No. 36.
29. G. I. Taylor, Aeronaut. Research Committee, R. and M., No. 345.
30. Th. Hesselberg and B. Bjorkdal, Beitr. Phys. fr. Atmos., 15 (1921).
31. A. Wagner, Gerlands Beitr. Geophysik, 24, 368 (1929).
32. A. Fage and H. C. H. Townsend, Proc. Roy. Soc. (London), A135, 656 (1932).
33. G. I. Taylor, Proc. Roy. Soc. (London), A92, 196 (1916).
34. R. C. Sutcliffe, Quart. J. Roy. Meteorol. Soc., 62, 3 (1936).
35. C. S. Durst, Monthly Notes Roy. Astron. Soc., 5, 369 (1949).
36. N. V. Piercey, "Aerodynamics" (London), 1947.
37. F. Pasquill, Proc. Roy. Soc. (London), A202, 143 (1950).
38. C.-G. Rossby, Ann. N.Y. Acad. Sci., 44 (1943).

39. WATTENDORF; see v. Kármán, J. Aeronaut. Sci., 1, 20 (1934).
40. O. G. SUTTON, Quart. J. Roy. Meteorol. Soc., 75, 335 (1949).
41. C. S. DURST, Quart. J. Roy. Meteorol. Soc., 59, 131 (1933).
42. O. G. SUTTON, "Atmospheric Turbulence" (London, 1949).
43. B. HOLZMAN, Ann. N.Y. Acad. Sci., 44, 13 (1943).
44. H. C. WILLETT, "Descriptive Meteorology" (New York, 1944).
45. W. J. PIERSON, JR., N.Y. Univ., Meteorol. Papers 1, 2 (1950).
46. F. DEFANT, Arch. Meteorol., A1, 421 (1949).
47. L. PRANDTL, "Strömungslehre" (Brunswick, 1942).

CHAPTER 8

DIFFUSION AND EVAPORATION

Problems of diffusion in the lower atmosphere fall into two main classes, depending on whether the rate of production of the diffusing substance is, or is not, affected by the properties of the ambient atmosphere. The diffusing substance may be gaseous or solid matter in a finely divided form. The typical problem in the first class is that of the spread of smoke from an industrial site, in which the strength of the source is effectively independent of meteorological conditions. In the second class the outstanding problem, that of evaporation from free surfaces of water or from the ground, amounts to the determination of the strength of the source in terms of wind, temperature, and humidity of the atmosphere.

Many of the experimental data on atmospheric diffusion available at the present time come from military sources, because of the need, in chemical warfare, for accurate estimates of the dispersion of toxic gases in various meteorological conditions. Such data usually relate to controlled sources and throw considerable light on processes in the turbulent lower atmosphere because of their precision and relative simplicity.

8.1. Characteristics of Clouds from Artificial Sources

The problem of atmospheric diffusion is most easily approached by considering the spread of smoke from a steady continuous source at ground level. In a moderate wind the smoke from such a source drifts down wind as a long, expanding plume. The frontispiece, an instantaneous photograph taken from the flank, shows a characteristic ragged top edge, sloping upward from the source at an angle which depends, to a greater or less degree, on the strength of the wind, the nature of the source (whether hot or cold), and the stability of the atmosphere. The plan of the cloud, as revealed by a similar photograph taken from above, shows a fan-shaped plume, with irregular boundaries. The cloud from a continuous point source thus expands vertically and laterally with distance from the source, and the particles move away from the point of emission with the speed of the wind.

The fundamental *theoretical* problem of atmospheric diffusion is to relate the spread of the cloud, and the consequent fall in the concentration, or density, of suspended matter, to the speed and turbulence of the

273

wind.   The *practical* problem is to find means of estimating the rate of
the diffusion from simultaneous measurements of purely meteorological
entities, such as wind, temperature, and humidity.   The concentration
of matter exhibits fluctuations at any point, but attention is invariably
directed toward the behavior of the mean concentration over a chosen
period of sampling.

   Nomenclature.   The following terms are used throughout the chapter.

   1. The *strength of the source Q* is the rate of production of matter as a
gas or in the form of a fine suspension (particulate cloud).   If matter is
formed instantaneously, as in an explosion, the source is simply the mass
of material (grams) which becomes air-borne.   When matter is being
evolved continuously at a point, as with a gas cylinder, smoke generator,
or chimney, Q is expressed in grams per second.   A cross-wind line source
consists of a number of point generators placed normal to the direction
of the mean wind, and Q is expressed in g sec^{-1} cm^{-1}, the rate of production of air-borne material per unit length of line.   An area source, such as
the rate of evaporation, means that Q is expressed as g sec^{-1} cm^{-2}.

   2. The *mean concentration*, or density, of suspended matter, whether
gaseous or particulate, is ideally expressed in grams per cubic centimeter.
To avoid very small numbers and troublesome negative powers of 10,
it is customary, in studies of chemical warfare, to measure concentration
in milligrams per cubic meter.   The stoichiometric system is also frequently used for true gases, especially in data relating to atmospheric
pollution.   In this, concentration is expressed in parts per volume,
usually as so many parts per million.   The relation between the density
and the stoichiometric ratio depends upon Avogadro's law that 1 gram
molecule of a true gas at normal temperature and pressure occupies
approximately 22.4 liters.   For sulfur dioxide (SO_2, molecular weight
64), the most common atmospheric impurity, the relation is

$$1 \text{ mg m}^{-3} = 0.35 \text{ ppm}$$

Throughout this chapter the absolute system of units is used, so that the
results are applicable to any true gas, or to solid matter in suspension,
provided that the particles are small enough to allow gravitational settling
to be ignored.

   3. The *dimensions* of a cloud (*height* and *width*) are conveniently
defined by the convention that the boundary of the cloud is found at
points where the concentration is a fixed fraction, usually one-tenth, of
the highest concentration in the same plane.

   Influence of the Period of Sampling.   Examination of the concentrations
from a fixed point source is usually carried out by placing sampling
apparatus along arcs, centered at the point of emission and extending
across wind, at fixed distances from the source.   With suitable apparatus

it is possible to take samples for periods varying from "instantaneous" (*i.e.*, the total time of sampling less than 1 sec) to minutes or hours. The results bring out very clearly the importance of the period of sampling in field work on diffusion. Instantaneous samples, when plotted against distance across wind, usually show a single-maximum curve of the "cocked-hat" type, with a relatively high peak and narrow base. A time-mean sample, extending over several minutes, with the sampling apparatus fixed in position relative to the source, shows a curve of the same general type, with a lower peak value and a broader base. The general character of the results is shown in Fig. 30, which refers to concentrations from a point source of chemical smoke in conditions of small temperature

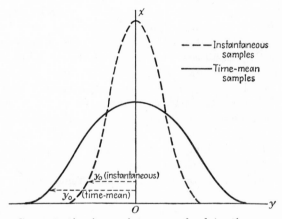

Fig. 30.   Concentration in a point-source cloud (section across wind).

gradient. The total width of the instantaneous cloud at 100 m from the source is about 20 m, but that of the time-mean cloud is 35 m. There is evidence of a similar effect in the height of a cloud, but it is not so pronounced. Measurements show that the width of a point-source cloud increases fairly rapidly as the period of sampling increases from zero to about 2 min, but for longer periods of sampling the rate of increase becomes much less, and consistent results may be expected provided that the mean wind is steady in direction and the period of sampling is not less than 3 min. This is well established for conditions of small temperature gradient (Sutton[1]), but not for large lapse rates and large inversions, and it is possible that in these conditions longer samples are required to eliminate completely the effects of change of period of sampling.

The effect of the period of sampling reflects the wide range of frequencies in the eddy spectrum of the natural wind. The instantaneous aspect is due to many small eddies and one or two large eddies, resulting in a single narrow cone of smoke. This cone swings slowly over a wide front under the influence of the larger eddies, so that the time-mean aspect involves diffusion due to both small-scale and larger scale turbulence. This is the same phenomenon as that found with the bidirectional vane (Chap. 7) and may be compared with the beam of a searchlight which is being moved in a jerky and random manner. At any instant, the beam has a definite width and a definite distribution of intensity of illumination, but the integrated effect over any lengthy period of time is compounded of the normal spread of the beam and the wide swings of the projector.

The published work refers, in the main, to the time-mean distribution, the period of sampling being not less than 3 min.

Empirical Relations for Diffusion in Small Temperature Gradients. The following data for time-mean samples have been established for clouds of smoke and gas over level downland in conditions of small temperature gradient (Sutton[1]). In all cases the sources were placed at ground level.

1. At any point down wind of a continuous source, the concentration varies directly as the strength of the source, provided that the source does not cause appreciable convection currents.

2. The time-mean concentration at any point down wind of a continuous source varies approximately inversely as the mean wind velocity.

3. The time-mean width and height of a continuously generated cloud show little variation with mean wind speed.

The values obtained in conditions of small temperature gradient are given in Table 30.

TABLE 30. DATA FOR DIFFUSION FROM STEADY CONTINUOUS POINT AND LINE SOURCES (ACROSS WIND) AT GROUND LEVEL IN CONDITIONS OF SMALL TEMPERATURE GRADIENT, AFTER SUTTON

Type of source	Strength	Wind velocity at 200 cm, cm sec^{-1}	Distance from source, m	Peak concentration, mg m^{-3}	Width, m	Height (from ground), m
Continuous point...	1 g sec^{-1}	500	100	2	35	10
Continuous infinite line, across wind.	1 g sec^{-1} cm^{-1}	500	100	3500		10

The results may be extrapolated to greater distances by the following empirical relations:

Continuous point source. The central or peak concentration decreases with distance down wind, x, according to the law

$$\frac{\chi(x_1)}{\chi(x_2)} = \left(\frac{x_2}{x_1}\right)^{1.76} \tag{8.1}$$

where $\chi(x)$ is the concentration at $(x,0,0)$.

Continuous infinite line source, across wind

$$\frac{\chi(x_1)}{\chi(x_2)} = \left(\frac{x_2}{x_1}\right)^{0.9} \tag{8.2}$$

where $\chi(x)$ is the concentration at $(x,0)$.

The above data and empirical laws apply only to conditions of small temperature gradient (overcast skies and moderate or high winds). As yet, no corresponding set has been published for large temperature gradients.

The variations of concentration across wind and in the vertical follow approximately the normal law of errors. Thus if the cross-wind variation of concentration at a fixed distance and height is represented by

$$\chi(y) = \chi(0) \exp(-ay^2)$$

it follows that the semiwidth of the cloud, y_0, is given by

$$\exp(-ay_0^2) = 0.1$$

or

$$y_0 = \sqrt{\left(\frac{1}{a}\ln 10\right)} \simeq \sqrt{\left(\frac{2.30}{a}\right)}$$

A similar relation holds for the height z_0. It should be noted that the width and height defined in this way are independent of the strength of the source. In general, these dimensions bear no definite relation to the visible outline of the cloud, which is determined by the "optical" properties of the smoke, such as its obscuring and light-scattering qualities, as well as by the attenuation of the cloud.

8.2. Theoretical Studies of Diffusion from Artificial Sources

The coordinate system employed in the mathematical analysis is that of Chap. 7, in which the x axis is in the direction of the mean wind, supposed horizontal, the y axis across wind, and the z axis vertical. The mean wind is assumed steady and dependent only on height above ground ($z = 0$) so that $\bar{u} = \bar{u}(z), \bar{v} = \bar{w} = 0$. The ground is supposed to be non-absorbent and impervious to the diffusing substance.

The problems considered in this section relate to steady continuous point and infinite (cross-wind) line sources maintained indefinitely. Expressions for concentrations in clouds from sources lasting for limited periods can be obtained by standard mathematical methods from the

basic solutions, but since these introduce no new meteorological principles and are of interest chiefly in military applications, they will not be
considered here.

Problems of this type involve, in the first place, the solution of the
equation of diffusion in a turbulent wind,

$$\frac{d\chi}{dt} = \frac{\partial}{\partial x}\left(K_x \frac{\partial\chi}{\partial x}\right) + \frac{\partial}{\partial y}\left(K_y \frac{\partial\chi}{\partial y}\right) + \frac{\partial}{\partial z}\left(K_z \frac{\partial\chi}{\partial z}\right) \qquad (8.3)$$

(see Chap. 4), where $\chi(x,y,z,t)$ is the mean concentration of the diffusing
substance and K_x, K_y, K_z are the eddy diffusivities in the direction of
the principal axes. Since $\bar{v} = \bar{w} = 0$, it follows that

$$\frac{d\chi}{dt} = \frac{\partial\chi}{\partial t} + \bar{u}\frac{\partial\chi}{\partial x}$$

and in the steady state, $\partial\chi/\partial t = 0$.

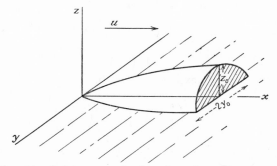

FIG. 31. Point-source cloud generated at ground level.

The boundary conditions for an instantaneous source have been discussed in Chap. 4. For continuous sources placed at ground level the
relevant conditions are

(1) $\qquad \chi \to 0 \qquad$ as $x,\ y,\ z \to \infty$

(2) $\qquad K_z \frac{\partial\chi}{\partial z} \to 0 \qquad$ as $z \to 0$, $x > 0$ (ground impervious to gas)

(3) $\qquad \chi \to \infty \qquad$ at $x = y = z = 0$

(4) The continuity condition:

$$\int_{-\infty}^{\infty} \int_{0}^{\infty} \bar{u}\chi(x,y,z)dz\,dy = Q \qquad \text{for all } x > 0$$

Condition (4) expresses the fact that matter is neither lost (deposited)
nor created during the passage of the cloud.

Solutions for Constant Eddy Diffusivity. The main features of the
mathematical problem emerge in an examination of the solutions of

equation (8.3) given by O. F. T. Roberts[2] for K_x, K_y, K_z constant and $\bar{u}$ independent of z. These solutions have already been derived in Chap. 4 [Eqs. (4.46) and (4.47)]. From the definitions of the semiwidth y_0 and the height z_0 of the cloud given above, the exponential terms in the solution yield

$$y_0 = \left(\frac{4 \ln 10\, K_y}{\bar{u}} x\right)^{\frac{1}{2}} \tag{8.4}$$

$$z_0 = \left(\frac{4 \ln 10\, K_z}{\bar{u}} x\right)^{\frac{1}{2}} \tag{8.5}$$

For $x = 10^4$ cm, Table 30 gives $y_0 = 1.75 \times 10^3$ cm, $z_0 = 10^3$ cm, and the trials were conducted in a mean wind of about 500 cm sec^{-1}. These data, and Eqs. (8.4) and (8.5), yield $K_y = 1.6 \times 10^4$ cm^2 sec^{-1}, $K_z = 5 \times 10^3$ cm^2 sec^{-1}, values in good agreement with those derived for the eddy viscosity and the eddy conductivity on the same hypothesis. The cross-wind and vertical distributions of concentration follow the normal law of errors, in agreement with the observations.

An examination of the results for concentration as a function of distance down wind, however, shows that the hypothesis of constant eddy diffusivity is unacceptable. The peak concentrations in a point-source cloud are found on the line $y = z = 0$, and for an infinite cross-wind line source on the plane $z = 0$. From the solutions (4.46) and (4.47) it follows that

Continuous point source:

$$\chi_{\text{max}} = \frac{Q}{4\pi x (K_y K_z)^{\frac{1}{2}}} \tag{8.6}$$

Infinite line source:

$$\chi_{\text{max}} = \frac{Q}{\sqrt{(2\pi K_z x)}} \tag{8.7}$$

Comparison with the empirical formulas (8.1) and (8.2) shows that the theoretical rate of decrease of concentration with distance from the source is much too slow. The observations indicate that, in neutral equilibrium, the ground concentration from a point source decreases very rapidly, as $x^{-1.76}$, whereas in the theoretical expression the rate of decrease is as x^{-1}. The same kind of discrepancy is found in the expression for the line source. Hence, numerical values of K_y and K_z, determined from observations of peak concentrations and expressions (8.6) and (8.7), increase indefinitely with distance from the origin. No physical meaning can be assigned to a quantity whose value depends on the distance of the point of observation from an arbitrary origin, and the result simply reflects the conclusion that the approximation $K_y = $ constant, $K_z = $ constant is unacceptable in problems of diffusion in a turbulent atmosphere, except as a means of providing expressions which give a qualitative description of the process.

Solutions for Variable Eddy Diffusivity. Two-dimensional problem. The steady-state equation of diffusion in two dimensions is

$$\bar{u}(z)\frac{\partial \chi}{\partial x} = \frac{\partial}{\partial z}\left[K_z(z)\frac{\partial \chi}{\partial z}\right] \tag{8.8}$$

neglecting the term $\dfrac{\partial}{\partial x}\left(K_x\dfrac{\partial \chi}{\partial x}\right)$. The problem considered here is that of diffusion from a line source of infinite length along $x = z = 0$, emitting at a constant rate Q for a long time. The boundary and continuity conditions are

(1) $\qquad\qquad\qquad \chi \to 0 \qquad$ as $x, z, \to \infty$

(2) $\qquad\qquad K_z\dfrac{\partial \chi}{\partial z} \to 0 \qquad$ as $z \to 0, x > 0$

(3) $\qquad\qquad\qquad \chi \to \infty \qquad$ along $x = z = 0$

(4) $\qquad\qquad \displaystyle\int_0^\infty \bar{u}\chi(x,z)dz = Q \qquad$ for all $x > 0$

Observation shows that, in neutral equilibrium, the height of a cloud generated at ground level is of the order of 5 to 10 per cent of the distance traveled. Hence, for x not exceeding a kilometer, diffusion takes place within the layer of constant shearing stress, and Schmidt's conjugate-power laws (Chap. 3) apply. If the eddy diffusivity is assumed to obey the same law of variation with height as the eddy viscosity, it follows that

$$K_z = \text{constant} \cdot \left(\frac{\partial \bar{u}}{\partial z}\right)^{-1}$$

At this point a mathematical difficulty enters. In conditions of neutral equilibrium, the velocity profile $\bar{u} = \bar{u}(z)$ is most accurately represented by a logarithmic function (Chap. 7). This implies that $K_z(z)$ is proportional to z, but the solution of Eq. (8.8) for $\bar{u} = \log z$, $K_z = z$ has not yet been found. On the other hand, if

$$\bar{u}(z) = \bar{u}_1\left(\frac{z}{z_1}\right)^m \tag{8.9}$$

and

$$K_z(z) = K_1\left(\frac{z}{z_1}\right)^n \tag{8.10}$$

(where $\bar{u}_1$ and K_1 are the values of $\bar{u}$ and K_z, respectively, at a fixed reference height z_1, which, for convenience, may be supposed to be unity), the equation can be solved very easily in terms of elementary functions. The solution, writing $s = (m + 1)/(m - n + 2)$, is

$$\chi(x,z) = \frac{Q}{\bar{u}_1 \Gamma(s)} \left[\frac{\bar{u}_1}{(m - n + 2)^2 K_1 x} \right]^s \exp \left[- \frac{\bar{u}_1 z^{m-n+2}}{(m - n + 2)^2 K_1 x} \right] \quad (8.11)$$

provided that $m - n + 2 > 0$. In the special case where the shearing stress is invariable with height, Schmidt's conjugate-power-law theorem implies the relation

$$n = 1 - m \qquad (0 \leq m \leq 1)$$

and Eq. (8.11) reduces to

$$\chi(x,z) =$$
$$\frac{Q}{(2m + 1)^{2(m+1)/(2m+1)} \Gamma[(m + 1)/(2m+1)] K_1^{(m+1)/(2m+1)} u_1^{m/(2m+1)} x^{(m+1)/(2m+1)}}$$
$$\exp \left[- \frac{\bar{u}_1 z^{2m+1}}{(2m + 1)^2 K_1 x} \right] \quad (8.12)$$

Over a smooth or short grass surface, in neutral equilibrium, the wind structure approximates to the familiar seventh-root profile. For $m = \frac{1}{7}$, Eq. (8.12) becomes

$$\chi(x,z) = \frac{Q}{(1\frac{2}{7})^{16/9} \Gamma(\frac{8}{9}) K_1^{8/9} \bar{u}_1^{1/9} x^{8/9}} \exp \left[- \frac{\bar{u}_1 z^{9/7}}{(1\frac{2}{7})^2 K_1 x} \right] \quad (8.13)$$

If K_1 is assumed to be proportional to $\bar{u}_1$, expression (8.13) is in good agreement with the observations on diffusion from a continuous infinite line source, across wind. The theoretical result indicates that the ground concentration is inversely proportional to $\bar{u}_1$ and decreases as $x^{-8/9} \simeq x^{-0.9}$. The height of the cloud is independent of the wind speed and increases with distance down wind as $x^{7/9}$. These properties have been verified by measurements of the diffusion of smoke over level downland in small temperature gradients (page 276).

The above analysis is applicable to any surface for which the simple power law (8.9) gives an adequate representation of the wind profile, and in particular for smooth terrain. The magnitude of K_1 can be found if τ_0 (or u_*) is known. For rough surfaces, K. L. Calder[3] has proposed an approximate solution which depends primarily on evaluating u_* and z_0 from the logarithmic profile

$$\frac{\bar{u}}{u_*} = \frac{1}{k} \ln \frac{z}{z_0}$$

valid for neutral equilibrium. To avoid the mathematical difficulties encountered when $\bar{u}$ is expressed as the logarithm of height in the term $\bar{u}\,\partial\chi/\partial x$, Calder replaces the accurate profile by an approximate power law

$$\frac{\bar{u}}{u_*} = q\left(\frac{z}{z_0}\right)^{\alpha}$$

where q and α are numbers chosen to give the best fit to the logarithmic profile. Since a power cannot equal a logarithm for all values of the variable, q and α vary with the depth of the layer concerned, and therefore with the distance of the plane of observation from the origin. This means that a preliminary estimate of the height of the cloud must be made before q and α can be found, but in practice this is not a serious difficulty, since at large distances (≥ 100 m) from the source, q and α vary only slowly with the upper limit of z. When the power law has been determined, it follows that

$$K_z = \frac{u_*^2}{\partial\bar{u}/\partial z} = \frac{N}{\alpha q}\left(\frac{z}{z_0}\right)^{1-\alpha}$$

where $N = u_* z_0$ is the macroviscosity. The solution of the two-dimensional diffusion problem is now given by Eq. (8.12) with the value of K_1 appropriate to the above expression.

For surfaces covered with high vegetation, Calder uses the empirical profile

$$\frac{\bar{u}}{u_*} = q'\left(\frac{z-d}{z_0}\right)^{\alpha'}$$

where d is the zero-plane displacement and q' and α' are numbers chosen, as before, to give the best fit to the modified logarithmic profile

$$\frac{\bar{u}}{u_*} = \frac{1}{k}\ln\left(\frac{z-d}{z_0}\right)$$

Neither profile is defined for $z < d$, and Calder therefore moves the origin of z to the plane $z = d$, which thus becomes effectively the surface of the earth. Solution (8.11), applied in this way, gives results which are in practically perfect agreement with observation (Calder[3]), but the method is open to the objection that the plane $z = d$ is not a real impervious surface in the same sense as the ground, and applications of this solution to conditions which require large values of d are of doubtful validity.

The main results of this work are twofold. In the first instance, it has been shown that in conditions of neutral stability, at least, momentum and mass are exchanged by the same processes and follow the same laws. Second, the concept of roughness length established for wind-tunnel work is directly applicable to the atmosphere and plays an important part in problems of diffusion.

Three-dimensional problems. The typical three-dimensional problem is that of the continuous point source, but this raises mathematical difficulties which have yet to be overcome. The equation of diffusion, disregarding the term $\dfrac{\partial}{\partial x}\left(K_x \dfrac{\partial \chi}{\partial x}\right)$, as before, is

$$\bar{u}(z)\frac{\partial \chi}{\partial x} = \frac{\partial}{\partial y}\left(K_y \frac{\partial \chi}{\partial y}\right) + \frac{\partial}{\partial z}\left(K_z \frac{\partial \chi}{\partial z}\right) \tag{8.14}$$

The functional form of K_z is settled, as before, by the conjugate power-law relation, but there is no similar way of finding K_y. It is obvious that K_y cannot be treated as a function of y, because this implies that lateral diffusion depends on the distance of the diffusing particles from an arbitrary plane, and the only rational possibility is that K_y, like K_z, is a function of height. The obvious suggestion is to assume a power-law variation for K_y. The equation

$$\bar{u}_1 z^m \frac{\partial \chi}{\partial x} = \frac{\partial}{\partial y}\left(az^p \frac{\partial \chi}{\partial y}\right) + \frac{\partial}{\partial z}\left(bz^{1-m} \frac{\partial \chi}{\partial z}\right) \tag{8.15}$$

does not appear to have been discussed for unrestricted values of p. If $p = m$, a solution appropriate to the continuous point source can be found without difficulty in terms of powers of x and exponential functions but such a solution does not agree with observation. It appears that the index p must be either slightly greater or slightly less than $1 - m$ to secure any measure of agreement with the experimental data. The whole problem stands in need of a thoroughgoing mathematical investigation.

Statistical-theory Method. An alternative approach to the problem, which enables approximate solutions to be found for two- and three-dimensional problems, was evolved by Sutton[4] in 1932. The method consists essentially in finding an appropriate form for $R(\xi)$, the correlation coefficient between eddy velocities at times t and $t + \xi$ (Chap. 3) by dimensional analysis, the theory being afterward developed on lines suggested by Taylor's work.

So far, no expression has been found for $R(\xi)$ in a nonisotropic field by exact analysis. By definition

$$R(\xi) = \frac{\overline{w'(t)w'(t + \xi)}}{\overline{w'^2}}$$

where $\overline{w'^2}$ is supposed constant. For motion near a smooth surface, the correlation between the fluctuating velocities at successive instants of time may be supposed to depend primarily on the intensity of the turbulence, as measured by the mean eddying energy $\rho\overline{w'^2}$, the viscosity μ, which is ultimately responsible for the decay of a fluctuation, and the time ξ. The only nondimensional group which can be formed from these constituents is $\mu/\rho\overline{w'^2}\xi$, and hence

$$R(\xi) = f\left(\frac{\nu}{\overline{w'^2}\xi}\right)$$

where f is an undetermined function. Obviously, $R(0) = 1$, and it is reasonable to expect that $R(\xi) \to 0$ as $\xi \to \infty$. The simplest function which has these properties is

$$R(\xi) = \left(\frac{\nu}{\nu + \overline{w'^2}\xi}\right)^n \tag{8.16}$$

where n is some positive number. [An exponential form for $R(\xi)$ has been shown to correspond to Brownian motion—see Chap. 3.]

The introduction of an explicit form for $R(\xi)$ enables the theory of turbulent exchange to be developed in two ways. The first of these follows the mixing-length concept. If mixing is defined as a gradual decay of correlation between the fluctuations which affect an element of fluid at different times, the mixing length may be defined as the distance over which an eddy moves during the time t_0 for the correlation to have fallen to zero or to some agreed small value. Thus

$$K_M(z) = \overline{w'l} = \overline{w'^2} \int_0^{t_0} R(\xi)d\xi$$

$$\simeq \frac{\nu^n}{1-n} (\overline{w'^2}t_0)^{1-n} \tag{8.17}$$

if $\overline{w'^2}t_0 \gg \nu$. From v. Kármán's expression for the mixing length,

$$l = k\frac{\partial\bar{u}/\partial z}{\partial^2\bar{u}/\partial z^2}$$

and the Maxwellian law of distribution relating $\overline{w'^2}$ to $\overline{|w'|^2}$, it may be shown that

$$K_M(z) = \frac{(\frac{1}{2}\pi k^2)^{1-n}}{1-n} \nu^n \left(\left|\frac{\partial\bar{u}}{\partial z}\right|^3 \left|\frac{\partial^2\bar{u}}{\partial z^2}\right|^{-2}\right)^{1-n} \tag{8.18}$$

Since $K_M(z)$ is essentially positive, it follows that $0 \leq n \leq 1$.

When the velocity profile is given by Eq. (8.9), it is easily seen that

$$m = \frac{n}{2-n} \tag{8.19}$$

This relation enables n to be found from observations on wind structure near the ground, *e.g.*, if the seventh-root profile is used, the value of n is $\frac{1}{4}$. From the profile

$$\bar{u}(z) = \bar{u}_1 \left(\frac{z}{z_1}\right)^{n/(2-n)} \tag{8.20}$$

and Eq. (8.18), it follows that

$$K_M(z) = \left[\frac{(\frac{1}{2}\pi k^2)^{1-n}(2-n)n^{1-n}}{(1-n)(2-n)^{2(1-n)}}\right] \nu^n \bar{u}_1^{1-n} z^{2(1-n)/(2-n)} z_1^{-n(1-n)/(2-n)} \tag{8.21}$$

Expression (8.21) enables the eddy viscosity to be evaluated for flow near an aerodynamically smooth surface, provided that the velocity profile can be expressed as a power law of the type (8.20). If the seventh-root profile applies, it follows that

$$\frac{\tau}{\rho} = K_m(z)\frac{\partial \bar{u}}{\partial z} = 0.020\nu^{\frac{1}{4}}\bar{u}_1^{\frac{7}{4}}z_1^{-\frac{1}{4}}$$

The experimental result for the shearing stress near a smooth surface is[†]

$$\frac{\tau}{\rho} = 0.0225\nu^{\frac{1}{4}}\bar{u}_1^{\frac{7}{4}}z_1^{-\frac{1}{4}}$$

Hence the expression (8.16) gives satisfactory results for aerodynamically smooth surfaces.

For fully-rough surfaces, it has been shown by Sutton that the appropriate form of $R(\xi)$ is

$$R(\xi) = \left(\frac{N+\nu}{N+\nu+\overline{w'^2}\xi}\right)^n \simeq \left(\frac{N}{N+\overline{w'^2}\xi}\right)^n \tag{8.22}$$

if $N \gg \nu$, where N is the macroviscosity (Chap. 3). The introduction of the macroviscosity, which involves the roughness-length and the friction-velocity, both of which are defined only for the logarithmic profiles, necessitates the use of a power-law profile which approximates closely to the Rossby profile [Eq. (7.3)]. Such a profile is

$$\bar{u} = \frac{\bar{u}_1}{\left(\dfrac{z_1+z_0}{z_0}\right)^p - 1}\left[\left(\frac{z+z_0}{z_0}\right)^p - 1\right] \tag{8.23}$$

where p is a positive number, not to be confused with the index m of Eq. (8.9). For $z_0 = 2$ cm, $u_* = 50$ cm sec^{-1} (values appropriate to downland) Sutton shows that the Rossby profile is closely approxi-

[†] See Prandtl's article in "The Physics of Solids and Fluids" (Ewald, Poschl, and Prandtl), p. 282.

mated by taking $p = 0.08$. From Eq. (8.22) it is easily shown that $p = n/(2 - n)$, as in the smooth-surface problem, so that in this example $n = 0.15$. With this value, the solution of the infinite-line-source diffusion problem in the form (8.12) yields satisfactory agreement with the observed values given in Table 30. This method is an alternative to that given by Calder, and both give adequate representations of diffusion in two dimensions over an aerodynamically rough surface in conditions of neutral stability. For the actual formulas used in computation, which are somewhat cumbersome in both methods, the reader is referred to the original papers.

The second method of developing the theory makes use of Taylor's theorem (Chap. 3), that if σ be the standard deviation of the distances traveled in a time T by particles originally concentrated on the (x,z) plane,

$$\sigma^2 = 2\overline{w'^2} \int_0^T \int_0^t R(\xi)d\xi\, dt \qquad (8.24)$$

The solution of the diffusion problem is thereby reduced to that of finding functions representing the distribution of concentration which, for a given $R(\xi)$, satisfy Eq. (8.24), the equation of continuity, and the boundary conditions. The asymmetrical nature of diffusion near the ground is allowed for by the introduction of three separate correlation coefficients for the three component fluctuations

$$\left.\begin{aligned}
R_x(\xi) &= \left(\frac{\nu}{\nu + \overline{u'^2}\xi}\right)^n \\[4pt]
R_y(\xi) &= \left(\frac{\nu}{\nu + \overline{v^{2'}}\xi}\right)^n \\[4pt]
R_z(\xi) &= \left(\frac{\nu}{\nu + \overline{w'^2}\xi}\right)^n
\end{aligned}\right\} \qquad (8.25)$$

These expressions apply to aerodynamically smooth surfaces. For fully-rough surfaces the kinematic viscosity ν is replaced by the macroviscosity N, as before.

From Eq. (8.24) it follows that

$$\begin{aligned}
\sigma_x^2 &= 2\overline{u'^2} \int_0^T \int_0^t \left(\frac{\nu}{\nu + \overline{u'^2}\xi}\right)^n d\xi\, dt \\[4pt]
&= \frac{2\nu^n}{(1 - n)(2 - n)\overline{u'^2}} (\nu + \overline{u'^2}T)^{2-n} - \frac{2\nu^2}{(1 - n)(2 - n)\overline{u'^2}} - \frac{2\nu T}{1 - n}
\end{aligned}$$

In this equation terms of order ν may be neglected in comparison with $\overline{u'^2}T$, and for sufficiently large T the expression reduces to

$$\sigma_x^2 = \frac{2\nu^n}{(1 - n)(2 - n)\overline{u'^2}} (\overline{u'^2}T)^{2-n} \qquad (8.26)$$

$$= \tfrac{1}{2}C^2(\bar{u}T)^{2-n} \qquad (8.27)$$

where

$$C^2 = \frac{4\nu^n}{(1-n)(2-n)\bar{u}^n} \left(\frac{\overline{u'^2}}{\overline{u^2}}\right)^{1-n} \tag{8.28}$$

is a generalized coefficient of diffusion. Similar expressions hold for σ_y and σ_z. In isotropic turbulence $\sigma_x = \sigma_y = \sigma_z$, and $C_x = C_y = C_z = C$ (say). This condition may be regarded as applying to the atmosphere above the surface layers.

Equation (8.27) indicates that the size of a moving cluster of particles increases as a certain power of the distance from the origin. For $n = 1$, this law resembles that given by Einstein for Brownian motion,

$$\sigma^2 = 2Kt$$

and, at the other end of the scale, the case $n = 0$ indicates that, for all degrees of turbulence, the radius of the cluster will not increase more rapidly than the distance traveled. It has been shown by Sutton that the expression for $n = \frac{1}{4}$, namely,

$$\sigma^2 = \text{constant} \cdot (\bar{u}T)^{\frac{7}{4}} \tag{8.29}$$

gives a reasonably accurate description of diffusion in the atmosphere for distances varying from meters to tens or hundreds of kilometers. There are good reasons for believing that the law (8.29) gives a useful approximation for all small-scale and large-scale diffusion processes in the free atmosphere.

In the application of this method to diffusion near the ground, consider the problem of the instantaneous point source (Chap. 4). The expression

$$\chi(x,y,z,t) = \frac{Q}{\pi^{\frac{3}{2}}C_xC_yC_z(\bar{u}t)^{\frac{3}{2}(2-n)}} \exp\left[(\bar{u}t)^{n-2}\left(\frac{x^2}{C_x^2} + \frac{y^2}{C_y^2} + \frac{z^2}{C_z^2}\right)\right] \tag{8.30}$$

where x, y, z, are measured from an origin moving with the cloud at constant speed, $\bar{u}$, is of the type required. The boundary conditions for an instantaneous source and the continuity condition are satisfied, and the distributions of density along the axes follow the law (8.27). The solution previously obtained for constant eddy diffusivity in a uniform steady wind [Eq. (4.47)] is obtained from (8.30) by putting $n = 1$ and taking $C^2 = 4K/\bar{u}$.

From Eq. (8.30), solutions for continuous point, finite line, and infinite line sources in a uniform wind $\bar{u}$ are obtained by integration. These are:

Continuous point source:

$$\chi(x,y,z) = \frac{2Q}{\pi C_yC_z\bar{u}x^{2-n}} \exp\left[-x^{n-2}\left(\frac{y^2}{C_y^2} + \frac{z^2}{C_z^2}\right)\right] \tag{8.31}$$

Continuous cross-wind finite line source of length $2y_0$:

$$\chi(x,y,z) = \frac{Q \exp\left(-z^2/C_z{}^2x^{2-n}\right)}{\sqrt{\pi}C_z\bar{u}x^{1-\frac{1}{2}n}} \left[\text{erf}\left(\frac{y_0 - y}{C_yx^{1-\frac{1}{2}n}}\right) + \text{erf}\left(\frac{y_0 + y}{C_yx^{1-\frac{1}{2}n}}\right) \right] \quad (8.32)$$

Continuous cross-wind infinite line source:

$$\chi(x,z) = \frac{2Q}{\sqrt{\pi}C_z\bar{u}x^{1-\frac{1}{2}n}} \exp\left(-\frac{z^2}{C_z{}^2x^{2-n}}\right) \quad (8.33)$$

The factor 2 in the numerator of expressions (8.31) and (8.33), and the omission of the same factor in the denominator of (8.32), expresses the "reflection" of the smoke by the impervious ground.

The above expressions constitute the simplest possible generalizations of the solutions for constant eddy diffusivity in a uniform mean wind which can be derived from the expression (8.16) for $R(\xi)$. They are not unique, since it is possible to satisfy Eq. (8.27) by expressions involving terms of the type $\exp\left(-y^s/ax^p\right)$, where $s/p = 2/(2 - n)$. Extended formulas of this type have been obtained by Sutton,[1] who shows that improved agreement with observation can be secured by their use, but for most purposes the simpler solutions (8.31) to (8.33) are adequate and have the merit of being easier to compute.

Turbulent diffusion as a random walk process. Recently, E. Knighting has shown† that (8.30) can be derived by an extension of the random walk concept, *i.e.*, by a discontinuous process. If a particle moves in a series of steps, a_ν, in any direction, the probability P_ν that it will be at (x,y,z) after ν steps is

$$P_\nu(x,y,z) = \frac{1}{4\pi} \int_0^{2\pi} \int_0^{2\pi} P_{\nu-1}(x - a_\nu \sin\theta \cos\phi,$$

$$y - a_\nu \sin\theta \sin\phi, z - a_\nu \cos\theta \sin\phi)d\theta\, d\phi.$$

[This expresses the fact that the particle comes from any point on the surface of the sphere of radius a_ν centered at (x,y,z).] By the method of the Laplace transform, Knighting shows that

$$P_\nu \sim \left(\frac{3}{2\pi\nu\sigma^2}\right)^{\frac{3}{2}} \exp\left[-\frac{3(x^2 + y^2 + z^2)}{2\nu\sigma^2}\right]$$

where σ is defined by

$$\Sigma a_\nu{}^2 = \nu\sigma^2$$

If the steps a_ν are all equal, and τ is the time taken to complete a step, the interval of diffusion is $t = \nu\tau$. The above expression for P_ν then leads

† Available as M.R.P. 728 (April, 1952) in the Library of the Meteorological Office, London.

to that for the distribution of matter around an instantaneous point source in Fickian diffusion (4.36). It is clear from physical requirements that Σa_ν must diverge (otherwise the particles could not diffuse outside a sphere of finite radius) but apart from this, a_ν is unrestricted. Suppose $a_\nu = k\nu^\alpha$, so that $\nu\sigma^2 = (k^2\nu^{2\alpha+1})/(2\alpha+1)$ and $t = \nu\tau$ as before. The expression for P_ν becomes

$$\left[\frac{3(2\alpha+1)\tau^{2\alpha+1}}{2\pi k^2 t^{2\alpha+1}}\right]^{\frac{3}{2}} \exp\left[-\frac{3(2\alpha+1)\tau^{2\alpha+1}(x^2+y^2+z^2)}{2k^2 t^{2\alpha+1}}\right]$$

This gives (8.30) if the condition of conservation of matter is introduced and α is put equal to $\frac{1}{2}(1-n)$. Hence Sutton's diffusion formula can be derived from a random walk process provided that *the length of the steps increases with the interval of diffusion*. This may be regarded as equivalent to the familiar concept that, in the atmosphere, the influence of the bigger eddies is increasingly felt as diffusion proceeds, but the exact physical interpretation of such a random walk process is not completely clear.

Extension to Nonadiabatic Gradients. The determination of the rate of spread of smoke in extremes of temperature gradient is of considerable importance in practical applications, but a satisfactory treatment has yet to emerge. The two-dimensional problem has been considered by E. L. Deacon,[5] who makes use of the generalized velocity profile [Eq. (7.6)], which is stated to be valid for all degrees of stability. In the layer of constant shearing stress this profile implies the relation·

$$K_M(z) = kN\left(\frac{z}{z_0}\right)^\beta$$

where $N = u_* z_0$, is the macroviscosity, and k is Kármán's constant. The index β is less than unity in inversions and greater than unity in large lapse rates. This expression is adopted for K_z in the diffusion problem, assuming that momentum and mass are transferred in exactly the same way in all conditions of temperature gradient. As in Calder's treatment, the velocity profile in the term $\bar{u}\, \partial\chi/\partial x$ is replaced by

$$\frac{\bar{u}}{u_*} = q\left(\frac{z}{z_0}\right)^\alpha$$

where q and α are found by comparison with the accurate profile (7.6). The solution (8.12) may then be expressed in the form

$$\chi(x,z) = \frac{Qq^{s-1}}{ANX^s}\exp\left(-\frac{qZ^p}{kp^2 X}\right)$$

where $X = x/z_0$, $Z = z/z_0$

$p = 2 + \alpha - \beta$

$s = (1 + \alpha)/p$

$A = k^s p^{2s-1}\Gamma(s)$

$N = u_* z_0$

Deacon compares this expression with the integrated cross-wind concentrations from a continuous point source, measured over prairie ($z_0 = 0.7$ cm) at Alberta, Canada. In these trials the Richardson number varied from $+0.02$ to -0.8, the corresponding range for β being 0.97 to 1.135. The results are inconclusive, since they show good agreement between theory and practice for small departures from neutral stability but considerable discrepancies for large instability, where the observed concentrations are somewhat irregular. The comparison also shows that, in large lapse rates, the rate of decrease of concentration with distance is more rapid than the theory predicts.

The observations referred to above demonstrate very clearly the effects of stabilizing gradients on vertical diffusion. At 100 yd down wind of the source, the change of Ri from -0.25 to $+0.02$ was accompanied by an increase of the integrated cross-wind concentration from 155 to 1360 mg m^{-3} for the same mean wind velocity at 2 m. Meteorological literature contains very few examples of accurate measurement of diffusion in stable conditions, and the above illustration, although isolated, indicates the necessity of specifying accurately the temperature gradient (or, better, the Richardson number) in all numerical work on diffusion near the ground.

The formulas obtained by the statistical method [Eqs. (8.30) to (8.33)] provide, at first sight, a simple means of estimating the effects of temperature gradients, whether stabilizing or destabilizing, provided that the quantity n can be found as a function of temperature gradient. In practice, this is not easy, and the difficulties encountered in this work are discussed in the next section.

8.3. Diffusion Formulas in Field Work

The theories of diffusion described above involve the assumption that the transfer of mass follows the same laws as the transfer of momentum, and their practical application therefore depends on accurate measurement of the velocity profile in the layer through which the diffusing substance spreads. In the early development of this work, prior to the publication of the researches of Nikuradse and Schlichting on flow over rough surfaces, the influence of the nature of the ground on the velocity profile was not fully realized, and expressions for diffusion in smooth flow were compared with measurements of diffusion over rough ground. Accounts of this work have been given by Sutton[1] and Calder.[3]

The generalized diffusion coefficients C_x, C_y, and C_z in the statistical diffusion theory depend on the gustiness components, the mean velocity at a fixed level, and the quantity n. Gustiness can be measured in a variety of ways, and the bidirectional vane is a particularly useful instrument for field work provided that some rule can be evolved whereby *mean* values of the gustiness components can be found from the records. The main difficulty undoubtedly lies in the determination of the appropriate value of n, which must be accurate because of the sensitivity of the formulas to small changes in n.

A direct evaluation of n from measurement of $R(\xi)$ is clearly impracticable for routine field work. The method originally used was to assume that n is determined by the velocity profile

$$\bar{u}(z) = \bar{u}_1 \left(\frac{z}{z_1}\right)^{n/(2-n)}$$

derived by the mixing-length method. This procedure is inconsistent with that used in deriving expressions (8.31) to (8.33), in which the mean wind is assumed invariable with height, but it can be shown that the error introduced in this way is small. The cloud from a continuous source is attenuated by cross-wind and vertical diffusion, and by dilution by the mean wind, the second process being represented by the term $\bar{u}\,\partial\chi/\partial x$ in the diffusion equation. The statistical method involves the assumption that the variation of wind with height can be ignored in this term, a statement likely to be true for all conditions except those of very steep inversions. The method therefore uses the variation of wind with height solely as a measure of the rate of transfer of momentum (and hence of mass) and disregards other effects of wind gradient as second-order.

If the power-law profile were strictly valid, the measurement of the ratio of wind speed at any two convenient heights would suffice to determine n but in practice it is found (in conditions of neutral equilibrium at least) that n not only changes rapidly with height in the layer 0 to 200 cm but is also affected by the size and distribution of the surface irregularities. At greater heights, the power law is closely followed, and in these layers the value of n is primarily determined by stability. Changes in surface roughness have thus a first-order effect on the wind profile very near the ground but exercise only a second-order effect on the diffusion of the cloud as a whole. On the other hand, stability has a first-order effect on both the velocity profile and the rate of diffusion, and it is difficult, if not impossible, to disentangle the two influences by the use of a simple profile expression which does not introduce specifically any function of the surface irregularities.

A method has been suggested by Sutton[6] for diffusion over fully-rough surfaces which overcomes these difficulties in conditions of neutral stability. This involves replacing the kinematic viscosity in the expression for $R(\xi)$ by the macroviscosity, so that the generalized diffusion coefficients are given by expressions of the type

$$C_y{}^2 = \frac{4N^n}{(1-n)(2-n)\bar{u}^n}\left(\frac{\overline{v'^2}}{\bar{u}^2}\right)^{1-n}$$

With this definition, and the value $n = \frac{1}{4}$, corresponding to the profile found by Scrase for the height interval $300 \leq z \leq 1300$ cm, over downland, the diffusion formulas (8.31) and (8.33) give results in good agreement with observation for $N = 10^2$ cm^2 sec^{-1}. The replacement of ν by N in the expression for $R(\xi)$ means that the approximations used in the derivation of Eq. (8.26) necessitate larger values of T than in the smooth-surface case, so that over very rough ground the solutions of the statistical theory cannot be expected to yield satisfactory results very near the source.

For diffusion over level surfaces, such as downland, in conditions of small temperature gradient and moderate wind, formulas (8.31) to (8.33) will give satisfactory results up to several kilometers from the source if the following values are used:

$$n = \tfrac{1}{4}, \qquad C_y = 0.4 \text{ cm}^{\frac{1}{8}}, \qquad C_z = 0.2 \text{ cm}^{\frac{1}{8}}$$

The above values are based on data obtained at Porton, England. No reliable values are yet available for large lapse rates and large inversions.

8.4. Diffusion from Elevated Sources

The solutions discussed in the previous section are applicable to clouds generated at ground level. In problems of atmospheric pollution the sources are usually at considerable heights above the ground, and the main problem to be solved is that of finding the concentration of smoke at ground level resulting from the emission of smoke or gas from an isolated industrial stack.

The mathematical setting of this problem has been discussed in Chap. 4, and the solution obtained below is derived on the same lines as for the constant-diffusivity case. The outstanding difficulty in the problem for a real atmosphere, in which diffusivity cannot be regarded as independent of height, is that no exact solution for a point source in a variable wind and for variable diffusivity is known, and the approximate solution (8.32) must be employed.

The treatment of the problem given by Sutton[7] is as follows: Observations on shell bursts at considerable heights show that diffusion in the free atmosphere satisfies Eq. (8.29), but the values of C are much smaller than those found near the ground. The coefficient C has been found to decrease with height according to the empirical law

$$C = C(0) - 0.075 \log_{10} z \tag{8.34}$$

where $C(0)$ is the ground level value of C and z is measured in meters (Sutton). Smoke emitted from a stack orifice at considerable height above the ground diffuses at first in a wind of relatively small gustiness, behaving as if the ground were absent, but with increasing distance down wind the effect of the ground is increasingly felt. This shows itself, not only in the "reflection" of the smoke particles by the impervious surface, but also in the increasing turbulence of the wind in the lower layers. This introduces severe mathematical difficulties, which may be partially overcome by the use of a mean diffusion coefficient appropriate to the layer defined by the height of the stack. Such a procedure is justified by the relatively slow variation of C with height [Eq. (8.34)]. Thus the scale of diffusion decreases with the height of the source, but the solutions used are those which correspond to the diffusivity increasing with the interval of diffusion. In this sense the lower atmosphere may be compared to a series of layers of gases whose intrinsic diffusivity steadily decreases from the surface upward, with the same type of non-Fickian diffusion in each layer.

Consider a rectangular system of axes Ox in the direction of the mean wind (assumed horizontal), Oy across wind, and Oz vertical. The plane $z = 0$ is taken to be the surface of the earth. A continuous point source placed at $x = y = z = 0$, allowing for the impervious surface $z = 0$, gives rise to a concentration $\chi(x,y,z)$, where

$$\chi(x,y,z) = \frac{2Q}{C_y C_z \bar{u} x^{2-n}} \exp\left[-x^{n-2}\left(\frac{y^2}{C_y^2} + \frac{z^2}{C_z^2} \right) \right] \tag{8.31}$$

This expression assumes (1) that the mean wind is uniform and steady, (2) that there is no rising of the cloud because of buoyancy, and (3) that the cloud is formed of particles which do not fall out. If a similar source is placed at $x = y = 0$, $z = h$, the problem is to find an expression for $\chi(x,y,z)$ which becomes infinite as $x^{n-2} \exp\left[-(z - h)^2/x^{2-n} \right]$ as $x \to 0$, $z \to h$ and allows for the impervious nature of the surface $z = 0$. This latter condition implies that

$$\int_0^\infty \int_{-\infty}^\infty \bar{u}\chi(x,y,z)dy \, dz = Q$$

for all $x > 0$. The required solution is obtained by the method of images (Chap. 4) and is

$$\chi(x,y,z) = \frac{Q \exp\left(-y^2/C_y^2 x^{2-n} \right)}{\pi C_y C_z \bar{u} x^{2-n}} \left\{ \exp\left[-\frac{(z - h)^2}{C_z^2 x^{2-n}} \right] + \exp\left[-\frac{(z + h)^2}{C_z^2 x^{2-n}} \right] \right\} \tag{8.35}$$

For $h = 0$ this expression reduces to that for a source at ground level (8.31).

The following properties of the solution are easily deduced:

1. Maximum concentration at ground level

$$\chi_{max} = \frac{2Q}{e\pi\bar{u}h^2} \left(\frac{C_z}{C_y}\right) \tag{8.36}$$

2. Distance of point of maximum concentration on ground from foot of stack

$$x_{max} = \left(\frac{h^2}{C_z^2}\right)^{1/(2-n)} \tag{8.37}$$

These expressions indicate the most important features of the distribution. These are:

1. The concentration of smoke at ground level rises to a maximum at a distance roughly proportional to the height of the stack and then falls to zero with increasing distance down wind.

2. The maximum concentration at ground level is directly proportional to the strength of the source and inversely proportional to the wind speed and the square of the height of the stack.

The inverse-square law (2) for the effect of stack height was first enunciated by C. H. Bosanquet and J. L. Pearson[8] and is of fundamental importance in problems of atmospheric pollution.

The results obtained on this theory are shown in Tables 31 and 32.

TABLE 31. CONCENTRATIONS AT GROUND LEVEL DOWN WIND OF AN ELEVATED SOURCE FOR $Q = 1$ G SEC^{-1}, $\bar{u} = 100$ CM SEC^{-1} AND NEUTRAL STABILITY
(In mg m^{-3})

Height of stack, m	Distance from source, m					
	0	50	100	500	1000	2000
0	∞	26.9	8.0	0.48	0.14	0.04
10	0	0.02	0.89	0.42	0.137	0.04
25	0	0	0	0.37	0.195	0.07
50	0	0	0	0.01	0.088	0.07
75	0	0	0	0	0.009	0.04
100	0	0	0	0	0	0.007

The variation of concentration down wind is similar to that shown in Fig. 16 (Chap. 4).

The extended problem of the deposition of grit from a stack emitting smoke containing particles of appreciable size has been considered by Bosanquet, Carey, and Halton.[9] The rate of dust deposition at a point

TABLE 32. DISTANCE OF THE POINT OF MAXIMUM CONCENTRATION AT GROUND
LEVEL FROM STACK BASE, x_m, AND CONCENTRATION AT THIS POINT, χ_m
FOR $Q = 1$ G. SEC^{-1} AND $\bar{u} = 100$ CM. SEC^{-1}

h, m	x_m, m	χ_m, mg m^{-3}
0	0	∞
10	158	1.34
25	439	0.375
50	1224	0.094
75	2350	0.042
100	4070	0.023

on the ground distant x from the foot of the stack is stated to be given
by the expression

$$0.0032 \, \frac{Qb(20h/x)^{(20f/u)+2}}{h^2\Gamma(20\,f/u)} \, \exp\left(-\frac{20h}{x}\right)$$

where f = terminal velocity of the particles
h = height of stack
Q = rate of emission
u = horizontal wind speed

expressed in self-consistent units. The quantity b denotes the fraction
of time the wind is in a 45° sector from the stack enclosing the point
considered; b thus corresponds, in a sense, to the gustiness factor in
Sutton's solution. The derivation of the formula is not given in the
published paper.

8.5. The Free-convection Jet in the Atmosphere

Much of the pollution found in the atmosphere originates in the form
of plumes of heated smoke-laden air from industrial stacks, and the
study of the dynamics of such jets is of considerable importance. Hill,
Thomas, and Abersold[10] have produced evidence that the effect of adding heat to a source of sulfur dioxide is to reduce the concentration of
the gas at ground level down wind of the stack. High stacks, designed
to conserve as much heat as possible, are to be recommended as a means
of securing maximum dispersion of the effluent.

The behavior of a jet of hot gas in a gravitational field is a particularly
difficult problem in fluid dynamics, especially in the presence of a horizontal wind. If the atmosphere is at rest except for the convection currents, the jet rises vertically, with entrainment of the cool air at its
boundary. The upward velocity exhibits a continuous shear from the
boundary to the center of the jet, so that the mixing process which
brings in the cool air is similar to that which takes place in the turbulent
boundary layer adjacent to a solid surface. In the presence of a hori-

zontal wind the jet is inclined to the vertical, resulting in a greater tendency for the stream of hot air to be broken up by thermal currents, and in this case the entrainment process involves both dynamic and thermal instability.

The problem of the plume in a calm atmosphere has been solved by Schmidt[11] on the lines of Prandtl's mixing-length hypothesis. Schmidt considers the two-dimensional problem of the jet above a long line source and the three-dimensional problem of the jet from a point source of heat.

Line Source of Heat. Take the z axis vertical (direction of motion) and the y axis perpendicular to the z axis and the heated line. The upward acceleration of a particle is $g\alpha\theta$, where α is the coefficient of expansion and θ the difference between the temperature of the jet and that of the ambient air (Chap. 4). The equations of motion, conduction of heat, and continuity are

$$w\frac{\partial w}{\partial z} + v\frac{\partial w}{\partial y} = \frac{1}{\rho}\frac{\partial \tau}{\partial y} + g\alpha\theta$$

$$c_p\rho\left(w\frac{\partial \theta}{\partial z} + v\frac{\partial \theta}{\partial y}\right) = \frac{\partial q}{\partial y}$$

$$\frac{\partial w}{\partial z} + \frac{\partial v}{\partial y} = 0$$

where ρ is the density of the gas, w and v the velocity components in the z and y directions, respectively, τ the shearing stress and q the flux of heat, per unit area.

The complete problem involves the solution of these equations for the appropriate boundary conditions, but it is possible to obtain the main properties of the distribution by a simple application of dimensional analysis and dynamic laws. Schmidt assumes dynamic and geometrical similitude for the mixing processes in transverse sections of the jet perpendicular to the direction of motion and follows Prandtl in taking the mixing length l to be proportional to the width of the jet, b, at all levels. It is easily seen that b is proportional to z, and hence $l = cz$, where c is a constant of proportionality.

If the strength of the source is constant, Q, the heat transported through any cross section is

$$Q = wb\rho c_p\theta = \text{constant} \tag{8.38}$$

giving

$$w = \text{constant } (\rho\theta z)^{-1} \tag{8.39}$$

The change of momentum J along the path dz is equal to the lifting force along this length, so that

$$\frac{dJ}{dz}\,dz = \frac{d}{dz}\,(\rho b w^2)dz = bg\rho\alpha\theta\,dz \tag{8.40}$$

Writing $\theta = Dz^{-m}$, where m is unknown and D is a constant of proportionality, it follows that

$$J = \text{constant } (\rho D^2 z^{2m-1})^{-1} \tag{8.41}$$

If the difference between the temperature in the jet and that of the ambient air is small enough to make $\alpha\theta$ negligible compared with unity, the density ρ may be taken to be the (constant) density of the ambient air. The lifting force is then proportional to z^{1-m}, and hence, from Eqs. (8.40) and (8.41),

$$2m - 2 = 1 - m$$

or

$$m = 1$$

Hence the excess temperature in the jet, θ, decreases as $1/z$, where z is height above the source, and from Eq. (8.39) it follows that the velocity w is independent of z.

Point Source. The treatment of the point source is on similar lines. Schmidt writes $\theta = Dz^{-m}$, as before, and puts $w = \text{constant} \cdot z^p$. From the condition that the heat transported across any section of the jet is constant, it follows that

$$Q = \rho\pi b^2 w c_p \theta$$

where b is the radius of the jet. Hence

$$2 + p = m \tag{8.42}$$

The rate of change of momentum is

$$\frac{dJ}{dz} = z^{2p+1}$$

and the uprising force is

$$b^2 g\alpha\rho\theta = \text{constant} \cdot z^{2-m}$$

so that

$$2 - m = 2p + 1 \tag{8.43}$$

From Eqs. (8.42) and (8.43)

$$m = \tfrac{5}{3}, \qquad p = -\tfrac{1}{3} \tag{8.44}$$

so that the temperature excess in the jet decreases as $z^{-\frac{5}{3}}$ and the velocity as $z^{-\frac{1}{3}}$.

The determination of exact expressions for the velocity and temperature necessitates the solution of the differential equations. This can be done only in the form of infinite series, and the computation is somewhat laborious. The reader is referred to Schmidt's original paper for the details.

Alternative Treatment. The following analysis of the three-dimensional problem, due to Sutton,[12] reaches much the same results but avoids the difficulties of computation inherent in Schmidt's treatment. Consider an atmosphere at rest, and of uniform potential temperature, which may be supposed to be zero without loss of generality. As in Schmidt's theory, the excess temperature in the jet, θ, is supposed small compared with the absolute temperature of the air as a whole, and the analysis applies only to jets in which the gases have been considerably mixed with air.

Sutton follows Schmidt in taking the mixing length l to be proportional to the radius r of the jet at any level but departs from the Prandtl theory by supposing that the velocity fluctuations in the jet are given by $w' = l\,dw/dz$, that is, proportional to the rate of decrease of velocity *downstream.* The rate at which air is entrained by the turbulent mixing process on the boundary of the jet depends on the area A exposed, the velocity fluctuation w', and the mixing length l. On the above hypothesis

$$\text{Rate of entrainment} = \text{constant} \cdot \rho A l \frac{dw}{dz} = \rho A c r \frac{dw}{dz}$$

where c is a constant of proportionality.

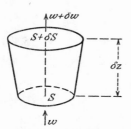

FIG. 32. Flow in a convection jet.

Consider (Fig. 32) an elemental slice of the jet lying between the planes z and $z + \delta z$. Inflow through the lower surface is $\rho w S$, outflow through the upper surface is $\rho(w + \delta w)(S + \delta S)$, where S is the cross-sectional area πr^2 and variations in ρ are disregarded. The difference is $\rho(S\,\delta w + w\,\delta S)$, retaining only infinitesimals of the first order, and this must be equal to the air entrained, which, by the fundamental hypothesis, is $\rho A c r\,dw/dz$, where A is the surface area of the elemental cylinder, $2\pi r\,\delta z$. Hence

$$\pi r^2\,\delta w + 2\pi r w\,\delta r = 2\pi r^2 c \frac{dw}{dz}\,\delta z$$

or, in the limit as $\delta z \to 0$,

$$r\frac{dw}{dz} + 2w\frac{dr}{dz} = 2rc\frac{dw}{dz} \tag{8.45}$$

The second fundamental assumption is that the radius of the jet, r, is related to the height above the source by an equation of the type familiar in the theory of the diffusion of smoke in a horizontal wind, *viz.*,

$$r = (\ln 10)^{\frac{1}{2}} C z^{\frac{1}{2}m} \simeq 1.5 C z^{\frac{1}{2}m}$$

where C is a generalized diffusion coefficient, the factor $\ln 10$ entering because of the convention that, in a normal error distribution of density, the boundary of the jet is determined by the points at which the concentration falls to one-tenth of the central concentration. The index m is unspecified.

Substituting this value of r in (8.45) and solving the resulting first-order equation gives

$$w = w_1 z^{m/(1-2c)} \tag{8.46}$$

where w_1 is a constant of integration whose value is found later.

If $\bar{\theta}$ is the mean temperature excess over any cross section, the condition of constancy of source gives

$$\bar{\theta} = \frac{Q}{\pi r^2 c_p \rho w} \simeq \frac{Q}{2.3\pi C^2 z^m c_p \rho w}$$

The upward velocity is determined by the principle enunciated by Taylor, that the intensity of the convection currents is determined by the balance between the rate of dissipation of energy by the breakdown of the heated mass into smaller eddies and the rate of loss of potential energy. Hence (Chap. 4, page 150)

$$w^2 = \text{constant} \cdot \frac{\bar{\theta} g l}{T_a}$$

where T_a is the absolute temperature of the undisturbed air. Taking the "constant" as unity,

$$w^2 = \frac{Qgcr}{2.3\pi C^2 z^m c_p \rho w T_a}$$

or

$$w^3 = \frac{Qgc}{1.5\pi C c_p \rho T_a z^{\frac{1}{2}m}}$$

Hence, from Eq. (8.46),

$$\frac{3m}{2c-1} = \tfrac{1}{2}m$$

or

$$c = \tfrac{7}{2} \tag{8.47}$$

The problem is now completely solved in a closed form if C and m are regarded as known. The solution is

$$\bar{\theta} = \frac{Q}{2.3\pi c_p \rho C^2 w_1 z^{5m/6}} \tag{8.48}$$

$$w = w_1 z^{-\frac{1}{3}m} \tag{8.49}$$

$$w_1 = \left(\frac{7Qg}{3\pi c_p \rho T_a C} \right)^{\frac{1}{3}} \tag{8.50}$$

In Schmidt's solution, r is proportional to z, and thus $m = 2$. Observations on smoke clouds give more support to the value $m = 1.75$ (page 277). The two solutions are thus

Schmidt

Sutton

$$\bar{\theta} = \text{constant} \cdot z^{-\frac{2}{3}}$$

$$\bar{\theta} = \frac{Q}{2.3\pi c_p \rho C^2 w_1 z^{1.46}}$$

$$w = \text{constant} \cdot z^{-\frac{1}{3}}$$

$$w = w_1 z^{-0.29}$$

(Constants expressed as series)

$$w_1 = \left(\frac{728.5Q}{c_p \rho T_a C}\right)^{\frac{1}{3}}$$

Sutton compares his solution with experimental data given by Schmidt for laboratory experiments with the jet produced by a small heating coil and shows that, on the whole, there is slightly better agreement than with Schmidt's original solution. A point of particular interest is that the value of the generalized diffusion coefficient C deduced from Schmidt's experiments is about 0.26 cm$^{\frac{1}{3}}$, which is much the same as that found for diffusion of smoke near the ground in conditions of neutral equilibrium (see page 292). This leads to the striking conclusion that the same coefficient of diffusion applies to the mixing of a tiny column of hot air with the cold air of a laboratory as for the travel of smoke over hundreds of meters.

Sutton has applied the theory to the case of a typical industrial stack, taking $Q = 5 \times 10^7$ Btu hr^{-1} = 3.5×10^6 cal sec^{-1} and finds that the upward velocity within about 10 m of the stack orifice is about 6 m sec^{-1}, that is, comparable with the average speed of the natural wind. This appears to be borne out by observation.

Plume in a Horizontal Wind. An exact solution of the behavior of a jet of heated air in a side wind appears to be impossible in the present incomplete state of knowledge of turbulence associated with the simultaneous appearance of thermal and dynamic instability. Sutton has applied the theory given above to obtain a relatively crude approximation to the solution by assuming that the shape of the plume axis resembles the trajectory of a particle subjected to a constant horizontal velocity (the natural wind) and an upward velocity which decays with distance along the trajectory according to the laws established above. If Schmidt's solution is adopted, the formulas can be given in a closed form.

If s is distance along the trajectory, $w = w_1 s^{-\frac{1}{3}}$ the vertical velocity, and $u(= \text{constant})$ the side wind, it is easily shown that

$$s = (w_1/u)^3 \cot^3 \psi \qquad (8.51)$$

$$z = \frac{3}{2}\left(\frac{w_1}{u}\right)^3 [\cot \psi \operatorname{cosec} \psi - \ln (\cot \psi + \operatorname{cosec} \psi)] \qquad (8.52)$$

where ψ is the inclination of the trajectory to the horizontal when the particle has reached a height z above the source. For a typical industrial stack, Sutton finds that the plume is virtually horizontal ($\psi < 10°$) when $z = 100$ m, $s = 400$ m if $u = 5$ m sec^{-1}, but for $u = 10$ m sec^{-1}, the plume is horizontal when $z = 12.5$ m. The height attained varies as u^{-3}, illustrating the marked effect of the side wind in forcing the plume from the vertical, a result also seen in the guttering of a candle flame in a slight current of air.

Formulas for the calculation of the path followed by the smoke trail in a side wind have also been given by Bosanquet, Carey, and Halton,[9] who consider the extended problem of hot gas emerging with a forced velocity v and a temperature difference Δ between the flue gas and the ambient air T_a. The expressions given are as follows:

Rise caused by forced velocity alone

$$z = z_{\max}\left(1 - 0.8\frac{z_{\max}}{x}\right) \qquad \text{when } x > 2z_{\max}$$

$$z_{\max} = \frac{4.77}{1 + 0.43u/v}\frac{\sqrt{(Qv)}}{u}$$

x being the horizontal distance from the stack down wind.

Rise due to excess temperature of the effluent. The path of the plume is given by

$$x = 3.57\frac{\sqrt{(Qv)}}{u}X$$

$$z = 6.37\frac{Q\Delta}{u^3 T_a}Z$$

when $u^2 > (\Delta g/T_a)(Q/v)^{\frac{1}{2}}$. X and Z are quantities whose relation is shown in graphical form. The derivation of these expressions is not given in the published paper. It is stated that the formula for the velocity rise agrees with experimental results obtained in a wind tunnel and that comparisons of the combined formulas with observations made on real stack plumes are satisfactory.

Effect of Adding Heat to a Source of Pollution. Suppose a stack of height h is emitting matter at air temperature at the rate Q_M g sec^{-1}. From Eq. (8.36), it follows that the maximum concentration at ground level $\chi_{\max}$ is proportional to Q_M/uh^2, where u is the horizontal wind. If a source of heat Q_H cal sec^{-1} is added, the result will be to lift the axis of the cloud so that the source is effectively at height $h + \delta h$. From Eq. (8.52), δh is proportional to $(w_1/u)^3$, which in turn is proportional to $Q_H u^{-3}$ [Eq. (8.50)]. Hence

$$\text{New } \chi_{\max} \propto \frac{Q_M}{u(h + aQ_H u^{-3})^2} = \frac{Q_M}{uh^2(1 + 2aQ_H h^{-1}u^{-3} + a^2 Q_H h^{-2} u^{-6})}$$

where a is a constant. Neglecting the term $a^2 Q_H h^{-2} u^{-6}$ (a procedure valid for all except the lightest winds), it follows that

$$\frac{\text{New } \chi_{\max}}{\text{Old } \chi_{\max}} = \left(1 + \frac{2aQ_H}{hu^3}\right)^{-1} \simeq 1 - \frac{2aQ_H}{hu^3}$$

This shows that the result of adding a source of heat of strength Q_H is to cause a reduction in the maximum concentration at ground level proportional to $Q_H/u^3 h$ or, if u is regarded as constant, to Q_H/h. Despite the slow increase of the convective velocity with additional heat, the reduction in ground concentration is directly as the magnitude of the heat source, the effect being most pronounced for low stacks. Hence, adding heat to a source of pollution is an effective way of minimizing objectionable concentrations at ground level. The advantage so gained is reduced by high winds, but in these circumstances the cloud is usually sufficiently dilute to be tolerated.

8.6. Theoretical Study of Evaporation

In the atmosphere, evaporation of water proceeds from free-liquid surfaces, such as seas, lakes, and rivers, from solids, such as soil, vegetation, snow fields, and glaciers, and from waterdrops, snowflakes, and ice crystals in the upper air. The discussion given below is confined to a process which is fairly common in the lower atmosphere, the removal of water vapor from a free-liquid or permanently saturated solid surface. The extended problem of the drying of a solid is extremely complicated, involving not only the mechanism of diffusion of vapor at the air-solid interface but also the motion of the liquid from the interior of the solid to the boundary, and as yet little progress has been made toward a comprehensive mathematical theory.

A rough total of water evaporated from a reservoir or lake can be obtained by measuring the inflow and outflow, precipitation, and water level during the period under review. Estimates of this type are often sufficiently accurate for the needs of civil engineering, but such results shed little light on the complexities of the meteorological problem. Evaporation from small isolated tanks, estimated in a similar fashion, is a routine observation at certain meteorological observatories, but the results are of doubtful value (see page 315). Methods of this type are purely observational and involve little or no theory.

The theoretical study of evaporation is approached in two quite distinct ways. The first method concentrates attention on the mechanism of the removal of vapor by diffusion and is primarily applicable to the determination of local rates of evaporation. The second approach does not require any knowledge of the details of the evaporation process but relies on estimating the amount of energy used in the change from the liquid to the vapor phase, and hence the rate at which water is being removed. This method finds its natural application to large areas. The two approaches will be referred to as the *diffusion method* and the *energy-balance method*, respectively.

Evaporation as a Diffusion Process. Limited Areas. In the absence of wind, water vapor is removed from a volume of liquid by molecular diffusion in a manner analogous to the cooling of a body. If V is the mass of water vapor per unit mass of air, the equation of diffusion in the steady state is

$$\nabla^2 V = 0$$

This is Laplace's equation, and the evaporation problem is most easily solved by consideration of a well-known problem in electrostatics, that of the distribution of potential in the neighborhood of a charged plate, which involves similar boundary conditions. The solution of the evaporation problem is that E, the rate of evaporation, is given by the analogue of a familiar formula in electrostatics, *viz.*,

$$E = -\iint \kappa\rho \frac{\partial V}{\partial z} \, dS = 4\pi\kappa\rho C V_0 \tag{8.53}$$

where dS is an element of area, κ is the coefficient of molecular diffusion of water into air, C is the electrostatic capacity of the surface area, and V_0 is the difference between the value of V at infinity and on $z = 0$ (Jeffreys[13]). Since C is proportional to the linear dimension of the charged plate, it follows that evaporation into a still atmosphere is proportional to the linear dimension of surfaces of similar shape.

Evaporation into a steady wind presents much greater difficulties. Mathematically, the problem is the inverse of those studied in the previous sections, in which the source is given and the concentration has to be found at all points. In the evaporation problem the source has to be determined, so that additional information concerning the concentration of vapor must be given beforehand, in the form of boundary conditions.

The diffusion process is specified, as in the constant-source problem, by the general equation of diffusion

$$\frac{d\chi}{dt} = \frac{\partial}{\partial x}\left(K_x \frac{\partial\chi}{\partial x}\right) + \frac{\partial}{\partial y}\left(K_y \frac{\partial\chi}{\partial y}\right) + \frac{\partial}{\partial z}\left(K_z \frac{\partial\chi}{\partial z}\right)$$

For the steady two-dimensional case, $d\chi/dt = \bar{u}\,\partial\chi/\partial x$, and there is no term in y. Neglecting, as usual, the down-wind diffusion term in x, the equation becomes

$$\bar{u}(z) \frac{\partial\chi}{\partial x} = \frac{\partial}{\partial z}\left(K_z \frac{\partial\chi}{\partial z}\right) \tag{8.8}$$

This equation has been considered above for an infinite cross-wind line source but is now to be applied to evaporation from an area which is infinite across wind and finite down wind. Such an area is defined by $0 \leq x \leq x_0; z = 0$. For $x > x_0$ or $x < 0$, it is supposed that the ground is dry (Fig. 33).

The boundary conditions have to be specified carefully. It is evident that $\chi = 0$ if $x < 0$, for all z, and that $\chi \to 0$ as $z \to \infty$ for $0 \leq x \leq x_0$, but these conditions are insufficient to specify the problem since they

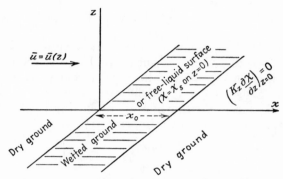

FIG. 33.   Two-dimensional evaporation problem.

leave undecided the behavior of χ as $z \to 0$ for $0 \leq x \leq x_0$. Three types of condition are possible:

1. The value of χ is prescribed at all points on the evaporating surface, *i.e.*,

$$\lim_{z \to 0} \chi(x,z) = \chi_s = \text{constant} \qquad \text{for } 0 \leq x \leq x_0$$

2. The local rate of evaporation is prescribed, *i.e.*,

$$\lim_{z \to 0} \left(K_z \frac{\partial \chi}{\partial z} \right) = f(x,\bar{u})$$

where f is some explicit function of position and wind velocity.

3. A combination of (1) and (2) (like the radiation condition in the theory of heat, Chap. 4), *viz.*, that the value of χ on the evaporating surface and the local rate of evaporation are joined by a linear relation.

The condition chosen by Sutton[4] is (1), the constant concentration being identified with the saturation value χ_s, which depends only on the temperature of the surface and the nature of the evaporating liquid. Evidence supporting the correctness of this assumption comes partly from laboratory measurements of humidity in the close vicinity of an evaporating surface and partly from the success of the solution in predicting rates of evaporation from small saturated surfaces in wind tunnels. With this formulation, the problem of evaporation amounts to the determination of the area source which maintains a constant concentration of vapor on the plane $z = 0$ despite the removal of vapor by the turbulent air stream. Condition (2) has been used by Giblett,[14] who employs an empirical relation devised by Bigelow to specify the local rate of evaporation in terms of the vapor pressure and the wind speed, any variation of evaporation with distance from the upwind edge of the source being disregarded. This treatment cannot be supported on mathematical grounds or by an appeal to observation. The radiation type of boundary condition does not seem to have been used by any writer.

A detailed account of the theory of the two-dimensional diffusion equation and the associated boundary conditions has been given by W. G. L. Sutton,[15] whose treatment is a generalization of that of Goursat for the equation of conduction of heat. Reference should also be made to the work of Gevrey,[16] Jaeger,[17] and Köhler[18] on the same equation.

Solution of the two-dimensional problem. The problem of evaporation from a saturated or free-liquid plane surface, extended indefinitely across wind and of finite length down wind, has been solved by Sutton for the wind profile (8.20) and the eddy diffusivity (8.21). The boundary conditions adopted for a substance which is not present in the air upwind of the evaporating strip are

(1) $\lim_{z \to 0} \chi(x,z) = \chi_s$ for $0 \le x \le x_0$

(2) $\lim_{x \to 0} \chi(x,z) = 0$ for $z > 0$

(3) $\lim_{z \to \infty} \chi(x,z) = 0$ for $0 \le x \le x_0$

For a substance which is normally found in the air (such as water), conditions (2) and (3) must be replaced by

(2′) $\lim_{x \to 0} \chi(x,z) = \chi_0$ for $z > 0$

(3′) $\lim_{z \to \infty} \chi(x,z) = \chi_0$ for $0 \le x \le x_0$

where χ_0 is the (uniform) concentration in the air before it reaches the strip. In the formulas which follow, this simply means replacing χ by $\chi - \chi_0$ and χ_s by $\chi_s - \chi_0$.

It is important to note that the solution gives the vapor concentration only over the wetted area. The total rate of evaporation is

$$E(\bar{u},x_0) = \int_0^\infty \bar{u}\chi(x_0,z)dz \qquad (8.54)$$

since the integral obviously represents the total mass of vapor carried across the plane $x = x_0$ by the wind. The solution of Eq. (8.8), for K_z

given by the expression (8.21), and subject to the above boundary conditions, is

$$
\chi(x,z) = \chi_s \left\{ 1 - \frac{1}{\pi} \sin \frac{2\pi}{2+n} \, \Gamma\left(\frac{2}{2+n}\right) \right.
$$

$$
\left. \Gamma\left[\frac{\bar{u}_1{}^n z^{(2+n)/(2-n)}}{\left(\frac{2+n}{2-n}\right)^2 a z_1{}^{n/(2-n)} x}, \frac{n}{2+n} \right] \right\} \quad (8.55)
$$

where

$$
a = \frac{(\frac{1}{2}\pi k^2)^{1-n}(2-n)^{1-n} n^{1-n} \nu^n z_1{}^{(n^2-n)/(2-n)}}{(1-n)(2-2n)^{2-2n}} \quad (8.56)
$$

and $\Gamma(\theta,p)$ is the incomplete gamma function defined by

$$
\Gamma(\theta,p) = \int_0^\theta x^{p-1} e^{-x} dx
$$

The total rate of evaporation per unit of cross-wind length is

$$
E(\bar{u},x_0) = A \bar{u}_1{}^{(2-n)/(2+n)} x_0{}^{2/(2+n)} \quad (8.57)
$$

where

$$
A = \chi_s \left(\frac{2+n}{2-n}\right)^{(2-n)/(2+n)} \left(\frac{2+n}{2\pi}\right) \sin\left(\frac{2\pi}{2+n}\right)
$$

$$
\Gamma\left(\frac{2}{2+n}\right) a^{2/(2+n)} z_1{}^{-n^2/(4-n^2)} \quad (8.58)
$$

These expressions show that the rate of evaporation from a smooth surface can be calculated knowing n, $\bar{u}_1$, and the Kármán constant k.

Expression (8.57) enables a quick check to be made from laboratory data. For $n = \frac{1}{4}$ [for which Eq. (8.20) becomes the seventh-root profile], it follows that

$$
E = \text{constant} \cdot \bar{u}_1{}^{0.78} x_0{}^{0.89} \quad (8.59)
$$

The value 0.78 of the wind-velocity exponent has been verified experimentally by Himus,[19] Powell and Griffiths,[20] Thiesenhausen,[21] and Hine[22] (data analyzed by Sutton[4]). Dörffel's[23] experiments gave the power as 0.71, but Mrose,[24] using the same apparatus, found 0.75. For the index of x_0, Lettau and Dörffel[25] found 0.873, which is very close to the theoretical value. Powell and Griffiths[20] found that in their experiments the power of the down-wind dimension varied with the cross-wind dimension, indicating that in their arrangement diffusion was not truly two-dimensional.

The most satisfactory test of the solution is that carried out by Pasquill[26] in a very careful and comprehensive study in a specially designed wind tunnel, using a variety of liquids. In these experiments,

considerable care was taken to avoid spurious effects caused by ~~~
from the lip of the evaporation vessel and to ensure that the turbu~~
boundary layer over the saturated surface was fully developed. The
results show close agreement between theory and practice, not only as
regards the functional form derived for E, but also in respect of absolute
values (Fig. 34).

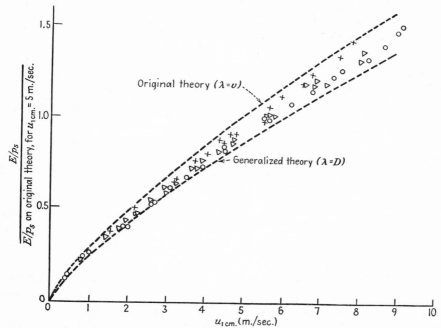

Fig. 34. Experimental and theoretical values for the rate of evaporation of bromo-
benzene into a turbulent air stream $\odot$ = observed values for surface 24 cm diameter;
$\triangle$ = observed values for surface 19 cm square; $\times$ = observed values for surface 20 cm
cross wind by 10 cm down wind. [*Proc. Roy. Soc.* (*London*), A 182 (1943).]

The curve marked $\lambda = D$ refers to a modification of the original theory
proposed by Pasquill. The expression (8.21) for the eddy diffusivity
may be written

$$K_z = f(n)\bar{u}z\left(\frac{\nu}{\bar{u}z}\right)^n \tag{8.60}$$

using (8.20). Pasquill suggested that the kinematic viscosity ν in this
expression, which is derived from consideration of the transfer of momentum, should be replaced by a general coefficient λ and that $\lambda = D$, the
molecular coefficient of mass diffusion for the transfer of matter, and
$\lambda = \kappa$, the thermometric conductivity, for the transfer of heat. The data

ıot indicate a significant improvement when D is
comparison with results obtained for other liquids
ification of the original formulas has a sound basis.
afforded by Pasquill's use of (8.57) and (8.58) to
t by forced convection from a plane surface main-
ıperature in a fast moving air stream. If the con-
ed by $c_p\rho T$ and ν by κ, the differential equation
ions for the diffusion of vapor become those for
heat transfer. ıne rate of loss of heat can then be calculated if the
velocity profile is known, and Pasquill found good agreement between
the theoretical result and the measurements of Elias on forced convection
from a metal plate in a high wind (about 35 m. sec^{-1}). A high velocity is
essential to minimize free convection effects, and it is noteworthy that,
in such conditions, Elias found almost complete similarity between the
profiles of velocity and temperature over the plate.

These results show that the solution (8.55) is sufficiently accurate for
the prediction of evaporation from a smooth surface in laboratory work
whenever lateral diffusion can be neglected. Experiments in the open
air with small saturated surfaces of blotting paper on glass and mounted
on a faired surround in the middle of a close-cut sports field also give
satisfactory agreement in conditions of small temperature gradient
(Sutton[1]).

The consequences of this theory for meteorology should be carefully
noted. In the first place, the rate of evaporation is proportional to the
saturation concentration or, for a substance such as water which is already
present in the oncoming air, to the difference between the saturation concentration at the temperature of the surface and the concentration in the
air upwind of the surface. Second, the rate of evaporation is directly
proportional, not to the down-wind dimension, but to a power of the
down-wind dimension less than unity. This means that the local rate
of evaporation decreases with distance from the upwind edge, so that
the phrase "evaporation per unit area" is ambiguous unless the complete
size of the area is specified. The decrease in the rate of evaporation with
distance down wind is due to the air becoming enriched with vapor as it
moves away from the upwind edge, and if the wetted surface extends
indefinitely down wind, a stage will ultimately be reached when the air
over the surface is saturated and evaporation ceases. Mathematically,
this is shown by the fact that for $0 < z < \infty$, $\chi(x,z) \to \chi_s$ as $x \to \infty$.
The variation of E with wind speed shows that the simple relation
assumed in many empirical studies of evaporation, that the rate of
removal of vapor is directly proportional to the wind velocity, is not
strictly true.

Rough surfaces. The above solutions apply to aerodynamically smooth flow.   For flow of the fully-rough type Calder[3] has used the same methods as in the infinite-line-source problem, *viz.*, replacement of the logarithmic profile by an approximate power law (see page 281).   The expressions so obtained are virtually identical with those given above but were derived by the method of sources, leading to an integral equation of the Abel type.   For the full formulas, which are somewhat complicated, the reader should consult the original paper.

Calder has compared the solutions with observations of the vapor concentration over areas of downland uniformly sprinkled with aniline, in conditions of neutral stability.   The results show reasonably good agreement with observation for heights up to about 2 m.

Concentrations outside the evaporating strip.   For $x > x_0$ the ground is supposed dry, so that in this region the boundary condition (1) is replaced by the condition that the local rate of evaporation is zero.   The expression for $\chi(x,z)$ in this part of the (x,z) space was obtained by W. G. L. Sutton,[15] and later by Calder[3] (using the method of sources), in the form

$$\chi(x,z) = \chi_s \sin\left(\frac{2\pi}{2+n}\right) \int_0^{x_0} \theta^{-n/(2+n)}(x-\theta)^{2/(2+n)}$$

$$\exp\left[-\frac{\bar{u}_1{}^n z^{(2+n)/(2-n)}}{\left(\dfrac{2+n}{2-n}\right)^2 a(x-\theta)z_1{}^{n/(2-n)}}\right] d\theta \quad (8.61)$$

So far, this integral has not been reduced to a tabulated function.

The above solutions are applicable to areas which are extended indefinitely across wind or to conditions in which lateral diffusion may be ignored.   The three-dimensional problem of evaporation from an area which is finite across wind as well as down wind still awaits a satisfactory solution.   D. R. Davies[27] has considered Eq. (8.15) for $p = m$ and has found the solution for a semiinfinite area bounded by a parabolic curve, but the assumption that K_y increases with height at the same rate as the mean wind speed has no theoretical foundation and is known to lead to an incorrect result in the case of a continuous point source (see page 284).   C. J. Tranter[28] has recently studied the problem as a corollary of that of the flow of heat in a solid bounded internally by an elliptic cylinder, the solution of which is given formally as an infinite series of integrals involving Mathieu functions.   Tranter's method of deriving the solution of the evaporation problem for constant K_y and K_z is as follows:

Consider a saturated or free-liquid strip of width $2h$ lying in the plane $z = 0$, the longer side being parallel to the mean wind direction.   The equation of diffusion is

$$\bar{u}\,\frac{\partial\chi}{\partial x} = K_y\,\frac{\partial^2\chi}{\partial y^2} + K_z\,\frac{\partial^2\chi}{\partial z^2}$$

with the boundary conditions:

$$\lim_{x \to 0} \chi(x,y,z) = 0 \qquad z > 0$$

$$\lim_{z \to 0} \chi(x,y,z) = \chi_s \qquad x > 0, \; -h \leq y \leq h$$

$$\lim_{z \to 0} K_z \frac{\partial \chi}{\partial z} = 0 \qquad x > 0, \; -h > y > h$$

and $\chi \to 0$ at large distances from the strip. The substitution $x = \bar{u}t$, $y = K_y^{\frac{1}{2}} \cosh \xi \cos \eta$, $z = K_z^{\frac{1}{2}} h \sinh \xi \sin \eta$ yields

$$\frac{\partial^2 \chi}{\partial \xi^2} + \frac{\partial^2 \chi}{\partial \eta^2} = \frac{h^2}{2} (\cosh 2\xi - \cos 2\eta) \frac{\partial \chi}{\partial t}$$

This equation is similar to that for the heat-conduction problem, and the same solution (with certain minor alterations) applies to the evaporation problem. Hence the formal solution is known for constant diffusivities but involves untabulated Mathieu functions, so that no practical application can be made at present.

Unlimited Areas. In meteorological applications, it is necessary to note that the solutions given above apply only to areas with a definite upwind edge, such as lakes and reservoirs. Evaporation from regions of ocean remote from land or from saturated soil which is part of a very large similar area is an entirely different problem. In these cases there is no ambiguity in speaking of the rate of evaporation per unit area, since properties are the same in all horizontal planes.

In such conditions the vapor concentration depends only on height and time and the equation of diffusion is

$$\frac{\partial \chi}{\partial t} = \frac{\partial}{\partial z} \left(K_z \frac{\partial \chi}{\partial z} \right)$$

The solution of this equation requires a knowledge of the diurnal variation of K_z at all heights, and at the present time there is insufficient information to justify such an approach. Most of the studies deal with the steady state $(\partial \chi / \partial t = 0)$, when it follows that

$$K_z \frac{\partial \chi}{\partial z} = \text{constant}$$

Since $(K_z \, \partial \chi / \partial z)_{z=0}$ is the local rate of evaporation, this treatment implies that the flux of water vapor is independent of height, and if K_z is identified with the eddy viscosity, it follows that the water-vapor profile is simply the wind profile adjusted to meet the different boundary conditions. From

$$\bar{u} = \bar{u}_1 \left(\frac{z}{z_1} \right)^m$$

it follows that

$$\chi_s - \chi = \text{constant} \cdot F_0 z^m \qquad (8.62)$$

where $F_0 = (K_z \, \partial\chi/\partial z)_{z=0}$ is the flux of water vapor at the surface. Such a power-law expression agrees reasonably well with observations of humidity in lapse conditions and rather better in inversion conditions (Sheppard[29]). If K_z is taken to be directly proportional to the height, the difference $\chi_s - \chi$ is proportional to the logarithm of the height, which agrees well with observations in small temperature gradients, but not in large lapse rates and large inversions (Sverdrup,[30] Firesah[31]).

The best-known and most widely tested evaporation formula derived on these lines is that of Thornthwaite and Holzman,[32] published in 1939, and afterward generalized by Holzman[33] in 1943. In adiabatic gradient conditions, when the wind profile is logarithmic, the expression for the rate of evaporation becomes

$$E = \frac{\rho k^2 (q_1 - q_2)(u_2 - u_1)}{(\ln z_2/z_1)^2} \qquad (8.63)$$

where q_1, q_2 and u_1, u_2 are the specific humidities and mean wind velocities, respectively, at heights z_2 and z_1, and k is Kármán's constant. This follows without difficulty from the usual logarithmic profile for a fully-rough surface [Eq. (7.2)] and the assumption that K_z may be identified with the eddy viscosity and thus given by

$$K_z = \frac{u_1 k^2 z}{\ln (z_1/z_0)}$$

As pointed out by Pasquill,[34] expression (8.63) may be written with sufficient accuracy in the more convenient form

$$E = B u_2 (e_1 - e_2) \qquad (8.64)$$

where

$$B = \frac{k^2 M}{RT} \frac{(1 - u_1/u_2)}{(\ln z_2/z_1)^2}$$

(M = molecular weight of water, R = gas constant, T = absolute temperature of the air, e_1 and e_2 = vapor pressures) is virtually constant for any site of fixed roughness. This is because, in adiabatic gradient conditions, u_1/u_2 depends only on the roughness of the surface, assumed constant. Hence there results a particularly simple expression in which the rate of evaporation per unit area can be estimated from measurement of the wind speed at some convenient low height and the vapor pressure at two heights.

Pasquill has examined these expressions in a series of papers, and has considered the modified form for very rough surfaces, *viz.*,

$$E = \frac{\rho k^2 (u_2 - u_1)(q_1 - q_2)}{\left[\ln \left(\dfrac{z_2 - d}{z_1 - d} \right) \right]^2} \tag{8.65}$$

where d is the zero-plane displacement (Chap. 7). The theoretical formula, which involves only meteorological measurements, was compared with the rate of evaporation found by removing soil cores and weighing the samples at regular intervals. Such a procedure demands careful control, and the precautions necessary to ensure the reliability of the technique have been discussed by Pasquill. The final result, based on 41 comparisons of the rate of evaporation, E_c, calculated by Eq. (8.65), and the rate found by loss of weight in the soil samples E_o, in effectively adiabatic gradient conditions, with wind speeds varying from 300 to 900 cm sec^{-1}, indicated a mean value of $E_c/E_o = 0.99$. The individual deviations from perfect agreement were within 10, 20, and 30 per cent in 24, 66, and 90 per cent of occasions. This implies that in neutral stability the estimation, from profile measurements, of mean rates of evaporation over periods of the order of hours would be in error by not more than 20 per cent on about 70 per cent of occasions, a satisfactory result.

Holzman,[33] using the empirical relation for the mixing length in non-adiabatic conditions discussed in Chap. 7, has given an expression for evaporation in any condition of stability, similar to that for neutral equilibrium, *viz.*,

$$E = \frac{\rho k^2 (q_1 - q_2)(u_2 - u_1)}{\ln \dfrac{z_2}{z_1} \ln \dfrac{z_2(1 - sz_1)}{z_1(1 - sz_2)}} \tag{8.66}$$

where s is an experimentally determined stability parameter. In adiabatic lapse-rate conditions, $s = 0$, and Eq. (8.66) reduces to Eq. (8.63).

R. B. Montgomery[35] has examined evaporation from the ocean. In this work, the humidity profile is described in terms of the *evaporation coefficient* Γ_E defined by

$$\Gamma_E = - \frac{1}{(e_0 - e_z)} \frac{de}{d(\ln z)} \tag{8.67}$$

where e_z is the vapor pressure on the plane z. For a smooth surface Montgomery takes into account the existence of the laminar sublayer and writes

$$K_z = D + k\bar{u}z \qquad \text{for a smooth surface} \tag{8.68}$$
$$K_z = D + k\bar{u}(z + z_0) \qquad \text{for a fully-rough surface} \tag{8.69}$$

where D is the molecular diffusivity of water vapor into air. In the laminar sublayer, all properties vary linearly with height, and so

$$E = \frac{5\rho D}{8p}\left(\frac{e_0 - e_\delta}{\delta}\right) \tag{8.70}$$

where δ is the thickness of the laminar sublayer and p is the atmospheric pressure. For δ, Montgomery uses the equation

$$\delta = \frac{7.8\nu}{u_*} \tag{8.71}$$

In the turbulent layer

$$E = \frac{5\rho k u_*(e_\delta - e_z)}{8p \ln \dfrac{D + k u_* z}{D}} \tag{8.72}$$

using Eq. (8.68). Eliminating δ between Eqs. (8.70) and (8.72) and using Eq. (8.67), Montgomery deduces that

$$E = \frac{5\rho k u_*(e_0 - e_z)}{8p}\,\Gamma_E \tag{8.73}$$

The evaporation coefficient may also be expressed in terms of the skin-friction coefficient of the surface.

To allow for the effects of waves, Montgomery considers three layers, proceeding upward from the surface: (1) a laminar layer, with a linear velocity profile; (2) an intermediate layer, with the smooth-surface logarithmic profile; (3) the turbulent layer proper, with a fully-rough logarithmic profile. The depth of the intermediate layer is equal to the wave height, and the analysis is based on continuity of velocity, but not of shearing stress, at the junction of the layers. The final result is an expression analogous to (8.73).

Montgomery's method leads to the result that the evaporation coefficient for a fully-rough surface is one-half of that for a smooth surface, but since the friction velocity increases in passing from a smooth to a rough surface, it is concluded that evaporation from a smooth sea is much the same as that from a rough sea, except for the contribution from spray. This does not agree with the work of Norris,[36] who assumes that the ratio of the flux of vapor in the intermediate and turbulent layers is proportional to the ratio of the shearing stress in these layers, and therefore to the square of the ratio of the friction velocities appropriate to the two layers. On this basis, Norris concludes that the rate of evaporation from a fully-rough surface is four times that for a smooth surface. Somewhat similar expressions have been given by Sverdrup.[37] On the whole, the weight of observational evidence is in favor of the theories of Norris and Sverdrup and against Montgomery. For winds (at 6 m) less than 800 cm sec^{-1}, all three theories lead to much the same result and are in moderate agreement with observation. For winds exceeding 800 cm sec^{-1}, Montgomery's formula gives rates of evaporation far below those observed, whereas there is a measure of agreement with the estimates of Sverdrup and Norris.

Energy-balance Method. The energy-balance method is based on the principle of conservation of energy. For a sheet of stagnant water or a layer of soil,

$$F_I = F_R + F_B + F_H - F_S + F_E \qquad (8.74)$$

where F_I = incoming radiation from the sun (direct and diffuse)

F_R = reflected solar radiation

F_B = upward flux of (long-wave) radiation

F_H = flux of energy from the surface as sensible heat

F_S = flux of heat into, and stored by, the body

F_E = heat used in evaporation

all the above being expressed in g cal cm^{-2} min^{-1}. It is assumed that no heat is advected into or out of the lake and that absorption of radiation by vegetation (photosynthesis) may be neglected. The problem is to determine F_E.

The quantities F_I, F_R, F_B have been discussed in Chap. 5, and values of F_S for soil are given in Chap. 6. The main difficulty lies in the accurate evaluation of F_H, the rate of transfer of heat by conduction and turbulence. Rewriting Eq. (8.74) in the form

$$F_H + F_E = F_I - F_R - F_B + F_S \qquad (8.75)$$

and introducing the so-called *Bowen ratio* $R = F_H/F_E$ (the ratio of the heat loss by conduction and turbulence to the loss of heat by evaporation), Eq. (8.75) becomes

$$F_E = \frac{F_I - F_R - F_B + F_S}{1 + R} \qquad (8.76)$$

Hence, with L, the latent heat of vaporization, the rate of evaporation per unit area is

$$E = \frac{F_I - F_R - F_B + F_S}{L(1 + R)} \qquad (8.77)$$

The problem now turns, effectively, on the determination of R, since all other quantities are known or fairly easily measured.

In the early work of Schmidt,[38] R was given values ranging from about 2 to 0.3. Ångström[39] later concluded that these values are too high and gave reasons for believing that R was about 0.1. Subsequently, Bowen[40] attempted to express R in terms of easily measurable quantities, so that Eq. (8.77) could be used without difficulty. He considered two limiting conditions, as follows:

CASE I. The wind speed does not vary with height in a thin layer adjacent to the surface, with stagnant or very slowly moving air above the top of the layer. The entire volume of air inside the layer is changed as regards temperature and humidity to that of the air in direct contact with the evaporating surface, and diffusion across the upper surface of the layer does not enter into the problem.

CASE II. It is supposed that there is a layer of stagnant air adjacent to the surface, with a high wind above. The heat and vapor diffused through the stationary layer are carried away immediately by the upper wind. Here diffusion is the dominating factor.

For these two extreme cases, Bowen found

CASE I

$$R = 6.6 \times 10^{-4}p \left(\frac{T_s - T_A}{e_s - e_A}\right) \tag{8.78}$$

CASE II

$$R = 5.8 \times 10^{-4}p \left(\frac{T_s - T_A}{e_s - e_A}\right) \tag{8.79}$$

where T_s, T_A, e_s, e_A are temperatures (degrees centigrade) and vapor pressures at the surface and in the air, respectively, and p is the atmospheric pressure. For the practical case, which is intermediate to cases I and II, Bowen chose

$$R = 6.1 \times 10^{-4}p \left(\frac{T_s - T_A}{e_s - e_A}\right) \tag{8.80}$$

These equations assume molecular diffusion and conductivity and therefore apply only to conditions of laminar motion. Bowen conjectured that the ratio of the heat losses will be much the same in turbulent motion. This supposition has been examined by Cummings and Richardson,[41] who conclude, as a result of comparisons between a small insulated evaporation dish and a large tank, that Bowen's theoretical conclusions are supported by the observations. Cummings has prepared a monogram which enables the Bowen ratio to be determined quickly and accurately.

8.7. Observations of Evaporation

Reference has already been made to the routine observation of rates of evaporation by direct measurement of the net loss of water from freely exposed small dishes or tanks ("evaporimeters"). Apart from the purely technical difficulties of securing consistent data (and these are by no means negligible), the question arises whether or not such observations serve any useful purpose in meteorology. There is no obvious reason why evaporation from a tank should be uniquely related to loss of water from the upper layers of the soil, but there is the possibility of a useful correlation with evaporation from a large enclosed sheet of water, such as a reservoir.

Experiments by Pasquill,[1] using saturated surfaces exposed on level ground in conditions of small temperature gradient, show agreement with Sutton's solution (8.57), which, strictly, is valid only for smooth flow and neutral equilibrium. Subsequent experiments, with the same apparatus, but in conditions of large temperature gradients, showed no significant difference from the rate of evaporation measured in neutral stability. If this result be accepted at its face value, it would imply that evaporation is unaffected by changes in stability, but the immediate effect is to throw doubt on the reliability of evaporimeters as meteorological instruments.

Sutton[1] has suggested that such results indicate that the diffusion of vapor from a *small* surface placed on the ground is primarily determined by the boundary layer formed by the test surface, and not by the properties of the earth's boundary layer, so that extrapolation to large areas is unsound. On the other hand, it is known that conditions very near the earth's surface do not depart markedly from those typical of neutral equilibrium even when there is a well-defined temperature gradient in the deeper layers. Pasquill's experiments indicate that the expression (8.57) will allow the rate of evaporation from a small saturated surface to be calculated from measurements of temperature, wind, and humidity to the order of accuracy obtained by direct measurements of the loss of water from such a surface, so that there is little point in using an evaporimeter. The question has not been definitely settled, but the status of the conventional evaporimeter as a worth-while meteorological instrument is more than doubtful.

Estimates of the amount and diurnal variation of evaporation from a clay-land pasture in fair spring weather in England, using only meteorological observations, have been published by Pasquill,[34] whose diagram is reproduced as Fig. 35. These values are based on the Thornthwaite-Holzman formula, since the effects of departures from strict neutral equilibrium are not significant provided that the formula is evaluated in terms of observations made close ($z < 50$ cm) to the surface. Effects of stability are apparently uniquely determined by the Richardson number, which decreases as the surface is approached. Penman[42] has published theoretical average values of annual evaporation from the British Isles, based on long-term averages of air temperature, duration of sunshine, vapor pressure, and wind speed, using a form of the heat-balance equation and an empirical relation for wind speed and vapor-pressure effect based on water and soil tank measurements.

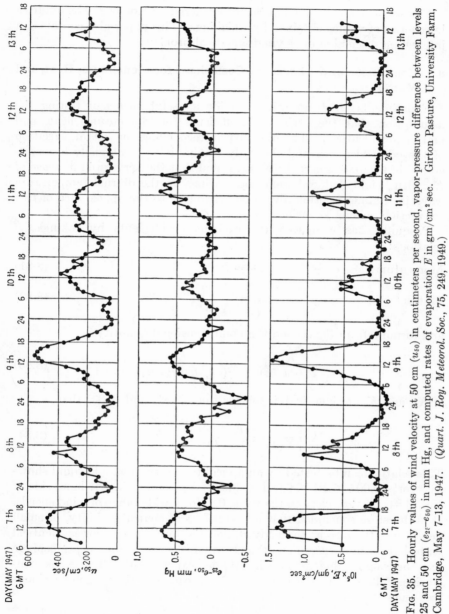

Fig. 35. Hourly values of wind velocity at 50 cm (u_{50}) in centimeters per second, vapor-pressure difference between levels 25 and 50 cm ($e_{25}-e_{50}$) in mm Hg, and computed rates of evaporation E in gm/cm² sec. Girton Pasture, University Farm, Cambridge, May 7–13, 1947. (*Quart. J. Roy. Meteorol. Soc.*, 75, 249, 1949.)

Evaporation from snow has been considered by Köhler,[43] who quotes a long series of values obtained by weighing. This paper also contains an interesting discussion of the mathematical problem.

8.8. Comparison of the Exchange Coefficients for Momentum, Heat, and Matter

Experiments on evaporation provide a useful means of testing the assumption that the exchange coefficients for momentum, heat, and matter are identical. The difficulty in reconciling the height variation of the eddy viscosity and the eddy conductivity has already been discussed in Chap. 6, where it was suggested that the very rapid increase of K_H with height deduced from observations on the diurnal temperature wave in summer is primarily to be attributed to the appearance of free convection on such occasions.

Pasquill[44] has compared the exchange coefficients by taking the relations:

Momentum:
$$K_M = k^2 z^2 \frac{\partial \bar{u}}{\partial z} \tag{8.81}$$

Matter:
$$K_z = -\frac{E}{\partial \chi / \partial z} \tag{8.82}$$

and forming from the second the nondimensional quantity

$$\frac{K_z}{z^2 (\partial \bar{u} / \partial z)} = \frac{-E}{z^2 (\partial \bar{u} / \partial z)(\partial \chi / \partial z)} \tag{8.83}$$

If K_M and K_z are identical, it follows from (8.81) and (8.83) that

$$\left[\frac{-E}{z^2 (\partial \bar{u} / \partial z)(\partial \chi / \partial z)} \right]^{\frac{1}{2}} = k \tag{8.84}$$

This relation can be tested by an appeal to observation. Pasquill shows that for $-0.004 \leq \mathrm{Ri} \leq 0.004$, values of k given by the left-hand side of Eq. (8.84) lie very close to the value 0.4, for a wide range of wind speeds. It is therefore concluded that in conditions of neutral stability, or small departures therefrom, the eddy diffusivity for water vapor is identical with that for momentum and that Kármán's constant for the atmosphere has the same value as in wind-tunnel experiments. The same conclusions follow from the study of the spread of artificial smoke clouds (see page 282).

In other conditions, Pasquill finds that there is a very striking agreement between $K_M/(z^2 \, \partial \bar{u} / \partial z)$ and $K_z/(z^2 \, \partial \bar{u} / \partial z)$ in *unstable* conditions, almost as good as that found in neutral stability. In stable conditions there is a considerable disparity, which Pasquill considers to be consistent with the breakdown of the Deacon profile [Eq. (7.6)], with the roughness length independent of stability, in large inversions.

From the equation for heat flux,

$$q = -\rho c_p K_H \left(\frac{\partial \bar{T}}{\partial z} + \Gamma \right)$$

Pasquill derives values of K_H and finds that these are of the same order of magnitude as K_z at $z = 75$ cm above grassland. A more critical comparison, when the nondimensional quantities

$$\frac{K_H}{z^2 \, \partial \bar{u}/\partial z} \quad \text{and} \quad \frac{K_z}{z^2 \, \partial \bar{u}/\partial z}$$

are plotted against the Richardson number, shows, however, a close identity between K_H and K_z in *stable* conditions but a marked disparity in large lapse rates, when $K_H > K_z$. The deduction is therefore that $K_H > K_M = K_z$ in unstable conditions and $K_H = K_z > K_M$ in stable conditions. The former conclusion is consistent with the results indicated in Chap. 6 on the propagation of the diurnal wave of temperature from the ground.

8.9. Diffusion in the Similarity Theory of Turbulence

In 1926, L. F. Richardson[45] published an unusual theory of diffusion which in some ways anticipated many of the concepts of the similarity theories recently advanced by Kolmogoroff, Weiszäcker, Heisenberg, and others (see Chap. 3). In any type of diffusion, the distance between any pair of marked particles will tend to increase as time proceeds. The characteristic feature of Fickian diffusion is that the rate of separation of two such particles is, on the average, independent of the distance between them. In his "distance-neighbor graph" Richardson studied a more general type of diffusion, which is claimed to be appropriate to a turbulent fluid. Let l be the projection of the distance between any pair of marked particles onto a fixed direction Ox, and let q, the "number of neighbors" per unit of l, be defined by

$$q(l) = \int_{-\infty}^{\infty} \chi(x)\chi(x + l)dx$$

where $\chi(x)$ is the concentration of particles at x. If the cluster of particles is symmetrical in the sense that $\chi(-x) = \chi(x)$, it can be shown that the inverse transformation, starting from $q(l)$, gives a unique $\chi(x)$. Richardson deduces that q satisfies the parabolic partial differential equation

$$\frac{\partial q}{\partial t} = \frac{\partial}{\partial l} \left\{ F(l) \, \frac{\partial q}{\partial l} \right\}$$

where $F(l)$ is a kind of diffusion coefficient. The nature of $F(l)$ can be elucidated by observations on pairs of particles. Let l_0 be the initial value of l and l_T its value T sec later, T being chosen so that $l_T - l_0$ is measurable, but small compared with l. Averaging over many such pairs, it can be shown that

$$F(l_0) = \frac{\text{mean of } (l_T - l_0)^2 \text{ for all pairs}}{2T}$$

For the atmosphere Richardson, using rather coarse data, deduced that

$$F(l) = 0.6l^{\frac{4}{3}} \text{ cm}^2 \text{ sec}^{-1}$$

for $10^2 \leq l \leq 10^6$ cm. If atmospheric diffusion were Fickian, $F(l)$ would be independent of l. Hence, in the atmosphere, the rate of separation of two particles increases with their distance apart, a result which reflects the wide range of length scales associated with the fluctuations of velocity.

In a later investigation, Richardson and Stommel,[46] by observing pairs of floating objects in Loch Long, Scotland, found that

$$F(l) = 0.07l^{1.4}$$

for both large and small l_0. This agrees with the result for the atmosphere as regards the power of l. Richardson's original theory does not predict the precise functional form of $F(l)$, and the merit of the new similarity theories is that they enable such relations to be deduced theoretically. Richardson and Stommel claim that the empirical laws given above are supported by the theories of Weiszäcker and Hessenberg, who are stated to have deduced theoretically a "four-thirds law."

The matter has been further considered by G. K. Batchelor[47] in relation to Kolmogoroff's formulation of the similarity theory. Batchelor divides the problems into (1) diffusion from a fixed source and (2) diffusion of a cloud drifting with the wind. In the first type of problem, the distribution of concentration about the source is known, theoretically, from the statistical behavior of *one* particle initially at the source; for example, by the relation between the mean-square displacement $\overline{X^2}$ of the particle from the source and the interval of diffusion t. From Taylor's theorem [Eq. (3.60)], $\overline{X^2}$ is given by

$$\frac{d\overline{X^2}}{dt} = \overline{2X(t)u(t)} = 2\int_0^t \overline{u(t')u(t)dt'}$$

where X and u are the projection of the displacement and the component of the velocity on Ox. The quantity $\overline{u(t')u(t)}$ depends chiefly on $\xi = t - t'$, and writing $S(\xi) = \overline{u(t')u(t)}$, it follows that

$$\frac{d\overline{X^2}}{dt} = 2\int_0^t S(\xi)d\xi$$

For the valid application of Kolmogoroff's theory, it is necessary to ascertain the range of eddy sizes likely to influence the process (see Chap. 3). For $\xi = 0$, $S(\xi) = \overline{u^2}$, which involves the total eddying energy of the system and therefore is not strongly dependent on the small eddies. As ξ increases, $S(\xi)$ tends to be even more influenced by the larger eddies, which are outside the range of the theory. The conclusion is that the Kolmogoroff similarity theory cannot be applied legitimately to the determination of $d\overline{X^2}/dt$.

The problem of diffusion from a center drifting with the wind is similarly reduced, in theory, to the discussion of the statistics of the behavior of *two* marked particles relative to each other, as in Richardson's theory. If $\xi(t)$ is the projection of the separation l on a fixed axis, and if $\delta u(t)$ is the x component of the relative velocity of the particles t sec after release, it follows that, averaging over many pairs,

$$\frac{d\overline{\xi^2(t)}}{dt} = 2\overline{\xi(t)\,\delta u(t)} = 2\int_0^t \overline{\delta u(t)\,\delta u(t')}dt'$$

For small t, $\delta u(t')$ is approximately equal to $\delta u(0)$, and hence

$$\frac{d\overline{\xi^2(t)}}{dt} \simeq 2t\overline{\delta u^2(0)} = 2t\,\overline{[u(x+l_0) - u(x)]^2}$$

The quantity on the right-hand side of this equation has been discussed in Chap. 3, where it is shown to be chiefly determined by small eddies when l_0 is sufficiently small. As t becomes large, the particles drift far apart and their relative behavior is determined by the large eddies, or, in symbols,

$$\lim_{t\to\infty} \frac{d\overline{\xi^2(t)}}{dt} = 2\frac{d\overline{X^2(t)}}{dt}$$

the system thus ultimately passing outside the range of applicability of the similarity theory. This shows that the Kolmogoroff theory can be applied to $d\overline{\xi^2}/dt$ for a limited range of values of l_0 and t only. From dimensional arguments it follows that

$$\frac{d\overline{\xi^2}}{dt} = \nu f\left(\frac{l_0\epsilon^{\frac{1}{4}}}{\nu^{\frac{3}{4}}}, \frac{t\epsilon^{\frac{1}{2}}}{\nu^{\frac{1}{2}}}\right)$$

where ϵ is the average rate of dissipation of energy per unit mass of fluid and f is a universal function. Batchelor considers a number of cases (t small, intermediate, and large, l_0 not large and also in the inertial subrange) and gives the various forms deduced from the hypothesis of the theory. The most important predictions are:

t small ($\ll l_0^{\frac{2}{3}}\epsilon^{-\frac{1}{3}}$)　　$\dfrac{d\overline{\xi^2}}{dt} = 2c_1 t(\epsilon l_0)^{\frac{2}{3}}\left(1 + \tfrac{1}{3}\dfrac{\xi_0^2}{l_0^2}\right)$　　　　(8.85)

t large ($\gg l_0^{\frac{2}{3}}\epsilon^{-\frac{1}{3}}$)　　$\dfrac{d\overline{\xi^2}}{dt} = c_2 \epsilon t^2$　　　　　　　　　(8.86)

where c_1 and c_2 are constants, provided that $\sqrt{\overline{\xi^2}}$ is much below the upper limit of eddy size to which the Kolmogoroff hypotheses apply.

These predictions have been compared with the Richardson-Stommel data on floating pairs. The observed variation with l_0 is not verified,[†] but the values deduced for ϵ are of the right order of magnitude for the conditions of Loch Long. On the other hand, Batchelor argues that the process of computing scatter about a mean position employed by Richardson in his earlier work on atmospheric diffusion effectively eliminates the influence of the large eddies, so that Eq. (8.86) is appropriate to these results. This equation is equivalent to the relation

$$K = \text{constant} \cdot \epsilon l_0^{\frac{4}{3}}$$

so that there are grounds for claiming that Richardson's empirical relation for the diffusion coefficient is consistent with the similarity theory. The agreement extends to the order of magnitude of the multiplier of $l_0^{\frac{4}{3}}$ (Batchelor[47]).

As yet, there is no unassailable evidence to support either of the predictions (8.85) or (8.86), and such evidence is difficult to obtain. Measurements of the scatter of clusters of free balloons are reliable only when the number of balloons is large and the effects of systematic errors are eliminated. Photography of puffs of smoke offers better prospects, but the results need very careful interpretation. The outstanding feature is undoubtedly that the similarity theories open up promising new lines of approach and are therefore to be welcomed in a subject in which much remains obscure.

BIBLIOGRAPHY

1. O. G. SUTTON, Quart. J. Roy. Meteorol. Soc., 73, 257 (1947).
2. O. F. T. ROBERTS, Proc. Roy. Soc. (London), A104, 640 (1923).
3. K. L. CALDER, Quart. J. Mech. Applied Math., 2, 153 (1949).
4. O. G. SUTTON, Proc. Roy. Soc. (London), A146 (1934).
5. E. L. DEACON, Quart. J. Roy. Meteorol. Soc., 75, 89 (1949).
6. O. G. SUTTON, Quart. J. Roy. Meteorol. Soc., 75, 335 (1949).
7. O. G. SUTTON, Quart. J. Roy. Meteorol. Soc., 73, 426 (1947).
8. C. H. BOSANQUET and J. L. PEARSON, Trans. Faraday Soc., 32, 124 (1936).
9. C. H. BOSANQUET, W. F. CAREY, and E. M. HALTON, Proc. Inst. Mech. Eng., 162, 355 (1950).

† Batchelor contests Richardson and Stommel's statement that their empirical law for $F(l)$ conforms to the similarity theory as advanced by Weiszäcker.

10. G. R. HILL, M. D. THOMAS, and J. N. ABERSOLD, Ind. Hyg. Foundation Am., Proceedings of 9th annual meeting, 1944.
11. W. SCHMIDT, Z. angew. Math. Mech., 21, 265, 351 (1941).
12. O. G. SUTTON, J. Meteorol., 7, 307 (1950).
13. H. JEFFREYS, Phil. Mag., 35, 270 (1918).
14. M. A. GIBLETT, Proc. Roy. Soc. (London), A99, 472 (1921).
15. W. G. L. SUTTON, Proc. Roy. Soc. (London), A182, 48 (1943).
16. M. GEVREY, "Sur les équations aux dérivées partielles du type parabolique" (Paris, 1915).
17. J. G. JAEGER, Quart. Applied Math., 3, 210 (1945).
18. H. KÖHLER, Arkiv Geophys., 1, 8 (1950).
19. G. HIMUS, Inst. Chem. Engrs. (London), Conference on vapor absorption and adsorption, 1929.
20. R. W. POWELL and E. GRIFFITHS, Trans. Inst. Chem. Engrs. (London), 13, 175 (1935).
21. R. THIESENHAUSEN, Gesundh. Ing., 53, 113 (1930).
22. T. B. HINE, Phys. Rev., 24, 79, (1924).
23. F. DÖRFFEL, Veröffentl. Geophys. Inst. Leipzig, 6, 4 (1935).
24. H. MROSE, Jahrb. Sachs. Amtes. Gewasserk (1936).
25. H. LETTAU and F. DÖRFFEL, Ann. Hydr. u. marit. Meteorol., 64, 342, 504 (1936).
26. F. PASQUILL, Proc. Roy. Soc. (London), A182, 75 (1943).
27. D. R. DAVIES, Proc. Roy. Soc. (London), A190, 232 (1947).
28. C. J. TRANTER, Quart. J. Mech. Applied Math., 4, 461 (1952).
29. P. A. SHEPPARD, Meteorological Factors in Radio Wave Propagation, Phys. Soc. (London) (1947).
30. H. U. SVERDRUP, Geophys. Pub., 11, 7 (1936).
31. A. M. FIRESAH, London University, Ph.D. thesis.
32. C. W. THORNTHWAITE and B. HOLZMAN, Monthly Weather Rev., 67, 4 (1939).
33. B. HOLZMAN, Ann. N. Y. Acad. Sci., 44, 13 (1943).
34. F. PASQUILL, Quart. Roy. Meteorol. Soc., 75, 249 (1949).
35. R. B. MONTGOMERY, Papers Phys. Oceanog. Meteorol. Mass. Inst. Technol. and Woods Hole Oceanog. Inst., 7, 4 (1940).
36. R. NORRIS, Quart. Roy. Meteorol. Soc., 74, 1 (1948).
37. H. U. SVERDRUP, J. Meteorol., 3, 1 (1946).
38. W. SCHMIDT, Ann. Hydr. u. marit. Meteorol., 43, 111 (1920).
39. A. ÅNGSTROM, Geog. Ann., 11, 237 (1920).
40. I. S. BOWEN, Phys. Rev., 27, 779 (1926).
41. N. W. CUMMINGS and B. RICHARDSON, Phys. Rev., 30, 527 (1927).
42. H. L. PENMAN, Quart. J. Roy. Meteorol. Soc., 76, 372 (1950).
43. H. KÖHLER, Arkiv Geophys., 1, 159 (1950).
44. F. PASQUILL, Proc. Roy. Soc. (London), A198, 116 (1949).
45. L. F. RICHARDSON, Proc. Roy. Soc. (London), 110, 709 (1926).
46 L. F. RICHARDSON and H. STOMMEL, J. Meteorol., 5, 238 (1948).
47. G. K. BATCHELOR, Quart. J. Roy. Meteorol. Soc., 76, 133 (1950).

NAME INDEX

A

Abbot, C. G., 171
Abersold, J. N., 295
Akerblom, F., 245
Ångström, A., 164, 165, 186, 314

B

Barkat, Ali, 238
Batchelor, G. K., 86, 100, 320
Beckmann, W., 118
Bénard, H., 118
Bernoulli, D., 15
Best, A. C., 197, 202, 205, 207–209, 213,
    230–233, 239, 252–254, 261
Bezold, W. v., 199
Bjorkdal, B., 253
Blasius, H., 53
Bosanquet, C. H., 294, 301
Boussinesq, J., 68
Bowen, I. S., 314
Boyden, C. J., 186
Brunt, D., 33, 102, 119, 131, 146, 147,
    168, 170, 204, 225, 230, 267

C

Calder, K. L., 79, 154, 240, 281, 290, 309
Callendar, H. L., 193
Carey, W. F., 294, 301
Carslaw, H. S., 112, 113, 125, 140
Chandra, K., 123
Cowling, T. G., 215
Cummings, N. W., 315

D

Dassanayake, D. T. E., 123
Davies, E. Ll., 186, 196
Deacon, E. L., 231, 233–237, 261, 264,
    289, 319

Defant, F., 267, 270
Dennison, D. M., 168
Dines, J. S., 249
Dörffel, F., 306
Durst, C. S., 256, 264

E

Eaton, G. S., 196
Einstein, A., 91, 287
Ekman, W. V., 71
Elias, F., 308
Elsasser, W. M., 171
Ertel, H., 79, 148, 225
Euler, L., 15

F

Fage, A., 255
Field, J. H., 196
Fishenden, M., 117, 201
Flower, W. D., 180, 186, 202, 205, 209
Fowle, F. E., 169
Fransilla, M., 184
Frost, R., 238

G

Geiger, R., 196, 197
Gevrey, M., 305
Giblett, M. A., 239, 263, 305
Ginsburg, N., 168
Glauert, H., 30
Goldstein, S., 54, 88, 95
Goursat, E., 305
Griffiths, E., 306
Groen, P., 181

H

Halton, E. M., 294, 301
Haude, 201

SUBJECT INDEX

Page numbers in **boldface** type refer to the more important discussions.